Tudors and Stuarts on

Tudors and Stuarts on Film

Historical Perspectives

Edited by

SUSAN DORAN AND THOMAS S. FREEMAN

palgrave
macmillan

First published 2009 by
PALGRAVE MACMILLAN

Palgrave Macmillan in the UK is an imprint of Macmillan Publishers Limited, registered in England, company number 785998, of Houndmills, Basingstoke, Hampshire RG21 6XS.

Palgrave Macmillan in the US is a division of St Martin's Press LLC, 175 Fifth Avenue, New York, NY 10010.

Palgrave Macmillan is the global academic imprint of the above companies and has companies and representatives throughout the world.

Palgrave® and Macmillan® are registered trademarks in the United States, the United Kingdom, Europe and other countries.

ISBN-13: 978–1–4039–4070–4 hardback
ISBN-10: 1–4039–4070–3 hardback
ISBN-13: 978–1–4039–4071–1 paperback
ISBN-10: 1–4039–4071–1 paperback

This book is printed on paper suitable for recycling and made from fully managed and sustained forest sources. Logging, pulping and manufacturing processes are expected to conform to the environmental regulations of the country of origin.

A catalogue record for this book is available from the British Library.

Library of Congress Cataloging-in-Publication Data
Tudors and Stuarts on film : historical perspectives / edited by Susan Doran and Thomas S. Freeman.
    p.   cm.
Includes index.
ISBN 978–1–4039–4070–4
1. Historical films—Great Britain—History and criticism.   2. Historical films—United States—History and criticism.   3. Kings and rulers in motion pictures.
4. Elizabeth I, Queen of England, 1533–1603—In motion pictures.
I. Doran, Susan.   II. Freeman, Thomas S., 1959–
PN1995.9.H5T83 2009
791.43'694205—dc22   2008038390

10   9   8   7   6   5   4   3   2   1
18   17   16   15   14   13   12   11   10   09

Printed and bound in China

IN MEMORY OF CHRISTOPHER DURSTON
OUR COLLABORATOR AND FRIEND 1951–2005

Contents

List of Illustrations

Acknowledgements

The authors and publishers wish to thank the following for permission to use copyright material:

BFI and The Kobal Collection for the image of Jonathan Walton, Muriel Higgins and Don Higgins from the motion picture *Winstanley* (1975) on p. 233

British and Dominions and The Kobal Collection for the image of Anna Neagle and Cedric Hardwicke from the motion picture *Nell Gwyn* (1934) on p. 247

Columbia, Irving Allen and The Kobal Collection for the image of Alec Guinness and Richard Harris from the motion picture *Cromwell* (1970) on p. 205, and for the image of Timothy Dalton and Vanessa Redgrave from the motion picture *Mary Queen of Scots* (1971) on p. 137

Gaumont British Picture Corporation of America and Photofest for the image of John Mills and Nova Pilbeam from the motion picture *Nine Days a Queen* aka *Tudor Rose* (1936) on p. 77

The Kobal Collection for the image of Paul Scofield and Robert Shaw from the motion picture *A Man for All Seasons* (1966) on p. 47

Miramax Films, Universal Pictures, The Kobal Collection and Laurie Sparham for the image of Colin Firth and Judi Dench from the motion picture *Shakespeare in Love* (1998) on p. 179

National Portrait Gallery, London, for the image of Henry VII and Henry VIII by Hans Holbein on p. 31

Paramount Pictures and Photofest for the image of Cary Elwes and Helena Bonham Carter from the motion picture *Lady Jane* (1986) on p. 77

Polygram, The Kobal Collection and Alex Bailey for the images of Cate Blanchett from the motion picture *Elizabeth* (1998) on pp. 107 and 123

United Artists and The Kobal Collection for the image of Flora Robson and Vivien Leigh from the motion picture *Fire Over England* (1937) on p. 89

Universal Pictures and The Kobal Collection for the image of Genevieve Bujold from the motion picture *Anne of the Thousand Days* (1969) on p. 61

Warner Bros., First National, The Kobal Collection and Bert Six for the image of Errol Flynn and Bette Davis from the motion picture *The Private Lives of Elizabeth and Essex* (1939) on p. 191

Warner Bros. and The Kobal Collection for the image of Flora Robson and Errol Flynn from the motion picture *The Sea Hawk* (1940) on p. 151

Every effort has been made to trace the copyright holders but, if any have been inadvertently overlooked, the authors and publishers will be pleased to make the necessary arrangements at the first opportunity.

Notes on the Contributors

Will Coster teaches at the University of Bedfordshire. He has written on popular culture in early-modern England and his books include *Family and Kinship in England, 1450–1800* (2001) and *Baptism and Spiritual Kinship in Early Modern England* (2002).

Susan Doran is Senior Research Fellow in History at Jesus College, Oxford and teaches at Christ Church and St Benet's Hall. Her many publications include *Monarchy and Matrimony: The Courtships of Elizabeth I* (1996), *Elizabeth I* in the British Library Historic Lives series (2003) and *Mary Queen of Scots: An Illustrated Life* (2007).

Christopher Durston was, until October 2004, Professor of History at St Mary's College Strawberry Hill before moving to the University of Plymouth. His works include *Cromwell's Major-Generals: Godly Government during the English Revolution* (2001) and *Princes, Pastors and People* co-written with Susan Doran (2003). For Palgrave he co-edited *The Culture of English Puritanism, 1560–1700* (1996).

Thomas S. Freeman is Research Editor for the British Academy John Foxe Project and he is affiliated with the University of Sheffield. He is the co-editor (with Susan Doran) of *The Myth of Elizabeth* and (with Thomas F. Mayer) of *Martyrs and Martyrdom in England, c.1400–1700*. He is the co-author (with Elizabeth Evenden) of *Religion and the Book in Early Modern England: The Making of Foxe's 'Book of Martyrs'*.

John Guy is Fellow of Clare College, University of Cambridge, where he teaches part-time so he can devote more time to his writing and broadcasting career. He has published 16 books and numerous academic articles. His book *My Heart is My Own: The life of Mary Queen of Scots* (2004) won the 2004 Whitbread Biography Award and was a finalist in the USA for the 2004 Biography/Autobiography of the Year Award (National Books Critics Circle).

Christopher Haigh is Tutor in Modern History at Christ Church, University of Oxford. He has published numerous articles and his books include *English Reformations: Religion, Politics and Society under the Tudors* (1993), *Elizabeth I* (1998) and *The Plain Man's Pathways to Heaven: Kinds of Christianity in Post-Reformation England* (2007).

Paul E. J. Hammer is Professor of History at the University of Colorado at Boulder, and is the author of *The Polarisation of Elizabethan Politics: The Political Career of Robert Devereux, 2nd Earl of Essex, 1585–1597* (1999) and *Elizabeth's Wars: War, Government and Society in Tudor England, 1544–1604* (2003), as well as numerous other publications. He is currently completing a book on the Earl of Essex and the late-Elizabethan crisis of 1598–1603.

Ronald Hutton is Professor of History at Bristol University, where he has taught since 1981. He is the author of 13 books on various different fields of history, including 6 on the Stuart period.

Carole Levin is Willa Cather Professor of History at the University of Nebraska. She is the author of a number of books, including *The Heart and Stomach of a King: Elizabeth I and the Politics of Sex and Power* (1994), *The Reign of Elizabeth I* (2002) and *Dreaming the English Renaissance* (2008). She has also co-edited several collections of essays on Elizabeth I.

Peter Marshall is Professor of History at the University of Warwick. His books include *Beliefs and the Dead in Reformation England* (2002), *Religious Identities in Henry VIII's England* (2006) and *Mother Leakey and the Bishop: A Ghost Story* (2007). He is a contributor to the forthcoming *Cambridge Companion to Thomas More*.

John Morrill FBA is Professor of British and Irish History at the University of Cambridge and a Fellow of Selwyn College. His research interests cover the whole of the period 1500–1750, but he is best known for his work on the Revolutions of the mid-seventeenth century. His biography of Cromwell – with a section on his posthumous reputation – was published by Oxford University Press in their VIP (Very Interesting People) series in 2007.

Judith Richards of La Trobe University has published on various aspects of early-modern English monarchy, including gender issues up to the accession of James VI and I, and on definitions of allegiance after 1603. Her biography of Mary Tudor was published in mid-2008.

Glenn Richardson is a Senior Lecturer in History at St Mary's University College, Strawberry Hill, London. He is the author of *Renaissance Monarchy: The Reigns of Henry VIII, Francis I and Charles V*

(2002) and co-editor with Susan Doran of *Tudor England and Its Neighbours* (2005). He is the editor of *Contending Kingdoms: France and England, 1420–1700* (2008) and is currently preparing a new study of the Field of Cloth of Gold.

David L. Smith is Fellow and Director of Studies in History at Selwyn College, Cambridge, and Affiliated Lecturer in the Cambridge History Faculty. He has won the Royal Historical Society's Alexander Prize and Cambridge University's Thirlwall Prize for Historical Research. His publications include *Constitutional Royalism and the Search for Settlement, c. 1640–1649* (1994), *A History of the Modern British Isles, 1603–1707: The Double Crown* (1998), and *The Stuart Parliaments, 1603–1689* (1999) and (with Patrick Little) *Parliaments and Politics during the Cromwellian Protectorate* (2007).

Brett Usher is Visiting Research Fellow in History at the University of Reading. His many publications include *William Cecil and Episcopacy, 1559–1577* (2003). He is Research Associate of the Oxford DNB.

Vivienne Westbrook is a graduate of the London Film School and an Associate Professor at National Sun Yat-Sen University, Taiwan. She has lectured and written extensively on Renaissance representation and reception.

1

Introduction: It's Only a Movie

Thomas S. Freeman

On 18 February 1915, President Woodrow Wilson, along with his Cabinet, gathered at the White House to view D. W. Griffith's Civil War epic, *The Birth of a Nation*. Wilson reportedly declared that Griffith's film 'is like writing history with lightning. And my only regret is that it is all so terribly true'. There is considerable doubt that Wilson actually made this remark; a fact which in itself ironically epitomizes the problematic, but not entirely unfruitful, relationship between history and cinema.[1] Today no scholar would contemplate hailing Griffith's interpretation of American history as 'true'. Yet almost everyone would acknowledge that, if Wilson did indeed compare *The Birth of a Nation* to history written with lightning, then he was prescient about the new medium. For the comparison is surprisingly apt; films have a remarkable ability to illuminate and animate past events, but they also distort our perception of them. Film may be history written with lightning, but is lightning, with its brilliant but erratic flashes of light, the best illumination for studying a dark and unfamiliar landscape?

In this collection we probe aspects of the relationship between film and history by examining historical films set in Tudor and Stuart Britain. These films are analyzed by scholars who teach and research this period of history. The authors make no claims to be film critics and do not judge the films on the basis of their artistic merits. We also are not providing biographies of actors or histories of film studios. Nor are we considering the development of the film industry in any particular country. All of these are elements which may be considered in the chapters in this book, but they are not the primary focus of these chapters. Instead the contributors to this volume are all concerned to treat historical films about early-modern England in the same ways in which we, as historians, examine texts, whether they be fact or fiction, dealing with a period of the past. In part, this means situating the films in their contexts by discussing the preoccupations of the filmmakers, the sources they used, the state of historical knowledge when the films were produced, and the reception of the films when they were first screened.

But which films are we examining? What is a historical film? The most obvious definition would be that it is a film dealing with the past. But this is a hopelessly broad category which covers everything from film adaptations of Shakespeare's history plays to *Indiana Jones and the Last Crusade*. Our remit has been considerably narrower. In the first place, we are focusing on films that are (at least ostensibly) classified as entertainments, not with documentaries or educational series such as those of David Starkey or Simon Schama. Beyond this, a possible approach would have been to distinguish between films set in the past, but dealing with fictitious people, from films dealing with historical figures and events. The problem is that the same film often contains fictitious people intermingled with actual historical figures and, even more frequently, fictitious plots interwoven with historical events.

The historian Robert Toplin has suggested that there should be a separate category of films dealing with the past, that of 'faction' films or 'faction-based movies' for such pictures and that they should not be treated or assessed as historical films.[2] This distinction, however, is unduly restrictive. Arguably the three most accurate films about the US Civil War, and the most insightful about important dimensions of the conflict, are *Glory*, about the exploits of the Fifty-Fourth Massachusetts Volunteer Infantry, a regiment of black soldiers, *Ride with the Devil*, about guerrilla warfare in Missouri, and *Pharoah's Army*, about a Union foraging party and the civilians they encounter in Kentucky in 1862. The first two contain largely fictional characters interacting with a few historical figures such as Robert Gould Shaw, the commander of the Fifty-Fourth Massachusetts, Frederick Douglass and the Confederate guerrilla leader William Quantrill. *Pharoah's Army* consists entirely of fictional characters. Yet to eliminate these from a survey of historical films about the Civil War would be misguided pedantry. Similarly, we are unwilling to omit consideration of such films as *The Sea Hawk* and *Fire Over England,* which have been extremely influential in shaping popular views of Elizabeth I and which are very revealing of attitudes towards her reign on the eve of World War II, simply because fictitious characters and plots are foregrounded in both films.

Another historian, Robert Rosenstone, has drawn a distinction between the 'costume drama' and the 'historical film' on the basis of their involvement with historical discourses. As examples Rosenstone contrasts *Gone with the Wind* to *Glory*, maintaining that the former is a costume drama because it ignores the issues involved in the Civil War, particularly slavery and race, 'and uses the exotic locale of the past as no more than a setting for romance and adventure'. *Glory*, on the other hand, is – according to Rosenstone – a historical film because it poses and attempts to answer questions about race, slavery and the Civil War.[3] These examples demonstrate the dangers in this distinction. A focus on romance and adventure does not preclude a film's dealing with historical topics. *Gone with the Wind* has a coherent, if tendentious, view of the Civil War and Reconstruction, and while the film's discussion of these subjects is limited – it says little about the causes of the war and, apart from Sherman's Atlanta campaign, little about its events – its presentation of slavery, antebellum Southern society and Reconstruction have proven to be remarkably influential.[4]

Nevertheless, Rosenstone's definition of a historical film is useful: 'To be considered "historical" rather than simply a costume drama, a film must engage the issues, ideas, data and arguments of that field of knowledge. A historical film does not indulge in capacious invention, and does not ignore the findings and assertions of what we already know'.[5] These basically are our criteria in selecting films: they all engage with historical issues through the presentation of historical events and personages and, at a minimum, they appear to do so in a factual manner. These criteria exclude films such as *The Pirates of the Caribbean* trilogy, which, although set in the past, do not depict historical people or events, and cannot be regarded as factual by any audience unwilling to believe in the actual existence of such plot devices as Aztec curses, the Flying Dutchman and undead monkeys. They also exclude films such as *Sense and Sensibility, A Room with a View* or *Howard's End* which, while set in the past and anchored to it by meticulously accurate sets and costumes, do not deal with historical people or events.

With these criteria, it should also be clear that this book is not about the 'heritage' film, although a number of the films we examine – for example, *Elizabeth, Shakespeare in Love* and *Restoration* – fall into this category.[6] But a number of other films discussed in this book, notably *Winstanley, Carry on Henry* and *Witchfinder General*, cannot be regarded as heritage films, even by the most inclusive definition of this term. We have also made the painful, but necessary, decision largely to ignore television programmes about the Tudor and the Stuart epochs. A number of television programmes, notably *The Six Wives of Henry VIII, Elizabeth R* and *Blackadder,* conform to our definition of the historical film and have proven to be quite influential in shaping popular perceptions of early-modern England. Some of these programmes will be referred to in this volume. However, detailed consideration of television, in addition to cinema, treatments of events and people in sixteenth- and seventeenth-century Britain would increase the size of this book beyond its feasible limits.

II

This then is neither a book of film criticism nor a book about film-making. It is instead a book discussing historical films as part of Tudor and Stuart historiography – that is, as part of the interpretation of British history during the two reigns. This does not mean that these films are histories, rather they are presentations of history, as are historical novels, historical dramas or paintings and poems on historical subjects. As a result of this approach, we will explore certain topics usually untreated in books about historical films. The first of these is a consideration not only of why certain figures and topics of early-modern Britain have been the subject of films, but also why certain others have been partially or entirely passed over. By any standard, for example, the Protectorate of Oliver Cromwell is a crucial period in British history, yet it has been ignored by the cinema.[7] Moreover while Henry VIII, Elizabeth I and Charles II have attracted the most cinematic coverage of any early-modern English monarchs, this coverage has fluctuated very considerably; in this book we will try to explain the circumstances which led to this inconstant and inconsistent awareness and recognition.[8]

Any examination of historical texts, whether they are histories or some variant of historical fiction, necessitates the examination of the sources on which these works are based. From *The Birth of a Nation* onwards, historical films have often been based, not on academic histories, but on popular biographies, historical novels and dramas. We will be looking closely at these biographies, novels and dramas as well as the films on which they were based in order to ascertain how filmmakers have used their chosen sources. And because historical texts need to be analyzed in the context in which they were created, our contributors will be examining the circumstances in which historical films were created.

Above all, in this volume we are concerned with analyzing the accuracy of historical films in dealing with early-modern Britain. Here we run the risk of being considered pedantic and of being accused of taking light entertainments far too seriously. After all, to quote Alfred Hitchcock, it's only a movie. Since the goal of historical films is to entertain, and only secondarily (at best) to instruct, then surely, many people feel, it is captious to judge them by the standards of academic history. Pierre Sorlin, a distinguished historian of film, articulates this widely held opinion, maintaining that since historical films do not claim to reproduce the past accurately, 'when professional historians wonder about the mistakes made in an historical film, they are worrying about a meaningless question'.[9]

Yet scholars have devoted considerable amounts of time and energy to examining the historical inaccuracies in the history plays of Shakespeare, the novels of Walter Scott and countless other literary and artistic representations of history that do not claim to be accurate representations of the past. Why then should film not be subject to the same critical scrutiny? In fact, such analyses would seem to be more necessary for historical films than for representations of the past in other media because of the greater ability of film to counterfeit reality. A theatregoer is always aware that he or she is looking at props and a set, but cinemagoers can easily forget that they are not viewing actual people and events.

Moreover, Sorlin is incorrect in maintaining that films do not claim to represent the past accurately. In fact, the makers of historical films have often gone to some lengths to blur the lines separating their films from historical reality. Everyone is familiar with the announcements preceding historical films that proclaim that these films are based on what actually happened. Occasionally filmmakers have thrown caution – and reality – to the winds, in their efforts to assure viewers of the total accuracy of particular films. Roberto Rossellini's *The Rise to Power of Louis XIV* opens with the unqualified assertion that 'It is all in the documents, nothing is invented'. Roland Joffé's *The Mission*, commences with the bold, and unfounded, claim that 'the historical events represented in this story are true and happened in Paraguay and Argentina in 1758 and 1759'.[10] Costa-Gavras's film *Missing*, (dealing with the 1973 coup that brought Augusto Pinochet to power in Chile), began with a notice declaring that 'This film is based on a true story. The incidents and the facts are documented'. When this

assertion was vigorously challenged, Costa-Gavras responded by insist-
ing that he was an artist, not a journalist, and that he could not be
expected to vouch for the accuracy of 'secondary details'.[11]

But such confident, yet spurious, claims are only the tip of an
iceberg of pretence, as filmmakers have made claims to accuracy a
routine part of the publicity for historical films. In 1938, MGM, in its
publicity for its 'prestige film', *Marie Antoinette*, boasted of the 'infinite
historical research' they devoted to the film, which included 'compil-
ing a bibliography of 1538 volumes, gathering 10,615 photographs,
paintings and sketches, and mimeographing 5000 pages of manuscript
containing more than 3,000,000 words'.[12] In the same spirit, Alfred
Ybarra, the set designer for John Wayne's film *The Alamo*, claimed,
falsely, that he had travelled to Spain and searched in Franciscan
archives to find the original designs of the mission building where
the Texans made their last stand.[13]

An instructive example of Hollywood's efforts to crown its historical
films with educational laurels was the common practice by film studios
of sending 'study guides' to American schools, which were really
thinly disguised press kits touting new releases. For example, when
Shenandoah (a film recounting the tribulations of a family in West
Virginia during the Civil War) premiered in 1965, its producers sent a
'Classroom Study Guide to Shenandoah' to high school and elementary school teachers across the United States. Apart from describing
the painstaking research that the studio had purportedly commissioned
as part of the making of the film, the guide extolled the long line of
Hollywood films that had – it maintained – presented the past accurately to the general public. These included the *Scarlet Empress* (in
which Marlene Dietrich played Catherine the Great), *The Private Lives
of Elizabeth and Essex*, *Broken Arrow* (in which Jeff Chandler played the
Apache chief Cochise), *Hudson's Bay* and *Custer's Last Stand*. 'In learning history, nothing beats a good Hollywood film' the guide crowed.[14]
Surprisingly this exploitation of the educational system continued as
late as 1997, when publicists for *Amistad*, a film about a mutiny of
blacks on a slave ship in 1839, sent out thousands of study guides to
American schools. A leading historian, Eric Foner, sharply and publicly objected to this, in particular to the guides having recommended
discussion of Theodore Joadson, a fictitious African-American abolitionist invented for the film, as if he were a historic figure.[15]

In general, the makers of historical films engage in an opportunistic
fan dance, strutting and vaunting the accuracy of their work, but con-
cealing themselves behind artistic license when this alleged accuracy is

challenged. In initial interviews, Arthur Penn, the director of *Bonnie and Clyde*, insisted that there was no major incident in the film that had not actually taken place and that his intention was to depict the outlaws as 'historical figures in the social-political situation in which they found themselves'. But as criticism of the veracity of the film mounted, Penn declared that his film was 'not a case study of Bonnie and Clyde' and he justified having invented incidents and details on the grounds that he was not attempting a historical portrayal of the couple but was instead portraying the 'mythic aspects of their lives'.[16] In a book about the making of the film *Titanic*, designed to accompany the film's release, James Cameron, its director, is quoted as saying 'Accuracy is a big challenge for us... Wherever possible we want our story within an absolutely rigorous, historically accurate framework, complimenting [sic] history rather than distorting it'.[17] Yet when the film's accuracy became the subject of sharp controversy, a producer of the *Titanic* declared that 'The film was entertainment. It was not made to be a documentary'.[18] As the Shekhar Kapur film *Elizabeth* was about to be released, a writer for the *Daily Mail*, obviously regurgitating publicity material, burbled that the 'in-depth research' that Cate Blanchett did for her role 'could have garnered her another degree in Elizabethan social politics'. Blanchett was quoted as saying that she had 'read 600 pages of Elizabeth's letters'.[19] One wonders why she bothered, since Kapur declared that 'Historical facts are only a constraint if you stick to them. If you are saying I have to tell history absolutely correctly, than I can't make an emotional movie'.[20]

There is one fundamental reason for this bait and switch: audiences expect historical films to be accurate and they want to believe that they are. Filmmakers go to the trouble of maintaining the illusion of fidelity to history, because this illusion sells films. As the director John Sayles has observed:

> There's a certain power that comes from history. I mean, I've heard producers say many, many times that the only way a movie is going to work is if the ad says 'Based on a true story'. Audiences appreciate the fact that something really happened.[21]

III

Often journalists and critics dismiss inaccuracies in historical films as trivial.[22] Yet if particular passions are invoked or particular sensibilities offended, journalists can become strident in their insistence that historical films remain true to historical fact. Thus Oliver Stone's *JFK* provoked a reaction from the American press that bordered on the hysterical. One syndicated columnist and television commentator charged that *JFK* contained 'countless buckets of manure, large measures of legitimate doubt, drippings of innuendo and pages of actual history'.[23] Another declared that Stone was 'an intellectual sociopath, indifferent to truth'.[24] One journalist implicitly compared Stone to Hitler, by denouncing his 'big lies', while Jack Valenti, president and chief executive of the Motion Picture Association of America, explicitly compared *JFK* to Leni Riefenstahl's *Triumph of the Will*.[25]

British reaction to the film *U-571* was equally intense. In a bid to ensure the film's popularity at the American box office, *U-571* depicted an American crew, not a British one, capturing the Enigma encryption machine, the central component of Nazi military communications, from a German submarine. This appropriation of an exploit that remains a considerable source of British national pride ignited enough of an explosion from the press and MPs to rattle the windows of Downing Street. Tony Blair told the House of Commons that the film was 'an affront' to the British sailors killed in the operation, while Chris Smith, then the Culture Secretary, declared that 'I think one of the things we need to make clear to Hollywood is, yes you're in the entertainment business but people see your movies, they're going to come away thinking that's information not just entertainment. You've got to make it clear where the dividing line lies'.[26]

Similar controversy swamped *Titanic* in regard to scenes in which the ship's Third Officer, William Murdoch, was shown accepting bribes to let wealthy passengers into the lifeboats and then shooting passengers desperately rushing the lifeboats, before committing suicide. After a press campaign had stirred up a certain amount of outrage in the officer's native Scotland (the children of Murdoch's hometown of Dalbeattie, inspired by the headmistress of the local school, even wrote letters to Twentieth Century Fox, the studio that distributed *Titanic*, protesting the film's portrayal of Murdoch), MPs protested in the Commons, and one tabled a motion asking that the House seek to compel the studio to rectify the slur on Murdoch's name.[27] Although Twentieth Century Fox would not admit that the depiction of Murdoch was inaccurate and refused to apologize, they did make a payment of £5000 to a school prize fund, which had been established to memorialize him. At least one Scottish columnist complained that this payment was not enough to assuage the 'terrible anguish' the film had inflicted on the residents of Dalbeattie.[28] And an editorial in *The*

Mirror on the affair, pontificated that '*It is time that Hollywood learnt the difference between fact and fiction*'.[29]

These examples of anger at historical inaccuracies in film could easily be multiplied; historical films such as *Missing*, *Mississippi Burning*, *Nixon*, *The Patriot*, *Gangs of New York*, *Downfall* and *The Passion of the Christ* all provoked widespread protests at their deviations from the historical record. When the issues are important to people, then they expect accuracy from historical films. And when people treat the accuracy of a historical film as an irrelevance, then what they are saying is that the particular historical issues in the film do not matter to them. There is considerable danger here. Hollywood film has traditionally been inclusive; it has had to be, because its economic viability depended on appealing to the tastes of a vast and heterogeneous nation. But it has been exclusive as well in its ethnocentricity and racism. Hollywood's indifference to much of the past, partially stemmed from, and has been intertwined with, an indifference to the sensibilities of other nations and cultures as well as, for much of its existence, an indifference to the sensibilities of the non-white populations of America. Saying that a particular history does not matter is often a shorthand way of saying that other people do not matter.

Pierre Berton, a Canadian journalist, has argued that the distortion of Canadian history in American films has been partially responsible for Canadians having a poorly developed sense of national identity.[30] One does not have to accept this argument completely to recognize the resentments that can arise from the distortions in historical films, particularly when those distortions reflect on people of nations, ethnicities and cultures other than those of the historically dominant American film industry. Moreover, the treatment of Canadians in US films has been relatively benign. American film treatments of Mexicans have veered from portraying them condescendingly (*Juarez* or *Vera Cruz*) to unsympathetically (*The Treasure of Sierra Madre* or *Villa*) but it is almost impossible to think of a favourable film about Mexican history produced in Hollywood.

Contempt is one of the few things that people give that is always fully repaid. Hollywood portrayals of Arabs have invested heavily in hostile stereotypes, and the animosity and disdain have been repaid with interest.[31] Historical films, moreover, have often been a reliable vehicle for Hollywood to denigrate racial minorities. Malcolm X described his feelings of humiliation at being black, while he watched *Gone with the Wind* as a 14-year-old boy; his feelings of debasement and mortification must have been felt by countless members of racial minorities across the decades as scenes from historical films such as *The Birth of a Nation* and *Gone with the Wind* danced across the screen.[32]

Nor has the denigration or vilification of religious, ethnic and national groups in historical films ceased. The two Shekhar Kapur films about Elizabeth I both portray Roman Catholic priests as ruthless assassins at the service of a totalitarian hierarchy. This may seem harmless, but is it? Imagine the reactions to a movie that portrayed sixteenth-century rabbis as assassins and an international Jewish conspiracy to kill European monarchs. Not that the anti-Semitic film is a thing of the past, as *The Passion of the Christ* demonstrates. In fact, Mel Gibson's film may well be the harbinger of an increase in the use of the historical film as propaganda against other groups. Commercial films made by major studios may have reinforced prejudices held by their mainstream audiences, but they rarely pursued unpopular ideological vendettas and their reluctance to stir up controversy often muzzled their readiness to snap at other groups. Individuals able to finance films may not show similar restraint.

In the past, individuals with sufficient resources have produced historical films in order to promote various causes. John Wayne produced and directed *The Alamo* as a patriotic wake-up call to an America which had, in his view, grown hedonistic and undisciplined.[33] In 1982, the Unification Church, headed by the South Korean minister, Sun Myung Moon, financed *Inchon*, a virulently anti-Communist film about the Korean War. *Inchon* was a box-office disaster and *The Alamo* barely recovered its costs. Yet *The Passion of the Christ* proved that an individual could make an inflammatory historical film and achieve considerable popular success. It may well be that other individuals will finance historical films that contain controversial and divisive themes and messages.

Certainly governments have done so. It is well known that two of the most repellent regimes in human history, the Third Reich and Stalin's USSR, were both pioneers in sponsoring historical films – such as *Alexander Nevsky*, *Ivan the Terrible*, *Ohm Krüger* and *Jud Süss* – for propagandistic purposes. It is less frequently remembered that governments have continued to do this down to the present day. Gamal Abdul Nasser's government produced an epic film *Saladin* and Indira Gandhi's government quietly financed one-third of Richard Attenborough's film *Gandhi*.[34] Francisco Franco's ministers were directly involved in the making of Anthony Mann's *El Cid* (which was filmed in Spain) and Franco's government was indirectly involved in financing it. Unsurprisingly the film contains a vision of

Spanish history congenial to the Nationalists.[35] As national film indus-
tries undergo mushroom growth throughout the world, challenging
North American and European dominance of the medium, the use
of historical films as propaganda, and the controversies and passions
enflamed by them, are likely to increase to the point where it will be
difficult for anyone to say they are only movies.

The content of historical films is actually a matter of considerable
importance since they reinforce and perpetuate, if not actually create,
myths about the past that are very difficult to shift or dislodge. Thanks
to Hollywood, everyone *knows* that Native Americans were nomads
who lived on the plains, hunting buffalo on horseback and living in
tepees. In actual fact, this was only true of a small minority of the
indigenous inhabitants of North America during a restricted period of
history but cinema has stamped these images indelibly on generations
of film audiences. Similarly, thanks to film, the French Revolution
is seen almost exclusively through the eyes of Charles Dickens and
Baroness Orczy. Apart from Jean Renoir's *La Marseillaise* (a film that
epitomizes the aspirations of the Popular Front) and, to a lesser degree,
Abel Gance's *Napoleon*, I cannot think of a film that is not wholly
negative about this seminal event in world history. These examples
could be multiplied endlessly; film has fostered countless pervasive
historical myths that remain all the more powerful because they are
accepted without reflection or examination.

Two recent examples demonstrate the way in which film injects
'history' into popular awareness. In January 1999, the late Congress-
man Henry Hyde declared in his speech at the beginning of President
Clinton's impeachment trial that Thomas More told his daughter
Margaret that 'When a man takes an oath, Meg, he's holding his own
self in his hands, like water, and if he opens his fingers *Then* – he
needn't hope to find himself again . . . '.[36] These words, however, are
not those of Thomas More, but of the playwright Robert Bolt. Hyde's
misattribution of this quote points to his having learned it either from
Bolt's play about More or (much more likely) from the film based
on the play and to his having uncritically assumed that what the film
depicted More as saying was something that More actually said. In the
autumn of 2002, Michael Portillo, a prominent Tory politician turned
media commentator, hosted a television special on Elizabeth I. In it,
he made the remarkable (and totally baseless) claim that Jesuit priests
sent into England during the queen's reign were trained assassins.
Almost certainly this canard was derived from Kapur's *Elizabeth*, in
which a Jesuit casually commits murder immediately upon landing in

England. The power of film is such that a rather mischievous invention can become common knowledge.

The previous examples illustrate the source of this power. It stems from the fact that far more people watch historical films than read academic histories, articles and essays. Almost 30 years ago, one scholar estimated that the average first-year American college student read only one novel for every 25 films he or she watched.[37] The imbalance between the audiences for film history and academic history becomes readily apparent when one remembers two things. Firstly, that the initial comparison was between films and novels, not films and academic works. Secondly, that in the years since this comparison was made, the audience for films has increased due to the proliferation of cable and satellite television channels and the advent of DVDs. Film is the primary medium by which people learn about the past and this is even true of films which have minimal claims to being factual; one study has documented the pervasive influence of the film *Forrest Gump* on the ways in which US high school students in the 1990s viewed the history of their country.[38]

As a result, the social and political impact of historical films has been considerable. *The Birth of a Nation*, for example, has been credited (if that is the appropriate word) with the revival of the Ku Klux Klan and its renewal as a political force in the 1920s.[39] This may be an overestimation of the film's impact, but there is no doubt that Griffith's portrayal of the Ku Klux Klan as chivalric defenders of Southern women glamourized the organization and made it, in what might be called reactionary chic, respectable in the North as well as the South. In the autumn of 1915, just after the release of *The Birth of a Nation*, members of several sororities at the University of Chicago jointly staged a Halloween dance in which everyone was dressed in a Klan outfit. The Rev. Lyman Rutledge, pastor of the prestigious Harvard Street Unitarian Church in Cambridge, Massachusetts, wrote that Griffith's film presented 'the glory of the Ku Klux Klan' which represented 'that divine spirit which is above the law'.[40]

The reception of *The Birth of a Nation* is a part of one of the most striking and important aspects of the social influence of historical films; their effect on race relations in the United States. 'Millions of Americans have had their vision of the South, race relations, and even the entire panorama of our past shaped if not wholly defined by the movie business'.[41] In this area, as in many others, film drew on both current conceptions of history and popular attitudes but gave them both different emphases and new power. Films 'did not merely reflect

America's racist stereotypes; they intensified them and turned them into a new kind of black, who bore little resemblance to anybody's history, black or white. The overwhelming power of the new film medium dwarfed small-circulation magazines and hardcover books and virtually entrenched the idea of Rastus, Sambo and Mammy in the American psyche.'[42]

It is important to remember that this racist interpretation of America and American history was not only supported by historical films, it was supported by historical films that were designed as lightweight entertainments. For example, the film *Santa Fe Trail*, a 1940 Western, had the future Confederate cavalry commander 'Jeb' Stuart (played by Errol Flynn) ahistorically teaming up with George Armstrong Custer (Ronald Reagan) to thwart the abolitionist John Brown (Raymond Massey). This film depicts blacks in Kansas, on the eve of the Civil War, as lacking the ability to cope with their new-found freedom (slavery was banned in Kansas) and longing for their former masters in the South, who treated them kindly. The film also maintains that Southerners wished to phase slavery out gradually and that the Civil War was caused by extremists trying to force the sudden abolition of slavery on the South. In its attitudes towards racial history and its interpretation of the Civil War, *Santa Fe Trail* was not an aberration, but rather entirely typical. Films such as *So Red the Rose* (1935), *Gone with the Wind* (1939), *Belle Starr* (1941), *The Undefeated* (1969) and numerous others provided the same depiction of slavery and race relations. These films were made during the Depression, World War II and the Vietnam War; they taught white audiences that pesky issues like slavery and racial equality should not be allowed to distract Americans from uniting to deal with the crises they faced. And they instructed black audiences that they were incapable of handling equality and that their interests would be best served accepting the *status quo*. Is it pedantic to examine the accuracy of films that are insubstantial entertainments, when they convey such consequential 'lessons' from history?

Historical (or pseudo-historical) lessons have also been both absorbed and manipulated by political leaders. Richard Nixon incessantly invoked the film *Patton* to justify his invasion of Cambodia in 1970. But more than that, he apparently was inspired by the film to make his extremely controversial decision. Nixon watched the film twice in the fortnight before he announced the invasion. After the invasion was announced, Nixon had *Patton* shown to the White House staff.[43] Henry Kissinger observes the powerful influence this particular film had on the President, noting that when Nixon was under pressure, he tended to think of himself as 'a beleaguered military commander in the tradition of *Patton*'.[44] If the people with the power to wage war and negotiate peace are drawing their knowledge of history from films, can we afford to neglect the content of these films?

Of course filmmakers, like playwrights and novelists, should be able to alter the historical record in order to enhance the drama or to make the author's point clearer. But, given the influence of film, it is difficult to accept that historians should not examine them. The editors of this volume do not maintain that historical accuracy is the sole, or even the most important, criterion by which a film should be judged. But we do feel that the purported facts of a historical film are worthy of consideration, correction and analysis. Yet too often, film scholars dismiss the accuracy of historical films as unworthy of consideration. For example, there are these strictures by one authority on *The Birth of a Nation*:

> In terms of film history, Griffith's opinion and treatment of blacks is not all that important. But inasmuch as *The Birth of a Nation* is quite possibly the single most important film of all time, and a film that is rarely regarded objectively *because* of its racial content, it is important to clarify Griffith's *intent* and to stress that, while difficult it should be shown in an atmosphere that tries to separate form from content.[45]

Comments like this tend to marginalize film studies. Of course, it is important to appreciate both the aesthetic qualities of *The Birth of a Nation* and its seminal importance in film history. But should one completely separate form from content? I have trouble imagining an art historian writing that because it is difficult to view Picasso's *Guernica* objectively, we should only view its form and try to ignore the messages it is conveying. As for the comment that Griffith's opinion and treatment of blacks is – even judged solely in the context of film history – unimportant, it is morally and intellectually obtuse. One of the purposes of the film was to depict blacks in a certain manner and this purpose affected the content, form and reception of the film. It is wrongheaded to assess films solely by their quality as depictions of historical reality, but it is also wrongheaded to assume that that the aesthetic qualities of a historical film are the only qualities worthy of discussion. The claim to historical accuracy is inherent in both the genre and purpose of historical films, and the validity of this claim requires assessment.

IV

But what is historical accuracy? It is an interesting paradox that while filmmakers, as we have seen, often boast of their painstaking research in making historical films, the inaccuracy of historical films has become almost proverbial not only among academics, but among the general public as well.[46] (Although, also paradoxically, this reputation for error and inexactitude has protected filmmakers from criticism as historians have tended to dismiss historical films as unworthy of serious analysis.) But, while audiences accept the principle that historical films are frequently inaccurate, they tend to accept the 'facts' depicted in them uncritically.

Admittedly, historical filmmakers often do take considerable efforts to be accurate in showing what people wore, what particular buildings looked like, and other physical details of life in past times; so much so, that the generic name for films set in the past is 'costume pictures'. Partly this is because this particular form of virtue has its own rewards, obtained through merchandising opportunities and commercial tie-ins.[47] Partly this attention to sets and costumes occurs because these are areas where the technical skills of studio personnel, used to creating backgrounds for everything from prison films to science fiction adventures, can readily be brought to bear. But this concern for physical details is frequently combined with a disregard for fidelity to what actually occurred or how people really behaved in a past epoch.

Historical films often win Oscars for costume and set designs, but unfortunately the Academy does not give out awards for accuracy in historical research or avoidance of anachronism. In order to recreate the semblance of New York in the 1840s for Martin Scorsese's film *Gangs of New York*, 45 life-sized buildings were constructed on a set outside of Rome. To ensure verisimilitude, bricks, made to match the physical appearance of those used in nineteenth-century buildings, were imported from New York.[48] Yet the film also contained numerous historical errors and distortions, some minor, some significant.[49] Having gone to enormous expense to ensure that the sets for the film looked authentic, the cavalier approach the filmmakers took to what people actually did and how they behaved, makes for a striking contrast.

Even when filmmakers try to get the manners and behaviour of historical characters correct, their good intentions are often built on shifting sands. For *Titanic,* James Cameron spent lavishly in an impressive effort to recapture the appearance of the doomed ocean liner and to recreate the costumes worn by its passengers.[50] To his credit,

Cameron also determined that the actors in the film had to depict convincingly the everyday demeanours and conduct of the passengers. In Cameron's words: 'In addition to how things looked, every nuance of human behaviour had to be examined. How people moved, how they spoke, their etiquette . . . all these things had to be known before a single scene could be filmed'.[51] In order to ensure that these commendable standards were met, Cameron hired an etiquette coach who instructed the actors in 'proper behavior'. In addition to giving the actors a three-hour course, the etiquette coach also produced a training video which was replayed on a loop in the wardrobe building.[52] Yet in the film, the heroine, played by Kate Winslett, smokes in a public restaurant and makes an obscene gesture with her finger; both actions unthinkable to an Edwardian lady.

The Kate Winslett character, a young socialite named Rose Bokater, is also shown responding at a dinner to the boasts of J. Bruce Ismay, the owner of the White Star Line, about the size of the *Titanic*, by commenting that 'Freud's ideas about the male preoccupation with size may be of interest to you'. Ismay, unaware of who Freud is, asks 'Is he a passenger?', while the other diners chuckle. Don Lynch, the historical consultant for the film, describes this as a 'wonderful line where Rose gets to show how educated she is'.[53] She certainly is. Unless Rose was a reader of the *American Journal of Psychology* – as so many Edwardian socialites were – which, in its April issue in 1910, printed an English translation of a lecture by Freud on 'The Origin and Development of Pyschoanalysis', she would have had to be able to read German to have been aware of Freud's views.[54] At the very least, Ismay's ignorance regarding Freud is perfectly comprehensible and the line is a clumsy anachronism.

All of these mistakes are quite venial. But the readiness of the filmmakers to let these anachronisms through, for the sake of a dramatic gesture or a feeble witticism, is indicative of the relative importance that filmmakers attach to the authentic-looking costumes and sets, on the one hand, and to historical veracity on the other. Historians would reverse this set of priorities. Simon Schama, after praising the meticulously researched sets of the film *Amistad* and after criticizing the anachronisms in it, observes, 'A true feeling for period, then, should never be confused with pedantically correct costume-and-décor detail. It's possible to get all the minutiae right and still get the dramatic core of a history wrong'.[55] Another historian is more caustic, denouncing the 'misplaced sense of historical values' which leads filmmakers to lavish huge sum of money on 'accurate' costumes and sets, as reflecting 'a crude empiricism and antiquarianism'.[56] It is revealing that one historical film, Carl Dreyer's *La passion de Jeanne d'Arc*, which is admired by critics and scholars alike, eschewed accurate period detail in sets and costumes; for example, the English troops in this 1928 film wore helmets like those worn by German soldiers in World War I.

The sort of historical accuracy admired by historians, that is, fidelity to fact together with a sensitivity to the beliefs and values of past generations, seems to be regarded by filmmakers as being rather like frugality in running a five star restaurant: perhaps an admirable virtue in itself, but not one appropriate to this particular business. And the fact that filmmaking is a business has made it difficult to produce a historically accurate film commercially. Furthermore, the pressure on commercial filmmakers when making historical films is magnified by their cost. Because of the expenses in creating sets and costumes, and in filming in suitable locations, historical films are often a significant financial gamble. When they succeed, as *Titanic* and *Braveheart* did, fortunes are made. When they fail the results can be disastrous, as happened with *Heaven's Gate*. As Martin Scorsese explained, in reflecting on *Gangs of New York*, 'With a budget of $96 million or something you have to be responsible for that money. So you have to try to combine what interests you with some elements of box office and some responsibility to the studio'.[57]

To make a profit, films need to be entertaining to the widest possible audience. An important part of this is for the scriptwriters to create characters that the audience can understand and with whom they can empathize. In a historical film, this can be problematic as people in the past had attitudes towards sexual mores, religious tolerance, as well as political, racial and gender equality that modern audiences find alien, barely comprehensible, indeed, in some cases, actually abhorrent. All too often, filmmakers respond to this challenge by depicting people in the past as having the same beliefs and opinions as the filmgoers. The excesses of films such as *Braveheart* or *Robin Hood: Prince of Thieves* (which managed to introduce feminism, multiculturalism and democracy into late twelfth-century England) are too well-known and obvious to deserve discussion here. But even more thoughtful and carefully researched films often fall into this trap. Natalie Davis, for example, observes that *Amistad*, despite the care lavished on accurate sets, makes 'patterns of alliance and friendship in New England in 1839–40 resemble egalitarian hopes in late twentieth-century America'.[58]

There are a number of areas where filmmakers have consistently tended to flatten differences between past and present, in order to make the former accessible, but religion is perhaps the most flagrantly and anachronistically mishandled. Perhaps no aspect of the past resonates less with modern audiences than the religious views and zeal of the past and no aspect of the past has been treated so carelessly by filmmakers. At times these sins are sins of commission, as in Luc Besson's *The Messenger: The Story of Joan of Arc*, in which the duke of Burgundy coolly tells Joan that he doesn't believe in God or the Devil – an almost inconceivable sentiment in the fifteenth century and one which, even if held, would not have been casually admitted. (For the record, Philip the Good, the duke in question, was ostentatiously, if conventionally, pious). But more often, the sin is one of omission and religion is either unmentioned or de-emphasized. A notable recent example of this is *Kingdom of Heaven*, a film which removes religious motivations from the Crusades and replaces them with political correctness and a quest for religious tolerance. In this volume, Peter Marshall points out that Thomas More's religious zeal is barely hinted at in *A Man for All Seasons*, while David Smith discusses the reluctance of filmmakers to treat the complicated religious makeup of the historical Oliver Cromwell.

Race and slavery are also often taboo subjects in historical films, at least in so far as they are part of American history. In the film *The Patriot*, the hero, a South Carolina planter who fights the British during the American Revolution, has free black labourers – the film insists that they are not slaves – who loyally support him during the conflict. In *Somersby*, a Confederate veteran returns from the Civil War and establishes an agricultural co-operative on a former plantation, where the former slaves now have a chance to own their own land and are treated equally with white farmers. In this respect, historical films have done a good deal to impede our understanding of history because they reinforce a prevalent misconception about the past: that it offers an exact mirror to the present.

Audiences also expect historical films to communicate clear moral certainties and a plot that resolves the dramatic issues unambiguously.[59] Since the past, while full of drama, is also conspicuously lacking in moral certainty and neat resolutions of complex problems, filmmakers often tailor the past to meet both dramatic necessities and audience expectations. Daniel Walkowitz relates that when he was participating in a film for American public television about working-class life in a nineteenth-century city, the screenwriter was tempted throughout 'to reduce history to dramatic conflicts between good and evil. In order that the viewer has a clear-cut identification with the workers, he was determined to make the bosses nasty and brutish. In the belief that audiences find ambiguity unappealing, he wanted to substitute personality for political positions'.[60] As one scholar has observed, 'When historians call for "historical accuracy" in this context, what they want, more than precision of detail, is acknowledgement of the ambiguity and complexity of the past'.[61]

A major respect in which historical films oversimplify is to interpret historical change as being driven by individuals and their personal desires. As Rosenstone has observed, it is possible to make historical films that foreground impersonal processes rather than individuals; in fact, he cites Sergei Eisenstein's *Battleship Potemkin* and *October* as examples.[62] However these were films that were officially subsidized and were not dependent on making a profit. And even non-commercial filmmakers are often reluctant to deal with a historical subject which cannot readily be oriented to individuals. Geoffrey Ward, the writer for Ken Burns's phenomenally successful documentary series *The Civil War*, responded to criticism that the series neglected the experience of slaves with the revealing admission that 'nothing we could find provided enough information about any *individual* slaves to sustain the sort of first-person self-portraits over five years of war that we were able to create for many of our white protagonists'.[63]

Historical accuracy is also frequently sacrificed to 'Hollywood's faith that historical events rise to the occasion of exceptional human romance'.[64] A love story is gilt-edged box-office insurance and, as the examples of *Braveheart, Reds* and *Titanic,* among many others, demonstrate, romances are worked into historical events on the flimsiest of pretexts and given centre stage. Before *La Reine Margot,* a 1994 film version of Alexandre Dumas's novel about the infamous St Bartholomew's Day massacre, was released in the United States, Miramax, the American distributor for the film insisted that it be re-edited to highlight its romantic elements, a decision that speaks volumes about how market forces determine the contents of historical films.[65] The emphasis on romance has tended to add further layers of schematic artificiality into historical films as cinema love stories have their own conventions – initial interest, physical confrontation, obstruction and eventual denouement – and historical events are shoehorned into conforming to these conventions.

Everyone loves a lover, but every filmgoer also loves a satisfactory ending; that is, one in which the good are rewarded, the evil punished and righteous causes prevail. Unfortunately, these happened no more frequently in the past than they do in the present and filmmakers often feel compelled to rewrite history to supply satisfactory conclusions where providence has failed to do so. Toplin has described how he changed the ending in a documentary that he produced for American public television on Denmark Vesey, who led a slave revolt in Charleston, South Carolina, in 1822. Because the revolt was brutally suppressed and Vesey executed, the producers worried that 'audiences would reject the film because of its gloomy ending'. Therefore an 'inspiring, uplifting finish' for the film was crafted, in which Vesey's wife reassured their son that his father would never be forgotten.[66] It should be remembered that this ending was contrived for a film that was not intended to make a profit; in a commercial film where the financial stakes are exponentially higher, the pressures to refashion the past must consequently be that much greater.

V

So far, we have been discussing ways in which films tend to misrepresent the past from commercial pressures and the resultant need to entertain mass audiences. But all films, even those which are not made in the hope of a large profit, or any profit at all, suffer from inherent limitations which prevent them from accurately representing the past. In the first place, the authenticity in recreating sets and costumes, in which filmmakers take such pride, is an illusion. The motion picture camera absorbs visual data in the same way that a black hole absorbs light, insatiably draining it all away. As the eminent medievalist David Herlihy has explained:

> In making the viewer an eyewitness to what purport to be past events, the historical film must pretend to show more about the past than its makers could possibly know. It must fill the field of vision with objects that will serve to maintain the illusion of reality. It is hard to choose appropriate objects, especially for events that occurred in the centuries or millenia before the very recent past .... For example, Charlemagne was crowned Emperor at Rome on Christmas night, 800; several chronicles record the event. But they do not describe what the interior of old St. Peter's – a church not now standing – looked like on that evening, what the courtiers and priests were wearing, what music was heard. To present this scene on film would require that the cinematographers supply all the missing information; they have no choice but to embroider spare records.[67]

L. P. Hartley's famous dictum that the past is a foreign country is only partially correct. It succinctly expresses an important truth: the past is alien to us. Not unrecognizably so, but it is true that they do things differently there. But one can visit a foreign country, one can even reside there and become acclimatized to it. The past is more like the ocean. Much of human history is irrecoverable, lost in profound darkness. For even greater portions of it, we have only scattered pieces of evidence comparable perhaps to those depths only known from beams of light shot out from bathyspheres. We cannot live in this environment, we cannot walk in it, we cannot touch anything in it. As we draw closer to the present we are entering the sunlit upper reaches of the ocean. Photography, phonographs, film, and even oral history combine to make this area more familiar – to extend the metaphor, we can now enter this realm, we can touch the objects in it, but it is still not our natural habitat.

Viewing films about any period before, say, 1850, audiences easily forget how much of what they are watching is pretence sustained by accepted conventions and a willing suspension of disbelief. One example of this concerns that most basic of human activities, speech. When Russell Crowe declaims in *Gladiator* or Charlton Heston pontificates in *The Ten Commandments*, their characters would not have been speaking in English. Interestingly, upon occasion, the makers of historical films have thought about the implications that the curse of Babel has for their work. In *Dances with Wolves*, much of the dialogue is spoken in Lakota, with translations provided in subtitles. In *Amistad* the African slaves continue to speak in Mende throughout the film and communicate with those who cannot speak their language through interpreters, gestures, sign language or drawings. In *The Thirteenth Warrior* (a film loosely based on Ibn Fadlan's well-known narrative of his encounter, in 921–22 C. E., with Vikings who had settled in what is now Russia), the Vikings speak their own language until Fadlan learns it, at which point the actors all speak English. The problem of languages does not prevent a film from being, in all but the most technical senses, historically accurate, but it is a useful reminder that all historical films are artifice and that the past cannot completely be recreated.

Herlihy has pointed out the difficulties in recreating events from periods where historians lack the evidence to supply the visual details that the camera demands. But what of a film trying to depict the coronation of Elizabeth II rather than that of Charlamagne? Since Westminster Abbey is still standing and since the ceremony was filmed, then surely this event could be accurately recreated? The coronation of 1953 can certainly be simulated with much more accuracy than that of 800, but it cannot be recreated with complete accuracy. The characters of the film would be inventions, since they would be played by actors, who even if they were mimicking the originals, would be, to a considerable extent using their own voices, gestures and movements. And we are now discussing the tiny minority of contemporary or nearly contemporary historical figures familiar to us, not the vast armies of such figures whose intonations, personal characteristics, even appearances, are largely or completely unknown.

All of this pertains only to the superficialities of visual details, yet the great gulf fixed between us and our ancestors lies in the realms of thought and feeling. Can modern Germans truly comprehend the mentalities of their Nazi grandparents? Can an American born within the last half-century fully assimilate the pervasive racism of a segregated society? Does anyone fully share the attitudes towards sex and gender of their forbears two generations ago? And this is still confining ourselves to the modern era, when we move back to the eras before Freud and Darwin, we are entering unfamiliar territory. It is difficult for scholars to set aside their own views on tolerance, religion, democracy and to enter into the mental worlds of past people, and no historical work has ever been completely free from anachronism. But the dangers of anachronism are particularly acute in historical films.

One reason for this has already been discussed: films that maximize the empathy between historical characters and the film audience, and which establish the relevance – be it real or fictive – between past and present tend to do better business. Another reason, more deeply rooted in the nature of the medium, rather than the business, of film, is that film can depict past events, but it cannot easily explain or contextualize them. Furthermore, while a film cannot contextualize what it depicts, it also has difficulty presenting variant interpretations of an event. Admittedly Akira Kurosawa's *Rashomon* famously related different versions of a single event from the perspectives of the main characters in the film. And *Reds* had witnesses to particular event's comment on both the events and the participants. But neither stratagem is completely successful. *Rashomon* took up an entire film to cover a single violent incident. And many critics and viewers felt that the commentary in *Reds* was artificial and slowed down the pace of the film.

Knowledge of the past is still most effectively conveyed in written words; no film can deliver the same levels of information without

seriously compromising its own aesthetic integrity and dramatic qualities. Ian Kershaw has observed – he is speaking of television but his
remarks apply with equal force to cinema – that film is at its weakest
'where an issue is highly contentious and subject to widely differing
interpretations. The lifeblood of a history seminar is disagreement and
problems of interpretation . . . . Television history is far more direc-
tive. Problems of interpretation tend to muddy the waters and leave
the viewer confused, baffled, or at least unable to decide which of
variant interpretations is most valid . . . in a ratings-led medium, there
is no room for this approach'.[68]

As Ian Jarvie has observed, while a particular viewpoint can be represented in a film, that viewpoint cannot be defended with citations
of sources, and objections to that viewpoint cannot be presented.[69]
Rosenstone has replied to this by maintaining that it is not necessary for historical works to assess or debate different interpretations of
historical topics. 'We all know many excellent narrative histories and
biographies that mute (or moot) debates by ignoring them or relegat-
ing them to appendices or burying them deep within the storyline'.[70]
Most histories or biographies deal with conflicting interpretations in
footnotes, although, as Rosenstone observes, some rely upon other
devices. But no historian or biographer completely ignores varying
interpretations of a topic and no film is able to employ devices such as
footnotes or appendices to discuss and evaluate debates on a historical
topic.[71] This inability to comment on events also prevents historical films from being able to evaluate the sources for the history they
present. When Oliver Hirschspiegel's *Downfall*, a brilliant evocation
of Berlin in the closing days of the Third Reich, was released, some
British historians criticized the film for its sympathetic portrayal of
Hitler's inner circle, particularly Albert Speer, who is depicted as defying the Führer in order to save German lives. The historians claimed
that there was a political agenda behind the film, in that it sought
to portray the Germans themselves as victims of Hitler.[72] In response
Hirschspiegel declared that he based his film on eyewitness sources
and that he was merely depicting what was in Speer's memoirs, one of
the few accounts from an eyewitness to Hitler's final hours.[73] I cannot
comment on the political agenda of the film, if there was one, but
the controversy demonstrates an important limitation in the depiction
of history on film. Speer's unreliability and self-serving motives can
be discussed in print, but how can they be presented on screen? In
portraying Hitler's last days on screen, the filmmakers effectively are
faced with a dilemma: they either ignore Speer's account which is

dramatic and *might* be accurate or they present what Speer says happened as actually having happened. If the testimony of self-interested
and biased witnesses is to be rejected then historians will be unable
to recount, much less analyze, many past events. But to present such
testimony uncritically is to perpetuate all sorts of distortions and false-
hoods. Cinema has, as of yet, devised no satisfactory solution to this
fundamental problem.

   Faced with the inability of film, because of commercial considerations and because of its inherent limitations, to present history
accurately, some historians have argued that the accuracy of historical
films should not be discussed at all. In the words of Toplin, '*Accurate*
strikes me as a troublesome and inappropriate word to employ in these
discussions about cinematic history. Our discussions about film would
profit greatly if we generally set this term aside, since it is not truly
applicable to the task of the filmmaker'.[74] (As has been observed,
historical filmmakers frequently claim otherwise.) The most forceful
exponent of this view is Rosenstone who demands that historians

> stop expecting films to do what (we imagine) books do. Stop expecting them to
> get the facts right, or to present several sides of an issue or to give a fair hearing
> to all the evidence on a topic, or to all the characters or groups represented in a
> particular situation, or to provide a broad and detailed historical context for events.
> Stop, also, expecting them to be a mirror of a vanished reality that will show us the
> past as it really was. Dramatic films are not and will never be 'accurate' in the same
> way as books (claim to be), no matter how many academic consultants work on a
> project and no matter how seriously their advice is taken.[75]

In Rosenstone's opinion any attempt to assess the accuracy of historical films is fundamentally misguided. He criticizes Natalie Davis for
her comments on particular historical films because

> Her judgements contain too much that derives from the standards of academic
> evidence. This puts as much of a burden on filmmakers as one would put on
> historians if we were to judge their renderings of the past in filmic terms and then
> to ask why are such works, compared to the colour, movement and excitement of
> the screen, so slow, stuffy, measured, colourless and silent?[76]

Like Sorlin, Rosenstone believes that historians should not judge the
historical accuracy of films. But Sorlin does not believe that historical
films are history, Rosenstone apparently does. In fact he goes so far as
to hail Oliver Stone's *JFK* as being 'among the most important works
of American history ever to appear on screen'.[77]

There is a problem here: the word 'history' has several different meanings and Rosenstone (and to a degree Toplin) are jumbling these distinctions together. On the one hand, the word signifies everything that has happened in the past. It can also signify the ways in which the past is interpreted and understood. And 'history' is also the name for an academic discipline that seeks to understand what happened in the past and to interpret it in the light of available evidence. For reasons discussed above, no film can be a work of history according to the third definition of the word, because a film cannot adhere to the methodological standards of the discipline. When Rosenstone hails a movie as a work of history, he is using the second definition, that of history as how the past is interpreted. This is manifest in Rosenstone's definition of a historian 'as someone who devotes a significant part of his or her working career to making meaning (in whatever medium) out of the past'.[78] This definition certainly includes filmmakers; it also includes historical novelists, dramatists, painters, politicians, theologians, philosophers and numerous others.

What Rosenstone and Toplin are essentially saying is that films are another artistic representation of the past and should not be judged by the standards of academic history. That is fair enough. But they should not confuse artistic representations of the past with the work of historians. Re-imagining the past is not the same thing as analyzing it. Of course, artists may – and frequently do – exceed historians in analytical sophistication, in the brilliance of their insights, or even the quality of their research. But artists are free to disregard or rearrange facts, historians are not. Of course, facts can admit of multiple interpretations. And of course bias and partisan zeal can lead historians to misinterpret those facts or even misrepresent them. But in order to gain acceptance, a historian's interpretation has to conform to all the known facts and more than this, it has to interpret them plausibly. Contrary to what some post-modernists maintain, one historical interpretation is not as good as another and David Irving's interpretation of the Holocaust is not as valid as Deborah Lipstadt's.

Nor do I think that it is correct to say that the accuracy of historical films is unimportant. Assessing how a historical film makes use of its sources is essential to assessing it as work of art. All historical films tell several stories simultaneously. One is of the events that they are depicting. Another story is about the creators of the film and another is about the periods in which they are created. To understand all of these stories, it is necessary to examine what is portrayed in historical films, but also to examine the film's misrepresentations and omissions. And most importantly, film is just too powerful a medium for its messages to be ignored and our understanding of the past too crucial for us to be indifferent to the errors, untruths and distortions conveyed in historical films.

VI

How then should scholars and those outside the academic community react to historical films? David Herlihy argues that historical films should not be used in classroom instruction or the subject of scholarly investigation, since, he maintains, the suspension of rational thought entailed in watching a historical film undermines true historical understanding.[79] This is an extreme, and somewhat impractical, reaction to a genuine concern. Film is far too pervasive a part of popular cultures across the globe to be so casually dismissed, and historians should be paying more attention to historical films. It is paradoxical that historians of early-modern Britain – an epoch which has unusual prominence in popular culture – have been remarkably dismissive of the depictions of the Tudor and Stuart periods in film, television, historical novels, children's literature and other popular media. A number of American historical journals, notably the *American Historical Review* and the *Journal of American History* regularly print reviews of historical films written by qualified scholars. Is there a valid reason why the *English Historical Review* and the *Historical Journal* should not do likewise? (And given the number of programmes dealing directly with historical topics on television, the small screen should be covered as well.) And, as already been remarked, scriptwriters frequently base their work on historical novels and plays. These novels and plays should be treated in historiographical surveys and subjected to historical analysis. I have been struck by both the number of films discussed in this book, that were based on dramas by Maxwell Anderson, and also by how little attention historians have paid to his work.

Let us be clear here: greater attention paid by historians to historical films will not result in any changes to the ways in which these films are made. Any hopes that filmmakers will pay attention to academic criticism or praise are as unrealistic as tossing daisies off the Hollywood sign and waiting for the echoes. What increased academic attention to historical films can accomplish is to begin to place the study of them, and instruction about them, more firmly in the curriculum. This will hopefully help educate students in how to view these films critically and, at the same time, help remind historians of their importance. Furthermore, while historians should devote more time and energy to the study of historical films, film scholars should not dismiss the contents of historical films as trivial. When analyzing historical films, it is important that both the historical context in which a film was made and the historiographical traditions the film draws on be examined. This requires drawing on several disciplines; but it can and has been done: Greg Walker's study of *The Private Life of Henry VIII* and Julianne Pidduck's study of *La Reine Margot* are models to be followed in all analyses of historical films.[80]

Furthermore, while films cannot follow historical methodology, they are useful in presenting history and they should be utilized in classrooms. For one thing, they certainly arouse interest in a topic and can be used to focus debate or discussion. Historical films also convey a feeling for life in a distant past. The illusory nature of this need to be explained carefully to students, but the emotional appreciation of a historical situation can be valuable. The film *La Reine Margot* contains many fictive elements – for example, Catherine de Medici did not poison her son, Charles IX – but it also provides a vivid picture of the tensions in Paris, and the fratricidal hatred between Catholic and Protestant, at the time of the St Bartholomew's Day massacre. Natalie Zeman Davis, although critical of historical inaccuracies in Stanley Kubrick's *Spartacus*, also praises it for its portrayal of the social divisions in ancient Rome, brought to life through the body language of the actors and the movements of Kubrick's camera.[81] A number of contributors to this book have admired aspects of films, even though in some respects these films presented distorted views of the past, because of emotional or dramatic truths that they presented.

Films can also be used in the classroom to show how historical figures and historical events are reinterpreted in different periods.[82] This can be used not only to examine a particular historical tradition or historical myths but to think about historical evidence and methodology. All of these are specific classroom uses for film and it is the hope of the editors and contributors to this book that it too might be of assistance to those teaching or studying the Tudor and Stuart epochs. But we also hope that this book might be of interest to those outside of schools and universities who, having seen these films, wish to learn more about what actually happened. The following chapters present painless – we hope – introductions to the topics addressed in these films and will provide guides for those interested in further investigation. Historical films have the power to kindle interest in and empathy for past people and epochs; we hope that this book might help some viewers of historical films to arrive at a greater understanding of them as well.

2

A Tyrant for All Seasons: Henry VIII on Film

Thomas S. Freeman

It all started with Hans Holbein. Although the original version of his famous portrait of Henry VIII, painted on a mural in the privy chamber at Whitehall Palace, has not survived, it was often copied and numerous reproductions seared it into the consciousness of subsequent generations. When preparing for the lead role in Alexander Korda's seminal film about the king, Charles Laughton grew his beard and cut his hair to match the appearance of Holbein's Henry. His efforts were appreciated; the *New York Times* film critic approvingly wrote that Laughton 'sometimes looks as if he had stepped from the frame of Holbein's painting'.[1] Virtually every cinema actor who has played Henry, from Emil Jannings to Sid James, has struck the accustomed pose of the Holbein portrait (see Plate 1), often several times in the same scene. The costume in Holbein's painting has been equally ubiquitous; every cinema Henry has worn the flat hat with plumes, the medallion and the dagger, although not even Sid James has dared to wear the codpiece.[2]

However, Holbein not only preserved the features of the royal Dorian Gray, he also partially shaped Henry's historical reputation. The king, standing like a defiant colossus, with his legs wide apart, supporting his massive torso, embodies pride, arrogance, authority, resolution and indomitable will. Yet if Holbein succeeded in creating an enduring image of Henry, he did not succeed in creating an endearing one. To the vast majority of those who view it, the Holbein Henry is a counterfeit, a heroic image stamped on the base metal of the king's

30

31

Plate 1   The cartoon – which is all that survives – of Hans Holbein's iconic portrait of King Henry VIII. Courtesy of National Portrait Gallery, London.

character. In large part, this was due to Henry's ruthless slaughter of both friend and foe. In Sir Walter Ralegh's words, 'if all the pictures and patterns of a merciless prince were lost in the world, they might all again be painted to the life out of the story of this king'.[3] Cruelty had transformed St George into a dragon and a royal hero into a tyrant.

Worse yet, in an era of religious polarization, Henry managed to alienate both sides of the confessional divide. To Catholics he was the ruler who led England out of the True Church into heresy and who initiated centuries of persecution and prejudice for those who remained loyal to the old religion. Yet Protestants did not champion Henry's memory either. For one thing, they also disapproved of his motives for abolishing papal authority in England, and of his methods in doing so. Moreover, Protestants remembered the all too numerous evangelicals and reformers whom Henry sent to the stake. John Foxe, the chronicler of the Protestant and proto-Protestant martyrs, caustically explained that Henry's failure to finish the religious reformation he had started was God's will, because the Lord wished to have the Reformation carried out by Edward VI and Elizabeth, 'whose hands were yet undefiled with any blood, and live[s] unspotted with any violence or cruelty'.[4]

Yet while Henry VIII was, and is, remembered as a bloodstained tyrant, there is both more and less to his popular reputation. This is because of the one fact about Henry that everyone remembers: he had six wives. On one level, this makes Henry look ridiculous. In the course of his matrimonial adventures he assumed a string of undignified roles: infatuated suitor, bullying husband and cuckolded spouse. And, since two wives were executed, along with a string of actual or alleged lovers and accomplices, there is a terrible aspect to this as well, and Henry would be popularly remembered as an English Bluebeard, wedding and beheading his brides with ruthless abandon. And yet, paradoxically, Henry's multiple marriages also humanized him, making it possible for the vast armies of people who have loved and lost, to empathize, if not sympathize, with someone who loved and lost repeatedly and conspicuously.

And mixed in with ridicule, abhorrence and empathy there was also an element of grudging admiration for the supposed virility and sexual prowess Henry displayed in his marital endeavours. This admiration, and Henry's reputation as a stud, are perfectly epitomized in the famous music hall song, whose protagonist, on the basis of his nuptials with the oft-married widow next door, proudly identifies himself as 'Henry the Eighth'. Films about Henry have frequently capitalized on his supposed sexual prowess. Publicity posters for *The Private Life of Henry VIII* read: 'What a King! What a Lover! What a Man!'. The publicists for *Carry on Henry* deftly wove together several strands of the mythic Henry – tyrant, Bluebeard and Lothario – with a slogan hailing the king as 'A Great Guy with his "Chopper"'.

II

The richness and complexity of the popular conceptions about Henry help explain the monarch's memorable but chequered film career. It would be affected by transient crises, such as the abdication of Edward VIII, and also by fundamental social and political transformations of the twentieth century: the evolving status of women, changes in sexual mores, the rise and fall of Fascism, the Cold War and the decline of the British Empire. At the beginning of the last century, Henry's reputation stood higher than at any point since his death. As the British Empire stood at its zenith, Albert Frederick Pollard composed one of the most influential biographies of Henry VIII ever written. In it he extolled Henry as the 'father of modern imperialism' (in late Victorian England this was praise) and also as a protector of parliamentary democracy.[5]

However, while Pollard's biography remained the standard academic work on Henry for decades, it did not directly influence most cinematic portrayals of the king. The scriptwriters for the films, and the dramatists who wrote the plays on which the films were based, drew their knowledge of Henry from other works. In 1934, Francis Hackett, a journalist and author, sued London Films, alleging that *The Private Life of Henry VIII* plagiarized his popular biography of the king. Korda, the producer of the film, denied Hackett's charge emphatically: 'in all the film, there is not one incident, not one line or phrase, borrowed from Mr. Hackett. If, by any chance, there are minor similarities – and I am not aware of any – that is because we both borrowed from history'.[6] In fact, the approach of Korda and his scriptwriters to historical fact was so cavalier (it included the invention of a fictitious lover for Henry's fourth wife, Anne of Cleves) that it is often difficult to ascertain from which sources they drew their 'history'.

However, it is fairly clear that they did draw on Hackett's biography (and it is worth observing that Korda never explicitly denied consulting it) for the film. The depiction of Anne of Cleves bargaining for generous terms for agreeing to divorce Henry echoes Hackett, and the terms of the agreement match Hackett's description of them.[7] Hackett describes Henry – in a 'mellow mood' after his marriage to Catherine Howard – ordering the release of Sir Thomas Wyatt; this is recapitulated in *The Private Life of Henry VIII*, only in the film Henry not only releases Wyatt, he also commutes all impending death sentences.[8] And Hackett's claim that Anne of Cleves, on her voyage to England, learned to play card games that Henry enjoyed, may have inspired one of the most famous scenes in the film, in which Anne and Henry pass their wedding night playing cards.[9]

Fifteen years later, in 1949, Hackett sued Maxwell Anderson, the dramatist whose play *Anne of the Thousand Days* (which would be the basis for the later film of the same name) was then enjoying considerable success on Broadway. Anderson furiously countersued for libel, and both suits were settled upon the playwright's payment of the token sum of $1 to Hackett.[10] In a newspaper article, written in response to the plagiarism suit, Anderson described the genesis of the play and listed the sources he had consulted. He admitted reading Hackett's biography but he declared that he had also read Martin Hume's *The Wives of Henry VIII* and maintained that it was Hume's book that had given him the idea for a play about Anne Boleyn.[11] Examination of *Anne of the Thousand Days* confirms that Anderson drew on Hume's book. The inaccurate claim in the play that Wolsey broke off the proposed marriage between Anne Boleyn and Henry Percy because Henry VIII was already smitten with Anne was taken from Hume.[12] At times Anderson follows Hume very closely. Hume describes Cromwell approaching Henry after Wolsey's fall, urging him to renounce papal authority over the English Church and papal jurisdiction over the king's marriage:

> Every Englishman is master in his own house and why should you not be so in England? Ought a foreign prelate to share power with you? . . . Sire you are but half a king, and we are but half your subjects.[13]

Anderson has Cromwell approaching Henry and saying:

> As matters stand you are but half a king. We are only half subjects to you. If you were truly king in England could a foreign prince call you to account?[14]

Nevertheless, Anderson also drew extensively upon Hackett's biography. It was almost certainly Anderson's source for his claims that Henry had been attracted to Anne Boleyn's mother and that Henry's passion for Anne led him to divorce Catherine of Aragon.[15] In his account of Wolsey breaking up the proposed match between Henry Percy and Anne Boleyn, Hackett describes Anne as a 'leggy girl'; dramatizing the same episode, Anderson has Wolsey call Anne a 'leggy girl'.[16] In *Anne of the Thousand Days*, Henry describes a letter he wrote to Anne: 'There's a heart drawn at the bottom of [one] letter, and in the heart "A.B." laboriously written. "Henry Rex seeks A.B., no other"'.[17] This letter, with the heart, the initials and Henry's inscription, is printed in Hackett's biography.[18]

Hackett is an obscure figure today, yet, through the cinema, he has powerfully shaped modern popular views of Henry, more so than any academic historian has. But what was his view of the king? Hackett saw Henry as a despotic, absolute ruler, but he focused on the feelings of inadequacy and weakness that he saw lurking beneath the king's supposed bluff and masterful personality. His Henry was insecure and oddly infantile – this may have been Hackett's most important contribution to Korda's film on Henry VIII – and bullied and blustered to reassure himself of his strength.[19] Hume's luridly written book, on the other hand, emphasized Henry's absolute power and its corrupting effect on the king's character; Henry began as a 'vain, brilliant sensualist, with the feelings of a gentleman, [but] ended a repulsive, bloodstained monster'.[20]

One other work powerfully influenced the ways in which Henry was portrayed in film: R. W. Chambers's biography of Thomas More, written in 1935, the year of More's canonization. Unlike the works of Hackett and Hume, Chambers's book not only gained a wide popular audience, it also won great acclaim among critics and scholars. And although Robert Bolt never discussed the historical sources he used for *A Man for All Seasons*, there is no doubt that he drew on Chambers's biography, not only for its data, but also for its portrayal of More as a martyr for free speech who died 'for the right . . . not to be compelled to say that which he does not believe'.[21] The obverse of envisioning More as a champion of individual liberty was conceiving of Henry VIII as a tyrant and Chambers, perhaps inspired by contemporary events and personalities, maintained that Henry 'succeeded in establishing a dictatorship' even though it 'revolted the consciences of his subjects'.[22] The three writers – Hackett, Hume and Chambers – who provided the foundation for cinematic portrayals of Henry all differed from Pollard in seeing the king as a brutal tyrant rather than a heroic monarch who paved the way for parliamentary democracy and the British Empire.

III

Cinema's first depiction of the second Tudor king was a filmed version of Sir Herbert Tree's production of Shakespeare's *Henry VIII*, made in 1911. But the first significant film about Henry was *Anna Boleyn*, directed by Ernst Lubitsch and starring Germany's leading film actor, Emil Jannings, as Henry VIII. Jannings's performance established a number of features that would characterize later cinema portrayals of the king: the physicality, the carnal appetites, the brutality, the capriciousness and the sexual aggressiveness. Charles Laughton studied Jannings's performance and imitated many aspects of it; in particular, Jannings apparently inspired the notorious eating scenes of *The Private Life of Henry VIII*.[23]

As this suggests, the chief importance of *Anna Boleyn* was its influence on Korda's ground-breaking film. For the first, but not the last, time, the life and matrimonial adventures of Henry would prove to be a cinematic goldmine. *Anna Boleyn* cost a massive eight million marks, but the U.S. distribution rights alone were sold for 14 million marks.[24] Korda was working in Vienna when *Anna Boleyn* was released and the success of Lubitsch's film inspired him to make his own Tudor film in 1920, a version of Mark Twain's novel, *The Prince and the Pauper*, and the part of Henry was a major one in the picture.[25] It was shown in England in 1927 and received favourable critical notices; this success helped to influence Korda's decision, after he had established his own production company in England in 1932, to make a new film about Henry VIII.

When this film, which Korda produced and directed, was released in 1933, it showed strong signs of the influence of the Lubitsch film. Nevertheless, in several crucial respects, *The Private Life of Henry VIII* differed from its predecessor. One of the most basic was in its depiction of Henry himself. While Jannings portrayed Henry as an amoral predator, Charles Laughton's Henry was more of a victim than a victimizer.[26] This effect was partly achieved through the ways in which Henry's wives were presented. In *The Private Life*, Henry is manipulated by Anne of Cleves, cuckolded by Catherine Howard and nagged, in his dotage, by a domineering Catherine Parr. Catherine of Aragon and Jane Seymour were difficult to cast as tormentors of a hapless Henry: the former because of the king's brutal treatment of her and the latter because of the quiescence of her brief marriage. Tellingly, these two queens barely figure in *The Private Life*; Catherine is flippantly dismissed in the first frame of the film with a title card declaring that 'her story is of no particular interest – she was a respectable woman' – while Jane is restricted to four brief appearances.[27]

Korda's film does present Anne Boleyn sympathetically and the viewer is encouraged to believe in her innocence of the crimes for which she was executed. Yet, as Greg Walker observes, 'our sympathy for Anne is never allowed to harden into dislike for, or even resentment of, Henry'.[28] Anne's appearances in the film all occur in its first 15 minutes. Moreover, Korda emphasizes glamour and stylishness, rather than terror or tragedy, in his depiction of her death. Anne (played by the strikingly beautiful Merle Oberon) is shown carefully arranging her hair in mirrors held by her attendants and wondering if the execution will disarrange it. Immediately after she is beheaded one spectator comments to his wife, 'One must admit she died like a queen' and his wife replies 'Yes, and that frock – wasn't it too divine?' Such scenes went some distance towards diminishing the horror of her death and went even farther in diminishing any sense of her as a victim.

Henry's brutality was further undermined by Laughton's insistence on playing Henry as a comic figure. Korda apparently wanted Laughton to eat with some decorum during the banqueting scenes, but Laughton chose instead to stuff the food into his mouth, belch, and then to deplore 'the decline in good manners'.[29] Moreover, Laughton's performance – possibly inspired by Hackett's biography – infantilized Henry, portraying him as both emotionally and sexually immature.[30] Laughton's Henry had the voracious appetites of Jannings's Henry, but where Jannings was aggressive and menacing, Laughton was energetic but ultimately ineffectual. This diminished Henry's stature but also diminished his culpability. This portrayal of Henry had an enduring influence on popular images of Henry; when Robert Bolt described Henry as 'the monstrous baby whom none dared gainsay' he was almost certainly thinking of Laughton's portrayal of the king.[31]

However, the infantilization of Henry undermined some of the messages that the film was apparently intended to convey. At one point, Henry orders Cromwell to triple the size of the fleet and fortify Dover, concluding ominously that 'To leave ourselves unguarded will cost us England'. Moreover – in a direct jab at proponents of collective security and disarmament – Henry brushes aside Cromwell's suggestion that security could best be achieved through diplomacy: 'Diplomacy? Diplomacy me foot! I'm an Englishman, I can't say one thing and mean another'.[32] Such lines had unmistakeable resonances in the 1930s and placed Korda's film firmly on the side of those, led by Winston Churchill, who argued that England needed to rearm in the face of potential German aggression.[33]

Such a position was in accord with the anti-Fascist sentiments which were a consistent feature of subsequent Korda films.[34] The outspoken advocacy of rearmament also reflected the extensive financial, social and political relationships that developed in this period between Churchill and Korda.[35] But if Korda wished these foreign policy precepts to be taken seriously – as he almost certainly did – why did he continually depict the monarch who uttered them as childish and absurd? Greg Walker maintains that Henry represents 'Churchillian patriotic opposition to "foreign" tyranny' and claims that 'the film seeks to evoke genuine sympathy for the ageing monarch'.[36] The second assertion may be largely true, but it is not necessarily consistent with the first assertion; in fact, sympathy for Henry is largely evoked by emphasizing qualities which throw his judgement, if not his qualities as a statesman, into doubt.

Another possibility is that Korda's opposition to dictatorship impelled him to accentuate the ridiculous aspects of Henry's character. It would have been characteristic of Korda; he inspired *The Great Dictator* (1940) by suggesting to Charlie Chaplin that he capitalize on his physical resemblance to Hitler and make a satirical comedy about the German dictator.[37] Korda may have intended to ridicule contemporary tyrants obliquely by producing an irreverent film about a famous historical tyrant. Henry's speeches about not relying on diplomacy and the imperative need for a navy are somewhat awkwardly inserted into the dialogue and they were extensively rewritten; they may have been late additions to an already conceived script. In any case, Korda's film illustrates the difficulty in presenting Henry as a prescient, patriotic monarch when his matrimonial career suggested that he lacked the necessary prudence and foresight. It is worth noting that despite the vocal support *The Private Life* gave to rearmament, Churchill does not seem to have been impressed with the film, while other potential supporters of the film's political positions were repelled by its levity and irreverence.[38]

Despite these criticisms, *The Private Life* was an overwhelming popular and financial success. It launched the careers of Laughton, Robert Donat (who played Thomas Culpepper, Catherine Howard's ill-fated lover) and Merle Oberon as major film stars.[39] It was also the first, and one of the greatest, international successes ever achieved by the British film industry. And, since imitation is the sincerest form of filmmaking, it inspired an ephemeral boom in English film biographies. Among the most notable of these was Herbert Wilcox's *Nell Gwynn* (1934), which is heavily indebted to Korda's film, particularly in the ways in which gastronomical appetites were used to represent sexual desires. But this trend was short-lived; the British film industry, and British society itself, were undergoing changes that would banish Henry VIII from films for years to come.

IV

These changes were apparent in the next film in which Henry played a significant role: *The Tudor Rose* (1936). Although largely forgotten, this film, relating the short life, and much shorter reign, of Jane Grey, was both popular and critically acclaimed; in fact, contemporary reviewers praised it more warmly than they praised any of Korda's historical films.[40] Its solemnity and respect for authority made it the antithesis of *The Private Life* and it may well have been a response to Korda's film. *The Tudor Rose* opens with crowds of people kneeling in the rain, as they cluster outside the Royal Palace, praying for their dying monarch. (This was a scene which must have resonated with audiences for whom the death of George V was a recent memory.) With Henry dying as thunder roars and lightning flashes, the leading nobles of the realm are clustered around the royal sickbed to hear the king name his successor. Sir John Gates, the henchman of John Dudley, the Earl of Warwick (as he is titled in the film, in reality, Dudley did not become an earl until shortly *after* Henry VIII's death) whispers to his master, 'The passing of a tyrant'. Warwick (Cedric Hardwicke) solemnly corrects him: 'Before he came each man fought for himself under the White Rose or the Red, and when he goes there will be many struggling to grasp the threads of power that fall from those hands'. Henry VIII (Frank Cellier) raises himself on the bed and, as the thunder rolls, utters his last words, a curse against anyone who plots against the line of succession he has established. Warwick dismisses the curse as empty words, but as the film unfolds it moves inexorably to destroy the Seymours, and then Warwick, when they attempt to seize power for themselves.

Henry not only proves to be an accurate prophet, but as Jeffrey Richards acutely observes, the king's death in the midst of a great storm, along with the curse and its fulfilment, establishes 'the throne's magical powers'.[41] There was every reason to do so in 1936, as the crisis caused by Edward VIII's determination to marry Wallis Simpson unfolded. The themes of *The Tudor Rose* – the sacral power of the crown and the inviolability of the succession – were efforts to shore up traditional respect for the monarchy in the face of rising tides that threatened to inundate it. At the same time *The Tudor Rose* was also part of an increasingly conservative trend in English historical films. As the worldwide depression bit deeply into the economy and the international situation worsened, English films became more support-ive of the government, the Establishment and the Empire.[42] Anna Neagle moved from playing a rambunctious, high-living, lower-class Nell Gwyn in 1934, to playing a regal Queen Victoria in two films whose titles admirably summarize their approach: *Victoria the Great* (1937) and its sequel, *Sixty Glorious Years* (1938).

In this political and social climate, Henry VIII was a most unsuit-able subject for films. It was almost impossible to make a film about Henry which did not inflame the still sensitive subject of royal mar-ital scandal and bring the monarchy into disrepute. The risqué, and also somewhat comic, aura surrounding the king – particularly in the wake of Korda's film – also undermined any chance that Henry had of becoming a patriotic icon during World War II. When filmmak-ers sought historical figures to glorify for wartime propaganda, they looked to Henry V, to Nelson and, above all, to Elizabeth and her sea dogs, rather than to the king who was, after all, credited with founding the royal navy. The wartime need for unambiguously heroic figures to rally the nation sealed Henry's cinematic fall from grace; apart from two rather idiosyncratic exceptions, he would not be seen in cinemas for three decades.[43]

If World War II was partially responsible for terminating Henry's screen career, the preoccupation with totalitarianism that pervaded lit-erature of the Cold War era, helped to revive it. But the Henry whose film career would be resurrected in the 1960s was markedly different from the comic, not uncongenial and intermittently patriotic monarch portrayed on screen in earlier decades. When Henry returned to the silver screen, he would be portrayed more consistently, yet even less sympathetically.

V

Two plays written in the aftermath of the Second World War, and in the long shadows cast by Hitler and Stalin, decisively shaped sub-sequent film portrayals of Henry. The first of these was Maxwell

Anderson's *Anne of the Thousand Days*, which opened on Broadway in 1948. Anderson declared that he had been attracted to the subject by his conception of Henry as a 'Sexual Everyman' whose 'excesses were the results of greater temptations, not of greater lust, rapacity or malice'.[44] As a result, his drama focuses on Henry's decline into tyranny with the decisions to divorce Catherine of Aragon, to break with Rome and to execute Anne Boleyn, as turning points, which transformed Henry from a young king, who genuinely wishes to rule well, into a conscienceless tyrant. As Anne Boleyn tells him at the end of the play,

> You're not old. You've been long a king.
> But you're still young and could change.
> You said – on that one day when we loved each other –
> you remember – that one day when I loved you
> and you loved me – that you would change – would
> seek justice – would be such a king as men hoped you'd be
> when you came to the throne?
> It's not too late for that.
> Only if you harden in your mind toward me . . .
> then I think it will indeed be too late.
> The king – the great king
> you might have been, will have died in you.[45]

In Anderson's portrayal, the slide into tyranny is made irreversible by Henry's having to wade through rivers of blood to attain his goals. There is a repeated emphasis in *Anne of the Thousand Days* on the slaughter Henry wreaks to eliminate opposition to his divorce. It is certainly true that there was opposition to Henry's policies and that he crushed it mercilessly, but when Anderson has Henry tell Anne that 'The altar at St. Paul's will stand ankle-deep in blood. The shop-keepers will mop blood from the floors. . . . But it must be done if we're to marry' or that it would take 'unlimited murder' to legal-ize their marriage, it is obvious that the dramatist was thinking of twentieth-century regimes, not sixteenth-century ones.[46]

Similar themes dominate Robert Bolt's drama about Thomas More, *A Man for All Seasons*. Like Anderson, Bolt was also concerned to emphasize Henry's degeneration into tyranny, and like Anderson, Bolt saw Henry's decision to marry Anne Boleyn as its beginning. Bolt's stage instructions describe More's sovereign: '*Not* the Holbein Henry, but a much younger man, clean-shaven, bright-eyed, graceful and ath-letic. The Golden Hope of the New Learning throughout Europe.

Only the levity with which he handles his absolute power foreshadows his eventual corruption'.[47] In reality, Henry was around 40 when
the events recounted in the play occurred, and he was bearded, bald-
ing and tending towards corpulence. Moreover, after the execution of
Buckingham, a series of European wars and heavy taxes (notably the
hated 'Amicable Grant') to finance them, the golden hope had long
since lost most of his lustre. But Bolt wished to accentuate Henry's fall
from grace, and the importance of his execution of More in causing
that fall, and this entailed exaggerating Henry's youth, innocence and
potential for enlightened rule on the eve of his break with Rome.
Bolt's drama was a considerable international success, but it reached
an even wider audience when it was made into a film in 1966. And
since Bolt wrote the screenplay for the film, there was an unusual
consistency between the depiction of Henry in the play and the film.

The critical, and unexpected financial, success of *A Man for All
Seasons* revived Hollywood's interest in Henry VIII. Three years later,
in 1969, a film version of Anderson's drama, *Anne of the Thousand
Days*, was released. (It is indicative of the influence of *A Man for All
Seasons* on *Anne of the Thousand Days*, that More appears in a number of scenes that were not present in Anderson's original drama.)
Although made with a larger budget than *A Man for All Seasons*, and
boasting a major star, Richard Burton, in the role of Henry, *Anne
of the Thousand Days* was something of a disappointment, at least in
terms of its critical reception. A fundamental problem was that the
film ignores or blurs some of the themes that made Anderson's play
dramatically effective, if not historically accurate. The degeneration
of Henry from a potentially enlightened prince into a tyrant is largely
omitted. Nevertheless, Henry is still depicted as an autocrat. Although
the film omits many of the play's references to purges and wholesale
slaughter, the executions of individual opponents are mentioned, and
More's execution is actually shown on screen. The portrait of Henry
in the film is not as incisive as that in the play, yet both versions
do agree on Henry's tyranny and dismiss both his doubts about the
validity of his first marriage and his religious scruples as hypocrisy.[48]

VI

Yet while Henry might not have been depicted as a heroic figure, he
was, at this point in time, thriving in both cinema and television. *Anne
of the Thousand Days* received only lukewarm critical reviews but, if it
was not the spectacular success the studio had expected, it nevertheless

turned a profit. A year later, in 1970, the BBC had a considerable triumph, on both sides of the Atlantic, with a television series, *The Six Wives of Henry VIII*. Keith Michell, the Australian actor who portrayed the king, played him in the Laughton tradition (although with more subtlety and less bravado) emphasizing both the comedic aspects of the king's marital adventures and his emotional vulnerability. In 1972, there was an attempt to repeat the television success on the big screen, with Keith Michell reprising the role of Henry in a film with the same name as his television series. However, this film was an abject critical and financial failure.

But the year would see the king return to the silver screen, if not exactly in triumph, then certainly with considerable fanfare. *Carry on Henry* starred Sid James as Henry, and presented a version of Tudor history tailored to meet the talents of the Pinewood repertory company. Sid James's performance was the last gasp of the music hall Henry: lusty, bluff and aggressively lecherous. (The film even depicts the king hunting – quite literally – women through the forest.) Yet Henry was about to be swept from his cinematic throne by a revolution: the sexual revolution which began in the late 1960s. Although *Carry on Henry* was successful at the box office, it was the last film incarnation of Henry as a hearty, masculine rogue. Henry had never been renowned for being uxorious, but whereas in past centuries patriarchal values made Henry's treatment of his wives seem somewhat amusing and even admirably virile, changing sexual attitudes and evolving gender relations created a climate in which bluff, philandering Henry now seemed an egregiously abusive husband and father.

As revulsion replaced grudging admiration towards Henry's marital career, the tensions of the Cold War eased, and much of Henry's relevance as a surrogate for contemporary tyrants or tyrannies melted away. As a result, Henry was again exiled from the silver screen, this time for the remainder of the twentieth century. But the post-war depictions of the king in cinema left an indelible, bloody stain on Henry's popular reputation. Thanks to Robert Bolt, Thomas More became a figure known to large sections of the general public and Henry was transformed from Pollard's champion of parliamentary democracy into the epitome of authoritarian oppression. Yet if Henry was gone from the cinema, he was not forgotten. His hold on the popular imagination continued, and still continues, to be as powerful as ever. And the continuing fascination with the king and his wives has ensured his recent return to film. But the strength and ubiquity of Henry's image has meant that he has recently been depicted in two radically different ways.

The conception of the king as a ruthless tyrant is very apparent in the Granada TV series *Henry VIII*, shown in 2003. Henry was chosen as the subject for this series because his reputation allowed the producers to combine two popular genres: the gangster film and the Tudor period piece (which had undergone a revival with the twin successes of *Elizabeth* and *Shakespeare in Love* in 1998). In the words of Andy Haines, the executive producer of the *Henry VIII*, it was 'the *Sopranos* meets the Tudors basically'. The director, Peter Travis, made the same point, calling *Henry VIII*, 'the *Godfather* in tights'.[49]

Ray Winstone, who played the king, stayed faithful to this conception of Henry as a crowned Kray; his king is as uncomplicated as a butcher's thumb and as deeply immersed in blood. There is nothing essentially inaccurate in portraying Henry as brutal (a strength of this drama is that it is almost unique among films in showing Henry's combination of duplicity and savagery in dealing with Robert Aske and his followers), but it is an error to underestimate Henry's sophistication. Winstone's Henry would have had difficulty reading a book of theology, much less writing one. To see Henry as simply a power-hungry, ruthless thug, not only fails to do justice to his formidable ability to rationalize even his basest actions, it makes much of his behaviour incomprehensible.

The most recent television portrayal of Henry, in a ten-part series, *The Tudors*, on the American cable network Showtime, is strikingly different from the tyrannical alpha male of almost all post-war film depictions of the king. This portrayal of Henry confirms the persistent power of the pre-existing stereotype of the king by apparently outflanking it. A narrative during the opening credits assures the audience that they *think* they know the story, but that they only know how it ends. The first season of the show was devoted to the early portion of Henry's reign, ending before his second marriage. In an effort to exorcize the spectre of the Holbein portrait, Jonathan Rhys Meyers, the actor who plays the king, is smaller than Henry, his hair is dark rather than auburn and he is clean shaven. In place of Sid James's dirty old Henry, we now have a lusty young Henry. In fact, the series places a considerable emphasis on the king's youth; in it events are telescoped so that while it covers a period of around 15 years – from when Henry was 25 until when he was about 40 – Henry never ages. (In reality, Henry was bearded through most of this period and, before Wolsey fell from power, he had already been afflicted with the ulcer on his leg, which was the first stage in the slow deterioration of his once splendid physique.) It will be interesting to see how Henry is portrayed in future episodes of the series as he ages and embarks on his tumultuous marital career.

And this is one of the two potential weaknesses of the non-traditional portrayal of Henry: its power is largely based on the audience's pre-conceptions about him. A considerable part of the interest in the *The Tudors* comes from watching Jonathan Rhys Myers gradually (very gradually) change into Holbein's Henry – as we know he will. The more the series subverts the traditional Henry, the more strongly it re-establishes it. The second weakness is demonstrated in the latest film incarnation of Henry VIII, in *The Other Boleyn Girl*. In this film, Henry is portrayed as the easily manipulated dupe of rival sisters and of a faction led by the Duke of Norfolk. This interpretation of Henry as being easily influenced by competing personalities actually has a respectable pedigree, going back to John Foxe, but it is less dramatic, and less compelling, than the lustful, bloodstained, masterful tyrant of popular history. Henry's first biographer, Edward Lord Herbert of Cherbury, concluded his work by wishing that he could leave the king in his grave.[50] Filmmakers have not shared this sentiment nor is it likely that they will any time soon, but it seems that each time they open his tomb, they will find Holbein's Henry inside.

Suggestions for Further Reading

Michael A. R. Graves, *Henry VIII* (London, 2003).

Diarmaid MacCulloch (ed.), *The Reign of Henry VIII: Politics, Policy and Piety* (Basingstoke, 1995).

Richard Rex, *Henry VIII and the English Reformation*, Second edition (Basingstoke, 2006).

J. J. Scarisbrick, *Henry VIII* (London, 1968).

3

Saints and Cinemas: *A Man for All Seasons*

Peter Marshall

Historians often have a love–hate relationship with films about the past, but most of us do not take them too seriously much of the time. Every so often, however, a historical film comes along which gets under the skin of the scholarly community even to the extent that it becomes part of the process of historical debate and explanation itself. Perhaps the best example of this for the early-modern period is Fred Zinnemann's 1966 feature *A Man for All Seasons*, an adaptation of Robert Bolt's 1960 stage play about Thomas More, the early-sixteenth-century humanist scholar and former English Lord Chancellor, beheaded in 1535 for refusing to recognize Henry VIII's divorce from Catherine of Aragon and replacement of the pope with himself as head of the Church in England. While most of Hollywood's forays into history are either ignored or disdainfully dismissed by experts in the field (sometimes after their advice as consultants has been ignored), Bolt's drama, and the film for which he wrote the screenplay, have for a generation and more been regularly referenced and critiqued in works of serious historical scholarship. We might expect More scholars to owe Bolt and Zinnemann a debt of gratitude. The sub-genre of historical biography in film nearly always reflects the acknowledged importance of the subject: Churchill, Gandhi, Oliver Cromwell, JFK. *A Man for All Seasons*, by contrast, took a figure familiar only in educated literary and pious Catholic circles and made him into a household name. In the words of Hugh Trevor-Roper, More had been 'made famous by Mr Robert Bolt's play and Mr Zinnemann's

Plate 2   Sir Thomas More (Paul Scofield) weighs his conscience under the watchful gaze of Henry VIII (Robert Shaw). Courtesy of The Kobal Collection for the image from the motion picture *A Man for All Seasons* (1966).

film'.[1] Or as another More scholar put it in the aftermath of the film's release, 'the man on the street, who once said "who?" at the mention of More's name, now says "oh!"'.[2] Yet by no means all Tudor specialists subscribe to the axiom that no publicity is bad publicity. This chapter examines their reactions, treating *A Man for All Seasons* as an influential historical 'text', and tracing its relationship to the development of scholarly studies of Thomas More in the second-half of the twentieth century. Though some assessment of historical 'veracity' is unavoidable in this context, this will not primarily represent an exercise in awarding points and spotting mistakes. Rather, I want to consider this powerful and unusual film as a site for assessing the potential, and the pitfalls, for creative exchange between popular and scholarly perceptions of the past.

Bolt's play about More's conscience-driven stand against Henry VIII opened in London in July 1960 and transferred to Broadway the following year, with the British stage actor Paul Scofield in the title role. It was both a critical and commercial success, and in 1965 the film rights were sold to Columbia Pictures. Bolt had wanted to direct himself, cheaply in black and white, but Columbia's executives were looking for a more appealing product and a more experienced hand at the tiller. The job went to Fred Zinnemann, who had made his name with the classics *High Noon* and *From Here to Eternity*. Nonetheless, expectations were modest. Zinnemann later recalled that Columbia Pictures considered it a 'totally unpromising project' which promised 'very little action, let alone violence; no sex, no overt love story and, most importantly, *no stars*, in fact hardly any actors that the US public had ever heard of'. The result of the studio's lack of interest was a restricted budget, but also a large degree of creative freedom.[3] The pessimism was unfounded. For almost a year after its release, the film remained near the top of the box office. It was nominated for eight Oscars, and won six of them, including best film, director, actor and screenplay. Critics were lavish with their praise, some even considering the movie to be better than the play, though the *New York Times* reviewer, in praising the film, found it 'full of long theological discourses and political implications that you must know your history to understand'.[4] Audiences, however, seemed happy enough to take their dose of history, and the film was a surprise hit. In retrospect, the success seems less astonishing. The film combines remarkably beautiful cinematography with fine performances from a superb ensemble cast, many of them survivors from the Broadway production. Like Paul Scofield himself, most were virtual unknowns to cinema-goers, though Orson Welles's brief cameo as Cardinal Wolsey may have done as much to create a lasting popular image as Scofield's acclaimed portrayal of More. The film's central theme of heroic nonconformity clearly resonated in the era of Civil Rights, and of growing disquiet about the war in Vietnam. Even the selection of a Catholic saint as lead protagonist looks less of a popular turn-off at a time when America had in John F. Kennedy recently lost a revered Catholic president, and the Second Vatican Council was blowing some of the cobwebs out of the Church.

Part of the explanation for the appeal of the film was that it was not simply a filmed performance of Bolt's play, but employed a series of strategic changes. Most obviously, the film dropped the character of 'the Common Man', a chorus-like figure who fills all the minor male roles and periodically informs the audience what is going on in the wider world. Ironically, it was the director who wished to retain this theatrical, Brechtian device in the film, and the writer who insisted on scrapping it in favour of greater naturalism.[5] Sparse, minimalist stage settings, for example, in the trial scene at Westminster Hall, gave way to elaborate set pieces with dozens of costumed extras. But the greater naturalism did not necessarily lead to a dilution of symbolic impact. In the play, Bolt constantly uses the imagery of water as a metaphor for 'the terrifying cosmos' threatening the order of society, though in the *Preface* he confesses that 'certainly no-one noticed'.[6] Through repeated visual references in the film, however, the River Thames assumes the status of a virtual character. Other changes are more likely to catch the attention of historians. The very first section of dialogue, for example, establishes More's credentials as a humanist reformer: he is shown relaxing with guests who jest about the moral fallibility of the clergy: 'every second bastard born is fathered by a priest . . . But in Utopia that couldn't be . . . For there the priests are very holy, therefore very few'. A few scenes from the play are cut out of the film, such as the episode, borrowed from William Roper's *Life of More*, depicting the household desperately searching for Sir Thomas as they await the king's 'surprise' visit at Chelsea. He is in fact in church helping to sing vespers in a surplice. 'A parish clerk, my lord Chancellor!', splutters More's friend, the Duke of Norfolk, 'you dishonour the King and his office!' 'The service of God', More calmly responds, 'is not a dishonour to any office'.[7] Compensation for the loss of this vignette is supplied by the memorable scene in which Henry leaps from the royal barge into the mud at More's Chelsea home, forcing dozens of peacock-pretty courtiers to follow suit, and thus effectively signalling the combination of good humour and menacing authority which constitutes the king's character in the film (and, arguably, in real life as well). An important new character is introduced: Vanessa Redgrave makes an uncredited and non-speaking 45-second appearance as Anne Boleyn, which nonetheless does a great deal to explain Henry's single-mindedness over the divorce.[8] Perhaps more significantly, an important historical character in the play is completely excised from the screen version: the imperial ambassador, Eustace Chapuys. This was an important interpretative step, for Chapuys's function in the play is to show More under pressure not just from the English government, but from the continental Catholic powers, eager to exploit his principled stand over the divorce for their own political purposes. 'The man's utterly unreliable!', Chapuys mutters to his attendant when More refuses to receive a supportive letter from his master Charles V.[9]

In the main, however, the film closely follows the structure and dialogue of the play. Certainly, both present the same essential picture of More. He is a successful man of affairs and a loving paterfamilias, but one who is forced to sacrifice everything, up to and including his life, rather than act against his conscience – something which, in Bolt's reading, would involve abandoning his very sense of self. More, however, is consistently circumspect. 'This is not the stuff of which martyrs are made', he tells his wife Alice. He will not swear the Oath of Succession,[10] but will not tell anyone why he will not swear, trusting in the letter of the law to shield him from its ultimate sanction. Some reviewers found this encryption of motivation problematic. The renowned theatre critic Kenneth Tynan detected in the play an intended analogy between More's predicament and that of the victims of McCarthyism: 'as a democrat, I detest such coercive investigations into a man's innermost ideas; as a playgoer, however, I feel entitled to know what his ideas were'.[11] It is a measure of Bolt's skill to have crafted a compelling drama out of a prolonged exercise in taking the Fifth Amendment.

The refusal to declare an opinion on the divorce and the supremacy was not Bolt's invention, but the tactic employed by the historical More. It is, of course, the issue of historical 'accuracy' rather than of artistic effect which has usually provoked historians to pronounce on cinematic representations of the past. Bolt never discussed his method of research, though it is often asserted that the near-contemporary *Life of More* by his son-in-law William Roper is the basic source text.[12] In fact, it seems virtually certain that he relied heavily on R. W. Chambers's classic biography of 1935.[13]

A Man for All Seasons contains numerous memorable incidents and lines of dialogue derived not just from Roper, but from Nicholas Harpsfield's mid-sixteenth-century biography, all of which are to be found in Chambers. Liberties are undoubtedly taken. Roper's marriage to More's daughter Margaret, which took place in 1521, is delayed by several years to allow More to veto it 'so long as you're a heretic'. Thomas Cromwell's promotion to the secretary-ship of the council, which happened in 1534, is accelerated. The 1532 Submission of the Clergy and the 1534 Act of Supremacy are conflated. There are a number of irregularities in the film's climactic scene, More's trial for treason in Westminster Hall, even without considering the detailed historical re-examination of the trial process, which has questioned the reliability of the accounts on which Bolt drew.[14] Thomas Cromwell, rather than the Attorney-General, is shown leading the case for the crown, and he conducts the prosecution in modern American fashion, striding back and forth as he addresses the jury. The mass ranks of spectators shown in the movie were not in reality there.[15] Yet in the main, *A Man for All Seasons* is remarkably free of the groan-inducing howlers which disfigure so many 'historical' films. In fact, it is possible that it is precisely because of the generally high level of veracity of Bolt's script, and the sumptuous verisimilitude of Zinnemann's cinematic eye, that so many scholars have found the play and film disturbing. At the heart of the indictment is the charge that Bolt presents a superficially plausible, but fundamentally misleading image of Thomas More, what he stood for, and what he died for.

At this point, we need to begin placing *A Man for All Seasons* within a context of scholarly approaches to the life of More. As we have seen, Bolt's text drew heavily on the biography by R. W. Chambers. This was published in 1935, the year when More was canonized by the Roman Catholic Church, and the process of his rehabilitation as an English hero got properly underway.[16] There was a trickle of publications on More in the 1940s and 1950s, but in the 1960s this turned into a veritable flood. Two developments in particular stand out. A major collaborative project began at Yale University to produce modern editions of More's complete works, the first volume of which was published in 1963. The same year witnessed the appearance of an international journal devoted specifically to More studies. *Moreana* was the organ of a network of scholars calling themselves the *Amici Thomae Mori*, whose moving figure was a French priest, Germain Marc'hadour. Unsurprisingly, it was in this quarter that scholarly enthusiasm about *A Man for All Seasons* was at its most marked. Over the course of 1967–1968, the editors of *Moreana* excitedly reported that 'news of Bolt's play and Zinnemann's film keep reaching us from all quarters', and they printed snippets from the film's many glowing reviews in the American and international press.[17] Marc'hadour later revealed that there had been anxieties among the *Amici* when news of a forthcoming film surfaced, but that these had rapidly subsided. Despite some minor historical departures, 'the voice of Thomas More rings true, and is recognized at once by those familiar with his life and works'.[18]

These words are either charmingly ingenuous, or intentionally polemical. For a cohort of scholars soon emerged who claimed not to recognize Bolt's More at all. Revisionist reassessment of More's career and character was initiated by the doyen of Tudor political historians, G. R. Elton. In a series of studies, Elton set out to demonstrate that far from withdrawing from public affairs at the time of the divorce, More remained up to his elbows in political intrigue with the crown's opponents; that far from being a reluctant courtier, More was an ambitious careerist who lied about the date of his entry into royal service; and that far from being the suave humanist of popular repute, More was an intolerant reactionary whose deep pessimism about human nature caused him to lose all sense of proportion when confronted with Lutheran heresy.[19] It seems virtually certain that Elton's entry into More studies was provoked by the popular success of the play and film. With considerable verve, he published a first version of his essay on More's active opposition (which flatly contradicts the image of passivity conveyed by Bolt) in that citadel of admiration, *Moreana*. Here it incongruously occupies space in a 1967 issue alongside glowing tributes to the virtues of Zinnemann's film.[20] Elton's irritation with *A Man for All Seasons* may have owed as much to its portrayal of Thomas Cromwell as of More himself. Elton devoted much of his life's work to exalting Cromwell as a selfless statesman and the architect of an admirable 'revolution' in Tudor government. Bolt, on the other hand, depicts Cromwell as a mirror image to More: a brutal pragmatist, whose *raison d'être* is to facilitate the king's desires whatever the cost. In this, Bolt clearly took his bearings from Chambers – 'we may think of the interview between More and Cromwell as one where the Utopian faced the Machiavellian' – though he effectively ignored Chambers's caveat that 'it was not necessarily idealism facing villainy'.[21] Elton too juxtaposed More and Cromwell, their portraits appearing side by side on the cover of his 1972 book *Policy and Police*. In a 1980 essay on 'the real Thomas More', Elton recalled spending half an hour 'before that splendid fireplace in the Frick Museum in New York above which Thomas Cromwell and Thomas More for ever stare past one another'. In a significant reversal of the classifications employed by Chambers, he commented that 'in the end I thought I understood the plain, straightforward man on the right', but not the other 'with that subtle Machiavellian smile, whose looks and look kept altering before one's eyes'. A subsequent conference paper comparing More and Cromwell opened with references to 'R.W. Chambers's disastrous biography', and 'Robert Bolt's more disastrous play'.[22]

There was further support for the idea of More as a more complex, and unattractive, character than most mid-twentieth-century scholarship had supposed, with the publication in 1984 of the first heavyweight biography to appear since Chambers. Despite his track record as an editor on the Yale project, Richard Marius's view of More was a surprisingly bracing one. Not merely conventionally misogynistic, More was tortured by a sexual drive which had prevented him becoming a priest. He was also driven by an obsessive, almost pathological hatred of heretics, and a desire to burn them which was 'almost the essence of the man'.[23] Inevitably, some reviewers explicitly contrasted Marius's More with that of the movie, a writer in *Moreana* observing that readers familiar with More's character from Bolt's 'magnificent screenplay' had probably been 'much dismayed' by the book.[24] In fact, Marius made only one passing reference to *A Man for All Seasons* in the course of his long biography.[25] But he was undoubtedly aware of the context of public awareness and expectation into which his iconoclastic study had been launched. In a published reflection (1989) on the work of the Yale Project, Marius confessed that

> I was never able to decide fully in my own mind whether Robert Bolt's *A Man for All Seasons* . . . was boon or disaster to More studies . . . The sudden attention to More now made our own studies more respectable; people stopped assuming that those of us who said we were working on Thomas More were laboring on the Irish poet . . .

But this higher profile carried a price: 'people already knew what we were supposed to find when we studied More. We were supposed to find Robert Bolt's More'.[26] When, a few years later, Marius was invited to contribute a short sketch of *A Man for All Seasons* for a volume examining the historical veracity of selected Hollywood movies, the tone had noticeably hardened. Marius excoriated the film's portrayal of More as 'a Catholic Abraham Lincoln, an icon of purity and principle', accusing Bolt of an inexcusable 'idolatry of More's character'. In particular, both the play and the film supply a 'saccharine picture' of More's religion, obscuring 'his furious and cascading hatred of the Protestants'. More's refusal to let Roper marry Margaret

> seems parallel to the polite but firm disdain we might expect of the head of a large corporation whose beloved daughter is about to marry a used-car salesman. Nowhere do we see the historical More who produced hundreds of pages of ugly polemics shrieking for the blood of Protestants . . . Nowhere in the film is the More who after his resignation as chancellor went on pouring out works against heresy.

Curiously, the quotation chosen from More's 'ranting works' to illustrate this pathology – 'the author showeth his opinion concerning the burning of heretics, and that it is lawful, necessary, and well done' – suggests a rather bland conventional viewpoint for the time. In the end, however, what Marius detested most was the moral complacency of the film's message: 'it leaves us not cleansed and thoughtful, but with glowing confidence that right-thinking people like ourselves would have voted for the hero'. It portrayed the common people as 'ignorant trash, gullible, unable to bear ambiguity, incapable of thought, self-righteous, and transfixed by appearances. *A Man for All Seasons* was designed for just such an audience. It succeeds brilliantly because it judges us so well.'[27] While this is rhetorically effective, it surely entails a significant misreading of the writer's intentions. As Bolt's *Preface* makes clear, the 'Common Man' (whose lines are parcelled out in the film) was supposed to embody the morally compromised attitudes and values of both author and audience, rather than to be a representation of 'that mythical beast The Man in The Street'.[28]

All in all, one is left with the sense of a scholar seriously rattled by what he perceives as the power of stage and cinema to propagate partial and misleading history. The desire to administer a sharp corrective appears still more strongly in a work appearing around the same time as Marius's seminal biography, Jasper Ridley's dual study of Wolsey and More, *The Statesman and the Fanatic*. The panegyrics accompanying the five-hundredth anniversary of More's birth in 1978 clearly provoked Ridley's literary attack on him as 'the worst kind of intolerant fanatic'. But the conclusion to the book is in no doubt that *A Man for All Seasons* remains the main obstacle to historical clear-sightedness.

With the help of Scofield's performance, Bolt created 'an image of More which is even more misleading than Chambers's – a brilliant and moving portrayal of More as he ought to have been but unfortunately was not'. In place of Bolt's splendidly upright hero, Ridley imagines a Thomas More who, had he lived in the twentieth century, would have justified the Nazi holocaust or the extermination of three-quarters of the world's population with nuclear weapons.[29] Ridley's one-dimensional diatribe, which opens by suggesting that the Protestant propagandist John Foxe had got More just about right, was thus hardly a model of dispassionate scholarship, even when (rather hilariously) the publishers re-titled the North American edition as *Statesman and Saint*.

But one of Ridley's charges against Bolt has been widely echoed by more responsible scholars: the notion that More resisted and died for the rights of individual conscience. As Anthony Kenny argued in an incisive short study of 1983, the consciences of Bolt's More and of the historical More are very different animals. In what is perhaps the most crucial passage in both play and film, Norfolk accuses More of being willing to forfeit all for the mere theory of the pope's apostolic succession. More responds that 'what matters to me is not whether it's true or not but that I believe it to be true, or rather not that I *believe* it, but that *I* believe it'.[30] This is the expression of the autonomous conscience, the irreducible self, which for Bolt's More is identical with the very soul. But it is hardly conceivable that Thomas More could have expressed himself in this way: conscience was belief about the law made by God. While it was always wrong to act against conscience, to act in accordance with it was not necessarily right, for one's moral convictions might be erroneous, as those of heretics were. More, it is true, did not condemn others who took the Oath: the legitimacy of the Act of Succession was a disputable matter where an erroneous conscience might be exercised without moral fault. But he certainly did not believe that conscience in itself was sufficient justification for action. Moreover, each person had the responsibility to inform their conscience. In More's case, this meant not turning in towards a private sense of self, but making the effort to shape it within an exterior forum of validation, the opinion of 'the whole corps of Christendom'. In Kenny's view, what More feared was the loss of God rather than a metaphysical loss of self. And he finds this figure a more convincing and consistent character than Bolt's creation, who combines 'a tender respect for his private conscience with an exaggerated deference to public law'. In fact, there was no real conflict between conscience and law, since for More 'true conscience is simply the right appreciation of God's law'.[31]

The theme is elaborated in the most recent major study of Thomas More to worry away at the Bolt legacy, John Guy's *Thomas More* (2000), which uses as the epigraph for a chapter entitled 'Whose Conscience?' the trial scene exchange between 'More' and 'Cromwell', culminating in More's declaration that 'a man's soul is his self!' References to *A Man for All Seasons* pepper Guy's text, appropriately enough for a volume in a series entitled 'Reputations'. Most of the book involves a careful examination and deconstruction of the primary sources for More's life, rather than a pioneering psycho-biography in the Marius mould, still less a Jasper Ridley-style polemic. Yet the pervasive influence of *A Man for All Seasons* supplies a kind of leitmotif for the book, and is addressed in its very last paragraph. A section of this text adapted as 'blurb' for the paperback jacket explicitly addresses itself to 'those who have seen the film *A Man for All Seasons*', people who want to investigate More further, but not to know too much. 'Their illusions might be shattered, their ideals infringed, their delight in a moral tale defaced.' Such faint-hearts, it is thoughtfully suggested, 'should not read this book'. That a work of scholarship from a leading academic historian should bill itself principally as a riposte to a Hollywood film made nearly 40 years before is a striking tribute to the depth of the latter's imaginative reach.

It is not of course surprising that historians should react to what they regard as misrepresentations of the past within contemporary culture. Whether contemporary culture pays any attention is another matter. In 1999, an American speechwriter, Joseph Roquemore, published the informatively titled *History Goes to the Movies: A Viewer's Guide to the Best (and Some of the Worst) Historical Films Ever Made*. *A Man for All Seasons* tops the poll, receiving five stars and the comment that 'the film industry has yet to produce a better movie'. Roquemore delights in pointing out anachronisms and inaccuracies in other movies, but finds none in this one.[32] Also in 1999, as the tragicomedy of Bill Clinton's impeachment unfolded in Washington, DC, the chairman of the House of Representatives' Judiciary Committee, Henry Hyde, quoted More in the opening speech of the trial. 'When a man takes an oath, Meg, he's holding his own self in his own hands'. Or rather, Hyde thought he was quoting More, he was of course quoting Bolt.[33]

Yet reactions to Bolt's More, and responses to those reactions, represent a partial exception to the usual pattern of academics fulminating impotently at the distortions of Hollywood. Scholarly revisionism could not of course change the print of Zinnemann's film, but by the late 1980s it was revealing an ability to affect readings of Bolt's play. The director of one amateur American production, for example, wrote a fan letter to Richard Marius, thanking him for helping her 'bring the necessary dramatic tension' to the staging of the play.[34] When *A Man for All Seasons* was professionally revived in New York in 1987, the actor playing More, Philip Bosco, gave an interview to the *New York Times*, in which he reported how members of the production were aware 'that Mr. Bolt's image of Sir Thomas More is conspicuously lacking warts'. The real More was 'immoderately proud of his high position in the realm and fierce, indeed, bloodthirsty on the subject of heretics'.[35] A production in London the same year received decidedly mixed notices, and not just for Charlton Heston's performance in the title role. The *Guardian* reviewer concluded that Bolt had failed 'to relate Sir Thomas More's crisis of conscience to the social and historical context in which he lived'.[36] This kind of reciprocal dialogue between scholarship and representation, history and drama, is decidedly unusual. In the field of early-modern and medieval history, it is virtually unique.

It is tempting in this context to see More's historical representation as a zero-sum game, a fixed asset boosted by the release and success of *A Man for All Seasons*, and then eroded by the wave of revisionist scholarship which followed. This is the impression one gets, for example, from Louis Martz's 1990 study of *Thomas More: The Search for the Inner Man*. Martz, then chairman of the editorial committee of the Yale edition, openly declared a desire to rehabilitate the battered image of More, an image 'shaped directly or indirectly by R. W. Chambers, or influenced by the similar figure created by Robert Bolt'.[37] Yet reactions to *A Man for All Seasons* have always been more diverse than this counter-revisionism would suggest, and informed critiques of Bolt's methods and intentions have not always come from the revisionist wing of More scholarship. In the aftermath of the film's release, the Catholic historian, E. E. Reynolds, author of several studies of More, complained that viewers of the film would most likely fail to 'come away with a clear sense of why Thomas More was executed', due to a failure to foreground the key issues of 'the spiritual supremacy of the Pope and the unity of the Church'.[38] In a *Moreana* essay of 1967, Majie Padberg Sullivan lamented the fact that Bolt, 'a self-confessed agnostic', had chosen More as his hero for his integrity, 'a quality secondary to his saintliness'.[39] From the perspective of the 1980s, a Catholic critic, Keith Mitchell, questioned whether *A Man for All Seasons* could in any sense be called a religious film, there being in it no 'real idea of the total self-surrender demanded by heroic sanctity'.[40] A more nuanced version of these objections was articulated at the end of the decade by the Yale edition editor, Clarence H. Miller. In his view, Bolt's characterization of More was imperfect 'in a radical and important way: it omits the religious dimension almost entirely'. The scene of More and his family at perfunctory night prayer Miller regards as 'faintly embarrassing'. The play thus fails to probe the deepest motives of More's death, his exertions to try to make sure that martyrdom was God's will for him, and his ultimate willingness to die, 'not for any theory of the papacy, or any idea or tradition or even doctrine or for his irreducible selfhood, but rather for a person, for Christ'.[41]

It appears then that where revisionists suspect the perpetuation of hagiography, Catholic scholars, and others attuned to the religious and devotional dimensions of the period, tend to fault the play and the film for failing to engage with the actual content of More's thought. They undoubtedly have a point. In his *Preface*, Bolt candidly conceded that he had 'appropriated a Christian Saint to my purposes'. These were to challenge the idea of the self as 'an equivocal commodity' in modern society, and to urge his contemporaries towards the realization of 'a sense of selfhood without resort to magic'. In an interview just before the first performance of the play in London, Bolt was still more explicit: More became a reluctant martyr because he had 'kept one small area of integrity within himself', and the powers-that-be could not rest until they had got at it. 'When he was attacked the Catholics thought he must be on their side. He was not. Both sides had the wrong end of the stick throughout.'[42] In veering into historical assertion of this order, it was Bolt who had the wrong end of the stick. The one thing we *can* safely say about Thomas More is that he was on the side of the Catholics.

Ultimately, therefore, what a spectrum of commentators have objected to in *A Man for All Seasons* is that the writer fails imaginatively to enter and explore the contemporary mindset of its central protagonist. The portrayal is not so much inaccurate as inauthentic. Here we come up against an inescapable dilemma of representations of the past, particularly the distant past, in popular cultural media. It is relatively easy to get the small details right – the costumes, the buildings, even (with a little care) the outlines of events and something approximating to the speech patterns of the characters. But why should we expect modern audiences to be engaged or entertained by the predicament of individuals whose actions are based on attitudes and values almost entirely alien to those by which they live their own lives? To writers of creative fiction, even subtle and imaginative ones like Robert Bolt, the dilemma is unlikely, however, to present itself in quite the same terms. Frequently, the appeal of a historical setting is that it allows moral and political issues of the day to be explored in an oblique, but fresh and refocused way (something, incidentally, it has in common with science fiction). An ability to recognize the present-mindedness informing nearly all historical fiction is a useful skill for students and practitioners of history to possess. Yet it should not induce feelings of complacency on their part. For the dilemma of historical film – how to respect the autonomy of the past while ratio-nalizing its representation in the present – is the dilemma of academic history also.

Suggestions for Further Reading

R. W. Chambers, *Thomas More* (London, 1935).
John Guy, *Thomas More* (London, 2000).
Anthony Kenny, *Thomas More* (Oxford, 1983).
Richard Marius, *Thomas More. A Biography* (London, 1985).

4

Anne of the Thousand Days

Glenn Richardson

Anne Boleyn is undoubtedly the most famous of Henry VIII's six wives. Her story remains one of the grand dramas of English history and has inspired countless biographies as well as plays and operas. It has all the right ingredients: glamour, power, lust, ill-starred love, a tragic end – but a glorious posterity. Anne was reviled in the years after her death, and still has her critics, but is now more usually celebrated both as a romantic heroine and as a feisty Tudor woman. She remains the star of Henry's court, as much in the tomes of professional historians as in the soap-opera retailed by the Tudor 'heritage' industry. And that is how she appears in *Anne of the Thousand Days*, a film that contributed significantly to modern perceptions of Anne Boleyn, even as it purported to tell the 'real' story of her ultimately fatal relationship with the King of England.

Released in 1969, the film was directed by Charles Jarrott and starred the young and beautiful Geneviève Bujold in the title role. Richard Burton, one of Britain's greatest screen idols (and no stranger himself to matrimonial shenanigans), played Henry VIII. The two principals were supported by a large and talented cast and the film was produced on a grand scale, bringing the story of Henry and Anne vividly to life on the big screen. The film's producer Hal B. Wallis had a good track record in films as different as *Gunfight at the OK Corral* and *Becket*. Fred Zinnemann's *A Man for All Seasons* which dealt with the same period of English history as *Anne of the Thousand Days* had swept the boards at the Oscars three years earlier and Wallis and Jarrott doubtless hoped that the starry cast and the story would secure similar critical acclaim for their film.[1]

Plate 3 Geneviève Bujold played a striking Anne Boleyn in Charles Jarrott's *Anne of the Thousand Days*. Courtesy of Universal Pictures and The Kobal Collection for the image from the motion picture *Anne of the Thousand Days* (1969).

The film's screenplay was by John Hale and Bridget Boland, based on Richard Sokolove's adaptation of the play *Anne of the Thousand Days* written in the 1940s by Maxwell Anderson and first staged in New York in 1948. Jarrott's film remained broadly faithful to its source insofar as it followed the same themes and the basic plot of the play. The precise sources employed by Anderson have proved elusive but, when defending himself in a suit for plagiarism brought by the journalist Francis Hackett, Anderson showed proof of his own research and the evolution of the play's ideas.[2] Whereas the play was a rather dark, introspective piece with minimal scenery and props, Jarrott's film is in the genre of the grand historical narrative.

Much of its ostensible appeal lay in the sheer spectacle of the events it portrayed. There was evident commitment from the production team to making a film which was dramatic, emotionally engaging and which brought before modern audiences the Tudor period in apparently authentic detail. The film's locations were impressive. They included Hever Castle, owned by the Boleyns during Anne's lifetime, Hampton Court and particularly the Sidney family seat of Penshurst Place whose grounds, battlements, Great Hall and rooms served as substitutes for the principal Tudor palaces which no longer survive.

The determination to interpret the Tudor period authentically to its audience was perhaps expressed most directly in the formal, somewhat arcane and occasionally poetic 'Tudor-esque' language of the film. In places the script's antique words, terms of address and grammatical constructions reproduce exactly the self-styled 'blank verse' of Anderson's play, but more often they merely echo it while lessening its complexity and pomposity. Equally important in this respect is the film's musical score by Georges Delerue. His neo-Tudor dance and ceremonial interludes go beyond mere pastiches. While it lacks the grandeur of the music he composed for *A Man for All Seasons* in 1966, the score for *Anne of the Thousand Days* still evokes the period well enough and contributes to the film's authentic tone and style.

Anne Boleyn had already been portrayed on screen several times before 1969 and has appeared in film and on television many times since. She first appeared in a silent movie of 1911, an adaptation of Shakespeare's *Henry VIII*. She was memorably played by Merle Oberon in Alexander Korda's 1933 classic *The Private Life of Henry VIII* which opened, like Anderson's play, with Anne contemplating her death. In 1966, Vanessa Redgrave made a cameo appearance as Anne in *A Man for All Seasons*. In the 1970s she was played by Dorothy Tutin in the BBC drama *The Six Wives of Henry VIII* and by Charlotte

Rampling in the 1973 film version of *Henry VIII and his Six Wives*. In 2003 she was played on television by Helena Bonham Carter and Jodhi May. In 2008 Natalie Portman played Anne in the film *The other Boleyn Girl* while Natalie Dormer played her in *The Tudors* on television. Yet, nearly 40 years after its appearance, *Anne of the Thousand Days* remains the most lavish and detailed cinematic account of Anne Boleyn's life ever produced.

The film centres on four questions. Why did Henry VIII want to have his first marriage annulled? Why did Anne Boleyn accept him as her lover and then her husband? Why did Henry break from Rome and why did Anne lose his favour and fall from power? That the film, like Anderson's play, simplified the answers to these questions in the interests of romantic drama is obvious. Yet, in striking contrast to many more recent cinematic and televisual offerings on Tudor history, Jarrott's film at least tries to be faithful to evidence as analyzed by historians and it presents a version of events that is broadly consistent with the record, interpreting them in an emotionally engaging way to twentieth-century cinema audiences.

Anne's story and the origins of the English Reformation are portrayed as a bitter personal and dynastic revenge tragedy between a powerful man and an ambitious, articulate woman – as the review of film in the *New York Times* called it, a 'Royal Battle of the Sexes'.[3] It has much in common with that other 1960s 'royal battle of the sexes' film, *The Lion in Winter*, which was released the previous year. Similar issues are dealt with in both films: fidelity and infidelity in royal marriage; the importance of a clear succession and so on. Like *Becket* before it (in which Burton had also starred), the film is an example of the 1960s vogue for 'popular' psychology in cinema and for getting under the skin of historical or contemporary personalities.

Yet, like all cinematic history, *Anne of the Thousand Days* struggles to get to grips with the intellectual, institutional and religious contexts of those whose lives it seeks to re-create on screen. It dresses them in the right costumes but puts 'updated' views and aspirations into their heads and suggests to its audience that they were really 'just like us', which in many important respects they were not at all. It only touches on the hierarchical nature of the Tudor world and the role of patronage in early-modern society, on the fundamental importance of religion in daily life and on the complex international, political and economic contexts in which Tudor England existed. Nevertheless, touch on all of these things it does and in the terms Robert Rosenstone has used to distinguish between the two, this film escapes the charge of being merely a classy 'costume drama' and deserves to be called an 'historical' film because it engages with the issues and debates raised by its subject.[4] One of the significant developments in Tudor historiography during the 1960s was an increased emphasis on understanding Henry VIII's personality in explaining the events of his reign. With its focus on seeing the institutional through the personal, the film may even be said, perhaps unwittingly, to have been well synchronized with the changing historical discourse.[5]

*   *   *

The character of Richard Burton's Henry is central to the drama. While he does not have quite the same sheer physicality as Robert Shaw's Henry in *A Man for All Seasons*, he intimidates those around him with his wit, his rages and his sense of his own authority. At first Henry appears as the bluff and jovial King Hal of folk memory who was, so he says, at 16, 'rogering maidens left, right and centre'. Yet Burton's Henry is actually more complex and 'modern' than he first appears and has much about him that might have been drawn from the writings of Professor G. R. Elton in 1962 and by Professor J. J. Scarisbrick, whose monumental *Henry VIII* appeared in 1968. Both wrote about a monarch who was imposing, who could be alternatively charming and menacing, and who had major limitations in his capacity for good kingship. This Henry certainly owes very little to that paragon of English Protestant royalty who dominated the earlier twentieth century in the work of A. F. Pollard.[6] As Anne herself asserts at their first encounter, Henry's 'hale fellow well met' persona masks a darker more insecure and more vindictive side to his character. Of this his entourage seems well aware and we witness the Tudor court in all its feathered and jewelled finery, dog the king's heels and curtsey at his frowns throughout the film.

The king's self righteousness is there from the start, an aspect of his monstrously large but fragile ego. As he tells Thomas Boleyn without a trace of irony: 'I'm the king of England – when I pray, God answers.' Meanwhile Anne, and the audience, quickly identify him as a man desperate to command hearts as well as minds and prone to masking his anxieties with bluster and bombast. Henry persuades himself that his decisions, including the pursuit of Anne, are those of a far-sighted visionary implementing change under God's direction and for the good of the realm. This was exactly the 'spin' placed upon the break with Rome by Henrician propagandists such as Richard Morison.[7]

This capacity for self-delusion, or at least confusion, about his motives dominates the portrayal of the king throughout the film, just as it has dominated more recent academic debate about him. Diarmaid MacCulloch finds a nascent anti-clericalism even in the young Henry and highlights his amateur, not to say amateurish, passion for theology as he grew older.[8] David Starkey also explores the contradictions of the king's character but rejoices more than do Elton and Scarisbrick in his follies and his grandeur, arguing that it was precisely Henry's obsessive, egotistical nature that made him as powerful as he was. With it, he renewed the strength of the English monarchy and laid the foundation for much of Britain's later greatness. His insecurities did make him a tyrant who brought down as many people as he raised but, for Starkey, as for Pollard in a rather different way, Henry VIII remains England's greatest king.[9]

* * *

As the king's infatuation with Anne develops, the film observes in some detail, just as professional historians have, Henry's dependence upon his two principal servants, Cardinal Thomas Wolsey and Thomas Cromwell. Henry relies on Wolsey for advice, and for a shoulder to cry on. Anthony Quayle's performance as Wolsey has energy, subtlety and exactly the mix of contradictory qualities possessed by the cardinal. He is forceful, arrogant and pompous and uses the king's authority freely, lording it over others and being every inch the 'alter rex' of contemporary descriptions.[10] But he is also dignified, charming, imaginative and humorous. Burton and Quayle capture well the mixture of respect, affection and even rivalry between the king and his chief minister.

Wolsey has divided historical opinion as much as Henry or Anne. Most historians have seen him as monopolizing royal favour for two decades, growing rich and powerful in the process, and creating enemies on every side.[11] Certainly he was instrumental in maintaining Henry VIII's high international profile and in extending the reach of Tudor government domestically. Wolsey did not agree with the annulment in principle and certainly had little time for Anne Boleyn and this is made clear in the film. But, as both David Starkey and Peter Gwyn have insisted, Wolsey never forgot that his power depended entirely on Henry. So he made Herculean efforts to secure the annulment by conventional means, despite a thoroughly hostile international environment. These are portrayed in the film through the invention of an unsuccessful mission to Rome by Wolsey in 1527. In fact Wolsey went to France that year, not Rome, and there allied Henry with King François I in the hope that they would, together, overpower the opposition to the annulment from Europe's most powerful monarch, and Catherine of Aragon's nephew, the Holy Roman Emperor Charles V. In the end the most Wolsey got from Pope Clement VII was permission to hold an annulment trial in England in 1529.[12]

When Wolsey's fall comes, as it must in the wake of Catherine's appeal directly to Rome from this annulment trial, Cromwell steps out from behind the disgraced cardinal's clerical skirts. With the demeanour of an English Iago, he explains, on his own initiative, to Henry and Anne that their matrimonial dilemma can be solved through recourse to the English parliament and that Henry can have the wealth of the monasteries into the bargain. John Colicos's Cromwell is very much the political 'fixer' of the story – nasty but effective. In presenting him thus the film mines an older seam of Tudor historiography. In 1969 Elton, then the doyen of Tudor historians, was a strong advocate of a rather more attractive and visionary Cromwell. He admired the minister's determination and competence, crediting him not merely with implementing the break with Rome and the dissolution of the monasteries but for initiating a bureaucratic 'revolution' in the government of Tudor England whereby it was strengthened and made more efficient. Elton saw this as setting a sure foundation for Britain's constitutional greatness. Most historians now judge Cromwell's aims and achievements to have been more modest and conventional but still agree that his success, like Wolsey's, came through giving the king what he wanted and that he fell when he displeased Henry once too often.[13]

* * *

When it comes to Anne Boleyn herself who is, after all, the star of this show, it is generally agreed among historians that she was an intelligent and articulate woman whose talents and sex-appeal attracted the king. Most agree that their relationship was genuine and passionate, if volatile. Anne's independence of mind appealed keenly to Henry as his lover, but less so as his wife. He had hoped to have a son by her and in order to secure the legitimacy of their initially bigamous marriage, he finally broke from Rome and established himself as the Supreme Head of the Church in England. When Anne was not able to give Henry the son she had promised him, Henry's attention turned to Jane Seymour. In May 1536, Anne Boleyn was found guilty of adultery with a number of Henry's courtiers and was executed for treason.[14]

So much is common ground and the basis of the film. On the whole, however, the Anne of the film appears much too pretty, and is too much occupied with her feelings to stand easily alongside the formidable politician and patron that Anne was to become in the historiography of the 1980s and 1990s. Eric Ives and David Starkey have argued persuasively that due to the nature of 'personal politics' at Henry's court, Anne Boleyn became a serious politician in her own right. She quickly understood the implications of his pursuit of her. She used her influence with Henry to place her friends and family in positions of responsibility around the king and spearheaded the efforts of this group or 'faction' first to undermine Wolsey and then to monopolize the king's favour to its own advantage from 1527.[15]

There is little of this, however, in the film, although we are at least given a sense that power depends on personal contacts and that getting the king's favour is the name of the game. Members of the Boleyn family, particularly Anne's father Thomas and her brother George, are to the fore in all court scenes. In the background are her mother and her sister Mary who is shown pregnant and abandoned by the king. With Peter Jeffrey's Duke of Norfolk, they comprise a familial clique who support Anne and push themselves forward. Through them we see glimpses of the gossiping, back-biting, plotting, anxieties and personal tragedies of which court life consisted. Both the film's script and Bujold's performance were calculated to make Anne an understandable, if not always entirely sympathetic, character for the audience. To achieve this, she becomes a sort of Tudor version of a sixties' 'every woman' who is moved by the king from the female, private, sphere to the male, public and aggressive world of the court.

As the story opens Anne has recently returned from France where she has been a Maid of Honour in the household of Queen Claude of France. Young Anne is in love with the young Henry Percy, the heir to the earldom of Northumberland. She teases him about how she prefers her 'northern clodhopper', despite his lack of personal adornments, to the fine young men she had met in France. This immediately identifies her to the audience as an essentially kind and unspoiled girl who falls for the Tudor nobility's equivalent of the 'boy next door' – admittedly one whose back garden consists of a sizeable chunk of northern England.[16]

But Anne also cheerfully tells Percy that she long ago lost her virginity, a revelation unthinkable for any real Tudor woman in her circumstances. This admission is designed precisely to give her that quality of dangerous exceptionality and indifference to conventionality that explains her rise to power. It also gives her a refreshing candour and apparent sexual sophistication which chimes with the rhetoric of sexual 'liberation' of the 1960s and of which the audience is presumably intended to approve. There is no evidence whatsoever for the film's claim that Anne Boleyn became sexually experienced in a libidinous French court, but it is at least reasonable to assume that she may have attracted flirtatious attention there and that she was not the blushing and confused innocent that Henry later found (to his horror) in Anne of Cleves.

Geneviève Bujold was 27 years old when she starred as Anne in 1969. The consensus among a majority of historians is that Anne Boleyn was born sometime between 1500 and 1501, and so by a nice coincidence Bujold was about the same age as the real Anne had been when she became the undisputed object of Henry's affections. However, Bujold's very youthful features enabled her to play, for the opening scenes of the film, a girl barely in her twenties and thus the age Anne had been when she had made her debut at the English court in March 1522 when she danced in a masque in which the king also participated.[17] With her Québecois French accent and her bright, slightly elfin, demeanour, Bujold gave her 'young Anne' an exotic and insouciant appeal which we might readily imagine the real Anne also possessed and which first attracted the king to her in the years after her return from France.

In the film, Anne's relationship with Henry Percy is suddenly ended by Wolsey at the king's insistence, Henry having already decided that he wants her for himself. The historical cardinal did indeed object to their relationship, principally because it was already intended that Percy should wed Mary Talbot, the daughter of the Earl of Shrewsbury. As he states bluntly, 'A half-grown steer and a leggy girl will not be allowed to overturn the policies of England.' The young couple protest that it is a 'good match', which, as far as the relative status of the partners is concerned, it certainly would have been for Anne, who is infuriated by Wolsey's intervention. According to Ives, this occurred late in 1523 when the king was still sleeping with Anne's sister Mary and it is unlikely that he had anything to do with ending the relationship. The film elides this episode with previous failed negotiations for a marriage of Anne to James Butler, heir to the earldom of Ormonde, and evidence of Anne's flirtatious and rather courtly friendship some two to three years later with Sir Thomas Wyatt, the first great poet of the Tudor age. Although he was very keen on Anne in 1526, Wyatt was warned off her, not by Wolsey, but by the king himself who by then definitely had taken an interest in Anne.[18]

In the film, however, Henry's first entreaties to her come hard upon the heels of Wolsey's rebuke, and her fury at being deprived in this way of her 'true love' is quickly turned on him and becomes the mainspring of the subsequent drama.[19] When Anne finally does accept Henry after their famously long courtship, it constitutes a type of perverse revenge because to get her he is forced to tear apart his own world in the way that he first tore apart hers. Although initially deeply hostile to Henry, Anne gradually accepts, then enjoys her combative banter with him and begins to feel some affection for her 'great royal fool'. As she listens to the king agonize over his lack of a son and regret his marriage, she responds with a mixture of sympathy and scepticism. In time, the wealth and privileges she obtains more than compensate for the loss of Henry Percy. Her innate ambition is engaged. As she tells her brother George: 'Power is as exciting as love, I discover, and who has more of it than the king.'

The exact time at which Henry first became interested in Anne, when he first offered to marry her and even the extent to which Anne was an active agent in his wish to have his first marriage annulled have recently been debated anew by historians. Starkey has argued that Anne's resistance to Henry was quite calculated and that she became, in effect, an active participant in Henry's decision to disown Queen Catherine. He maintains that they had committed themselves to each other as early as January 1527. Ives thinks that matters proceeded somewhat more slowly and that Anne was probably still following where the king led, albeit with increasing enthusiasm. He suggests that a decision to marry was not reached until the summer of 1527 and only after Henry had begun preliminary consultations with his counsellors about an annulment and Anne had refused an initial request that she become his *maîtresse en titre*.[20]

In the film Anne resists implacably until well beyond either of these dates. She believes (as the real Anne almost certainly did) that to yield to Henry as anything other than his wife would entail the eventual abandonment suffered by her sister Mary. Her resistance spurs the king on until finally he offers her the deal she wants in order to accept him: marriage and the succession settled upon her children, the prior claims of Princess Mary notwithstanding. Momentarily wrong-footed, because she doubts that Henry is genuine, she quickly recovers her customary defiance and agrees, daring Henry to set himself against the rest of the world. There is nothing remotely romantic about this marriage proposal – it is one dynastic politician bargaining with another.

On hearing her response Henry is equally exultant and terrified. He bellows at Wolsey:

> I shall make Anne queen
> If it breaks the earth in two like an apple
> And flings the two halves into the void.

This *cri de coeur* expresses Henry's determination to have his own way whatever the cost. But it also expresses Henry's rage at Anne and his sense of himself as a victim of her intransigence. Melodramatically self-pitying while theologically conservative to his shoe buckles and rosary beads, Henry bitterly resents the fact that his feelings for Anne force him into rejecting Catherine publicly, defying the papacy and propelling his kingdom into schism. Yet in order to have her he must do so. He begins to blame Anne as much as he loves her.

So Anne the very successful 'personal politician' does appear in the film but the implications of her bargain with Henry and the complexity of the period between 1529 and 1535 somewhat defeat the film's historical narrative. It is reduced and rearranged, resulting in some odd juxtapositions of characters or sequences of events which are either significantly at variance with the existing evidence or for which there is no evidence at all. Thus, following the failure of the Legatine Court at Blackfriars to resolve Henry's matrimonial difficulty Henry accepts, on Cromwell's advice and far more quickly than did the real Henry, that he must take another course. In the film, as best as may be judged from contextual references, Henry is armed with the Act of Supremacy and its concomitant oath recognizing him as the Supreme Head of the Church in England as early as 1531. With it he bullies and threatens with death all those who oppose his proposed marriage to Anne. The Act of Supremacy was not in fact passed until 1534 and it completed rather than initiated the break with Rome. The Act is made to stand for more than a dozen pieces of legislation which were required to secure his second marriage.

There are also references to Henry having already begun the dissolution of the monasteries and 'torn at the body of the Church' in order to get to Anne. In fact the Henrician dissolutions did not begin until about 1535 and there is no exploration of Anne's attitude to the Reformation. Here the film seems particularly dated. Based on evidence of Anne's connections in France, her patronage of certain academics and claims made about her religious sympathies after her death, a number of historians have argued persuasively that Anne was evangelical – that is, favoured a form of Christianity which emphasized bible-knowledge and teaching above rituals. They demonstrate that many of the lawyers (including Cromwell) and theologians whom Henry used to prepare his annulment case and then to enact the break with Rome, were Boleyn or Howard family clients. Men like Thomas Cranmer and Edward Fox worked with Anne, urging Henry to make himself Supreme Head of the Church and to implement evangelical reform, of which the dissolution of the monasteries became part.[21]

The break with Rome itself took six long, laborious and anxious years. But cinema abhors a vacuum, and so not simply the break with Rome but the entire Henrician Reformation is collapsed into the space of a year and we hear no more of it for the rest of the film. Instead, we move directly to its emotional climax. At Hampton Court, in Anne's presence, Henry sadly says farewell to Bishop John Fisher of Rochester and Sir Thomas More who has resigned the Chancellorship in protest at the king's intentions. Henry makes it plain that they will be executed if they continue to resist him. More's resignation puts us in May 1532. Immediately beforehand the couple have also said their farewells to Wolsey who has just made the palace over to Anne as a gift. Through the magic of cinema, Wolsey, who actually died in November 1530, has enjoyed an extra 18 months of life in order to meet with a triumphant, and uncharacteristically sympathetic, Anne. In a nice domestic touch, he leaves the keys to the front door on a table and, with a last, longing look, shuffles out – a broken and dispirited man.

Henry's determination to bring down and even kill his closest servants in order to get the woman he loves is now clear. Evidently impressed by the lengths to which he will go to make her his wife, Anne is suddenly and dramatically overwhelmed and makes the passionate declaration of genuine love for him which Henry has been waiting half-a-dozen years to hear. As the Tudor career girl *par excellence* goes for the top job, violins swell and soar and Anne falls at the king's feet, kissing his hands.

Two minutes later and lying, at last, in the royal four-poster in a state of post-coital bliss, Anne says she no longer cares about becoming queen so long as she can be with Henry. This moment of surrender and contentment redeems her from a somewhat bitchy self that was starting to grate on Henry – and the audience. It allows us to believe that her essential good nature, which we saw at the outset and which has been so long suppressed by the need to resist Henry, is emerging again, now that she has realized that he is her man after all. She even asks him to spare the lives of those under threat, to which he responds that a new golden age has dawned for them both – it could almost be from the pages of Jane Austen. But whereas Elizabeth Bennet got her Mr Darcy and his cash and lived happily ever after, Anne, as we know, did not.

The story of the sudden fall and death of Anne in May 1536 is as fascinating as it is appalling and no other aspect of her life so divides historians of the period. In keeping with their views on Anne as a politician and the reality of court faction, Ives and Starkey have both argued that her opponents, for a variety of reasons, took advantage of her failure to produce a male heir to manoeuvre Jane Seymour into Henry's view and then to plant charges of adultery and treason on Anne. It suited the king to believe that she was guilty because it enabled him to be rid of her.[22] Other historians, chiefly George Bernard, argue that Anne was guilty of adultery with at least some of her co-accused and that her opponents merely took advantage of her own folly to bring her down.[23] Yet another, extraordinary view is that Anne fell because she miscarried of a 'deformed foetus' in January 1536 which was taken by the king as proof in itself of Anne's involvement in witchcraft. He had to be rid of her and so accusations of adultery, and particularly incest, were made to substantiate the accusation of witchcraft and to distance Henry from the paternity of the foetus. In fact there is no evidence that the foetus was deformed, nor is there any evidence that in Tudor England witches were thought to give birth to deformed foetuses.[24]

More recently Greg Walker has advanced what might be called the 'cock-up' theory to set against the conspiracy ones. He maintains that it was not Henry's wish to be rid of her that finally did for Anne but some injudicious remarks she made to her brother and to Henry Norris about Henry's sexual inadequacies and possibilities for her after his death. These remarks, made in late April 1536, somehow got into the public domain and provoked an investigation by Cromwell. In an atmosphere of growing tension and hysteria, evidence of another oblique conversation Anne had with her musician, Mark Smeaton, gave them a credence and an implication of infidelity and plotting the king's death that they should never have had. She fell not for what she did but for what she said.[25]

In *Anne of the Thousand Days* Henry's wish to be rid of his wife comes remarkably soon after her coronation. Following his disappointment at Princess Elizabeth's birth and the subsequent still-birth of a male child, his infatuation with Jane Seymour begins. Anne first attempts to remove Jane from the court, then tries to bargain acceptance of her as Henry's mistress in return for his protection of Elizabeth's right to the succession. The real Anne is not recorded as having said anything in the days after her arrest about her daughter, but Elizabeth's succession becomes the sole aim of Bujold's Anne who grows increasingly defensive, calculating and strident in defence of her child. Having once pleaded for their lives, she now demands the deaths of all those, including More and Fisher, who refuse to subscribe to the 'the oath' accepting Henry's title and recognizing Elizabeth as his only legitimate heir.[26] In the days before her fall she also acquires in respect of her daughter what Vincent Canby in his *New York Times* review memorably called, 'the sort of foresight favoured in second-rate hindsight dramas: 'My Elizabeth', she screams at Henry, 'will be a greater queen than any king of yours!'[27]

As enraged by her as he was once captivated, Henry demands that Cromwell 'find a way' to get rid of her. The minister gets busy planting charges on Anne and her alleged accomplices. The scene of the trial of Anne and her brother George, reinforces the view that she and all her co-accused are innocent. The final twist in the exploration of the relationship comes when Henry visits Anne in prison, unsure whether he wishes to free her or merely to salve his conscience about killing her by hearing her admit that she was unfaithful to him. Of course this is something that Henry's patriarchal pride also hopes desperately is *not* true, even though a just conviction depends upon it. Anne's final vengeance on him is to say, in a way which signals to the audience that she is lying, that she has indeed been unfaithful and that Henry will go to his grave never really knowing how many times and with whom. The result, foreshadowed at the start of the film, is Henry's signature on her death warrant. Alone in the Tower, awaiting her fate, Anne sadly counts up (on Exchequer tally sticks, a nice touch) the 'thousand days' of her happiness, before the dramatic scene, absent from the play, of her execution by sword on Tower Green on the morning of 19 May 1536.

The film *Anne of the Thousand Days* is not especially innovative but it is a well-made historical picture. Again Vincent Canby put it succinctly, describing it as 'one of those almost unbearably classy movies . . . that have a way of elevating the reputations of moviemakers without doing much for the art'. Possibly for this reason and because it followed so close upon the heels of several other 'epic' historical films to which it owes significant stylistic debts, it failed to capture the imagination of the critics or the film academies on either side of the Atlantic.

The major contribution to the discourse of Tudor history of *Anne of the Thousand Days* is that it challenges the conventional, largely folk history, views of Henry VIII as a kind of brashly impressive Tudor 'Don Juan' and Anne Boleyn as his willing but unfortunate floosie. *Anne of the Thousand Days* offers a more interesting and more accurate view, portraying them as complex and rather fallible creatures. The film's 'revisionist' focus on the nature of Henry's personality in explaining his type of monarchy was in step with the direction Henrician studies were beginning to take in the 1960s. The film also reflects on the experience of women in Tudor England, viewed through the prism of a particular and exceptional woman. Whether the historical Anne was quite the proto-feminist that she is at times in the 1969 film may be doubted but she was, nevertheless, shown to cinema audiences for the first time as a person in her own right, not merely as the object of Henry VIII's passion. This worked with the grain of emerging feminist historiography even if, in the film, she is not quite the master politician, nor the innocent victim, nor yet the foolish sinner that modern Tudor historians have by turns made her.

That the film is ultimately on Anne's side in the conflict with Henry is clear and is reinforced when she posthumously triumphs over the king. In the final scene, as distant cannons thunder to signal Anne's death, the face of her two and a half-year-old daughter Elizabeth suddenly looks up to the camera, as if searching for the source of the noise. Blinking into the strong sunlight and into the camera's gaze, she holds our eyes for a compelling moment, then turns and toddles away, unsteadily but purposefully, into her glorious future.

Suggestions for Further Reading

E. W. Ives, *The Life and Death of Anne Boleyn* (Oxford, 2004).

J. J. Scarisbrick, *Henry VIII* (London, 1968).

D. R. Starkey, *Six Wives: The Queens of Henry VIII* (London, 2004).

D. R. Starkey, *The Reign of Henry VIII: Personality and Politics* (London, 1991).

G. W. Bernard, 'The Fall of Anne Boleyn', *English Historical Review*, 106 (1991), pp. 584–610.

5

Lady Jane Grey on Film*

Carole Levin

The natural pathos of the story of Lady Jane Grey, executed for a treason she had never wished to commit, would obviously lead to dramatizations. She was only 16 when she died, forced by her ambitious parents to be part of a plot to keep John Dudley, Duke of Northumberland, in power through her marriage to his youngest surviving son Guildford. Jane was the nominal queen of England in 1553 who 'ruled' for nine days. She was not only a pawn on the losing side of a political battle, but she was also a deeply religious Protestant. We can never truly or completely know the character of the historical Jane, but one Lady Jane Grey that most people in the late-twentieth and early-twenty-first centuries perceive comes from the cinematic presentations of her in the films *The Tudor Rose* (1936) and *Lady Jane* (1986). These depictions are far different from that sixteenth-century woman who, though caught up in the political crisis of 1553, was far more concerned about her commitment to her religious beliefs than the political situation. Executed by her Catholic cousin Mary I the following year, Jane departed her life a committed Protestant, believing that she died 'simply and purely for the Reformed Faith'.[1]

Studying the film presentations of Lady Jane Grey allows us to examine not so much the life of the historical person, but the life of a symbol. We might wonder whether it matters if these presentations are accurate or not; after all, they are fictional, but at least some of the presentations in historical dramas ask us to take them seriously in the authoritative way they present the material. However, these two films say more about views towards woman of the time period in which they were created than about a historically accurate depiction,

Plate 4 Two versions – each reflecting the fashions of the time when the film was made – of the doomed couple, Lady Jane Grey and Lord Guildford Dudley'. Courtesy of Gaumont British Picture Corporation of America and Photofest for the image of John Mills and Nova Pilbeam from the motion picture *Nine Days a Queen* aka *Tudor Rose* (1936) and Paramount Pictures and Photofest for the image of Cary Elwes and Helena Bonham Carter from the motion picture *Lady Jane* (1986).

and that is also useful to our cultural understanding. For each version of the cinematic Jane, love was the most important emotion. In the 1936 film Jane was kind and sweet and a bit spirited. By 1986 she was passionate about her studies, about her religious beliefs, and eventually about social reform – but most passionate about her husband Guildford. In both films John Dudley is the villain. He is presented as a man both clever and evil. At the end of his life, he abandoned his Protestant beliefs in an attempt to save his life, and, as Barrett Beer points out, 'after failing in his boldest enterprise surrendered to despair and humiliation'.[2] Dudley was not only the twentieth-century film villain; he also was strongly disliked by his contemporaries.

Lady Jane Grey's move to centre stage in history came about because of a dynastic crisis. Despite all of Henry VIII's marital adventures, at the end of his life he had one son Edward and two daughters, Mary and Elizabeth. Mary was a dedicated Catholic, but Henry had broken with the Papacy to annul his marriage to her mother Catherine of Aragon. Elizabeth was Henry's second wife Anne Boleyn's only surviving child, and after only three years of marriage Henry had Anne executed in 1536 for adultery and treason. By his third wife Jane Seymour Henry had the son he craved. Jane, Elizabeth and Edward were raised to be Protestants. Henry's will, supported by the Act of Succession of 1544, left the throne to Mary if Edward died without heirs, then to Elizabeth, and if she were to die without heirs, then to the descendants of his younger sister Mary. Because Jane, born the same year as Edward, was Mary's eldest grand-daughter, she too was in line of the succession for the crown.

Edward was only nine when he became king. After his maternal uncles, Edward and Thomas Seymour, were executed for treason, John Dudley took over ruling for the young king. When Edward grew sickly, Dudley feared greatly not only losing power but what Catholic Mary, next in line, might do to Protestants like him, who had forwarded the Reformation for his own ends. Whether the plan to have Edward's sisters cut from the succession in place of Jane originated with Dudley, as has been traditionally believed, or with Edward, as some scholars have more recently argued, Jane was married to Dudley's young son Guildford. Jane had vehemently protested against the marriage, and her parents had had her beaten until she agreed. While the dramatizations show a Jane who grows to love Guildford dearly, in reality Jane seems to have feared John Dudley and not cared for Guildford during their brief marriage. Once queen, Jane informed Guildford that the crown was not a plaything for boys and girls, and he could only be a duke, not a king. Before her death, Jane wrote to Mary about how she was ill-treated by her husband and his mother, and believed that Guildford's family had been attempting to poison her.

Jane was one of the most educated women of her time and though she died so young, we still have a small body of writings from her and some evidence about her character. Jane's story was very famous in the later sixteenth century, when editions of her last letters were published and her story presented in John Foxe's widely read *Acts and Monuments*. Foxe's Jane was strong and powerful and not afraid to talk back to anyone if it involved her faith. But this depiction of the fiercely devout Jane did not last long.

By the beginning of the seventeenth century Jane had become the heroine of a play, and this first dramatization began the pattern that has continued to the late twentieth century with the emphasis on romance rather her high intelligence and strength of character. In this earliest play about Jane, written in 1602 and published in 1607, Thomas Dekker and John Webster's *The Famous History of Thomas Wyat*, the young, passive, deferential woman is very much in love with Guildford. In the play Jane defers to her husband, whom she allows to speak for the two of them. On the day of their execution she tells him, 'My dearest Guildford, let us kiss and part'. Over the next few centuries more romantic plays about Jane were produced and she was depicted in film from very early in that format's history. The first of three films about her was the 1923 *Lady Jane Grey: The Court of Intrigue* but, apart from the cast, little else is known about the film.[3]

In the next decade, historical films were very popular. In 1933 Charles Laughton's *The Private Life of Henry VIII* was highly success-ful; it is not surprising that it was followed by other historical films of the Tudor period. 1936 saw the release of *The Tudor Rose*, also known as *Lady Jane Grey* or *Nine Days a Queen*. The film was directed by Robert Stevenson, who also co-authored the script with the actor Miles Malleson, who played Jane's father, Henry Grey, Duke of Suf-folk. This film, with some heavy-handed irony, presented a sweet, highly romantic Jane, who cares little about her studies. Jane, rather than Elizabeth who is absent from the film, has a somewhat flirtatious relationship with Tom Seymour; however, her real romance is with her husband. The cast was impressive with Cedric Hardwicke as the villainous John Dudley, referred to throughout as the Earl of Warwick, rather than Duke of Northumberland; Nova Pilbeam as Jane; and John Mills as her love interest, Guildford Dudley.

The Tudor Rose begins with prayers for the dying Henry VIII, played by Frank Cellier, who is characterized at that moment as a still powerful and terrifying monarch. In many ways this first scene appears as the sequel to *Private Life*. The deathbed is surrounded by the men who will rule for his young son Edward, including Thomas Seymour, his older brother Edward, Duke of Somerset, and John, Earl of Warwick. Henry proclaims his will, naming his successors, and the camera pans to portraits of Edward, Mary, Elizabeth, and Jane. Then Henry gives each of the three men his final analysis of their characters. He describes Thomas Seymour as someone of 'little wit but no judgment,' and suggests that Seymour 'Go where your wit will serve you and your lack of judgment won't bring you to disaster.' The statement evokes the statement supposedly made by Elizabeth after she heard of Seymour's execution: today died a man of much wit but very little judgment. Henry tells Seymour's older brother, Somerset, that he is 'such a hypocrite you deceive even yourself'. This film's Somerset, is indeed hypocritical, as well as easily manipulated. The characterization is unsympathetic, and far from the 'Good Duke', whose execution begins the 1986 film about Jane. As for Warwick, he is a man of 'no conscience, no fear'. Henry then thunders as his dying words: 'You heard my will. Edward. Mary. Elizabeth. Jane. And I lay my curse on any who abuse their power and intrigue against the succession as I have named it. . . . May he die a traitor's death. May his head be on London bridge.' The alert or knowledgeable moviegoer will already foresee what will take place for the rest of the film. But Warwick certainly does not share this insight and shows no concern for the words of the dying king. In words that eerily echo Dr Faustus, Warwick remarks: 'What is a curse but words . . . no I am not afraid.' Marlowe's scholar tells Mephistopheles, 'Think'st thou that Faustus is so fond imagine/That, after this life, there is any pain?/No, these are trifles, and more old wives' tales.' Both Marlowe's scholar and the film's evil earl learn all too late of the power of words, especially curses.

In this 1936 film, the innocent and sweet Jane is no match for Warwick, nor are the Seymour brothers or young King Edward. The clever, amoral Warwick stirs up rivalry between the two brothers and convinces Somerset that it is his higher public duty to arrest Thomas. The king, meanwhile, is powerless to intervene despite promising Jane to have Thomas spared. Warwick is shown to be ruthless and manipulative and so Edward shows no concern when the earl stages a coup and replaces Somerset. Indeed, Edward tells Jane that Warwick is his best Protector[4] ever, adding that the earl promised to spare Somerset.

Warwick of course is shown to be duplicitous, and when Jane and Edward hear the cannon which announces Somerset's execution, Edward is devastated, collapses, and soon is dying.

As Edward lies dying, Warwick decides to marry Jane to his son Guildford, in this film a decent and pleasant man, and subvert the succession. When, totally unhistorically, Edward refuses to make Jane his heir out of concern for her well-being, having too late recognized Warwick's monstrous character, Warwick simply forges the dying king's name. At first Jane screams her refusal to marry Warwick's son, the one time in the film when she is not the good docile and sweet-natured heroine; however, when she realizes he's the nice man who has been sympathetically listening to all her concerns about the court, and who hid her the night before from the guards when she tried to escape, she smilingly agrees, and she is back to presenting herself as the charming, high-spirited, but obedient girl. Frank Prochaska suggests that in this film 'Guildford and Jane are star-crossed lovers, though this is treated tamely and to little purpose.'[5] Their idyllic honeymoon that allows them to feel safe as they wander the countryside is short lived, however. With heavy-handed foreshadowing, Jane has just told Guildford how much she wants to stay in the country forever, when Warwick comes to tell her she must become queen. At first Jane is reluctant but Guildford manages to convince her that it is her duty. But Jane's rule is short lived too. While Jane is young and innocent, her cousin Mary is a clear thinking and stalwart adult. After Mary's forces defeat Warwick's army, both Jane and Guildford are beheaded. As the historical Charles I did on his way to his execution, the film character Jane asks for a cloak so people do not see her shiver and believe she is afraid.

Jane of *The Tudor Rose* is a pretty, sweet, rather flighty girl with a good heart, who is not much interested in her studies, and delighted to leave them behind for London. Though she at first resists the marriage with Guildford, when she realizes he is the stranger who has been helping her she falls immediately in love and is delighted to be married. She finally agrees to be queen out of a sense of duty and is more distraught about her beloved husband's death than her own. The 1930s were a time of great economic difficulty and political insecurity, and historical films were a popular escape mode in this time period. Their attraction may well have been to carry the viewer off to a far distant place with very different problems. Despite the different setting of time it also may well have been reassuring for a 1930s audience to have so quiet, modest, and sweet a heroine as Jane. Romances were

also a popular form of escapism in the 1930s. Jane is not so different in
her appeal from the heroine of the 1940 romance thriller film *Rebecca*,
where Maxim de Winter, played by Laurence Olivier, affectionately
calls his second wife, played by Joan Fontaine as a young naïve girl,
'little goose', and their love too is also put at great risk by larger events
she does not truly understand.

Fifty years passed before another film about the life of Lady Jane
Grey was made. This film, directed by Trevor Nunn, is gorgeously
filmed with beautiful costumes; the characterization of Jane is also
quite different. In the 1986 film *Lady Jane* the main character is far
more powerful than her predecessor in the 1936 *Tudor Rose*. This
Jane is passionate about her studies and speaks out far more vehemently against her parents. The film also has a very strong cast: Jane
is played by Helena Bonham Carter, Cary Elwes plays Guildford, and
John Wood is the Duke of Northumberland. Shakespearean actors
Michael Hordern, Jane Lapotaire, and Patrick Stewart, play Master
Feckenham, Princess Mary, and Henry Grey, Duke of Suffolk, respectively. But the two films do share a major plot theme that in no way
echoes the historical Jane. In both films Jane is at first appalled and
resistant at the thought of the marriage to Guildford, and in both films
by the end Jane is consumed by love of him and the love is equally
returned. As with the earlier film, *Lady Jane* also rather heavily foreshadows her tragic end from the beginning. But the 1986 film also has
a social agenda; it values youth as the ones who see the need for reform
clearly, in a way not at all suggested in the earlier film. The historical
consultant on the film, Frank Prochaska, confirms that 'Trevor Nunn
did not intend to present a historically accurate depiction of Lady
Jane'. Rather, 'suited to his own predilections', it was '1960s socialism
writ 1550s'. The screenwriter, David Edgar, 'was very much in tune
with this interpretation, which turned Lady Jane into a proto-socialist
feminist, a strange amalgam of Robin Hood and Beatrice Webb'.[6]

Unlike the earlier film, Jane's history in the film *Lady Jane* is greatly
foreshortened. *Lady Jane* begins toward the end of Edward's reign. Jane
is a passionate Protestant and a committed scholar who does not get
along with her parents. We see this the first time she appears in the film
sitting in a window seat by leaded pains of glass absorbedly reading.
She is disturbed by the visiting Master Feckenham, described in the
film as Mary's confessor, with whom she then discusses theology; in
reality Feckenham was in prison at the time. The scene is in some
ways modelled after the actual description by Roger Ascham of his
visit to the Duke of Suffolk's home of Bradgate Hall that he reports

in his later text, *The Schoolmaster*. While all the rest of household is out hunting, Jane is at home reading Plato's *Phaedro* in Greek with much pleasure. But while Ascham would have not only applauded Jane's love of learning, he also would have supported her religious ideals, which are challenged in the film by Feckenham, when he finds her reading Plato's description of the death of Socrates. Feckenham tells Jane this is a difficult text for someone of her age; when she shrugs, he asks her to read a passage aloud. The passage she reads is one of the touchstones of the film that will be referred to throughout: 'The soul takes flight to the world that is eternal, invisible but there arriving she is sure of bliss and forever dwells in paradise.' Since Jane is reading about the death of Socrates, Feckenham asks Jane for what would she be prepared to die. Jane's reading about death is another foreshadowing, but her answer suggests one important theme this film *Lady Jane* will develop. Jane responds: 'I would die to free our people from the chains of bigotry and superstition.' And truly, this is a response the historical Jane Grey might well have made; the reformed religion was probably the most important factor of her brief life.

While Jane and Feckenham did not meet at the time presented in the film, they did later. Soon before her execution they debated theology in the Tower. The film borrows briefly from this later actual exchange loosely following the account in Foxe. Feckenham demands to know what superstition is and Jane responds saying it is the idea that a piece of bread can become the body of our saviour. Feckenham replies: 'Did he not say at his last supper, take, eat, this is my body?' Jane's replies 'He says I am the vine, I am the door. Is he a vine? A door?' Though the two are in fundamental disagreement about theology, the encounter also foreshadows the later scene in the film when Feckenham shows kindness to Jane at the end of her life, and expresses his admiration for her: 'it is a privilege to talk to anyone whose love of learning shines like yours' he says. The 1986 film is asking its audience to take Jane's beliefs seriously, and presents enough of them with sufficient clarity to make this possible.

At the beginning of the film Jane's religious beliefs are the core of her being. This is the case for her cousin King Edward as well. The film depicts both as lonely young people who are fond of each other and have little that matters to them except their religious beliefs. Because of these beliefs, Northumberland easily convinces Edward to make Jane his heir. Her parents have more trouble convincing Jane to marry Guildford; though they beat her, it is only the dying king who finally convinces her as they sit on the floor together after one of her beatings. When Northumberland describes Guildford to Jane's father as a pious young man, the camera pans to him drinking and acting wild. Both Jane and Guildford are demonstrably miserable and alienated from each other at their wedding.

Nonetheless, after Guildford has explained to Jane his outrage over the poverty and injustice in England, the two newly married teenagers fall passionately in love as they spend time together in the country thinking of all the social injustice they would like to cure. There is a montage of scenes of them together growing in intimacy, making love, and debating societal wrongs. Just as they plan to run off together, they are brought to court where Jane is told she is queen. At first she refuses, but Guildford convinces her to agree, and instead of being Northumberland's pawn, she and Guildford begin the social improvements they wanted: reforming the currency with new non-debased Queen Jane shillings, freeing the prisoners over the objections of the Lieutenant of the Tower, and joyously giving food and her own royal clothing to the poor. But Mary is claiming that she is queen and soon defeats Northumberland.

After Jane and Guildford are arrested, to their great despair they are separated from each other. As Jane is taken into the Tower we see that she has in her hand the silver shilling. Mary promises to reprieve all who practise the true religion and Northumberland seizes the opportunity, hailing Mary as queen and making the sign of the cross. Jane meanwhile is in prison pacing her room. Finally she sits on the bed holding the pillow whispering, 'Guildford, where are you?' Elsewhere in the Tower Guildford lambastes his father for forsaking his religion; the duke tells Guildford that it is better to be a living dog than a dead lion, a comment truly made about the historical Northumberland and which is a verse from Proverbs. But Guildford soon emphasizes what is much more important to him, telling his father that they will not let him see Jane.

Mary is merciful and promises Jane she will be reprieved, but more important she allows Jane and Guildford to be together in the Tower. But again events beyond Jane and Guildford get them caught up in tragedy, this time fatally. And again, it is Jane's parents who fail her. Her father joins rebels who are massing against Mary's marriage to Philip of Spain, and the Spanish ambassador tells Mary that Jane and her husband must die before Philip will set sail for England. Mary considers that if she can get them both to convert, she could save them: 'these children [would] be less a threat if they embraced the true religion'. In an attempt to achieve this, she sends Feckenham to see Jane.

At their meeting, in contradiction to historical fact, Feckenham tells Jane that she will be executed unless she converts to Catholicism. Guildford, who is present, says nothing but stands by a large cross and watches his wife. Jane replies saying there is no point in discussing theology; she cannot go against her faith. Feckenham, though disappointed, shows his compassion and promises her, 'I will be with you 'til the end.' He then leaves the young couple alone for their last night together, which again combines romance with commitment to social justice. Guildford tells Jane, 'He came to me first. I'll stay firm for the sake of our nine days. To keep their memory true.' Jane agrees. 'They brought you here and told you to stay silent so I'd think they'd broken you but they were wrong. I could never stay true if you weren't here.' The young lovers beg to have their last night together and we see them romantically in front of the fireplace in Jane's cell. Jane promises Guildford, 'We'll both fly beyond their reach so their reach can't touch us. And at last we'll be nothing and nobody. We'll be each other. I need this time forever.' When the soldiers come in to take Guildford away, Jane promises him, 'Next time I see your face I want it for eternity.' Later Feckenham comes to Jane who is sitting and waiting, dressed well for her final performance. 'I promised and I'll repeat my promise up to the end.' But Jane is most concerned about Guildford. 'Tell me. I want to know.'

As Feckenham describes Guildford's death we see both Jane's face and Guildford bravely walking up Tower Hill. Feckenham is still telling how Guildford died while we see Jane doing the same. On the scaffold Jane tells Feckenham, 'God will requite you for your kindness sir', and she hands him something. Jane then forgives the executioner and blindfolds herself. But she cannot find the block. 'Where is it? Where is it? What do I do?' Feckenham leads her there. Jane puts her head down and just as she is about to be beheaded she calls, 'Guildford!' In the final scene we see what Jane had given Feckenham. It is a Jane shilling that he passes on to Mary, who, struggling not to cry, tells him, 'I am going to meet my husband.' In Foxe's text, shillings were occasionally handed out as tokens of remembrance by Protestant martyrs. In this context it is also a remembrance of Jane and Guildford's commitment to social justice, to efforts to restore a currency, to help the poor. The last words of the film are Feckenham's, and he repeats what Jane read to him in the opening scene: 'The soul takes flight to the world invisible but there arriving is sure of bliss and dwells forever in paradise.'

From eyewitness accounts, Feckenham was indeed kind to Jane before her death. She told him on the scaffold, 'God I beseech Him abundantly reward you for your kindness to me.' There never was, however, a Queen Jane shilling, and Jane not only did not spend her last night with her husband, but she refused to see Guildford before his death even though permission had been granted. She sent back word that she would prefer to wait and see him instead in heaven. Jane certainly did not say 'Guildford' as her final word; instead, making her faith clear to all witnesses to her execution, she asked, 'Good people, while I am alive, I pray you to assist me with your prayers.' As a Protestant, she did not believe in purgatory, and once she was dead, her soul would go to heaven or be damned for all eternity, so prayers would be only of value in these last dreadful minutes of her life. As the axe was about to come down she cried, 'Lord, into thy hands I commend my spirit.'[7]

The Jane of the film in many ways had the strength and spirit similar to what we know of the actual Jane, but the sixteenth-century Jane was not concerned with social issues, though in another century her personality might well have found complete dedication to social causes attractive. While religion is far more considered in *Lady Jane* than the earlier *Tudor Rose*, in both the films religion takes a back seat to romantic love; it certainly did not in her historical life.

Lady Jane is in some ways a precursor to the 1998 film *Elizabeth*: both movies are beautifully filmed with lavish costumes and a somewhat tragic love story. Yet Jane and Elizabeth are film parallels rather than connecting life lines. While the two cousins knew each other, neither appears as a character in the films about the other. But had the coup that attempted to put Jane on the throne succeeded, it would not only have meant the end of Mary but of Elizabeth as well. Though both films emphasize romance – Jane with husband Guildford and Elizabeth with Robert Dudley – the 1998 *Elizabeth* presents a far less politically committed heroine than the earlier film *Lady Jane*. While one may be as historically inaccurate as the other, *Lady Jane* has a determined heroine who wants her reign to have meaning and has learned to care deeply about the poor. We never see Jane dancing, ogling her courtiers, or involved in a lovers' spat the way the 1998 film depicts the young Queen Elizabeth. While *The Tudor Rose* has a sweet but weak heroine, *Lady Jane* is a film of a strong young woman who briefly comes into her own with the suggestion that the young have more understanding of the need for real political and social change than their cynical and corrupt elders. In the 1980s, when this film was made, Ronald Reagan was president of the United States and Margaret Thatcher Prime Minister of Great Britain; the poor were as criminalized in the public eye in that decade as Trevor Nunn presented the poor as viewed by the upper classes in the 1550s. His Jane and Guildford were a call to those of the 1980s to see the need for social change. While the actual Jane Grey was neither political nor romantic, in her own way she was also a strong young woman of deeply felt religious beliefs who met her death bravely. In certain ways the 1986 film brings the circle back to the original Lady Jane Grey.

Suggestions for Further Reading

British Academy John Foxe Project. http://www.shef.ac.uk/uni/projects/bajfp/

J. G. Nichols (ed.), *The Chronicle of Queen Jane, and of Two Years of Queen Mary, and Especially of the Rebellion of Sir Thomas Wyat* (New York, 1968).

Carole Levin, 'Lady Jane Grey: Protestant Queen and Martyr', in Margaret Hannay (ed.),*Silent But For the Word: Tudor Women as Patrons, Translators, and Writers of Religious Works* (Kent, OH, 1985).

D. M. Loades, *John Dudley, Duke of Northumberland : 1504–1553* (Oxford, 1996).

6

From Hatfield to Hollywood: Elizabeth I on Film*

Susan Doran

From one of the earliest silent films at the beginning of the twentieth century until two Oscar-nominated performances in 1999 and one in 2007, Elizabeth I has appeared as a character in over 20 films, whether as the female lead, in a supporting role, or as a non-speaking bit-player. Taking all these appearances into account, she must hold the record for the most cinematically exposed British monarch. The films cover a variety of genres: biopic, romance, the adventure/swashbuckling movie, and the 'heritage film'. This essay seeks to explain why so many 'Elizabeth films' were produced, how they reflected their own time, and how accurately their makers brought to celluloid the Elizabeth of historians.

Elizabeth's popularity as a screen subject began properly in the 1930s. What attracted filmmakers of that decade to the queen was her status as a national icon and the perceived importance of her reign in British history. As the film historian Marcia Landy noted, historical films of the interwar years focussed on the 'significant individuals and events associated with traditional and watershed moments in a country's past'.[1] And at that time Britain 'watershed moments' were thought to be those central to its rise as a great sea-faring nation and imperial power, and consequently events in Elizabeth's reign, notably Francis Drake's circumnavigation of the globe, Walter Ralegh's early colonization of Virginia and the defeat of the Spanish Armada.

This version of British history can be traced back to the mid-nineteenth century, when the historian James Froude's *Forgotten*

Plate 5   In *Fire Over England* Flora Robson conveys a mixture of pensiveness, personal loss and resilience that characterizes her pre-war portrayal of Elizabeth. Courtesy of United Artists and The Kobal Collection for the image of Flora Robson and Vivien Leigh from the motion picture *Fire Over England* (1937).

Worthies (1852) told the stories of lesser-known Elizabethan explorers and the novelist Charles Kingsley's *Westward Ho* (1855) spun tales of adventure around the Elizabethan Devonshire men who took to sea against the Spaniards. These books were immensely influential in encouraging Victorians to locate the origins of their own empire in Elizabeth's reign and to take pride in the naval feats of her seamen.[2] Writers and their readers somehow forgot that Virginia was not properly settled nor an overseas commercial empire established until the reigns of the early Stuarts.

The process of raising the profile of the Elizabethan period in the cultural identity of Great Britain was boosted towards the end of the nineteenth century by the 1888 tercentenary commemoration of the defeat of the Spanish Armada. In that year, a 'large company of Plymothians and visitors from a distance' attended both an exhibition and a ceremony at Plymouth Hoe when a memorial to Drake's victory was erected. Even more people attended a similar exhibition at the Drury Lane Theatre, and countless others purchased a commemorative medal in which a crown of glory was placed above two oval medallions containing the busts of Elizabeth and Victoria. Speeches marking the event praised the Armada as the central event of an age 'of great men and great thoughts', for the victory not only demonstrated English sea-power but also marked the defeat of 'the greatest conspiracy ever undertaken against human liberty'.[3]

Patriotic pride in the English victory was, thereafter, kept alive in the paintings of Seymour Lewis, Sir Henry Newbolt's *Drake's Drum* and the poems of Rudyard Kipling. Consequently, by the time that H. E. Marshall's children's book *Our Island Story* was published in 1905 the mythic status of Elizabethan England had been firmly established. The many children who obtained an early taste of British history from its pages[4] were treated in one chapter to the story of Ralegh's explorations and exposed in another chapter (significantly entitled 'Elizabeth – how England was saved from the Spaniards') to such iconic moments as Elizabeth's Tilbury speech, Drake's continuation of his game of bowls at Plymouth and the release of the fire-ships against the heavy Spanish galleons.

At about this time, Elizabeth herself became personally identified with these events and the achievements of her seamen. Before then, mid-Victorians had tended to be unsympathetic towards the queen;[5] Froude, so full of praise for Elizabethan explorers, had obviously not much liked their monarch. Although he admitted she was 'supremely brave' and hardworking, he also described her as cold, vain, unscrupulous, remorseless and full of artifice. The successes of her reign he credited to the policies of Sir William Cecil and to a lesser extent Sir Francis Walsingham. Left to Elizabeth, he thought, her navy would have been 'starved and mutilated' of resources.[6] Froude's harsh opinion, however, soon ceased to be fashionable. In 1896, the biography by Bishop Mandell Creighton set the tone for a reappraisal that came to dominate future writings. For Creighton, Elizabeth 'represented England as no other ruler ever did . . . She educated Englishmen', he wrote, 'to a perception of England's destiny, and for this purpose fixed England's attention upon itself'.[7]

During the 1930s Creighton's view was popularized by historians such as Arthur D. Innes in 1931 and John E. Neale in 1934. In his essays on important figures in English History, Innes announced that if his countrymen were asked 'To which of her monarchs does England owe her deepest debt', they would answer Elizabeth I: 'Somehow we feel, as with no other king or queen, that Elizabeth herself was the central figure inspiring the vision and directing the action' [of adventurers and writers].[8] Innes praised the queen on various counts, but reserved his hyperbole for the moment 'when the great crisis came' in 1588: 'Elizabeth rose to the occasion as she always did; again she became the Genius of England incarnate.'[9] Neale's highly acclaimed biography of the queen was equally complimentary. He too claimed that Elizabeth reached 'the heights of true greatness' in the summer of 1588 when undismayed by the threat of invasion she raised her troops' morale at Tilbury. Furthermore, Neale's Elizabeth showed 'consummate skill' in her government of England and captured the devotion of her subjects through her personal magnetism and style.[10] So, by the mid-1930s when talking cinema turned to Elizabeth, the queen had been re-established as Gloriana, the embodiment of her nation, 'the idol of her people', a ruler who had raised England to the height of power and shattered its enemies.[11]

The two British films depicting Elizabeth during the 1930s – *Drake of England* (1935) and *Fire Over England* (1937) – drew on this version of history, re-creating the pivotal moments when she knighted Drake, delivered the Tilbury speech and ordered action against the Armada. On screen Elizabeth was portrayed as the powerful ruler who stood for England; as she announces in *Fire Over England*, 'I *am* England'. In both films she demonstrably puts her duty to her nation before all other considerations and provides strong leadership at a time of crisis. Like Innes and Neale's Elizabeth, she bravely challenges Spanish power and stiffens English resolve in the face of invasion. Although two entirely fictitious romances take up a considerable proportion of screen-time (in *Drake of England* a secret marriage between Drake and one of Elizabeth's ladies-in-waiting; and in *Fire Over England* a love affair between two imaginary characters, Michael Ingolby and Cynthia, another lady-in-waiting, who was said to be the grand-daughter of Lord Burghley), Elizabeth's filmic presence is in no way diluted; indeed she provides the moral heart of each film.

In *Drake of England* Elizabeth's anti-Spanish stance went well beyond historical reality as it inaccurately filmed Elizabeth (Athene Seyler) meeting Drake before his circumnavigation and secretly agree-ing to his attack on Spanish treasure on the Isthmus of Panama.[12] Nonetheless, it created a picture of England's past that fitted well with the childhood lessons of its audience, capturing on film the memorable, if sometimes historically suspect, highlights (such as the bowls scene) of the privateer's career. As *The Times* reviewer pointed out, 'the incidents are related in much the same spirit as that of the more elementary histories for children'.[13] Presented as a pageant extolling Britain's greatness, the film was thoroughly appreciated in some quarters: not only was it selected for the opening gala event in a programme of films and lectures to mark George V's jubilee, but it also went down well with the right-wing press.[14]

The filmmakers of *Fire Over England,* however, intended to do far more than simply re-tell a familiar story and stimulate British patrio-tism. They saw in Elizabethan history a relevance to their own time and used the film to draw parallels between the international situation of the 1580s and that of their own day. Alarmed about the tyranny, racism and war-mongering of contemporary Fascist regimes, the pro-ducers (Alexander Korda, a Hungarian of Jewish origin, and Erich Pommer, a German Jewish refugee) presented Elizabeth as the staunch defender of the liberal values of a free society against an intolerant and tyrannical autocrat. This agenda was evident from the opening title-credits that announce the year to be 1587 when 'Philip II rules by force and fear' and 'Spanish tyranny is challenged by a free people of a little island'. This stark contrast between the tyrant and the English ruler of a 'free people' was sustained throughout the film. Elizabeth (Flora Robson) is constantly shown interacting with her courtiers and debating with councillors, whereas Philip II (played by a brooding Raymond Massey) sits in the shadows of his court, issuing commands to the handful of nervous men about him. Similarly, Elizabeth is humane and merciful (as when she allows a deranged assassin to go free and gives English spies the opportunity to redeem themselves), whilst Philip relies on torture and the Inquisition to suppress all opposition.[15]

In line with the film's propaganda purpose Elizabeth stands up to Spanish aggression and rejects the policy of appeasement whose leading spokesman is the elderly and gout-ridden Burghley (actually rather too elderly and ailing, for in 1587 he was just 67 and went on for another 11 years). Elizabeth initially draws laughter from her courtiers when she tells the Spanish ambassador that Philip is free to punish Drake as a pirate *if* the Spanish can capture him. Once the ambassador has left, she confides to Burghley that Drake's raids are 'privately agreed between us' even though she has publicly disavowed them. Then, after listening carefully to the arguments for appeasement, she reluctantly dismisses them and recommends the alternative policy namely a pre-emptive strike against Spain: 'I strike, or be struck' she tells her councillors. Finally, towards the end of the film, when the unprovoked Armada is sighted, Elizabeth dons a breast plate, mounts a white horse, and calls on her people to hold together and repulse the powerful invasion force.

The portrait of Elizabeth in *Fire Over England* was unquestionably idealized – after all, at her order John Stubbs lost his hand for writing a pamphlet against her marriage plans in 1579, and with her consent hundreds of Catholic priests, plotters, and rebels were executed. Nonetheless, the film did reflect a long-held and prevailing view that the queen was personally tender-hearted and unusually tolerant. Neale was but one of her many biographers who made much of the former trait, citing for example, Elizabeth's reluctance to order the executions of the Duke of Norfolk and Mary Queen of Scots.[16] As for her tolerance, Francis Bacon's dictum that she did not seek to make windows into men's souls was often quoted and sometimes falsely ascribed to Elizabeth. Historians noted too that she vetoed or mitigated the severity of anti-Catholic legislation brought before parliament.[17]

At its release, historians were in two minds about *Fire Over England*. On the debit side they disliked its use of fictional characters and picked holes in its historical accuracy. Professors F. J. C. Hearnshaw and J. E. Neale, who were commissioned by the English Historical Association to review the film for teachers, complained that 'history is once again violated for the sake of melodrama', and drew attention to several howlers they had detected: for example, that the on-screen Elizabeth thought up the use of fire-ships after her speech at Tilbury whereas in truth the ships had been used 12 days before her speech;

and then the Spanish ships were not burnt as shown in the film but in reality had cut their anchor and fled.[18] These changes, presumably deliberate, served to intensify the drama, but other more careless errors had also slipped in and were noticed; a well-informed, if pedantic, reader of *The Times* pointed out that the prayer of thanksgiving the queen recited after the Armada victory came from the 1661 Book of Common Prayer and could not therefore have been used in 1588.[19]

Despite these inaccuracies, Hearnshaw and Neale were almost ecstatic about the portrayal of Elizabeth:

> No one will go far wrong who takes his idea of the historical Queen Elizabeth from Flora Robson. Her interpretation, even her words, ring true; and indeed sometimes, as in the supreme moment of Tilbury, her words are the very words spoken by Elizabeth.[20]

Although historians are today less confident about what words Elizabeth actually spoke at Tilbury,[21] Hearnshaw and Neale's praise for Robson is both understandable and justified: understandable because the actress captured Neale's Elizabeth – rational, intelligent, witty, and majestic; justified because Robson brought an unusual restraint, dignity, and authority to the role. Although part of her interpretation seems anachronistic today, reflecting as it does the gender stereotyping and expectations of the 1930s, Robson characterized well a powerful woman without turning her into a monster or shrew. Her sympathetic portrayal may have resulted from a personal identification with Elizabeth. As she told *Film Weekly* in January 1937: 'Elizabeth was essentially a woman of action' and

> such women – women whose lives and works were far more important than their loves – are much more in tune with our modern idea and tempo of life than many of the sexy sirens who have figured as heroines of sexy and sentimental films in the past.[22]

But Robson had also done some homework. She had read a considerable amount about Elizabeth's character, and the previous year had turned out to watch Queen Mary in the Silver Jubilee production 'to see how a real Queen behaved'.[23]

On the basis of playing Elizabeth in *Fire Over England*, Robson was chosen to reprise the role in the Warner Brothers' production of *The Sea Hawk* (1940). Elizabeth had not been a character in the original Rafael Sabatini novel, on which the film was very loosely based, but she was written into an early draft of the script in 1935.

By then, several plays about Elizabeth, including Maxwell Anderson's *Elizabeth the Queen,* had enjoyed long runs in America and the historical character was considered to be sufficiently familiar to an American audience, the film's primary market. During the script development, her presence was retained as it came to suit the propaganda purpose of the filmmakers.[24] Like Korda and Pommer before them, Warner Brothers decided to make a film which had a political relevance. *The Sea Hawk*'s message, however, was to be more pointed, with the director (Michael Curtiz) and screenwriters (Howard Koch and Seton I. Miller) drawing an unmistakable comparison between Elizabeth's England threatened by the Armada in 1588 and Churchill's Britain about to be attacked in the Blitz.[25] Consequently, whereas the message of the earlier film had escaped the notice of most critics, some reviewers of *The Sea Hawk* were to comment upon the contemporary parallels.[26]

Despite their common purpose, Koch and Miller's approach to the queen also differed significantly from the one taken in *Fire Over England*. Elizabeth in *The Sea Hawk* does not save England from a Spanish invasion; that task is left to Geoffrey Thorpe, the hero based on Francis Drake and played by Errol Flynn. As the foreword to the script explicitly stated, 'The story of this picture finds its origin in the exploits of Sir Francis Drake, under whose leadership Elizabethan England challenged the supremacy of the great empire of Spain.'[27] The film follows this line exactly. Here Elizabeth is not by choice the founder of the British navy; she is only persuaded into that role by Thorpe. When Elizabeth first appears, she can be heard dismissing the advice of her Lord Admiral that she should build a fleet with the words: 'A large fleet is a luxury England can ill afford.' Nor does this Elizabeth secretly connive with English privateers in their attacks upon Spanish shipping; on the contrary, she initially upbraids Thorpe for assaulting and looting Spanish ships: 'Never again', she told the Sea Hawks in an early scene, 'will you dare in my presence to condone your crimes under the mask of patriotism . . . And in the future', she continued, 'let me warn each of you that any unwarranted attack upon the person or property of Spanish subjects will cost the guilty person his head'. Although this display of anger is designed largely for the benefit of the Spanish ambassador, Elizabeth has to be persuaded into privately endorsing Thorpe's plan to seize Spanish gold, and she seems to be influenced as much by her 'feminine' side – the sea captain's flirtatious charm and his gift of an exquisite West Indian pearl – as by 'masculine' considerations of strategy. Even then she is determined to avoid war at all costs: 'Our safety', she claims 'lies in diplomacy, not force'. When Thorpe is later captured, Elizabeth gives in to Philip's II's demand that she must disband her Sea Hawks, the one effective naval defence she possesses. She claims her instincts are 'to defy Philip; but the safety of my subjects constrains me to caution'. Only after Thorpe escapes and reveals Philip's Armada plans does she accept the need for war and 'pledge you [her countrymen] ships worthy of our seamen'. Moreover, unlike the Elizabeth in *Fire Over England,* who recognizes Sir Hillary Vane as a spy at her court, the queen in *The Sea Hawk* needs Thorpe to expose the dastardly plans of Philip II and his treacherous agent, Lord Wolfingham, who has been deceiving the queen successfully for years; and of course it is Thorpe who dispatches him in a swordfight.

Elizabeth in *The Sea Hawk* is, therefore, a well-intentioned but often misguided ruler. At one level she stands for the sympathetic face of appeasement, the policy that had understandably, if mistakenly, dominated British foreign policy during the 1930s;[28] at another she represents the passive woman who needed to be rescued by a man of action. In no case is she the queen of 1930s British historians. Interestingly the script writers did not consult Neale's work as a resource but relied instead on the undistinguished biography of Elizabeth by the American, Katherine Anthony, which had been published in 1929. There they found a paradoxical character, a queen who was coquettish yet mannish, daring yet prudent, and affable yet not affectionate. These qualities found their way into the film.[29]

It was not, however, only Elizabeth's mythic status arising from the Armada years that caught the interest of filmmakers in the 1930s; they were also attracted to the question of sex, or rather the absence of it, in the life of the Virgin Queen. As they saw it, Elizabeth's conscious decision to renounce sex and marriage opened up possibilities for psychological exploration. In the case of *Fire Over England* and *The Sea Hawk*, Elizabeth's virginity was not central to the plot, but it nonetheless informed her character and reinforced the theme of patriotic service to one's country; for in both films Elizabeth was shown to have suppressed her natural feelings and needs as a woman so that she could provide strong political and military leadership for her nation. In *Fire Over England*, though, the costs were seen to be higher than in *The Sea Hawk* where the unmarried queen displays little regret for her decision to renounce love in return for political power. When she hears the Spanish Dona Maria singing a love song in the latter film, Elizabeth is prompted to say to herself 'I dare say each of us must choose between loving a man or ruling him.' Then turning to the girl she said good-humouredly, 'I don't quarrel with your choice. You have your song and I have my sceptre.' By contrast, in *Fire Over England* Elizabeth expresses sadness, even bitterness, at the sacrifice she has made in putting duty to her country before the emotional satis-faction of love and marriage. These feelings are most apparent in two scenes where the queen displays irritation with the beautiful Cynthia (who is happily humming a love tune in the first and being embraced by Michael in the second) and in two further scenes where the queen looks sadly at her ageing face in the mirror. Yet here too, Elizabeth's virginity is portrayed sympathetically, since her brand of self-sacrifice and strong sense of duty seemed to represent exactly what Britain needed at times of national emergency – whether in the mid-1580s or the later 1930s.

An entirely different approach to Elizabeth's virginity, however, was taken in two other films of the 1930s, *Mary of Scotland* (1936) and *The Private Lives of Elizabeth and Essex* (1939). Both films were adap-tations of plays by Maxwell Anderson, a playwright who throughout his career demonstrated an intense dislike for Machiavellian politicians like Elizabeth, whom he branded as tyrants. Neither film, therefore, had time for the heroic Elizabeth; instead, each characterized her as a failure, if not as a queen then certainly as a woman. On screen she is a frustrated and emotionally damaged woman, who has made a Faustian bargain in giving up personal love and happiness in return for political power.

Both Anderson's original drama and the adapted screenplay of *Mary of Scotland* followed a well-established literary tradition which found the naïve Mary Stuart to be a far more likeable figure than the *realpolitik* Elizabeth. Anderson had probably read Sir Walter Scott and Friedrich Schiller, who exemplified this approach, although no evidence exists that they were his sources. It is known, however, that at university he had been influenced by a certain Professor Orin G. Libby who passed on 'the view unpopular with many other histo-rians of that day, which was that Elizabeth was far from being a virgin saint and that Mary was by no means a she-devil'.[30] As a Catholic Irish-American, the director John Ford probably shared Anderson's prejudice against Elizabeth. Consequently both screenplay and direc-tion turned Elizabeth into a thoroughly repellent character, if not a caricature.[31] Played by Florence Eldridge, she barks commands, abuses Leicester, spits venom at her women at court, and is of course vin-dictive towards her Scottish rival. In contrast to the principled, even saintly, Mary, Elizabeth is utterly amoral: in her political life she is engaged in 'a life and death struggle for supremacy' over Mary, for as she explains to her royal prisoner in a fictitious interview on the eve of her execution: 'You were born too close to my throne – it was you or I'.[32] As for religion, unlike Mary, Elizabeth has no conscience or faith, but rather treats belief systems as a cloak 'to be put on and taken off at will', consequently deciding at her accession to abandon the Catholic ship 'when it sinks'. Although 1930s historians might recognize here the *politique* queen who had little time for theological issues but understood the political uses of religion,[33] there was little else in Eldridge's portrayal that had any authenticity. Certainly Elizabeth's deep reservations about keeping Mary a prisoner in England and signing the warrant for her execution are entirely missing.

Another problem in the representation of Elizabeth arises from the film's presentism, for as well as being engaged in a political battle the two filmic queens are involved in a contest over their femininity, which Mary wins outright. Anderson's original script hinted at this theme but the film took it much further. With her soft-spoken voice and graceful movements, Katherine Hepburn as Mary represents a 1930s feminine ideal, whereas Eldridge's Elizabeth is naturally masculine – as seen in her body language when she leans heavily on the table and strides through the court. Mary therefore trounces Elizabeth where it counts. In their imaginary confrontation Elizabeth wistfully tells Mary 'I see now why men love you' while Mary tells Elizabeth 'you are not even a woman' (sentences which are not actually in the play). A little later Mary asserts that Elizabeth's life has been 'a magnificent failure', for she has suppressed all the natural female instincts and been condemned to live without having a fulfilling romantic relationship or bearing a child.

Elizabeth's sacrifice in *The Private Lives of Elizabeth and Essex* is even greater. Because she fears that the young, dashing, popular, and ambitious Earl of Essex will destabilize her realm and undermine her power, she cannot afford to express her love for him publicly and she therefore prefers to humiliate him. In her first speech, she lays down her dilemma and creed: 'the necessities of a queen must transcend that of a woman'. Made desperately unhappy by the consequent emotional conflict – smashing mirrors, cursing Essex's name and abusing her ladies – Elizabeth is a tragic, if somewhat monstrous, figure. As she tells her maidservant Margaret, 'To be queen is to be less than human'. At the end of the film, her lover is dead, her power is secure and England is safe from the ambition of Essex, but Elizabeth sits on the throne in total isolation, her face ravaged with pain.

The ahistoricity of the film is largely the fault of Maxwell Anderson's play of 1930 *Elizabeth the Queen*, on which it was closely based and Lytton Strachey's 1928 psycho-sexual biography, which had inspired Anderson.[34] Keen to outdo Lynn Fontanne who played the part on Broadway to great acclaim, Bette Davis attempted verisimilitude by working secretly with the make-up artist to devise a reincarnation of Elizabeth's face from the portraits.[35] However, few others at Warner Brothers, had any interest in re-creating the historical Elizabeth, although the screenwriters did introduce a number of superficial historical references that had been absent from Anderson's original script. Most of the production and artistic team were simply working to produce a Hollywood spectacle, and treated the film as 'a romantic swashbuckling sort of thing' rather than a historical drama. Once produced, its trailer tried to sell it as 'a battle royal of love' and 'the mighty story of a love affair that changed world history'.[36]

It was in order to market the film as a romantic swashbuckler that led many at Warner Brothers to push for the film to be called *The Knight and the Lady*. Their thinking was that *Elizabeth the Queen* and *Elizabeth and Essex*, the titles originally proposed, would be unappealing to a mass American, especially a Mid-Western, audience who had little interest in, and less knowledge of, British History. When Jack Warner personally intervened in the ensuing disputes over the film's title and decided upon *Private Lives*, at least one businessman at Warner Brothers questioned the commercial wisdom of the decision, maintaining that 'any other title which suggests romance and adventure will serve far better than the present title which positively identifies the material as an English historical drama'.[37]

1940 was the last year for Elizabeth to feature in a film for over a decade. By then the queen had probably been over-exposed, even as a wartime leader. Additionally, filmic tastes were changing. With the important exceptions of Westerns and adaptations of novels, 1940s films came to focus on the present rather than the past, while early 1950s period-epics were usually set within Ancient Rome, often with a biblical theme, or in the Middle Ages.[38] *Fire Over England* was re-released in 1947 but otherwise the only films before 1953 that were vaguely 'Elizabethan' were adaptations of Shakespeare.[39]

Why Elizabeth returned to the screen in *Young Bess* (1953) and *The Virgin Queen* (1955) is not entirely clear, but her reappearance may possibly have had something to do with the accession of Elizabeth II in February 1952 reigniting interest in the first Elizabethan Age.[40] Although plans for the adaptation of Margaret Irwin's novel predated

the death of George VI, the film's release was timed to be part of
the 'Coronation festivities' on both sides of the Atlantic. *The Private
Lives of Elizabeth and Essex* was reissued in 1953 in a similar attempt to
exploit the historical moment.[41] Both the new films also attempted
to piggy-back on the success of previous Tudor dramas, so in *Young
Bess* Charles Laughton was cast once more as Henry VIII, while Bette
Davis starred again as Elizabeth in *The Virgin Queen* with similar make-
up and wigs.

In *Young Bess* the general characterization of Princess Elizabeth as
impetuous and warm-hearted fitted reasonably well with descriptions
of her in popular biographies of the 1950s.[42] The idea, intimated in
the film's last shots, that the trauma of Seymour's execution had transformed Elizabeth from a headstrong and passionate girl into the severe
and resolute ruler of fame was also evident in some contemporary
profiles of the queen.[43] But, the more serious side to Elizabeth's character (including her intellectual pursuits) were ignored while the love
affair between Elizabeth and Seymour, as dramatized in the film, was
the stuff of romantic fiction not history; and the notion that the executed Admiral was Elizabeth's only love, spoiling her for other men
(whatever happened to Robert Dudley?) was just plain silly.[44]

The Virgin Queen was more historically situated in that it attempted
to debunk two central myths surrounding Elizabeth: The first was that
she chose to be the Virgin Queen because her patriotic duty to the
state was incompatible with a married life. Davis's Elizabeth, provides
a more prosaic and less noble reason for her perpetual virginity, when
she explains to Bess Throckmorton that physicians diagnosed her as
barren at the age of 18.[45] Although Elizabeth affects not to care, claiming 'I am glad, England was child enough for me', the narrative belies
her words, for she is shown to be guilty of sexual jealousy, beset by
frustrated desires, and exhausted by public affairs. Second, the film
implicitly rejected the epic Elizabeth and depicts her as anything but
Gloriana. As in *Private Lives,* Davis's queen is a capricious and mannish
bully, while her court is a feminized, oppressive space. This Elizabeth
turns her councillors into servile courtiers, and her favourites into
lap-dogs who sit on a cushion before the throne and lick the hand of
their mistress. Her court is described by various characters as artificial,
full of flattery, no place to speak truth, 'an aviary full of tame birds'.
Her body-language is graceless and unfeminine (watch her hitch up
her skirt to walk over Ralegh's cloak). Furthermore, England seems to
suffer from having an unmarried woman on its throne. Her policies are
penny-pinching and small-minded; she revels in putting one over the
French ambassador and prefers to engage in matrimonial diplomacy

rather than build up a navy to challenge Spain on the High Seas. While adept at managing the ambitious men at court, she stifles their imagination and saps their vitality – all but the 'blunt soldier', Walter Ralegh (played by Richard Todd), who resists her attempts to make him subject to her whim and command. 'It is no honour for a man to humble himself,' cries Ralegh at one crisis-point in their relationship before storming out of the queen's council room (please note Ralegh was never a councillor). 'I wish to serve not you, but England,' he then announces before giving a rousing speech about England's 'destiny and hope' to become a great maritime and imperial power to the strains of patriotic music. He, not Elizabeth, sets England on its path towards the New World.

While mirroring 1950s gender stereotyping about what happens when a woman becomes the boss, Davis's characterization of the queen in her court could be found in a number of Elizabethan texts as well as pre-Victorian works.[46] It also anticipated several later hostile biographies, in which Elizabeth's court was portrayed as a place of intrigue where courtiers had to fawn on the queen to survive, where their marriages were punished by exclusion or a spell in the Tower, and where the queen was always an unpredictable and domineering mistress. Even today, this version of Elizabeth and her court is alive and well. Witness Christopher Haigh's description of the Elizabethan court, where he tells readers: 'Elizabeth attempted to control her councillors and her magnates by drawing them into a web of personal, even emotional, relationships with her, in which she was by turn queen and coquette'. Courtiers, he claims, were forced 'into the role of worshippers at her shrine', while the queen herself displayed 'sexual jealousy', 'her natural ill-temper', and 'the bitterness of an ageing woman at the attractions of the young'. No wonder, that her court 'could produce apparently childish behaviour' from male courtiers.[47] Haigh's view, however, is by no means uncontested.[48]

The Virgin Queen provided the last memorable cinema depiction of Elizabeth, before Glenda Jackson in *Mary Queen of Scots* (1971) re-played in miniature her part in the widely viewed and much-admired 1960s television series, *Elizabeth R*.[49] The success of that series as well as cinema's fondness in the late 1960s for historical drama explains the production of this particular film. Jackson's portrayal in the film owed not a little to Neale and emphasized the queen's dedication to her state *á la* Flora Robson, but brought it up-to-date by excluding sentimentality. Jackson's queen is an independent, courageous and astute woman who unlike her cousin rules with her head. Yet this does not mean she has no heart, for this Elizabeth is not vindictive towards Mary, and she tries to save her from the scaffold. When in the last shot the camera lingers on the queen sitting alone on the throne, her sadness does not stem from her rejection of marriage and motherhood. Rather in this film her tragedy is that Mary forced her to execute a kinswoman and a monarch. Jackson's Elizabeth therefore portrayed a woman who could succeed in a patriarchal world while retaining some 'feminine' qualities and not greatly missing a husband and children. No wonder she became a role-model for many women in the feminist 1970s and 1980s.[50]

Cinematically more interesting, however, was Derek Jarman's inclusion of the figure of Elizabeth in *Jubilee* (1978). Here Jarman utilized the iconic status of the first Elizabeth to comment upon English society in the Jubilee year of the second. His Elizabeth, though, no longer represented the England of Drake and Ralegh, whose imperialism he despised. Instead she stood for the era of Shakespeare, Marlowe and Spencer, the Golden Age of English culture, and was employed as a voice to express his horror at England's degeneration into a state of violent anarchy and embittered punk culture.[51] Two decades on, Elizabeth's association with the Golden Age of English culture was exploited again in *Shakespeare in Love* (1998). The choice of the renowned Shakespearean actress, Dame Judi Dench, to play Elizabeth served to highlight the queen's mythical role as patron of the theatre and England's greatest playwright. Dench's persona, as well as the script, made her perhaps the most attractive of the filmic Elizabeths. Although she is far from being Gloriana (indeed the script deliberately subverts the Gloriana myth) she is kind-hearted, plain-speaking, humorous, self-knowing and perspicacious. As one commentator has observed, Elizabeth's virgin state may have come at a price but she pays it good temperedly; besides, Gwyneth Paltrow's Viola pays a much higher one in marrying the Earl of Wessex.[52]

By contrast Shekhar Kapur's *Elizabeth* of the same year suggests that the queen by renouncing her sexuality is stripped of her humanity and becomes a martyr to the state, her hair-cropping at the end of the film echoing that of the female heretic at its start.[53] Although determinedly modern, or rather post-modern, Kapur's *Elizabeth* was as much a product of the traditional myths surrounding the queen as were earlier films. Only because of her status as a national icon and the Virgin Queen could Kapur use the figure of Elizabeth to explore subversively issues of gender, sexuality, and Englishness. As far as the latter was concerned, the director later claimed that he had

conceived the film in part as 'the revenge of the colonials' and deliberately employed actors who were ex-colonial (Australian) to star as
Elizabeth and Walsingham.[54] Transgressive sexuality Kapur expressed
through the Duke of Anjou's cross-dressing, Walsingham's bisexual-
ity, and Mary of Guise's sexual voraciousness; and gender issues lay
at the heart of his emphasis on female empowerment. Because of this
strong presentism, as well as its deliberate trampling over historical fact,
the film is profoundly unhistorical.[55] Yet, perhaps surprisingly it still
reflects some historical concerns: first, the preoccupations with gender
issues that arose in many studies of Elizabeth during the 1990s;[56] and
second, a longer-established historical interpretation that the queen
consciously fashioned her own image, deliberately inventing herself as
The Virgin Queen to secure the adulation of her people and to fill
the void left when the cult of Virgin Mary was banned in Protestant
England.[57]

Kapur's second film equally relates to the issues of his day: in the
case of *Elizabeth: The Golden Age* his focus is on religious wars and
a tolerant ruler's response to international terrorism. But here too
gender issues are played out and, perhaps surprisingly for a twenty-
first-century film in a very traditional way. Elizabeth's bitterness at
being unable to enjoy a sexual relationship with Walter Ralegh turns
her into an unreasonable, vengeful harridan when she learns of his
sexual relationship with Bess Thockmorton. In the last scene, we are
left with a queen who is saddened by her lack of a fulfilling emotional life and weighed down with the onerous duty of ruling alone.
Looking into the eyes of Ralegh's baby, she murmurs 'Unmarried,
I have no master, childless, I am a mother to my people. God give me
the strength to bear this mighty freedom.' Kapur's Elizabeth is again
the subject of myth not historical reality: there is no evidence that she
was ever the lover of Dudley or yearned to be the lover of Ralegh.

To sum up, Elizabeth has appeared in so many films because their
makers found in the queen's character and career a relevance to their
own time. Her malleability can be explained by both her iconic
place in British History and her persona as the Virgin Queen. Her
mythical association with England's imperial past, England's apparently miraculous defeat of an invading force, and with the Golden
Age of English literature meant that screenwriters could use her as a
vehicle to comment upon contemporary political and cultural concerns. Furthermore, her position as unmarried ruling queen who
operated in a male-dominated environment enabled writers and directors to reflect upon or explore issues concerning gendered identities

and sexuality. These issues had particular significance for filmmakers and audiences because of the transformations in attitudes towards sex and gender as well as the changes in women's societal role during the last century.

Despite this presentism, filmmakers – especially British ones – seem to have had some awareness of the historical discourse current when their films were made. While they agree on certain aspects of Elizabeth's personality and character, such as her wit, intelligence, theatricality, vulnerability, and sense of duty, they also reflect the differing interpretations of biographers and historians, who either love or hate her. Some filmmakers, for example, emphasize her vanity, irritability and stinginess; others play down these characteristics and stress more attractive qualities, her sense of humour, lack of fanaticism, and gestures of kindness. Some see her in control of policy; others show her to be deceived and manipulated by a group of courtiers for their own ends.

Nonetheless, as will be even more evident from reading the other essays in this volume, filmmakers flagrantly disregard historical facts. Why is this? From my experience on working as a consultant on a film and a recent television drama, I am convinced that most inaccuracies do not arise because of ignorance or negligence. It is true that some screenwriters and directors simply plunder the past for interesting characters, good stories and visually arresting costumes and sets, but others are more respectful and ask historians to comment on their scripts and advise on costumes and interiors. But even these filmmakers believe history is incompatible with drama, and prioritize the drama. As many of them see it, an entertaining narrative requires compression, simplification and dramatization. So, because Elizabeth's long reign is dramatically unmanageable, events have to be compressed into a much tighter time-frame than actually occurred. Filmmakers also fear that the complexities of religion and European power politics cannot be conveyed easily to an audience, which helps explain why confessional issues are grossly over-simplified and why the Dutch Revolt is barely mentioned in films depicting Anglo–Spanish relations. Finally, drama requires personal confrontations and interactions; hence Elizabeth has to visit the imprisoned Mary Stuart, the disgraced Sir Walter Ralegh, and the condemned Earl of Essex to secure 'closure'. All this is disappointing for historians. We are uncomfortably aware that many people learn their history from film, and that future myths about the past are born in the film studios of today.

Suggestions for Further Reading

Susan Doran, *Elizabeth I,* British Library Historic Lives (London, 2003).
Christopher Haigh, *Elizabeth I* (London, 1988; 2nd edition, 2000).
Wallace MacCaffrey, *Elizabeth I* (Oxford, 1994).
John E. Neale, *Queen Elizabeth* (1934).

7

Lady in Waiting: Young Elizabeth Tudor on Film

Judith Richards

Despite the number of popular studies written about the few queens regnant in European history, surprisingly few films have been made about them. There has been, however, even less interest in making films about such women *before* they became queens. The first movie about the Lady Elizabeth, for example, was not screened until 1953; it came Eight years after the publication of Margaret Irwin's histori-cal novel *Young Bess*[1] on which it was based. *Young Bess* the film was, like the novel, an immediate success. But it apparently still needed defending against the suspicion of being tied to a specific historic past. *Variety Film Reviews* advised readers that although 'it was a roman-tic drama told against a Tudor setting', it was definitely 'no pompous, awe-struck and stilted period piece'. The plot summary of Elizabeth's unhappy childhood concludes: 'It was not until gracious Catherine becomes queen that young Bess, now fifteen, takes up a more or less permanent residence in the palace, finding love and happiness with the queen and her little step-brother, the sickly Edward.'[2]

The target audience would apparently not care that the historical Elizabeth was nine years old when her father married his sixth and final wife. To acknowledge her extreme youth would have been to present the origins of the romance at the heart of this film as much more dubious than the film planned. *Young Bess* starred Jean Simmons as Elizabeth[3] and Stewart Granger as Thomas Seymour. Individually popular romantic stars of their day, they were also a much-feted mar-ried couple. Once the casting for the female lead had been agreed,

Plate 6 In this fanciful scene from Shekhar Kapur's *Elizabeth*, Princess Elizabeth (Cate Blanchett) cavorts with her ladies in an anachronistic manner. Courtesy of Polygram, The Kobal Collection and Alex Bailey for the image from the motion picture *Elizabeth* (1998).

Granger was even more an obvious choice for the romantic, swash-buckling Seymour, destined to teach the difficult adolescent Elizabeth about love.

The film opens promisingly, if mysteriously, with a gleeful Kat Ashley and Thomas Parry, respectively, mistress and treasurer of Elizabeth's household since 1536, drinking to the news that 'Bloody Mary' is dying. Although Mary was obviously a Bad Thing, the audience is never given any indication why this was so. The bibulous encounters of those two, played by Kay Walsh and Cecil Kellaway, open and close the movie. From their first reminiscences, the movie fades into a lengthy retrospective in which Young Bess emerges as effectively the one true successor among Henry's children. Henry brandishes the infant Elizabeth before his courtiers, shouting 'Your future Queen Elizabeth!' Soon after, her mother is beheaded and the child summarily sent into the country. Deadly matter is handled with a light touch in the semi-cartoon succession of new stepmothers for the young Elizabeth. She is shown as growing into an increasingly sullen and defiant child, thereby apparently foreshadowing the great and independent queen she would become. Henry VIII, played (again!) by Charles Laughton, is apparently delighted by her wilfulness – 'spirit' – as he courts and discards successive wives.

As Henry's truest heir, Elizabeth demonstrates an impressively precocious mastery of court politics. On board ship at Portsmouth, and awaiting the attack of the French fleet, presumably in July 1545, her tense father turns on Elizabeth's beloved last stepmother, Catherine Parr. Her offence was having authorized the novelty of an English translation of the Bible while she was regent in 1544. While all other onlookers watch helplessly, Elizabeth provides a sufficiently powerful distraction for Henry to turn from the matter, and Catherine lives. As drama, the scene is quite effective; as history it conveniently overlooks the point that the Bible had been issued in English versions in 1535 and again in 1539; both of them had spectacular frontispieces of Henry transmitting the word of God in English. Similarly ahistorical is the scene where the dying Henry compares his children to sheep. He starts with the Crazy Sheep: the camera pans to a youngish woman dressed in purple, who we are left to guess is Mary, soon to become England's first queen regnant. That is her one appearance on the screen, so brief that the actress does not get her name in the credits. Henry then names the Frightened Sheep: whimpering Edward, looking even younger than his nine and a half years, before trying to identify Elizabeth, who helpfully reminds him she is the Black Sheep and proceeds to impress him so royally that he nearly dies, gasping with admiration. In the historical record, Edward was at Hertford when his father was dying, Elizabeth at Enfield, and Mary who *did* spend much of her time at court was, like almost everyone else, kept in complete ignorance of Henry's death for three days. After Henry's death, the focus of the movie shifts to Elizabeth's increasing attraction to Seymour. Then 14, and curiously unsupervised by any members of her household, she is shown as running to his bedroom in her nightclothes to deplore their imminent separation. She then fights a mighty fight for self-control as she learns that despite his attention to her, Seymour actually plans to marry Queen Catherine Parr.

Throughout the film, the viewer is constantly reminded of the role Elizabeth's love for Seymour ostensibly played in training her to be a queen, as well as wakening her most womanly instincts. He was already Lord Admiral when they met, and she quickly discovers her own interest in building up the navy. As Elizabeth explains to her tutor, long after the novelty of Cleopatra's youth and beauty had worn off, she had held Caesar's affection by sharing *his* interests. One evening on the Thames with Seymour, and once again unchaperoned, Elizabeth notes a light burning in Lambeth Palace, and muses on the new religion Archbishop Cranmer is making. That, she suggests to an unresponsive Seymour, may well become a new way of life in England. When, after Seymour's fall, Elizabeth is rigorously questioned about Seymour's courtship, she shows an impressive skill in countering her evil-wishers. And so the case is made that the Protestant queen of popular repute, who fostered England's sea-power as well as the (new) true religion and always outmanoeuvred her enemies by her wily ways with words, had learned much from her times with Seymour. There is also a suggestion that, in her curiously unattended state, she managed to spend at least one night with him in her bedroom. The trials follow quickly. The narrative leaps from Seymour's execution in March 1549 to Mary's death in November 1558. Then without further comment on how her transformation from moody, infatuated, adolescent took place, the film closes with a regal, reserved, controlled Elizabeth, moving to the window to receive the plaudits of her (already?) loving subjects.

The film's director was George Sidney, who had previously directed *Annie Get Your Gun* (1950), *Showboat* (1951) and *Scaramouche* (1952); after *Young Bess* he directed *Kiss Me Kate* (1953). Several of these were rollicking musicals; all of them had romantic storylines reflecting current major entertainment preoccupations. This version of the adolescent Elizabeth reflected a new interest, clearly definable in the United States by the mid-1940s, whereby teenage girls were increasingly identified as a distinct sociological group, and as a promising new market with distinctive consumer 'needs'. The preferred magazine images were increasingly of sexualized and narcissistic adolescents.[4] The associated message was neatly encapsulated in the 1959 film, *The Best of Everything,* which reiterated that women could indeed pursue a career, in such modern times, but always and only always providing they did not lose sight of the most important of their needs – that of being the 'loved individual' of their chosen man.[5] *Young Bess* conforms much more closely to these beliefs than to the historical records.

For students of history, a movie as purportedly historical as *Young Bess* raises other questions, quite distinguishable from those of initial viewer enjoyment: just how historically plausible is the film, and just how much does that question of historical plausibility matter? It is significant, therefore, that the love invoked in this film was that romantic love which acquired social legitimacy only in the later eighteenth century; the equivalent emotion in Elizabethan times was deemed socially dangerous, and likely to destroy the reputation of previously virtuous women – as indeed so nearly happened to the historical Elizabeth after Seymour's rumoured flirtation with her. The disgrace and execution of Anne Boleyn had left a difficult heritage for her daughter, who was always likely to be morally suspect. Many may have felt vindicated when the news broke so publicly of Elizabeth's rumoured escapades with Thomas Seymour. He was bundled into the Tower, for that and other treasonable offences. Their affair was discussed in England by the Privy Council, abroad by ambassadors. And hearing the rumours that she was with child by Seymour led to a furious plea by Elizabeth that she should be allowed to visit the court, and show herself as she was. Although there is no reliable evidence she was ever as abandoned as the movie implies, her flirtations with Seymour were very dangerous to them both (deadly for him), and rather than maturing her, marked her as having a dubious moral reputation – one which her opponents kept alive for the rest of her life. It is not surprising that by 2001, the critical evaluation of the movie was that *Young Bess* was 'historical fiction, wildly unreliable as to fact and dramatically not very rewarding. The character actors have the best of it.'[6] As indeed they do, especially Kat Ashley and Mr Parry.

A closer examination of the shifts between the film, the historical novel on which it was based, and the historian who provided the essential framework raises issues that challenge any historian. The film

was based on Margaret Irwin's historical novel *Young Bess* (1945). That
work in turn owed much to J. E. Neale's very influential biography of
Elizabeth, first published in 1934, and republished many times since.[7]
Neale was, at the time, a Tudor historian of particular eminence and
must have seemed an excellent source for the novelist. It is on Neale's
authority that both novel and subsequent film reiterate the case for
Elizabeth's precocity and independence of mind from an unusually
early age.[8] Neale argued for an Elizabeth who was an extraordinary
woman, uniquely able to provide 'romantic leadership to a nation in
peril', as he noted in his 1952 Preface.[9] Again setting a pattern for fiction and film, Neale devoted a whole chapter to the Seymour episode,
paying little attention to how much of it had no foundation beyond
rumour and hearsay; for him the episode was the preferred romantic
explanation for why Elizabeth never married. Irwin followed closely
the emphases Neale gave to the Seymour episode, placing it at the
centre of her novel. Irwin's Seymour was a seafaring swashbuckling
piratical romantic hero, and one 'gaily reckless of consequences'. Irwin
presents Elizabeth's love for him as foreshadowing her future attraction
to wild piratical types – presumably such as Drake, Ralegh and Essex –
and reiterates Neale's argument that the impact of his disastrous end
was the reason she never married. In such ways is the frequently pre-
posterous film also almost legitimized. There are, however, differences.
At least in Neale's biography, as in Irwin's book, Elizabeth is shown
as finally recognizing the harm her reputation suffered from her association with Seymour. She consciously remodelled herself, becoming
in the later part of Edward's reign the scholarly demure maiden of
Protestant hagiography. Irwin, however, may have had serious reservations about how complete the transformation was. As she wrote
it, when Elizabeth was waiting (in July 1553) to hear whether Jane
Grey would be accepted as queen by the people instead of the rightful
heir, Mary, she thought: 'Under Mary's essential goodness of nature
there lay the sickening uncertainty of hysteria'. Elizabeth then concluded that Jane Grey, whom she judged another religious bigot, was
possibly less dangerous than Mary. ' "May God preserve me from good
women!" sighed Bess.'[10] Clearly Irwin's Elizabeth had no wish to be
classified as 'a good woman', let alone a seriously religious one.

The early scene where Henry berated Catherine Parr for her
promotion of the Bible in English appears to be Irwin's own rework-
ing of a much more complex theological argument between the royal
couple. Despite such devices, a saving grace of Irwin's book is her
clarity that this *was* a more or less romantic, and more or less fictional,

history about Elizabeth. And her telling is always more nuanced, more complex, than that offered by the later movie. The girl's relations with Seymour and its aftermath, for instance, is only part of the story she tells. Irwin cast a wide net for sources and drew extensively on the contemporary ambassadorial reports which help build a plausible context even for the more implausible tales. She portrayed a much wider political context in which was set this particular destructive story of love and ambition and the making of a future queen. Because of that wider frame, it was a work which some members of two generations found sufficiently historically minded to turn them to reading more – and more seriously – about the history of the Tudors.[11] There is surely no more satisfying outcome than that for any historical novel.

No matter how problematically historical a movie may be (which is an issue quite separable from how successful the movie itself is) there is always a chance of fresh historical insights. When Natalie Zemon Davis wrote of her role in the making of the much more historically plausible *Le Retour de Martin Guerre* (1982), she was clear about one benefit: 'Writing for actors rather than readers raised new questions about the motivations of people in the sixteenth century'. But she also deplored the imperatives to keeping the film to a misleadingly simplified narrative line.[12] Even filmmakers who do consult qualified historians, it would seem, prefer to work in stereotypes, rather than spend too much time expounding complex individuals.[13] There are several necessary goals for any commercially targeted 'historical' film, to portray a past, to provide a compelling narrative, and to draw as large an audience as possible. In that context, the relation between popular depictions of historical characters and a more scholarly concern to interrogate and redefine historical understandings can be fraught.

This is an issue central to the second portrayal of the Lady Elizabeth before she became queen, in the opening half-hour of Shekhar Kapur's *Elizabeth* (1998). It also has the distinction of being the only one of the works discussed in this chapter which takes seriously the divisive potential of religion in the mid-sixteenth century. This might seem the more surprising since when both versions of *Young Bess* were produced at a time when mixed marriages between Protestants and Catholics were still very strongly discouraged in western countries, and there never had been a Catholic president of the United States – nor a Catholic monarch of England since 1688. Elizabeth herself, apparently, was far too sophisticated to suffer from *any* doctrinal affiliations at all. And what about the audience? Perhaps all moviegoers of the early 1950s were well schooled in the complexities of why one queen was called 'Bloody Mary'? They certainly got no help from the film script. It appears, rather, that the scriptwriters were concerned to discuss any religious question as little as possible, if at all.

Kapur's film *Elizabeth* (1998) has already become, for many, the definitive account of the best known of English female monarchs. It gives a fresh and modern edge to widely held beliefs about England's first Protestant queen regnant, and in the opening half-hour it revisits the equally traditional account of relations between the Princess Elizabeth and her half-sister Mary. But the historical past is again only one aspect of this ostensibly historical film. There are many indicators that this movie was also designed as a comment about contemporary women and the effects of power on their 'essential' femininity. Cate Blanchett has described in one extended TV interview how closely she studied Margaret Thatcher while preparing for the role of Elizabeth. Kapur had previously explored the issue of a woman's loss of innocence as she became powerful in his earlier *Bandit Queen*. Released in 1994 that film was based on the life of the low-caste one-time outlaw, Phoolan Devi, who after her capture and a prison term, became an Indian Member of Parliament. (She was assassinated in 2001, as revenge for acts committed while she was still an outlaw.) Historians might note Devi's complaint that Kapur took many liberties with the details of her life in that earlier film. The tension between any historical past and a filmmaker's more pressing imperatives appears to be a constant in biographical movies.

In Kapur's *Elizabeth* at least the audience is left in no doubt about the potential for horrible consequences of religious difference; but still the actual nature of Catholic/Protestant differences is once again quite unexplored. Some opening shots dwell for an uncomfortably long time on Ridley's death by burning, although his companions in this version unexpectedly include a much less heroic female victim. Maybe she is there to remind the audience that women are usually the weaker sex? Some of those shots of the martyrs are taken from Kapur's favourite overhead angle, and that angle is echoed when, later, Elizabeth undergoes examination about her role in Wyatt's uprising. The invitation to compare her with the religious martyrs is quite explicit – but then John Foxe encouraged the same idea in his formative account of the Marian persecutions in his *Acts and Monuments*. Kapur's Elizabeth, however, is far too savvy to fall victim to the kind of commitment the martyrs showed. Indeed, she later asks, 'Why must we tear ourselves apart for this small matter of religion?' So Neale's reductive view of Elizabeth's religious detachment perpetuated in both versions of *Young Bess* endures, despite the increasing complexity of more recent research about that queen's beliefs.

It would take about 30 seconds, no longer, for any student of Tudor history to work out s/he might as well just sit back and enjoy the movie in its own cinematic terms. Above all, any audience would be well-advised *not* to try unravelling Kapur's version of the chronology of Mary's reign. As already suggested, the film focuses on the process by which Elizabeth, first presented as a bundle of sensuality and very vulnerable in the wider world of politics, learns to become strong (for Kapur, that means to suppress her womanly nature), to make herself a queen. Indeed, the theme of innocence and its loss dominates the opening scenes of *Elizabeth*. So it was that Walsingham advises the young page/companion who has just failed to assassinate him, 'Innocence is the most precious thing you possess. Lose that and you lose your soul.' He then cuts the lad's throat. Perhaps he is saving the boy's innocent soul? Otherwise it looks like just another bit of gratuitous violence. Just before she wins the throne, Elizabeth is warned by Cecil, 'You are most innocent in the ways of the world.' The context makes it clear he was not referring to her sexual mores. To be knowing about the ways of the world means, it would seem, behaving like, for example, the Duke of Norfolk, who is throughout a splendidly sinister *eminence grise* in Mary's court. He seeks Elizabeth's death consistently until the last possible moment, and then triumphantly leads the celebration of her accession.

Much of the first 25 minutes of the movie are very dark – literally so dark it is hard to see. This is because the focus is on the reign of Mary Tudor who is shown as sometimes hysterical, or claiming to be pregnant to a man who, the audience is assured, found her so physically repulsive he refused to sleep with her. She is also, however, a quite tragic figure. Although there are many shadowy court women about her, the only person who shows any empathy for Mary is her fool Jane, as physically unattractive as Mary herself, as far as can be seen. Mary's court is always filmed indoors and in this film also had chronically bad acoustics, presumably to enhance the conspiratorial atmosphere. It is all very different from the colourful, bright outdoors world inhabited by the young Elizabeth, a world where twice there is so much light that the screen goes completely white. But Neale did write that the 'two half-sisters were a striking contrast. . . . The old world and the new; such were these two daughters of Henry VIII'.[14]

As noted, filmmakers do seem to favour the dramatic potential of his interpretations.

This *Elizabeth* is, despite those many reservations, a more interesting movie than *Young Bess* visually and historically. It is not just that Kathy Burke's Mary has a much larger role than in other studies of Elizabeth, nor even that some thought has been given to Mary's motivations. (Unlike Mary, young Elizabeth is curiously modern, easily understood in her hedonism, not at all part of an alien world – this, however, may not be quite what Neale meant when identifying Elizabeth with the new world in the quotation previously cited.) It is not in the details of individual lives, but in a wider sense of important historical issues that this film is most effective. Mary is often pathetic, and poignantly so, as her hoped for child proves to be a cancer. Even that hints at a world where medical knowledge was very differently constructed. Mary's personal trauma in handing her realm on to her heretic half-sister is clearly shown, but so is her reluctance finally to take the obvious way out of having Elizabeth killed – despite the religious implications, despite Elizabeth being the daughter of Anne Boleyn and despite the pressure on Mary on her deathbed, by the forceful Norfolk. The exposition of the atmosphere of a Tudor court, however dark, where power was personal, and the death of others an obvious solution to intransigent problems, is sobering. Like *La Nuit de Varennes* (1982), which includes a scene with Casanova and Tom Paine in the same coach, Kapur's *Elizabeth* is both historically inaccurate on many levels – often quite wilfully so – but also brilliantly suggestive about aspects of, in the one case Tudor England and in the other pre-revolutionary France. However, uncomfortable it might be for any historian to contemplate, such films suggest a filmmaker can indeed play fast and loose with historical detail and yet produce real historical insights.

*   *   *

Within days of her becoming queen, Elizabeth I was hailed for being 'mere English' and brought up 'in the sincere knowlege and following of God's holy word'.[15] She was thereby distinguished from the late Queen Mary (reigned 1553–1558), also the daughter of Henry VIII, but born of a Spanish princess, married to a Spanish king and always true to the Catholicism in which she had been educated. Logically, therefore, it might seem that relations between the half-sisters should always have been tense. The surviving records, however, sometimes challenge the traditional presumption of there being always bad relations between the king's daughters and the dramatic potential implicit in that. In late-1536 Mary reported to her father that her younger sister was 'such a child . . . as I doubt not but your Highness shall have cause to rejoice of in time coming'.[16] But thereafter it was Mary who occupied the position which both versions of *Young Bess* ascribe to Elizabeth, that of the daughter closer to Henry VIII. Henry's third wife Jane Seymour brought Mary back to court as soon as her husband permitted; the much younger Elizabeth remained in the country. The age difference between the two sisters meant that they did not see very much of each other; in effect they had separate households. During the brief queenship of Catherine Howard, Mary was almost continuously at court and accompanied the royal party in the 1541 progress to York; Elizabeth seems to have had little direct contact with her third stepmother. All three royal children attended their father's last wedding, to Catherine Parr. Thereafter, while Mary accompanied the newly-weds on their leisurely progress to Woodstock, Elizabeth and her brother stayed behind and continued their studies. It may have been a year before Elizabeth saw either parent again. None of this is surprising, given the age difference between Mary and her two siblings. But it does cast serious doubt on the widespread belief that her father particularly favoured Elizabeth. She was third in any line of succession and, because of her mother's reputation, of little interest on the international marriage market. Nevertheless, Elizabeth received a sound humanist education comparable to that of her elder sister – indeed, often with the same texts. As Maria Dowling has commented, this is the more remarkable since, unlike Mary, she was not educated in the expectation that she would ever rule.[17]

During the later years of Edward's reign (1547–1553) his relations with his elder half-sister became notoriously fraught, as she insisted on maintaining her customary religious observances in the face of the sweeping changes then introduced to the Church of England. Mary resisted in public as well as in private.[18] As the elder sister fell from favour, Elizabeth was more frequently seen at court, and even courted by some diplomats. Less is known about relations between the sisters. The two had certainly exchanged letters discussing possible responses to the remarriage of their stepmother Queen Catherine Parr to Thomas Seymour so soon after the death of their father. Elizabeth nevertheless moved into her stepmother's household and under her supervision had made good progress with her studies until rumours began to swirl around her, pointing to the attention which Catherine's ambitious husband was paying to the young woman now second in line to the throne. Increasing domestic tensions appear to have led to Elizabeth leaving the Seymour/Parr household and returning to Cheshunt, and then to Hatfield. After Catherine's death in childbirth, Seymour's attentions to Elizabeth were renewed.[19] His name, however, was also linked with that of Mary (who always kept her distance) and possibly Lady Jane Grey, and there were many rumours of his rather indiscreet questions to friends about their followers and the defences of their strongholds, as he apparently plotted a coup.

Although the royal half-sisters maintained separate households and seem to have met infrequently in the Edwardian years, this is not evidence that sibling relations were strained. Very few letters between Elizabeth and Mary have survived from the period, but one of them indicates clearly that, at a time when they were both much more independent women, Mary was a more frequent correspondent.[20] In the earliest days of Mary's reign (July, 1553) they were on entirely cordial terms, at least in public; Elizabeth was prominent in Mary's first entry into London and during Mary's coronation celebrations. Relations between them deteriorated soon after, in part because of Elizabeth's reluctance to follow her sister's return to more Catholic religious rituals, and in part because of Mary's growing reluctance to accept the formally illegitimate Protestant as her heir to the throne. She increasingly gave precedence to her Catholic cousin, Lady Margaret Douglas, daughter of Henry VIII's elder sister Margaret. Elizabeth withdrew from the court in early December to Ashridge, a monastery which had fallen into Henry's hands. She remained in the country until she was arrested on suspicion of her implication in the protests against Mary's proposed Spanish marriage, which culminated in Wyatt's uprising, ending with his failed assault on London in February 1554. Suspicion of Elizabeth led to her imprisonment in the Tower. That episode marks the beginning of the narrative of the Protestant princess suffering for her faith, on which so many subsequent histories have focussed. It also marks the end of any semblance of warm relations between the half-sisters.

Apart from the issue of recoverable historical information, there is also an issue of recoverable cultural values. Elizabeth has always been, and remains, a problematic heroine. Unlike most female heroines, she neither died young nor finally married. But she has not yet been shown as the feminist heroine one might expect this to make her. Twentieth-century versions of Elizabeth's early life have either made her a hoyden who defied the conventions of her time or, more recently, been explicit that whatever the reason she did not marry, it was not because she was sexually frigid. Moreover either of the solutions the two films offer raises another issue, about how much attention it is reasonable to expect modern filmmakers to pay to the very different cultural and social values of Tudor England. That, after all, is not what the directors of historical films think their work is about. For historians, on the other hand, exploring cultural and social differences is a major reason for studying other societies. Such visual issues as the richness of royal dress is seldom a problem – any film-maker worth his or her salt is happy to work on variations of that. But sixteenth-century expectations of how, for example, young well-born Tudor women should conduct themselves pose another kind of problem, for those were so very different from modern filmmakers' preferred models. Lady Grace Mildmay (born c. 1552) remembered for her grandchildren that her father

> could not abide to see a woman unstable or light in her carriage, to hold her head one way and her hands another and her feet a third way, her eyes tossing about in every place and the features of her face disfigured by evil countenances. But he liked a woman well graced with a constant and settled countenance and good behaviour throughout her whole parts, which presenteth unto all men a good hope of an established mind and virtuous disposition to be in her.[21]

Influential humanists like Vives and Erasmus had long agreed that all children should be taught from an early age the integral relation-ship between physical self-control and moral well-being; but female deportment was always expected to be quite distinctively chaste and demure, as an outward expression of that 'established mind and vir-tuous disposition' within. This deportment was one in which royal children were rigorously trained from earliest infancy; Mary, not yet three, was expected to remain perfectly quiet and still – and reportedly played her part well – during her lengthy betrothal ceremony to the then Dauphin of France.[22]

Such Tudor ideal deportment is consistently ignored in each work about the youth of Elizabeth discussed in this paper. In Irwin's book, the opening page has the 12-year-old heroine stamping 'like a wilful pony' and tossing her head before breaking another fundamental rule for young girls in Tudor society, and engaging in a private conversa-tion with Thomas Seymour. In the film of *Young Bess*, Jean Simmons tosses her head, swings her arms, takes great strides and stands arms

akimbo, before an admiring Seymour who tells her she is the image
of her father. Probably he was invoking Holbein's great master-image
of Henry, with arms akimbo and legs splayed. Anything further from
the way Elizabeth was actually taught to move and stand is hard to
imagine. In Kapur's movie *Elizabeth*, the young Elizabeth is indeed
'light in her carriage', her vulnerability being conveyed by her sensuality and in the early scenes her hair hangs loose. In Tudor times,
of course, such loose hair was a sign of a wanton woman, and probably a prostitute. Kapur shot many sequences of Elizabeth as princess
out of doors, free – and the women with her, all very young and
nubile, are like her dressed in pastel colours. The general effect is
more pre-Raphaelite than Tudor. But Elizabeth quickly retires from
all her companions/chaperones to a conveniently nearby building and
embarks on a passionate set of embraces with Robert Dudley, in a
way often seen on TV screens today – or in public parks, in summer.
Such behaviour was, however, quite enough, in Tudor terms, to justify the darkest suspicions of the morality of Anne Boleyn's daughter.
Moreover, in historical terms, Dudley's apparent attempt to seduce
the heir to the throne would have left him wide open to the charge
of treason – a similar concern was part of the reason for the execution
of Thomas Seymour. In Kapur's *Elizabeth,* not an eyebrow is raised at
her dubious behaviour, then or subsequently.

There are, however, films based on early-modern historical events,
which suggest that despite the many contrasts between their worlds
and ours good historical movies can be made. Despite Zemon Davis's
own disappointments with aspects of it, and probably because of her
involvement with its making, *Le Retour de Martin Guerre* has shown
the way, as both a popular success and an informative introduction
to the world of early-modern France. Although never a comparable
success with audiences, Kevin Brownlow's *Winstanley* (1975), about
the mid-seventeenth-century English social visionary, was another
rich reconstruction of a past society. For historians who still share
the views (if not necessarily the language) of older historians such as
G. M. Trevelyan and Hugh Trevor-Roper that 'the ultimate purpose
of history is to educate and edify a non-professional audience',[23] then
in contemporary society they need to confront the challenge of shaping visual images to their historical purposes. Of course it involves
selectivity in the narrative, but any history writing requires that. In
all cases the issue is the plausibility of and justification for the selection. Imagine a film which tells the history of an apparently demure
young Elizabeth who was her father's delight for some three years, and

comparatively ignored by him for the rest of her life, whose mother was widely regarded as scandalous and who was herself declared illegitimate, who had no natural group of supporters for the first 20 years of her life, whose reputation – and probably life – was endangered first by the schemes of an ambitious Thomas Seymour, and later by her own half-sister, and who still ascended the throne to reign for 45 years. Now that could be a film worth making. But the imperatives of commercial filmmaking suggest a very long wait for such a movie.

Suggestions for Further Reading

David Loades, *Mary Tudor: A Life* (Oxford, 1989).
J. E. Neale, *Queen Elizabeth I* (Harmondsworth, 1960).
David Starkey, *Elizabeth: Apprenticeship* (London, 2000).
Judith Richards, *Mary Tudor* (London, 2008).

8

Kapur's *Elizabeth*

Christopher Haigh

At the premiere of his film *Bandit Queen* in 1994, the director Shekhar Kapur claimed that he had told the truth about Phoolan Devi, the bandit queen: 'I had a choice between Truth and Aesthetics; I chose truth, because Truth is pure.' It was a film about survival and revenge: an innocent girl abandoned, abused by men, deliberately remaking herself, exacting retribution, and finally surrendering to the state. The novelist Arundhati Roy claimed that Kapur had misrepresented Phoolan's story, selecting and altering details of her life to fit a dramatic pattern and aiming for emotional impact at the expense of accuracy and perspective.[1] *Elizabeth* (1998) is another Kapur film, with the same dramatic structure of survival, revenge and, in a sense, surrender to the state. 'I think both stories are of women who survived and who had no choice but to survive. The only way they could live was through power. Otherwise they'd both be dead', said Kapur.[2] But what did he do with the story of Elizabeth Tudor? Did Kapur select and alter events in the interests of dramatic impact, or did he choose truth? And what, in a two-hour movie, can be true?

Elizabeth appears to be the true story of the early years of the queen's reign. The film is set in a real historical context. It begins and ends with historical statements – about the impact of Henry VIII's reign and the Reformation, and about Elizabeth's own rule. The main characters, and many of the lesser figures, really did play important roles in Elizabeth's life – Queen Mary (Kathy Burke), Robert Dudley (Joseph Fiennes), Francis Walsingham (Geoffrey Rush), William Cecil (Richard Attenborough), the Duke of Norfolk (Christopher Eccleston), Bishop Gardiner (Terence Rigby) and many more. The

Plate 7 The coronation of the queen in Shekhar Kapur's *Elizabeth*. The traitorous Duke of Norfolk (Christopher Eccleston) is on Elizabeth's left. Courtesy of Polygram, The Kobal Collection and Alex Bailey for the Image of Cate Blanchett from the motion picture *Elizabeth* (1998).

manners and modes of speech seem authentic; some of the dialogue is based on what we know Elizabeth said, and many reviewers, especially in the United States, assumed that the story was true. When Blanchett sits upon the throne at the coronation, she looks exactly like the 'coronation portrait' in the National Portrait Gallery. The splendid costumes and towering castles and cathedrals are there to convince us that this is what Elizabethan England was really like – and that the drama we see unfold really did happen.

That drama has two dominating themes. First, 'Why did she become the Virgin Queen?' – that 'seemed quite a good question to try to tackle and answer in our movie', said Tim Bevan, one of the producers.[3] The film suggests that Elizabeth the woman and lover had to become Elizabeth the queen and virgin: 'I have become a virgin,' she announces in the penultimate scene. Faced by a conflict between her attachment to Dudley and her role as queen, the emotional girl has to sacrifice the love of her life to become a career virgin, married only to England. The second theme is how Elizabeth survived dangers and plots against her: 'With the early part of her reign being filled with such uncertainty, we decided to structure it as a conspiracy thriller', explained Bevan.[4] Norfolk, Gardiner and Guzman de Quadra, the Spanish ambassador, wanted her executed to prevent her becoming queen; Norfolk, Sussex, Arundel and Quadra want to overthrow her when she is queen. Elizabeth survives these conspiracies by becoming ruthless, steeling herself to eliminate her enemies by using their methods; she will survive by recasting herself as an English replacement for the deposed Virgin Mary. Thus her question to Walsingham, 'Am I to be made of stone?' has two meanings – 'Must I have no emotions?' and 'Must I become an icon?' In the final scene she is a shining effigy-queen, with whitened skin and clothes, moving sedately towards the camera and ascending the throne. The opening credits call the film simply 'Elizabeth': at the close, it is 'Elizabeth: the Virgin Queen'.

So far, so good. The historical Elizabeth indeed did not marry, and, at least later in her reign, she was portrayed as a virgin queen. The historical Elizabeth indeed did face major political difficulties and, at least later in her reign, there were plots against her. But *Elizabeth* is a highly charged political melodrama, made by a production company that expects and achieves commercial success. Alison Owen, another of the producers, was quite frank about this. 'Although it is a film that is very true to the Tudor times, historical veracity has not been the main point of contact. We have not changed facts but manipulated time-periods. In doing so, we have given our film so many things to

attract an audience. At the heart of it is a wonderful love story.'[5] We
have messed about with the history for box-office success, she admits –
or rather, she claims, we have messed about with the chronology while
remaining true to the period.

The better-informed reviewers noted that events that historically
took place over 20 years and more have been crammed into the first
few years of Elizabeth's reign. (The time-span of the film is not entirely
clear. The closing remarks tell us that Elizabeth ruled for another 40
years after the movie ends; that is, the film finishes in 1563. But '40'
may be used loosely and the rush of dramatic events seems to take
up only a year or two of the reign.) So things that happened much
later are nevertheless included in the movie. The papal bull against
Elizabeth, *Regnans in Excelsis*, was not issued until 1570. The Duke
of Norfolk's plotting did not begin until 1569 and he was executed
in 1572. The assassination attempt on the Thames was in 1578, and
Robert Dudley's secret marriage was revealed to Elizabeth in 1579.
(The Dudley marriage that did fall within the time-span of the film
was to Amy Robsart: it was well known to the queen, and Amy died
in 1560. It was Dudley's second marriage, to Lettice Knollys, that was
used against him.) The Duke of Anjou's first visit to court Elizabeth
was not until 1579, and he was not rejected until 1581. And, a small
but illustrative matter – Elizabeth's rebuke that the word 'must' is not
used to princes was to Robert Cecil at the end of her reign, not to
William Cecil at the beginning.

Events have been compressed into *Elizabeth*; they have also been
re-ordered. The film opens explicitly in 1554, with the burning of
three Protestants: the burnings actually began in 1555. Wyatt's rebellion (which was in 1554) is placed after the burnings had started, so
it seems a response to the persecution. The war in Scotland (in 1560)
is put before the passing of the Act of Uniformity (which was in
1559), and the French proposal of the Duke of Anjou as husband for
Elizabeth was in 1570, not before the Uniformity Act. The dramatic
purpose was presumably to build up the problems Elizabeth faced at
her accession (Scotland, France, the marriage question and religion),
so that her calculated performance in the Uniformity debate can be
the first stage in the victory of Elizabeth the queen over her enemies
and over Elizabeth the woman. The errors in *Elizabeth* are not acci-
dental, they are quite deliberate adjustments of history to meet the
requirements of a drama.

Alison Owen told us 'We have not changed facts, but manipulated
time periods.' That is untrue: facts have been changed. The war against

the French in Scotland in 1560 was far from an English triumph, but it was not 'our miserable defeat' – as Cecil describes it in the film. The objective of the English invasion – the withdrawal of French troops – was achieved and the threat from France eliminated. So there was no need for Elizabeth to entertain Anjou's marriage proposal as the price for avoiding a French invasion from the north, as she does in the film. A real event, the war, has been altered to suit the drama – and the same happened to another real event, Robert Dudley's deal with Spain. In the film, Dudley tries to persuade Elizabeth into a diplomatic marriage to King Philip of Spain: Philip will stay in Spain, and Dudley can continue his relationship with Elizabeth. But Elizabeth will not play – 'Lord Robert, you may make whores of my ladies, but you shall not make one of me!' This is a neat readjustment of something that really did happen in 1561: Dudley had then sought Spanish backing for his own plan to marry Elizabeth, after the death of his wife Amy, in return for concessions to the Catholics. In the film, however, Dudley's first marriage serves as the reason why Elizabeth cannot marry him – so his project has to be Spanish-backed adultery not Spanish-backed marriage.

If events have been altered, so have characters. The Duke of Norfolk was not an active politician in Mary's reign, when he was only a teenager. He was not a Catholic, nor did he scheme to seize Elizabeth's throne for himself. The Earl of Sussex was not a Catholic either and, though Arundel perhaps was, neither he nor Sussex plotted the queen's overthrow. Sussex, indeed, commanded the army that put down a Catholic revolt in 1569. William Cecil was not an old man when Elizabeth came to the throne, but was only 38. Dudley did scheme with Norfolk in 1569, but it was to remove Cecil and not the queen. Francis Walsingham was not a political player until 1570, and was not a key advisor to Elizabeth until 1573. The priest allegedly sent to murder Elizabeth, revealed as John Ballard in the cast list, was barely born when the film ends: he was involved in the Babington plot of 1586, as a messenger and not a killer. The film's Duke of Anjou is a composite character: Henri d'Anjou (the first French suitor) was a transvestite, but it was François d'Anjou (the second suitor) who came to England to court the queen. The only central character who gets a fair representation in the movie is Elizabeth herself.

The screenplay for *Elizabeth* was written by Michael Hirst, who clearly did a lot of preliminary research. He collected scraps of bio-graphical information, poems, quotations and events, and wrote them out on the back of a sheet of wallpaper. He and the director seem to have then adjusted what Hirst had found to make a better story. Elizabeth and Dudley had a romantic relationship, certainly – but did they really have a full sexual relationship? 'In a film you have to push things a bit. It's not like writing a history book in which you can stand back and be cool and say perhaps or perhaps not', Hirst said. 'Obviously I needed to push the piece forward, I needed to push the drama and the tension and the love.' So he pushed: the film has a sex scene between Elizabeth and Robert – watched attentively by her maids and by millions of viewers. The likelihood that the queen really did make sexual love with Dudley is slim: the risks of scandal and of pregnancy were far too high. Hirst has suggested that 'There's plenty of circumstantial evidence that she did sleep with Dudley', especially that they sometimes slept in adjacent apartments. He admitted there is no evidence that she did, but said there is no evidence that she didn't. The sex 'was just a small nudge in the direction of romanticism'.[6] It also serves a key dramatic purpose: after sex with Dudley, Elizabeth can 'become a virgin'.

Although the sex scene provoked a good deal of fuss in the British press, in truth it was no more than 'a small nudge': the two behaved as lovers, whether they had consummated their love or not. But other scenes were more than nudges of reality; they were wild speculation and sheer invention. Francis Walsingham did not have a homosexual relationship with a French youth whom he then murdered – nor did he have a heterosexual relationship with a French queen whom he then murdered. The Catholic bishops did not demand Elizabeth's removal from the throne, and no priest tried to murder her. If Dudley ever had sex with one of Elizabeth's maids, he surely did not get her to pretend to be the queen – 'Say you're my Elizabeth!' No Maid of Honour died from wearing a poisoned dress belonging to Elizabeth. William Cecil was not sacked by the queen, but served on until his death in 1598. Bishop Gardiner was not murdered by Elizabeth's (or Walsingham's) agents, but died of illness in 1555 – three years before Elizabeth became queen. Ambassador Guzman de Quadra was not killed, and the Earls of Arundel and Sussex were not executed: Arundel died naturally in 1580, and Sussex in 1583. Of the five victims of Elizabeth's bloodbath near the end of the film – Norfolk, Arundel, Sussex, Gardiner and Quadra – only Norfolk died at her order (in 1572), and she gave that with the greatest reluctance.

There were some interesting cuts made to the original film before it was issued in video and DVD versions, which are four or five minutes shorter. The homosexual scene between Walsingham and a young Frenchman, and the sex scene between Walsingham and Mary of Guise were both removed (making the death of Mary almost inexplicable). Also cut were parts of the retribution sequence: the hanging of Catholic priests in their vestments and the obvious signs that Norfolk, Arundel and Sussex had been tortured. Perhaps the cuts were to make the home-entertainment versions suitable for 15-year olds – the sex and violence are both described on the video packaging as 'moderate'. But it is noteworthy that these deletions were of wholly invented parts of the story. We cannot be certain that Walsingham never had sex with a Frenchman, but we do know that he never met Mary of Guise. We also know that priests were not hanged in any number until 1581 (and then not in their robes), and that noblemen were not tortured. Did someone have a conscience?

Elizabeth was not made in ignorance. You have to know a lot of Elizabethan history to make these mistakes; you have to know what really happened (or probably happened) before you can turn it into this particular story. Real characters are adjusted, real events are amended and relocated, plausible incidents are invented – all to serve the drama. Tim Bevan described how the production team decided they would treat Elizabeth's reign: 'We wanted to find a spin on it', so they gave it a 'conspiracy-twist'.[7] Some nasty conspirators were needed – a fanatical bishop, a slimy foreign ambassador, and a few hard-faced aristocrats. What else should a successful historical drama have? Sex? – well, let's have Robert and Elizabeth in a big four-poster bed (and Robert and a maid groaning in a dark corridor). Rivalry? – well, let's make Norfolk the constant villain, seeking Elizabeth's throne and her life. Blood? – well, let's have the bad guys killed off in a final retribution (and let's have a few incidental murders along the way). Excitement? – well, let's have the killers getting close to the queen: a crossbow arrow just missing her head, a poisoned dress worn by someone else, a priest in billowing black robes heading straight for her. That'll work, won't it?

Elizabeth has quite a simple plot-structure: danger (will Elizabeth be tried for treason?); release (coronation and celebration); complications (Scotland, the marriage question and religion); threats (the papal bull and assassination attempts); retribution (the enemies meet their end); and redefinition – 'I have become a virgin'. The alterations and inventions are made to support this structure. Later events are brought forward to bolster the complications (defeat in Scotland and the Anjou proposal), the threats (the bull, the Ridolfi plot and the Thames attack), and the retribution (Norfolk's execution). Similarly, manufactured events are inserted to sustain the plot: opposition to Elizabeth's rule by the bishops (complications); the poisoned dress and the priest-assassin (threats); and the murders and executions (retribution). And the concluding redefinition is manufactured too: it has been argued that Elizabeth did not 'become a virgin' until 1578, when Protestants cast the queen in that role to scupper the second Anjou marriage. In Susan Doran's interpretation, Elizabeth did not choose to become a virgin: she was made a virgin.[8]

A major difficulty in making a history film is that much of the audience knows, or thinks it knows, the story already – so the producers need a 'spin', a 'twist', to make it different. In the case of *Elizabeth*, says Tim Bevan, 'We decided to structure it as a conspiracy thriller' – 'Let's try and make it a conspiracy-type movie'. Shekhar Kapur told an interviewer that 'The [directing] style is always dictated by the core. In each film, I try to find that core. For example, the core of *Elizabeth* was conspiracy. So the whole film was shot in a very conspiratorial tone.'[9] This was not to be a conventional English costume-drama of the Merchant-Ivory kind. 'We were a lot more influenced by films like *The Godfather* than by previous historical dramas', Alison Owen revealed[10] – and the result is a gangster-movie in tights. *Elizabeth* indeed follows the plot-structure of *The Godfather*: a sensitive innocent survives in a harsh environment by learning ruthlessness, and wins a succession war by eliminating rivals. The debt to Francis Ford Coppola's film is clearly acknowledged. In the 'retribution' scenes of *The Godfather*, the camera cuts between Michael Corleone at church and his henchmen doing the killings: in *Elizabeth* the camera cuts between the queen at prayer and the murders and arrests of the plotters.

Elizabeth is a very modern version of the queen's life. Kapur claimed that 'It's a story about survival, it's a story about love, and it's very contemporary.' Cate Blanchett was pleased that the film was 'not reverential at all' towards the past, and was 'incredibly contemporary'.[11] Such assertions of relevance were no doubt part of the promotional campaign – 'it's a history movie, yes, but it makes sense to a contemporary audience.' The central issues – love and rivalry – are timeless, and so relevant today and always. Kapur argued that 'People are always doing the same things for the same reasons – money, power, love, revenge – in only slightly different ways. Stress the similarities, and the differences become easy to explain.'[12] Not all historians would agree with that: some suppose that the cultural norms and social structures of the past were so distinct from ours that people were different – they had different beliefs, different emotions, different motives. But I'm with Kapur: the past was made by people like us, not by aliens in fancy dress; we can understand them, and they saw most things much as we do. In the film (if not in history), Elizabeth is torn between her love and her career; Dudley can't cope with a powerful woman; Norfolk wants the job for himself but is afraid to act decisively; Walsingham's worldly cynicism and callousness get him to the top; and poor old Cecil is just too cautious for the impatient younger generation. It may not all be true, but it's certainly plausible.

If the story is modern, the treatment is post-modern. It is a very self-conscious film, almost a film about filming. The shooting techniques are very obvious: lots of jump-shots and overhead views; the camera watches from behind a pillar; and camera angles are constantly shifting – 'look, we're making a movie!' The film's structure is obvious too: it begins and ends with hair-cuts, and it follows Coppola's pattern. There are moments of pastiche – the arrival of Anjou, and his cross-dressing at an orgy. The sets are stylized – low ceilings and gloom for Mary's court, vibrancy and colour for Elizabeth's. The characters are stereotypes: the besotted but weak lover; the wily Spaniard; the lascivious French; the Machiavellian spymaster; the old-buffer advisor inherited from the past. Of course, one could say this was just clumsiness, a lack of subtlety – the cliché-characters are just clichés, not parodies. But *Elizabeth* seems a highly intelligent and thought-out film, where nothing happens by accident.

The interpretation is also post-feminist. *Elizabeth's* Elizabeth does not triumph as a woman, but has to abandon her womanhood if she is to triumph. She reconstructs herself by a deliberate act of will: hair cut, big wig, big ruff, big gown, rigid stance, stern aspect, and, as she tells Cecil she is now married to England, a booming low-register Thatcher voice. When Elizabeth emerges from her makeover as a queen, she is no feminist heroine. Some commentators see her as a girl-power icon manipulating the media – appropriating the cult of Madonna rather than the cult of the Virgin Mary. There is, however, no trace of the assertive sexuality of girl-power. Instead, Elizabeth is de-sexed, a stiff, unapproachable, wax-works figure who generates awe but no affection. Robert Dudley could not love *that*.

The film is 'an imaginative interpretation', as Alison Owen described it – 'Michael [Hirst] and Shekhar's interpretation of how things could have been'.[13] Well, in some alternative world of virtual history Norfolk *could* have coveted the throne, Walsingham could have murdered his sexual partners, Bishop Gardiner could have lived another 8 years, and the Earl of Sussex could have been executed 10 years before he died naturally. Anything is possible in 'an imaginative interpretation', when the normal rules of historical investigation are suspended. Of course, historians construct interpretations too: they select what they regard as significant details and use them to sustain an interpretation. But they have a professional responsibility to try to get the facts straight and in the proper order – the right people alive at the right time, for example. The makers of *Elizabeth* do not claim to have got the detail right – but they do claim to have got the big picture. 'I had to make a choice, whether I wanted the details of history or the emotions and essence of history to prevail', Kapur reports[14] – and he chose emotions and essence.

> I decided that I could make a film about events or about humans. I was always bored with history. In school, I was taught history as events, and then my grandmother would teach me history as myth. Before the English came [to India] we never recorded our history so it became mythical. I've made the film an emotional telling of history.[15]

Does *Elizabeth*, for all its howlers, have something to tell us about history? A little, perhaps. Most films about Elizabeth – indeed, most television history series – show the great queen getting things right. She does have her problems – mainly coping with her own emotions and the men who claimed to love her – but she is a subtle politician who has the interests of England at heart and presides over a golden age of achievement. *Elizabeth*, however, gives a much bleaker picture of the early years of her reign: threats from stronger foreign powers, opposition to her religious programme, rivalry and faction in her court, and a Council that thought it knew better than she did. That is how many historians now see things. The film itself puts the marriage issue starkly: some want Elizabeth to marry a Habsburg, some want her to marry a French prince, and some want her to marry an Englishman – but the only Englishman she's at all likely to marry is unacceptable. Perhaps the best solution really was to 'become a virgin'.

But can 'the emotions and essence' be separated from 'the details'? Can we understand the emotions if the events that cause and reflect them are falsified? In the film, Elizabeth's love for Dudley falters when she learns he is married, and is extinguished when she discovers he has plotted against her: the end of (this particular) story. In history, however, Dudley was widowed in 1560, did not marry again until 1578, and did not plot against her (when he plots, as in 1561 and 1569, it is

to marry her). For nearly 20 years Elizabeth could have married him –
but she did not, largely because of the domestic political opposition to
the prospect of Dudley as consort. The emotions were different in film
and fact: in the film, Elizabeth is betrayed by her lover; in fact, she was
blocked by those who wouldn't accept her choice of husband. Dudley
did not kill off her love for him; she had to overcome it herself.

And can the 'essence' of a period be separated from its 'details'?
The filmmakers claim to have manipulated the facts of Elizabeth's
reign to show a fundamental truth about it. Kapur explained that 'the
core of *Elizabeth* was conspiracy'[16] – that is, the essence of the period
portrayed was seen as conspiracy. In the film, the conspiracy is to murder the queen and put her rival, Norfolk, on the throne – nobles, a
Catholic bishop, Spain, the papacy, and a priest-assassin conspire to
remove Elizabeth. In the politics of the 1560s, however, it was all very
different. Conspiracy was not against the queen, and rivalry was not
with her: Elizabeth herself was not at risk until after 1570, and then
not from within the court. Instead, rivalry was between politicians
for influence over Elizabeth, and any conspiracy was against political rivals – Cecil versus Dudley, Dudley versus Norfolk, Norfolk
and Dudley versus Cecil (and Walsingham nowhere). The 'essence'
may be conspiracy – but it was a totally different kind of conspiracy.
Conspiracy against the queen was treason: conspiracy against rivals was
politics.

Some of what we see happen on the screen in *Elizabeth* did not
happen at all, and much more did not happen that way. Does that
really matter? Can't we accept it as a work of art, a fiction that happens to use some historical characters? 'A work of art is not necessarily
about the subject', said Kapur, it's about those who make it.[17] But history does matter, and so does history on film: it's important to get it
right. History – our understanding of the past – matters because it provides the data on which we base our opinions in the present. History
on film – fictional or documentary – matters because it is the prime
source of information about the past for most of our citizens. Bad history produces ill-informed citizens, and ill-informed citizens can make
bad decisions. Consider the representation of religion in *Elizabeth*.

The film is, according to the *New York Times* reviewer, 'a resolutely
anti-Catholic drama'.[18] This is surprising, since the script was written
(according to Kapur) by a Catholic[19] – but it is certainly true. The
film begins with Catholic oppression and violence. Three Protestants
are burned at the stake: the crowd is horrified by the cruelty, riots in
protest, and is chased off by mounted troops. When Elizabeth is taken

from the Tower to meet Queen Mary, there are background flashes of soldiers beating civilians and dragging them away, and a woman screams at Elizabeth 'Help me! Help me!' Here we see an unpopular regime and an unpopular faith, sustained by fanaticism and force: the people want Protestantism and Elizabeth. But Mary's reign was not like that, and Catholicism was still the religion of the vast majority of the people. There was a good deal of popular support for the persecution of Protestants, especially in its early stages, and a lot of affection for the queen.

There is only one good Catholic in the movie, the Earl of Arundel – and even he commits treason for his beliefs. Gardiner is a fanatic: he wants Princess Elizabeth convicted of treason, and Queen Elizabeth murdered. He wants heretics and political rivals to burn in hell, and flogs his own back to atone for his sins. Norfolk is consumed by envy and ambition: he bursts into Elizabeth's bedroom to tell her there's bad news, he hectors her at the council table, and he plots her removal. He believes his faith justifies murder, and at the end hopes the people will remember him as a martyr. 'No, they will forget', Walsingham smugly tells him. The Catholic bishops howl at the queen in the House of Lords, and prevent effective military action against the French. Ballard, the priest sent to England by the pope, beats a man to death with a rock and means to kill Elizabeth himself. The foreign Catholics are a bad lot too – Quadra scheming with anyone who'll listen, Anjou a petulant fool who doesn't know how to behave, and Mary of Guise sleeping with the enemy. They get their deserts, however: Quadra and Mary get killed, and Anjou gets a cold.

Protestantism fares much better. When Elizabeth justifies the royal supremacy and the break with Rome in terms of loyalty to one master, a bishop cries 'Heresy!' 'No, your Grace', responds Elizabeth, 'it is common sense. A most English virtue.' The Lords smile, and nod approvingly – and we are meant to, too. Catholicism is the past, the religion of sterile old Mary; Protestantism is the future, the religion of lively young Elizabeth and her England. Of course, religious passions are now cooler, except perhaps in Northern Ireland, and a tendentious account of sixteenth-century religion may be less harmful. But the identification of Protestantism with England's interests and with progress is part of a nationalist interpretation of English history, one that still manifests itself in hostility to Europe and a conviction that Britain is different and better.

Some of the faults of *Elizabeth* are inherent in the genre. Film audiences expect 2 hours of spectacle and excitement or 2 hours of love and romance. *Elizabeth* delivered the lot, and got seven Oscar nominations and a clutch of other nominations and awards. The impact of the film owed something to its pace. This was no staid costume drama, with panning shots and rosy glows. Instead, we have cuts and contrasts, a rush of events, and nearly 30 years of history condensed to a short span. It makes great drama, but poor history. We are encouraged to feel that life was more feverish and exhilarating then, that things got done quickly, that somehow history happened faster. But students need to remember that the past was just as tedious as the present can be, and that a year had 365 dragging days then too. History happened slowly, a day at a time, change was gradual, and those who were there couldn't work out what was going on. By all means enjoy *Elizabeth*, I certainly did – but don't suppose that it's telling you anything much about history.

Suggestions for Further Reading

Christopher Haigh, *Elizabeth I* (London, 1988; 2nd edition, 2000).
Susan Doran, *Monarchy and Matrimony: The Courtships of Elizabeth I* (London, 1996).

9

Mary Queen of Scots (1971)

John Guy

Mary Queen of Scots, a British film made in 1971 at Shepperton Studios starring Vanessa Redgrave as Mary and Glenda Jackson as Elizabeth I, was released for general distribution the following spring. Among that year's box-office hits were *A Clockwork Orange*, *Dirty Harry* starring Clint Eastwood, and *Fiddler on the Roof*. It was also a vintage era for the theatre. Robert Bolt, fresh from winning six Academy Awards for the film version of *A Man for All Seasons*, had written a new stage-play *Vivat, Vivat Regina!* for the Chichester Festival. It had opened in May 1970, with Eileen Atkins as Elizabeth and Sarah Miles as Mary, winning critical acclaim before transferring to London. There it ran for 18 months before moving to Broadway, where audiences were equally enthralled. Tudor history was in vogue in New York, because the City Opera had lately put on Donizetti's *Roberto Devereux*, with Beverly Sills in the role of Elizabeth. And by the time *Vivat, Vivat Regina!* arrived – with Atkins again as Elizabeth but now Claire Bloom as Mary – the opera management had capitalized on its ear-lier success, staging Donizetti's *Maria Stuarda* with Sills as Mary and Pauline Tinsley as Elizabeth. Also at this time, Tom Foster, author of the award-winning *Tom Paine*, had an Elizabethan play in rehearsal. History, especially British history, had never had it so good; the crit-ics were buzzing about 'the emerging Elizabethan industry'. Hopes, indeed expectations, for *Mary Queen of Scots* were high.

Sadly they were dashed. So what happened? What are the film's strengths and weaknesses? The subject is a major challenge. It's a case where truth is not only stranger, but also more intensely dramatic than fiction. There is no shortage of documentary evidence, but Mary's is

Plate 8 Mary, Queen of Scots (Vanessa Redgrave) and Lord Henry Darnley (Timothy Dalton) embark on one of the most disastrous marriages of the early-modern period. Courtesy of Columbia, Irving Allen and The Kobal Collection for the image from the motion picture *Mary Queen of Scots* (1971).

an enigmatic, labyrinthine history. Even when stripped to its core, the
story involves two queens, three husbands, two murders, an alleged
rape, a forced abdication, and a regicide – not to mention interminable
conspiracies and revolts. The kaleidoscopic nature of Scottish politics, in which the nobles switched sides with breathtaking speed and
for the flimsiest of reasons, is potentially bewildering. Here the film's
approach is broadly narrative and chronological. Since, however, the
story is so convoluted, it naturally had to be cut. This was done indis-
criminately; it looks as if entire scenes were removed midway through
the production. In order to compensate, events still fundamental, but
now happening off-stage, had to be described through the notoriously
difficult medium of explanatory dialogue. The result is a cacophony
of words.

But we are getting ahead of ourselves. Films tell stories in pictures,
and the opening shots of the château de Chenonceau succeed brilliantly in recreating Mary's youth as a girlish idyll. In a brief space
of time, we learn that her marriage to her first husband, the young
François II, is a royal love affair. Whether or not this is historically
accurate, the scene works. It is one of the very few uncluttered by
dialogue. We seem to have entered a magical world. Only a cerebral
abscess breaks the spell. 'My head', screams François in an accent worthy of 'Allo 'Allo, as Mary rushes to cradle him in her arms. Inevitably,
the illness proves fatal, triggering in quick succession the regency of
Catherine de' Medici, the enemy of Mary's Guise family, and Mary's
return to Scotland.

From then on, the emphasis of the early scenes, in which we also
take our first glimpse of Bothwell – he appears (wholly inaccurately)
as the emissary of the 'Lords of the Congregation' – is dynastic. The
Cardinal of Lorraine, Mary's uncle, informs her that she is the Catholic
claimant to the English throne as a great-granddaughter of Henry VII.
'You are', he pedantically explains, 'Queen of Scotland by birth and
Queen of France by marriage. And the Queen of England by right.'
He elaborates on Elizabeth's heresy, bastardy and descent from Anne
Boleyn, the crux as it was grasped by contemporaries; historically, this
is impressive, but the creaking dialogue and Lorraine's resemblance to
a cliché out of *Les Quatres Mousquetaires* muffle these effects.

Across the Channel, the news of Amy Robsart's death has stunned
all at Elizabeth's court that are privy to the queen's nightly romps
with Robert Dudley. Sir William Cecil, Elizabeth's wily chief minister, talks of murder; Dudley is banished from court until the coroner's
verdict is returned. We discover that Elizabeth and Cecil can work

together, but enjoy a checkered, semi-antagonistic relationship. Cecil and Dudley are rivals (a traditional interpretation, but one that will cause a few modern scholars to squirm). Most emphatically, Cecil reminds Elizabeth of the danger of an international Catholic league centred on Mary and her Guise relations. They are allied to Philip II of Spain, the pope and the house of Savoy, threatening Elizabeth's 'safety' and England's national security. The 'safety' of the queen and the Protestant state must be protected – and subliminally we conclude that in Cecil's mind, he means 'protection' by fair means or foul. So far so good, since the film's depiction of Cecil as an unscrupulous, messianic Protestant is one of its strongest suits.

A lively battle of wits, first between Elizabeth and Mary, and then Elizabeth and Cecil, ensues, a strand running through the remainder of the film. It begins when Mary offers Elizabeth a fresh start in their relationship, linked to her request to travel home to Scotland through England, a request denied by Elizabeth. Since the treaty of Edinburgh (1560) is never mentioned, the significance of Mary's gesture is obscured. This treaty was the chief diplomatic obstacle to an accord between the two 'British' queens, because Cecil had negotiated it with Mary's rebels behind her back. Although Mary understandably refused to ratify a treaty she had never been allowed to discuss, her offer of a fresh start was a genuine olive branch. Still, we learn in general terms that she will not renounce her dynastic claim and refuses to be treated as an inferior. We glimpse something of her geniality, humanity, and willingness to compromise in the interests of a settlement with her cousin, but we also become aware of her wilfulness, determination, concern for honour and reputation, and sense of grandeur. Moreover, insofar as her illegitimate half-brother, James Stewart, Earl of Moray, is shown to be scheming and ambitious, secretly accepting English gold and colluding with Cecil at every turn against the interests of his sister, these scenes more than earn their place.

Later, the facts of history will be manipulated. It is made to appear as if Elizabeth has carefully planned Lord Darnley's release to Scotland over many months, calculating that Mary will misjudge his narcissistic, predatory character and marry him in preference to Elizabeth's cast-off lover Robert Dudley. In this section, it is Elizabeth (rather than Cecil) who has set out to destabilize Mary's rule. Mary is even offered a place in the English succession (apparently by name) if she will marry Dudley. Elizabeth sends Bothwell and Darnley to Mary with the 'deed of succession'. She wagers Cecil 50 gold crowns that Mary will marry

Darnley. This is where the film first diverges radically from the undisputed facts. The intention is to heighten the illusion of a confident, proactive, masterful Elizabeth – a woman who is monarch of all she surveys, who loves Dudley but never allows her love to distract her from her political ends – in contrast to a naive, emotional, idealistic Mary – a woman who allows romance to shape her aims, who lacks seriousness and giggles at the 'naughty' thought of marrying Darnley against her brother's advice. But this dramatic colour comes at a heavy price. The account of Darnley's arrival in Scotland is just the first in a series of distortions eroding our confidence in the film's historical credibility.

This comes on top of earlier dramatic licence. Already Lorraine is seen to nominate Father John Ballard, in reality one of the Babington plotters of 1586 but here one of Mary's lifelong companions, as her confessor on the eve of her departure from France. And Lorraine chooses David Rizzio to attend her. From the outset, Rizzio is cast as Mary's closest confidant, whereas in reality he was a valet and musician, who'd arrived in Scotland in the train of the Savoy ambassador, sang as a bass in Mary's choir, and was not appointed as her confidential secretary until after Darnley reached Scotland. Every good story needs a baddie, and Rizzio is set up for this role. He is said to be the pope's agent, a Catholic and a foil to the influence of Moray and the Protestant nobles. Lorraine advises Mary to promote Rizzio slowly but surely, creating the misleading impression that she seeks on her return to bypass her nobles and reverse the official Reformation. Since she ostensibly seeks to justify her rule in Scotland as moderate and benign, this is liminally as well as subliminally damaging. At best Mary appears emollient and irresponsible, at worst a hypocrite.

As Mary lands at Leith, her Scots nobles appear whooping on horseback over the brow of the sand dunes like Native Americans in a John Wayne movie. In this insensitively stereotyped image, Scotland is shown to be a tribal society governed by the blood feud, a barbaric realm alien to Mary's francophile values. In a fit of pique, she cries out that she will not 'drag out her days in this barren land'. And yet, she appoints Moray her chief adviser. Despite this, she shows herself to be spirited and courageous, a woman who is not afraid to speak her mind. Riding past what is meant to be Arthur's Seat on the approach to Holyrood, she encounters the Calvinist leader John Knox with whom she freely banters. She tells him she will not stand for threats and intimidation. She believes in the untrammelled exercise of conscience, the right of all her people to worship 'as they will'. 'Papist whore!', he suggestively retorts.

In politics and religion alike, the film's approach to Mary's personal rule in Scotland is strangely schizophrenic. At one level, Mary is depicted as a politique and a moderate, at another as a Catholic ideologue. Perhaps the intention is to try and reconcile conflicting historical traditions? For it is certainly true that Mary has been interpreted both ways by historians over the past 150 years. But not both at once! The film tantalizingly depicts a ruler who alternates between assertiveness and timidity, between knowing her mind and fulminating at the plotting and manoeuvring she knows she can't control. 'Did you hear him?', she demands of Rizzio and Ballard as soon as Moray leaves her apartments. And yet we've just seen her cravenly deferring to her brother. Visually, this ambiguity emerges when Mary is glimpsed wearing riding breeches. In real life she adored riding, for which she adopted the daring habit of wearing breeches of Florentine serge beneath her skirts. The fashion was introduced by Catherine de' Medici from Italy, and was *risqué* because it allowed the wearer to ride astride her horse and not side-saddle as female protocol required, a habit for which Mary would be greeted with suspicion in Scotland. It is a rare nuance, and yet it is over in a flash, far too quickly to register with an audience not already prepared for it.

The first and most successful four years of Mary's rule are skipped over, so that the Darnley marriage seems to have been settled within a few weeks of her return home. Mary is infatuated – unsubtle allusions are made to the love affair of her first marriage; the film's controlling idea is increasingly of a *femme fatale* who allows her heart to rule her head (this in sharp contrast to Elizabeth, whose head always rules her heart.) Whereas Elizabeth has refused to marry Dudley even after he is finally acquitted by the coroner's verdict, declaring that there will be 'one mistress and no master' in her household, Mary yearns for a man in her life to relieve her of the burdens of government so she can devote herself to luxury and pleasure. From this point onwards, the film succumbs to stereotypes.

Darnley, as soon as he is married, misbehaves himself. His character is fatally flawed. 'I will be the master', he shouts menacingly; 'I am the King . . . We will show this Queen who is the master'. The result is a murderous mayhem with overtly sexual overtones. When Mary, counselled by Rizzio, refuses to grant the 'crown matrimonial' to Darnley, the result is Rizzio's assassination, followed by Mary's latest infatuation: this time for Bothwell. Now the leading man in Mary's life, Bothwell is present throughout. And yet in reality, he wasn't even in Scotland then. He'd fled into voluntary exile in France, and had to be recalled to help lead Mary's forces against Moray, who had raised an army to resist Mary's marriage to Darnley in a revolt usually known as the Chaseabout Raid. The film's audience will be unaware of this, because Moray's revolt is omitted. Doubtless that was deliberate; Mary's resourceful, victorious, masculine response in which she rode at the head of her army wearing her steel cap and with a pistol in her saddle-holster conflicts radically with her image as a *femme fatale*. On the other hand, Moray's defeat led to his exclusion from power. This has to be covered somehow in the script, so Bothwell arrests him, lamely remarking, 'It was a bad day for you when you sold off my lands.' This doubly misses the point, because Moray had rebelled in the name of the Protestant religion, whereas Bothwell's attributed remark implies the revolt was a quarrel over property rights. Bothwell urges Mary to execute Moray, 'or else he will take revenge', but she exiles her brother instead. Once more the script has to show Mary as impractical and idealistic. She seeks to be merciful and just, but is characterized as a dreamer lacking Elizabeth's grit and foresight, her grip on the levers and realities of power.

Back at Elizabeth's court, Cecil has advance warning of the assassination plot against Rizzio, which he condones. Elizabeth – in reality, all knowledge of the plot was denied her by Cecil – objects to the murder, but finally declares, 'I leave it to God's hands.' Cecil wants Elizabeth to subsidize Moray and the rebels (it's not really clear why they *are* rebels, since the revolt has been omitted), and Elizabeth refuses. Or at least, she refuses until Robert Dudley intervenes, declaring boldly that if only Elizabeth would consent to marry him, the kingdom would be secure. Provoked by his presumption, Elizabeth changes her mind, offering to send the rebels £3000 in gold coins. The scene is fictional – its dramatic purpose seems to be solely to trigger the punch-line from Cecil, addressing the Almighty: 'I thank you for the endless ambition of Robert Dudley to be king!' But at least the joke works: the only example of successful humour in the script.

From here, the film becomes ever more reductionist. It's clear that the level of attention given to the Rizzio plot and its antecedents cannot be sustained if the audience is not to be detained in the cinema indefinitely. Rather than re-edit or re-shoot the earlier scenes, the producer, Hal B. Wallis, must have decided enough was enough. Now it was time to switch from Shepperton's approach to Hollywood's.

Although many details of setting, costume and gesture are meticulously choreographed to maintain a sense of historical authenticity, the story and (especially) its chronology are bowdlerized to achieve the desired effect: the fatal attraction of Mary and Bothwell, and the inevitability of their doomed love affair, leading to Mary's downfall, forced abdication and regicide.

So it is that Mary escapes from Holyrood after the Rizzio plot with Bothwell, and they ride to the Hermitage, Bothwell's border stronghold, where Mary has her baby, the future James VI and I. (In fact, Bothwell had already fled from Holyrood, and Mary rode with Darnley to Dunbar. She later had her baby at Edinburgh Castle.) Bothwell and Mary then ride in triumph to Edinburgh Castle, where Moray – seemingly captured in the course of his revolt – is in a dungeon. The facts are juggled to create a situation in which Moray can't be executed unless Darnley is condemned too, and Darnley can't be touched because he'll slanderously name Rizzio as the father of Mary's son. 'I will not risk my son even for the pleasure of killing you', Mary tells her brother. She then shows her baby to the cheering people. 'I shall be merciful', she says, and pardons Moray. It's a scene which conflates a series of events that lasted six months, ending with the grand ceremony of reconciliation that Mary staged for her nobles at Edinburgh in September 1566, except the characters and everything about them must be altered.

The screenwriter's way out is quickly to move things on, so the sulking and syphilitic Darnley declares his intention to leave the country. First, however, he insists that Mary joins him in bed. It seems he plans to rape her, so she drugs his wine. As soon as Darnley has spat out the line, 'Even though I disgust you, you will sleep with me', he falls to the ground. On cue, Bothwell enters. He kisses Mary, and leads her towards the bed. She yields; they consummate their love.

The conspiracy to murder Darnley in a gunpowder plot at Kirk o'Field ensues. The plan is masterminded by Moray and Bothwell, but Mary is fully implicated. Not only an accessory to murder, she is even seen to write the so-called 'Casket Letters' to Bothwell, planning Darnley's death and confessing her adultery, all the while nursing Darnley and sitting beside his bed. As Mary leaves her husband, the gunpowder trail is laid. Darnley hears a noise and looks out of the window. He sees men setting light to a fuse and rushes to the door. But the door is locked, so he jumps out of the window, making his escape a few seconds before the bang. At Holyrood, the explosion is heard and Bothwell and Mary exchange a knowing glance. Darnley's lodging is reduced to rubble. He's still alive, but as he picks his way out of the debris, he's surrounded and stabbed by Bothwell's co-conspirators.

At the English court, Elizabeth is dressed in black. She tells the French and Scottish ambassadors she is in mourning for the late King of Scots. Her long speech is lame and cumbersome, not surprisingly since most of it is a narration of events that have occurred off-stage – its purpose is to convey the news that Mary has married Bothwell. In a few seconds, we've skipped over three months and the most crucial part of the story. Such incidents as Mary's abduction at Almond Bridge in April 1567, her alleged rape by Bothwell at Dunbar, the proceedings to divorce Bothwell from his wife Jean Gordon, and Mary's threat to kill herself a day or so after her wedding to Bothwell, are omitted. The reason isn't hard to guess. There is no dramatic space for them. We've already been shown that Bothwell and Mary are head over heels in love, that their infatuation began shortly after the birth of her son, and that her guilt – as a murderess and adulteress – is beyond doubt. Every question, in short, that exercises any reputable historian concerned to investigate the truth about Mary's downfall has been begged. Of Mary's modern biographers, only Dr Jenny Wormald agrees with the film that Mary was solely and unequivocally responsible for her own ruin, a verdict endorsing that of Mary's enemies who reached it by restricting the agenda to events in Scotland, ignoring the scale of Cecil's cross-border collusion with Mary's rebels, and side-stepping the hornet's nest of the authenticity of the 'Casket Letters'.

The film gets sketchier and sketchier as episodes lasting a year are conflated. The Scottish nobles rise up against Mary and Bothwell, surrounding them at Borthwick Castle, where the lovers trade insults with them from the battlements. These rebels are led by Moray – no matter that he had already left the country for France or that the 'Confederate Lords' were opposed by an active Marian party. There follows the denouement at Carberry Hill and Mary's forced abdication at Lochleven Castle. These events are played out as if they had occurred at Borthwick. Moray presents Mary with a deed of abdication. When she refuses to sign, she is shown the 'Casket Letters' and threatened. 'Abdicate or I will publish them and have you tried for murder', crows Moray triumphantly. But when Mary persists in her refusal, Moray sends Bothwell to her (no matter that Bothwell had already fled to Denmark, never to return). Bothwell pleads with Mary, 'They will pardon me, spare you, give me a passage to Denmark if I can persuade you to abdicate.' And he holds out the prospect of freedom. If Mary complies, she'll be escorted to the English border and sent into exile.

(No such small inconveniences, then, as the need to escape in a boat across the loch from Lochleven Castle and fight the battle of Langside). It isn't a difficult choice, and soon we see Mary riding towards the border on a glorious spring morning with Moray at her side. 'We will bring up your son as a good Protestant . . . ', her brother tells her unreassuringly. 'My son, my son . . . ', Mary pleads, as if she had forgotten all about him until now. And then, she is across the border and made to say, 'I have my whole life before me, free, free . . . . !'

The climax is pure invention. A few days later, Elizabeth – just as in Donizetti's *Maria Stuarda* –happens to be riding close by with Robert Dudley, while out hunting. She encounters Mary in the forest. Mary, riding a white charger and dressed in black for the first time (and for no obvious reason), meets Elizabeth, who greets her with the line: 'I am here to meet you as you so urgently demanded . . . '

Yet the scene, theatrically, has its merits, if only because it closely follows the lines of Donizetti's 1834 opera. For Donizetti, despite numerous flights of fancy, had a firm grasp of character. His drama is impeccable, if not his history. Mary is fearful and resentful, but is sure of herself as a legitimate queen and therefore willing to go through with the interview. She eagerly appeals to Elizabeth's belief in the ideal of monarchy. They are 'sister queens' who need to safeguard each other from the threat of sedition and republicanism. Mary asks for money and an army, so that she can return to Scotland to recover her throne. The two queens know it is a defining moment. Their destinies are intertwined. Mary will humble herself, fulfilling what is needed to obtain a settlement, provided her grandeur is respected and she is not treated as an inferior. On the other hand, her compliance springs from her confidence in her unblemished royal status, unlike Elizabeth whose dynastic legitimacy is tainted by her father's adultery.

Elizabeth, however, is arrogant. She is jealous of Mary, who is nine years younger and more beautiful. Elizabeth finds her cousin's attitude strangely presumptuous. She rounds on her: 'When you are honourably acquitted of the crimes of which you are accused, you shall have your army and your money.' She then explains she will have Mary taken deeper into England, where she will be closely watched. Mary instantly retaliates that 'You are my equal. I am not your subject. You hope to dishonour me', but Elizabeth maintains 'It is you who are dishonoured.' Mary can no longer contain herself. She feels she has done everything possible to nurture reconciliation, and can no longer keep up the pretence. When Elizabeth declares, 'You are a pampered woman demanding that all indulge her. You are not fit for the high office to which you are called', we reach the point of no return. The unspeakable is spoken. Mary calls Elizabeth her 'mortal enemy . . . bastard, heretic, usurper' and Elizabeth too crosses the line when she calls Mary an 'infamous royal whore' and admits that she 'must keep her prisoner until the day of her death'.

We've reached the beginning of the end. The script shifts gear, the overriding theme is now that of sin and redemption. Mary sinned in marrying Bothwell, but she will redeem herself as a good Catholic. We catch glimpses of her in her gilded cage, dressed all in black apart from a white cambric cap on her head. Father Ballard in disguise visits her and hears her confession. Here, too, we find a striking affinity with Donizetti's *Maria Stuarda*, in which the character of 'Talbot' (George, Earl of Shrewsbury and Mary's custodian) is a disguised Catholic priest who hears Mary's confession and thus ensures that she can die a true Catholic martyr, absolved of mortal sin.

This theme is interspersed with the end game of the battle of wits between Elizabeth and Cecil over Mary's execution. Cecil wants Mary dead as a threat to England's security; Elizabeth has always realized that the ideal of monarchy is at stake. Monarchy is divine; Mary is an anointed queen. Like Elizabeth, she is accountable to God alone. Cecil offers to bring Elizabeth the proof of Mary's conspiracies against her. 'No forgeries!', insists Elizabeth. Ballard, meanwhile, is captured and racked in the Tower. Walsingham, who conveniently appears as Cecil's spymaster, has intercepted letters in Mary's own hand, endorsing Elizabeth's murder as 'the mainspring of the plot'. Cecil visits Mary – he has all the letters. He is the spider at the centre of the web that ensnares her. As ever, he is resolute and indomitable. 'Madam', he informs Mary, 'you cast an evil spell on all you meet except me.'

Will Elizabeth sign the death warrant? She is keeping her options open. 'If [Mary] begs forgiveness of me, she shall live'. But Elizabeth understands Mary's character and can read her like a book. She knows in her heart all hope of reconciliation is gone. Mary will never stoop to ask forgiveness; Elizabeth knows she will never pardon her. Nonetheless, Elizabeth meets Mary at Fotheringhay Castle. It might be said that one fictional meeting is dramatically justifiable, but two stretches credulity. This second set-piece clash is strangely anticlimactic, but serves to crystallize the issues. Mary offers to beg forgiveness verbally and in private – 'between these four walls'. Elizabeth refuses. Mary's submission must be in writing and in public. If it is not forthcoming, Elizabeth threatens to put her on trial and ruin her reputation by producing the 'Casket Letters' in court. Just to prove she has them,

Elizabeth has brought the letters with her: the Casket is laid on the table. But Mary is resolved to die a martyr for the Catholic faith. She will free herself from imprisonment and her sins, rising to heaven in glory, whereas Elizabeth is destined to kill her and so destroy the ideal of monarchy and the values for which she herself has earnestly striven. Mary will die unjustly, for she is not Elizabeth's inferior and cannot lawfully be judged by her or her court. 'It is your destiny to kill me', Mary almost spits out the words. 'So now it is I who pity you [for] the judicial murder of an anointed queen.'

Elizabeth turns fleetingly to Mary as she departs: 'If your head had matched your heart, I would be the one awaiting death.' The remark is saccharine, contrived and historically glib, but in the context of the film's crude stereotypes, it hits its mark. Mary prays and prepares herself for her execution. The sheriff of Northamptonshire knocks on the door, and Mary walks into the Great Hall with her prayer book and rosary beads. 'I hope', she says, quoting the diary of Bourgoing her physician, 'that death shall put an end to all my troubles.' And she ends with the motto that became her epitaph: 'For in my end is my beginning!' If Elizabeth triumphed in life, Mary would triumph in death. Far from disappearing into oblivion as Cecil had intended, she would rise like the phoenix from the ashes to go down as one of the most celebrated and beguiling rulers in the whole of British history.

Mary Queen of Scots was not long in the cutting room, and was released in March 1972 to a chorus of faint praise. Few critics felt it necessary to comment on its factual inaccuracies or the extent to which the key questions about Mary's character are begged. The consensus was more pedestrian – that the film made great history boring. As the critic for *The Times*, remarked, maybe

> it is not all that bad, in the sense that it is never less than quite respectable, reasonably literate, but it is certainly a long, dull plod. I cannot imagine why no filmmaker yet seems to have found the secret of making Mary a really interesting figure, when the fascination of the character should surely be built in.[1]

Failure must largely have been the responsibility of the screenwriter, John Hale, and the director, Charles Jarrott. Vanessa Redgrave is visually stunning as Mary, while Glenda Jackson took the part of Elizabeth fresh from her triumph in the title role of the BBC television mini-series, *Elizabeth R*. And if the female leads were already household names, the male actors would shortly become so and gave outstanding individual performances; in fact, considering the cast overall, this has to have been one of the most talented group of theatrical luminaries ever seen in a British historical film.

But maybe in the end, the casting *was* part of the trouble. Time and time again, Redgrave is upstaged by Jackson, exactly as audiences expected and demanded at the time. As the star of *Elizabeth R*, Jackson had gripped the nation. People were glued to their television sets. It was the first time total strangers had talked to each other in bars and on buses and trains about a TV mini-series, and the BBC captured viewing ratings never previously obtained by an historical drama. Forget King Arthur, Henry V and Nelson, thundered *The Times*: Jackson taught us history like no one else. 'Our national myth is really that of the slim, regal girl with red-gold hair and a golden tongue who threaded her way through dangers to the crown and led a united people to glory'.[2] All this tended to make Mary little more than a foil to her English counterpart, and since it has always been a screenwriter's first duty to dramatize the contrasts between the leading protagonists, it is easy to see how Mary became a *femme fatale* at a moment when the triumphalist reading of Gloriana was ascendant.

Something similar had happened to Robert Bolt in *Vivat, Vivat Regina!* Very few people know that this play, first conceived because Bolt's wife, Sarah Miles, wanted to act the part of Mary, did not originally have Elizabeth in it as a character. This came to light when Eileen Atkins gave an interview shortly after her last appearance in the role on Broadway. She acknowledged then that hers had been 'by far the better part'. But she insisted, no one who had read the earlier drafts of the script could ever have formed that impression. 'I knew Robert Bolt had written the play for Sarah Miles', she explained. 'Originally he didn't want to have Elizabeth in it at all, and when he found he had to put her in he kept it down to such a minimum that I found it interesting.'[3]

Vanessa Redgrave also gave an interview, interrupting the shoot at Shepperton Studios to talk to Michael Billington. Asked what she felt about the film's interpretation of history, she explained that in her opinion, it was 'all about loot'.[4] 'Mary is after England. Elizabeth and her advisers are out to get what they can out of Mary.' The scene where Rizzio is murdered 'has strong economic and class overtones'. As Mary's secretary and confidant, Rizzio 'occupies a position of extreme power and the Scottish nobility deeply resented the fact that he was an Italian who had risen from the professional classes.' Then, on the issue of Mary's character, she candidly confided: 'Characters don't emerge simply from reading all the books. I just get a sudden, lightening impression of some quality I'm after. Just a stray phrase from a speech or an odd sentence or two in a not very serious novel may do it.'

Redgrave's remarks are revealing. Very few who watch this film will ever consider it to be a story 'about loot', although this idea could explain the significance of Bothwell's jibe to Moray about his lands. Overall, its controlling idea is that Elizabeth ruled from the head, whereas Mary ruled from the heart. Many historians will be surprised, even shocked, to think that a leading actress, thinking about character, would gather inspiration from 'an odd sentence or two' in a trashy novel. Doubtless, Redgrave was dissembling. No one involved in making a major feature film, at the time of shooting, is likely to admit the influence of any one book or interpretation on the production. It is, however, widely supposed that the director and screenwriter drew to a greater or lesser extent on Lady Antonia Fraser's biography, published to rapturous reviews in 1969. This was beyond question the pre-eminent life of Mary Queen of Scots in the twentieth century: the book set a fresh standard for royal biography as a genre, as well as for its interpretation of Mary.

And yet, it isn't ultimately the film's relationship to the book that surprises, but the lack of it. One feels that Donizetti's *Maria Stuarda* may in the end have exercised a more powerful artistic influence. Only the earliest scenes in France and England owe anything of substance to Fraser's biography, where Mary's francophile values and the battle of wits between Elizabeth and Cecil plainly derive from the book. Beyond this, the distortions are legion, and it is pointless to dwell further on them. Suffice it to say that, when Fraser briefly commented on the 1971 film, she described it as 'rather unoriginal and unexciting'. She drew attention to its obsession with Mary as a *femme fatale*, before remarking of that idea: 'it has occurred to me in studying the many fictional forms of her life, that simply to concentrate on that element in Mary's character is to miss a great deal of interest.'[5] Faint praise indeed, and perhaps rather generously so.

Suggestions for Further Reading

John Guy, *'My Heart Is My Own': The Life of Mary Queen of Scots* (London, 2004).
Antonia Fraser, *Mary, Queen of Scots* (London, 1969).
Jenny Wormald, *Mary, Queen of Scots: A Study in Failure* (London, 1988).
Susan Doran, *Mary Queen of Scots: An Illustrated Life* (London, 2007).

10

The Armada, War and Propaganda in the Cinema

Will Coster

The Armada stands at the crossroads of a number of myths. The first is a specific form of xenophobia in the attachment to the Spanish of what historians usually refer to as the 'Black Legend'. Second is a sense of imperial destiny, linked to a view of the British as a sea power, in which victory in 1588 was for some the genesis. The final element is a view of the English character exemplified by the images of piratical sea dogs and Elizabeth I's defiant speech at Tilbury: the twin pillars of resistance to adversity. All this echoed the parallel slide to war in the middle decades of the twentieth century. The use and elaboration of these issues are nowhere more apparent than in films such as *Fire Over England* and *The Sea Hawk*, which marked important attempts to embody these myths and use them to provide both entertainment and a relatively subtle form of propaganda in the face of a gathering storm.

Both films present cases of what, in Nietzsche's terms, can be seen as classic examples of monumental history, engaging with 'greatness that once existed'.[1] Both have stories that revolve around the attempted invasion of England in 1588. Both share a common key cast member, providing Flora Robson with opportunities to pursue what is often said to be a remarkably subtle characterization of Elizabeth I.[2] Both films also focus on a male protagonist, in the case of *Fire Over England* Michael Ingolby, played by the Shakespearian actor Laurence Olivier and for *The Sea Hawk* the actor often seen as the embodiment of the swashbuckling hero: Errol Flynn as Geoffrey Thorpe. The two

Plate 9 Patriotism rewarded. Queen Elizabeth (Flora Robson) knights Geoffrey Thorpe (Errol Flynn), a fictitious stand-in for Francis Drake. Courtesy of Warner Bros. and The Kobal Collection for the image from the motion picture *The Sea Hawk* (1940).

films were made on different sides of the Atlantic and are separated by radical changes in the nature of global politics, yet both have considerable similarities in the circumstances in which they originated. The first, *Fire Over England* (released by London Film Productions in 1937) was, to the degree that its creators anticipated a war with Nazi Germany, looking forward to a conflict that most in Britain hoped to avoid. However, there is no doubt that the co-producer Alexander Korda, the dominant figure in the British film industry of the mid-twentieth century, as a Hungarian refugee of Jewish origin and a friend of Churchill, took a less optimistic view.[3] The director of the *The Sea Hawk* was Michael Curtiz, another figure who had once been dominant in the Hungarian film industry. When this film was released by Warner Brothers in 1940, the war in Europe had already begun, but this was the era of American isolationism and, like England three years earlier, many hoped to avoid involvement. By this point the anti-Nazi sympathies of the company were already clear. As a result of these circumstances both films can also be seen as a relatively subtle preparation of a peacetime audience for war.

Before moving any further in interpreting these films as propaganda, it is important to note that this was also popular entertainment. Warner Brothers in particular never knowingly undersold a film and *The Sea Hawk* was marketed with the tag line: 'Never before so many thrills! Never such adventure, such romance! Sail to high adventure with "The Robin Hood of the Sea" '. The reference to Robin Hood is a significant one as *The Adventures of Robin Hood*, the Technicolor smash of two years before, was clearly an important model for the film. Both movies dealt with a character who was a moral bandit; they shared cast and crew, most obviously Claude Rains playing his suave villain, Alan Hale as the perennial sidekick and Flynn himself as the hero. They also had very similar plots and devices, not least of which was the wooing of a reluctant heroine, who for a time was to be Olivia de Havilland reprising her place as Flynn's love interest. Two other Warner Brother movies were also significant, the first being the picture that made Flynn a star, *Captain Blood* (1935), which had long prompted the studio to cast Flynn in another nautical adventure, and *The Private Lives of Elizabeth and Essex* (1939), which shared with *The Sea Hawk,* not only a time period, but also a director, sets and costumes.

The Sea Hawk was the title of a silent film released in 1924, for which the ultimate source was a book by popular novelist Rafael Sabatini published in 1915.[4] However, the final script was based on a story about Francis Drake originally brought to the studio by Seton I. Miller, titled *The Sea Begger* or *Beggers of the Sea*.[5] After Miller had finished working on *The Adventures of Robin Hood*, he and Howard Koch revised the script, each draft building up the aspects of international politics and court intrigue, the very elements which tend to emphasize the links between the circumstances in the sixteenth and twentieth centuries.[6]

The pedigree of *Fire Over England* was a little less complex, based as it was on a novel by A. E. W. Mason which had been published only in 1936. Mason is more famous for what is often seen as an imperialist tract, *The Four Feathers*, which would be filmed by Korda in 1939. Here the modification of dialogue and indeed of the story in general is much less marked, although according to Gore Vidal, Churchill made an uncredited contribution to the script.[7] Whether this story is true or not, the depiction of events does seem to accord with a Churchillian view of British history, which itself borrowed from popular Victorian images of the past.[8] The degree to which these films were able to play directly into such an existing popular conception of the Tudor period was vital in their impact as both political statements and entertainment.

The Black Legend?

The existence of an historical conflict with Spain was incredibly fortuitous for filmmakers in the 1930s and 1940s. The more implacable historical enemy of the English was France, but the analogy between sixteenth-century Spain and Nazi Germany was more useful. The status of the Spanish under Franco, as neutrals with fascist politics, did the analogy no harm, but the roots of this depiction lay much deeper, beginning in the Tudor period itself with the set of associations usually known as the Black Legend.

To say the Black Legend is complex is something of an understatement, but its contours can at least be mapped fairly briefly.[9] Aside from the general distrust of aliens, which we might view as somewhat ironic given the nature of Nazi racism, the Legend revolved around the issues of religion and the treatment of subjugated peoples. For late sixteenth-century English Protestants, the Spanish came to encapsulate all that was to be feared about Catholicism, which had a direct expression in the shape of the Spanish Inquisition. Until the late twentieth century the image of the Inquisition was of implacable bigotry and cruelty, in particular associated with arbitrary imprisonment and the use of

torture. Important archival work has seriously challenged this view
and the Inquisition now has to be seen as just one more mechanism
for the judicial and legalistic maintenance of religious uniformity.[10]
But it was to these prejudices that *Fire Over England* referred by having Michael Ingolby's father killed by the Inquisition. *The Sea Hawk*
also alludes to the Inquisition as the cause of the slavery of Englishmen
on Spanish galleys, and they make up the court that sentences Flynn's
Captain Thorpe and his crew to the galleys in an interesting avoidance
of the Hay's Office usual strictures on depictions of religious figures.

The origin of the Legend is usually traced back to the former
bishop of Chiapas, Bartolomé de Las Casas, who in *A Brief Account of
the Devastation of the Indies* (1542), published in English in 1583, condemned Spanish brutality towards 'peaceful' natives in America and
the Caribbean.[11] This heritage is alluded to in *The Sea Hawk*, when
Flynn's Captain Thorpe justifies theft by noting the Aztec origins of
Spanish gold. In the sixteenth century this was exacerbated by incidents such as the so-called 'Spanish Fury' of 1576, in which soldiers in
the Netherlands rioted and massacred the citizens of Antwerp.[12] The
condemnation of Spanish imperial ambitions and methods seems particularly ironic to modern eyes, since the alternative was presumably
the imperialism on which the English were embarking and because
this was the very period when English sailors, those paragons of freedom and liberty, began to purchase slaves from Africa and ship them
to the New World. Nevertheless, in the mid-twentieth century, these
moral inconsistencies were less obvious to British and even American
audiences. In America attitudes to British imperialism were complex
and often coloured by ethnic origin, but audiences were generally very
willing to watch what now appear to be hymns to British imperialism
in very large numbers, including *The Lives of a Bengal Lancer* (1935),
Gunga Din (1939) and another Curtiz–Flynn project *The Charge of the
Light Brigade* (1936).

The useful contrast between the archetypal freedom of English
sailing ships and imprisonment on Spanish oared galleys is very clearly
expressed. This also had the useful effect of associating the Spanish
with a medieval form of technology and the English with modernity. In fact the Spanish routinely utilized sail when outside of the
Mediterranean, and even the Armada, where just about every available
vessel was pushed into service, contained only 8 oared ships out of 150
craft. Nevertheless, to most Western, mid-twentieth-century cinema
audiences, this was, of course, the worst form of slavery: the slavery of white people. Thus the dangers of Spanish rule incorporated a

common, if coded message that while British imperialism was focused on the wider world, Spanish ambitions aimed at the conquest of mainland Europe and possibly North America. The theme is best portrayed in the opening scene of *The Sea Hawk* in which Montagu Love, as Philip II, surveys a map of the world, noting that the Spanish are: 'invincible everywhere but on our own doorstep: only Northern Europe holds out against us'. Both Spain and England are highlighted on the map, but most significantly, when we move to a wide shot, the most noticeable area is not, as we might reasonably expect of Spanish cartography, Southern America or Southern Europe, but quite clearly North America, offering an almost subliminal message about the current Nazi threat.

It is also important to point to the more subtle ways in which the Spanish are characterized, which is far from implacably evil. In *Fire Over England* the need for Olivier's Michael Ingolby to sing while in Spain may carry suggestions of effeminacy and in *The Sea Hawk* we see an unkempt Spanish captain devouring a meal that connects with common stereotypes of Mexicans. However, Ingolby is aided by Spaniards, including a friend of his father and his daughter. The situation in *The Sea Hawk* is even more interesting where the major love interest is a Spanish noblewoman and her uncle, the ambassador to England, played by Claude Rains, is clearly sympathetic, if not towards the couple, then certainly towards his niece's dilemma. Even the obvious villains are limited in their evil. Philip II is represented in a very restrained way at the beginning of *The Sea Hawk* and Raymond Massey as Philip in *Fire Over England*, who we are told rules 'by force and fear', with much more time on screen, and the undoubted ability to be menacing, comes across as fervently Catholic but is best described as lugubrious, rather than megalomaniac. Antagonists like Captain Lopez, played by Gilbert Roland, who is Flynn's action counterpart in much of *The Sea Hawk,* are not simply stereotypical in their evil and give a sense of following their duty or of being crossed in love. Notably Lopez waits to be the last man to leave his sinking ship and his jump to safety is not accompanied by the traditional laughter of the crew which often marks a villain as a buffoon in a Hollywood film of this period. The key to attitudes here may be given in Flora Robson's final speech as Elizabeth I where she states that, 'we have no quarrel with the people of Spain or of any other country'. If we follow the analogy through, this may indicate a hope that the German population is merely being misled, or forced to follow, but cynically we could observe that only a foolhardy film distributor would have a quarrel with any nation that included potential ticket buyers.

Much more savage is the treatment of the English traitors who are essential to the plots of both films. In *The Sea Hawk* it is not Lopez who meets Flynn's character in the final duel, but Henry Daniell as the treacherous Lord Wolfingham. In *Fire Over England* a suitably shifty (and uncredited) James Mason as Sir Hillary Vane in the pay of the Spanish, is killed off in the first reel so that Olivier's Ingolby can impersonate him. In the more sedentary climax, five more traitors are caught in an assassination plot and denounced by the queen. Fascinatingly, against any form of logic in the plot, Flora Robson gives them to Ingolby to help in his fight against the Armada. Perhaps the analogy here is not to fifth columnists, but to appeasers, and there are evidently hopes that national unity may prevail. In as much as these films could shape popular perceptions about the Spanish, although they certainly fed from the Black Legend, they did little to intensify or extend it. Rather they may have helped it decline as they provided very English or American Spaniards with which the audience might well feel some sympathy.

Imperial Destiny and Sea Power

A large part of Korda's rationale in producing *Fire Over England* was to distribute it to both British and American audiences, thus emulating his greatest success with *The Private Life of Henry VIII* (1933), but also scoring a double propaganda victory by influencing sympathies on both sides of the Atlantic. For these reasons *Fire Over England* presents a rather restrained version of British national destiny. Notably Robson's Tilbury speech is couched much more in terms of defence than of the implications of conquest, as she swears that England will fight 'to the last ship and the last man'. This may have been aided by the fact that the multinational team that produced the film was headed by an American director, William K. Howard, and Korda's choice here may reflect an attempt to produce a film that would be acceptable to American audiences.

When we turn to *The Sea Hawk*, the use of the idea of national destiny is, against reasonable expectations, pushed very much to the fore. The central debate at the court throughout the film is whether England should build a navy that will enable it resist Spain, but by so doing antagonize Philip II and provoke attack. This theme of appeasement is introduced as soon as we encounter Elizabeth I and crops up perennially until the final scene. It is here, in the full version of the film that this argument suddenly merges into a statement of British destiny as Robson declares her intention to build 'a navy foremost in the world, not just in our time, but for generations to come'. The point was then underlined as the masts of the English galleons fade into the funnels of modern ships. This statement is somewhat ironic, since it is clear to historians that Britain had begun to lose this role and the war itself would demonstrate that she could no longer compete with America in this respect. What may be intended here, however, is a closer analogy with the need to build up American naval forces in the face of the potential Japanese threat.[13]

In addition, modern historians cannot see the Armada in such threatening terms. As Geoffrey Parker has suggested, the veteran Spanish *tercios* from the Netherlands would have had a considerable advantage over the militia-based armies of England, if not in numbers then at least in fighting ability, once they had landed, and in Alexander Farnese, the Duke of Parma, they were led by perhaps the greatest general of the age.[14] The problem was that landing was incredibly unlikely. Even the Spanish acknowledged this, setting sail, as one commander put it, 'in confident hope of a miracle'.[15] What was also not apparent is that the British in World War II were also relatively safe from direct military invasion. Despite the Blitz and Battle of Britain, not only did they retain superiority at sea, but eventually achieved one in the air. We now know that Hitler had no developed plans for invasion and no real interest in conquering Britain. Thus the situations in 1588 and the mid-twentieth century were similar in ways of which the filmmakers were unaware.

National Myth and Identity

The two films are guilty of considerable historical licence, even by the standards of what was known of the Tudor period by the 1930s and 1940s, but fall somewhere between the categories outlined by Natalie Zemon Davis of those based on documented persons and movements and those that deal with fictional characters in a clearly historical context.[16] Much of the historical licence comes from the tension between the use of historical and fictional events and persons, in particular the employment of a surrogate or composite figure that embodies many of the characteristics of the archetype of the 'Elizabethan sea dog'. Quite where the term originated is unclear, but it owed something of its currency to William Wood's

book of 1918, which used the phrase as its title and enthused about
Elizabethan captains, pointing in particular to their part in the origins
of North America and underlining the model of a loyal, resourceful
and relentlessly fearless leader.[17] The sea dogs included John Hawkins,
a Plymouth merchant who was the first Englishman to threaten the
Spanish monopoly over the New World slave trade in a series of
expeditions from 1563, but which cumulated in the disaster of a surprise attack by the Spanish at San Juan de Ulúa in 1568, from which
Hawkins reached England with only 1 ship and 20 men. Despite this
setback he became treasurer and controller of the English navy and is
usually credited with having built up English naval forces to a point
that made victory in 1588 possible, resulting in a knighthood after
the Armada campaign. This group also included Sir Walter Ralegh,
whose attempts at establishing colonies in North America and finding the fabled city of El Dorado both ended in failure, and eventually
resulted in his execution in 1613. Martin Frobisher's reputation largely
centres on his expeditions to find a north-west passage to the Orient
which resulted in the exploration of what is now the coast of Canada
in 1576 and 1577, but which brought very few financial or practical
gains. He participated in the successful expedition to the West Indies
in 1585 and was knighted for his part in the events of 1588. Unquestionably, the leading figure among the English sea dogs was Francis
Drake, a cousin of Hawkins and one of the few survivors of the 1568
debacle. This event coloured his attitude to the Spanish and marked a
shift to a far more aggressive policy. Drake led a series of expeditions
which sacked Spanish towns and shipping. In 1577 he led the first
English voyage to navigate the Straits of Magellan and circumnavigate
the globe, resulting in his knighthood. His 1587 attack on Cadiz was
a serious blow to Spanish pride and preparations for the Armada, and
although only one of three vice-admirals in the Armada campaign of
1588 he has often received the lion's share of credit for its defeat.

Drake's reputation was already cemented in his lifetime by Richard
Hakluyt's publication in 1589 of his *Principal Navigations, Voyages,
Traffiques and Discoveries of the English Nation,* which included a narrative of Drake's 1577 circumnavigation based on the notes of the *Golden
Hind*'s preacher, Francis Fletcher. The account of another eyewitness
Francis Pretty was published in 1580 and Fletcher's whole work was
subsequently published as *The World Encompassed* in 1630.[18] It seems
that Drake's reputation remained high in the subsequent centuries, but
reached its apogee in the late nineteenth century with works of popular fiction including Charles Kingsley's *Westward Ho!* and Sir Henry

Newbolt's poem *Drake's Drum*.[19] On the scholarly side this view is exemplified by Sir Julian Corbett's two-volume study of *Drake and the Tudor Navy* published in 1899.[20] Inevitably, in the general mood of a post-colonial world more recent works have been less generous, pointing to the immorality of piracy and slave trading which were part and parcel of the sea dogs' history.[21] The obvious geographical link between the modern United States and particularly Drake (resulting in considerable spilt ink over which bits of the American coastline he visited), has long helped in a process of naturalization of the sea dogs as models for American entrepreneurship. As Dobson and Watson have pointed out, despite the savaging that Drake has received as a heroic figure in recent years, his image in particular, and that of the sea dogs in general, continues to be linked to the idea of Elizabeth as a sort of managing director over enterprising freebooters that still appeals on Wall Street.[22]

In more general terms there has been a diversion in attitudes to the emerging naval power of England in the sixteenth century. David Loades retains a more optimistic attitude, suggesting that the Tudor period saw a key change in attitudes and organization. In contrast authors such as N. A. M. Rodger tend to see development in the era as only part of a long, protracted and faltering process.[23] The idea that the sea dogs had an immense superiority to the Spanish, that they were always successful and that this directly contributed to victory in the Armada campaign has all been abandoned for some time, although these powerful myths often resurface in popular history and depictions of the past.[24] Although able to prey on merchant shipping, despite some undeniable advantages in ship design in the relatively small numbers of English 'race-built galleons', which were faster and easier to manoeuvre, they were largely unable to take on and defeat Spanish warships when such confrontations occurred, as was to become obvious in the Armada campaign.

The use of the sea dogs also speaks to the class ideologies of mid-twentieth-century Britain and America. As the proliferation of knighthoods and acquiring of fortunes indicates, the sea dogs can also be seen as self-made men, and at the time were often regarded as parvenus, thus providing a prototype of the English middle class. It is not hard to see Ingolby as embodying the positive characteristics seen in other heroes of Korda-backed films, including the most famous homage to the white man's burden, *Sanders of the River* (1935), whose opening titles eulogize the 'handful of white men whose everyday work is an unsung saga of courage and efficiency'. Thus *Fire Over*

England subtly pours an historical archetype into the mould of a particular sort of twentieth-century Englishman.

Flynn presented a more problematic image to the English class system. His mixture of Irish ancestry, Australian birth, English upbringing and long-term residence in the USA, made him extremely difficult to place, contributed much to the appeal of his on-screen persona and to his ability to sell the role of aristocrats such as Robin of Loxley or the Earl of Essex to an American audience as an everyman. There is an obvious irony in Flynn's films that he often played an Englishman who combated those that were, if anything, more English than he, even if, like Claude Rains, they were playing the Spanish. Flynn's character is also more morally ambiguous than that played by Olivier. While exhibiting loyalty and generosity to his men and even his victims (at least the attractive ones) he is a strict disciplinarian, imprisoning a sailor in irons for excessive bravery. His speech to a potential recruit (and spy), who asks about the nature of their mission, elevates national survival to a justification for total obedience. Finally, when all is said and done, Geoffrey Thorpe is something that Michael Ingolby is not, a pirate. Thorpe's first act is an attack on the ship of a power with which England is not even at war and which contains a duly appointed ambassador. This again is justified in terms of national interest, but the line that 'Spain is at war with everyone' is hardly convincing and objectively this remains clearly an illegal act. Part of this may be a useful plot device to make mistrust of Thorpe by Brenda Marshall's Dona Maria Alvarez de Cordoba credible, and even to allow us to see him through her eyes. While this makes the plot less justifiable it does allow Flynn to play up his screen persona as a lovable rogue and provided audiences, particularly American audiences, with an outsider with whom they could sympathize. What is more interesting is that, in playing to these characteristics, Flynn was being more true to the nature of English sea captains who had, to put it mildly, a difficult moral record.

The Impact of the Films

How effective then were these two films in projecting images of Tudor England and therefore contributing to the willingness to fight among the general populations of Britain and America? The first observation must be that both films did good business at the box office. *Fire Over England* filled movie theatres in Britain, probably coming second only to *Victoria the Great* in 1937.[25] In the five Mass Observation

Exercises that were carried out between 1939 and 1945, the film was singled out for praise a number of times and only once treated negatively. Even here Flora Robson was described as giving 'a brilliant performance'.[26] It premiered in Los Angeles (the first British film to do so) in January 1937 and was distributed in America through United Artists. The impact within the American film industry may have been greater than with the public. Thanks to their performances in this film, Laurence Olivier earned his part in *Wuthering Heights* (1939) and Vivien Leigh her opportunity to audition for the coveted role of Scarlett O'Hara in *Gone with the Wind* (1939). Flora Robson also benefited, with her move to America and, fairly obviously, the invitation to reprise her role in *The Sea Hawk*, facilitated by the success of *Fire Over England*.[27]

The Sea Hawk managed better box-office returns, which is hardly surprising given the status of its star at the time. It cost a very high $1,701,000 to make, but earned $2,678,000, of which $1,631,000 (61 per cent) came from the domestic market. This made it the highest-grossing film of the year for Warner Brothers, fourth in total earnings out of the studio's cycle of six 'Merrie England' films, but second only to *The Adventures of Robin Hood* in the American market.[28] This domestic success was probably aided by the action/adventure status of the film, which made it stand out above the worthy and more explicit pieces of anti-Nazi propaganda of the same year, such as *The Mortal Storm, Four Sons* and *The Man I Married* (aka.*I Married a Nazi*). It also helped it completely dodge the attentions of the Hays Office, which attempted to enforce the neutrality laws and industry policy of isolationism at this time; notably the film was never cited in the Congressional inquiry into propaganda of 1941.[29]

In the period before Pearl Harbour there was an understandable reluctance in America to alienate audiences either at home or abroad. The result was a tendency not to stress the allegorical aspects of these films in publicity. When *Fire Over England* had been released in Britain the link was explicit, as a story in the pressbook quoted co-producer Erich Pommer's emphasis on the 'extraordinary parallel' between Britain's situation in the 1580s and the end of the 1930s. In contrast, the pressbook used for the release in the USA focused on the historical authenticity, the costumes, sea battles and pageantry. Partly as a result, American press stories concerning the film said almost nothing about its relationship to the events that were unfolding in Europe.[30]

Given the climate in America at this time it is surprising that the ending of *The Sea Hawk* was, as originally intended, if anything much stronger in its drawing of parallels with current events. After Flynn's Captain Thorpe has been knighted, he and the other actors virtually disappear from the screen to allow Flora Robson to provide an epilogue. Her call for her subjects to 'prepare for a war that none of us wants' is clearly not aimed at the characters around her. Her comment that, 'when the ruthless ambition of a man threatens to engulf the world', cannot be fitted with the aging and sedentary Philip of Spain, whom we have not glimpsed, except in a portrait, since the opening scene. There can be little doubt that the idea that 'it becomes the solemn obligation of all free men to affirm that the earth belongs not to one man, but to all men, and that freedom is the deed and title to the soil on which we exist', would be seriously at odds with an England about to begin an imperial adventure, and was clearly calculated to appeal to a nation for which freedom is a constitutional imperative and who might be encouraged to take on a dangerous dictator. However, this version was never seen by American and neutral audiences. Instead Warner Brothers, perhaps fearful of another battle with the Hays Office, perhaps concerned about box-office receipts, provided a different cut for domestic and neutral distribution, in which the film fades out after Thorpe has been knighted and the fleet is seen setting out to battle the Armada.[31]

It is important to note that *The Sea Hawk* was only one of a staggering 150 Hollywood films about Britain or British subjects made between 1939 and 1945.[32] Gore Vidal recalls of this period that British-made and -inspired films were a key element in emphasizing a special affinity between Americans and Britain. They helped give life to the image of a small, brave, island nation, striving to fight for liberty against the threat of dictatorship. In his words, 'on our screens, in the thirties, it seemed as if the only country on earth was England, and there were no great personages who were not English, or impersonated by English actors . . . the English kept up a propaganda barrage that was to permeate our entire culture, with all sorts of unexpected results. Since the movies were by now the principal means of getting swiftly to the masses, Hollywood was subtly and not so subtly influenced by British propagandists'.[33]

This was all the more notable as it is clear that the fit between the Black Legend and the Nazis was difficult territory; that this was the very point at which the imperial destiny of Britain was being challenged from both within and without; that the British sea power that these films celebrated was coming to an end; and that the class system in Britain was already undergoing fundamental change. Nevertheless, both films managed to produce something that was able to connect these myths and images with the contemporary world. In many ways it was these difficulties and complexities that helped those involved in the production of these films create something that may well have had more impact than the overt propaganda that would dominate film-making in the war years and would achieve what they seem largely failed to do, to help prepare the English-speaking peoples for arguably their greatest challenge.

Suggestions for Further Reading

Angus Konstam, *Elizabethan Sea Dogs* (London, 2000).
Colin Martin and Geoffrey Parker, *The Spanish Armada* (London, 1988).
Garrett Mattingly, *The Defeat of the Spanish Armada* (London, 1959).
John Sugden, *Sir Francis Drake* (New York, 1990).

11

Elizabeth: The Golden Age: A Sign of the Times?

Vivienne Westbrook

Representations of Elizabeth on film, from Sarah Bernhardt's 1912 performance in *The Loves of the Queen* through to Cate Blanchett's 1998 performance in *Elizabeth*, directed by Shekhar Kapur, have tended to focus on her primarily as a queen of hearts forced to rule with the stomach of a king. Thomas Betteridge has suggested that these films were not so intent on reproducing a historical queen as her myth, and have merely reproduced much of what can already be found in earlier representations of her.[1] *Elizabeth: The Golden Age* can also be accused of following tradition in representing her as a woman torn between love and duty, but Kapur makes some bold departures from that tradition in an attempt to create a queen not of an age but for our times.

Kapur's 1998 *Elizabeth* was set in the context of the Marian martyr-doms. Elizabeth herself faced execution, fell in love, was betrayed and as a result made a sacrifice that she thought would ensure her stability as the Virgin Queen of England. Dramatically it had all the right ingredients for a thrilling 2 hours. The sequel necessarily turned the first film into the back story. In *Elizabeth: The Golden Age* the elaborate red wig has now replaced Elizabeth's natural red hair to become part of the fabric of her public persona through which she conveys the power and the glory of England to the world. Inside this costume of state is a woman with ordinary desires and needs that threaten to fracture the iconic status that she has achieved.

Elizabeth won no fewer than 29 international awards. It established Kapur as a major new directing talent and launched the international career of Cate Blanchett. Anticipated for almost a decade, the sequel, *Elizabeth: The Golden Age* opened in the USA in October and in the UK in November 2007. With twice the amount of money invested and the return of much of the star cast, the film promised to be every bit as good as the last with spectacular Armada scenes and a steamy romance between Elizabeth, played by Cate Blanchett, and Sir Walter Ralegh, played by Clive Owen. When the film opened it was received with derision. It took $8,073,965 at the box office in the USA in the first week, but by the fourth week it had not even doubled its first week's takings and was fast slipping down the American charts. In England it took $4,614,317 in its first week and was in the number one box-office spot. By the fourth week it had managed to accumulate $9,830,016 but had already slipped to ninth position.[2]

Throughout the making of this film Shekhar Kapur set up a website through which he could answer questions from his fans and share his thoughts and aspirations for not just this film but his planned trilogy. In his diary entry of 22 May 2007, Kapur explained:

> Elizabeth was about Power. Survival in the context of Power. Love and Betrayal in the context of Power. And the trade off between the ruthlessness that is essential to gaining Power, against innocence, love, trust and joyfulness.

> Golden Age, on the other hand is about Immortality. It is about absolute Power and the aspiring to Divinity. To go beyond the ordinary and to be Divine. Almost immortal. It is about Elizabeth becoming the Divine, the Immortal being she is perceived as today.

> The third, when everyone is ready to do it, will be about Mortality. How do you face Mortality when you have been Divine? When you have been Immortal? Elizabeth, when she knew that her time was near, tried to impose her will upon Death itself. She stood for 12 hours (a tiny exaggeration I think!) refusing to lie down, knowing that if she did, the Gods would spirit her away.[3]

In an interview with Stephen Moss, Kapur explained that whilst the Elizabeth of his first film was based on Indira Gandhi, the Elizabeth of the second film was based on Princess Diana. In the first film he wanted to show how 'Virginity is a political statement', whilst in this second film he wanted to treat 'the difficulty of being a living icon'. Kapur added, 'If you can't see our own times and lives in a film ... there's no reason to make it.'[4]

Since it is Kapur's aim to make film relevant to our own times
it is useful to explore some of the ways in which he tries to
achieve this relevance. In both *Elizabeth* and *Elizabeth: The Golden
Age* Kapur employs opening caption sequences to establish the film
within an historical context. In *Elizabeth*, for instance, the caption sequence reads: 'England 1554 ... Henry VIII is dead ... The
country is divided ... Catholic against Protestant ... Henry's eldest
daughter Mary, a fervent Catholic, is queen ... She is childless ... The
Catholics' greatest fear is the succession of Mary's Protestant half-
sister ... Elizabeth.' These gobbets are already an uneasy marriage of
fact and fiction. Yes, Henry was certainly dead in 1554, but the
caption elides Henry's death with Mary's accession, thereby eras-
ing the Protestant reign of Henry's only son Edward VI. In spite
of her Catholic affiliation, Mary's right to the throne, over that of
the Protestant Lady Jane Grey, daughter-in-law of the ambitious John
Dudley, Duke of Northumberland, was supported by some prominent
Protestants.

Immediately following the captions a picture sequence depicts
handcuffs, head-shaving and the martyrdom of the Protestant bishops, Latimer and Ridley, together with an anonymous woman. But in
1554 no one was being burned for their faith, as Protestant Edwardian legislation had not yet been repealed. The first martyr of Mary's
reign to be publicly burned at Smithfield was the preacher and editor of the Matthew's Bible, John Rogers, but not until 4 February
1555.

In *Elizabeth: The Golden Age* the opening caption sequence similarly attempts to establish it as an historical film: 'A world divided by
religious hatred. The new Protestant faith is spreading ... The most
powerful ruler in Christendom, Philip of Spain, has sworn to return
all Europe to the Catholic Faith ... Only England stands in his way:
a weak impoverished nation ruled by a woman ... Philip prepares to
obey the will of his God'. Kapur inserts images of Philip praying in the
Escorial Palace before the caption sequence concludes with 'Escorial
Palace, Spain, 1585'. Interestingly, the date at which the film begins is
reserved for the final caption, suggesting that this war has been in process for some time already. The presence of the Spanish ambassador at
Elizabeth's court is therefore rendered problematic. If, in the caption
sequence to *Elizabeth,* the country was divided between Catholics and
Protestants, in *Elizabeth: The Golden Age* the problem has now esca-
lated somewhat. Religious hatred is now a global problem. Anyone
reading these captions as history will understand that Europe was at

this point in time the world, and that England was the last Protestant stronghold that had to be overthrown to make the world Catholic once more! This is not virtual history in the sense that the film is a more advanced way of representing history to the twenty-first century than writing books and putting pictures in them: this is virtual in the sense that it makes tenuous claims to being fact whilst paying its chief respects to fiction. Put more simply, what is presented as fact is, in fact, fiction.

Philip French suggested that Kapur's *Elizabeth* and *Elizabeth: The Golden Age* is more indebted to *The Godfather* than to history, which he considered to have been elided and truncated for the sake of drama. He argued that as in the case of *The Sea Hawk* (1940), in which the Spanish threat of 1588 is made to serve the needs of the moment, the Spanish are clearly identified with Nazi Germany, so: 'In the new film the Catholic fundamentalists in Spain and their exploitation of co-religionists in England reflect the current threat of Islamic fundamentalism.'[5] He hastened to point out that in this film Elizabeth refuses to punish her people for their religion, only for their actions against her and her realm. Of course, officially, this was Elizabeth's stance, although the increasing legislation throughout the 1580s that almost automatically made Jesuits traitors came alarmingly close to punishing people for their religious beliefs.

Both Mary Stuart and Philip II are tangible Catholic threats to Elizabeth's Protestant England, but Kapur exploits the post-9/11 fear of the unseen enemy, the network of infiltrators who are being hosted by the country they hope to ruin. The film clearly depicts a network of assassins who are able to reach the queen in spite of the security she has in place. The attempt on her life whilst at prayer in St Paul's is a surprise attack of the kind that cannot be intercepted. Elizabeth may understand this moment as a sign of her own invincibility, but we later learn from Walsingham that the gun simply wasn't loaded. Whilst this may be the equivalent of the suicide bomber who fails to press the trigger, it doesn't lessen the impact on the collective consciousness of a terrorist threat. However, the path to safety that depends on treating everyone as a potential threat is also the path that makes enemies of friends. The solution is as dangerous as the problem.

Roger Ebert complained that 'The film's screenplay, by Michael Hirst and William Nicholson, placed her [Elizabeth] in the center of history that is baldly simplified, shamelessly altered and pumped up with romance and action.' He suggested that this cavalier attitude to history ultimately undermined the capacity of audiences to 'get

involved in true historical drama, instead of recycled action clones'.[6]
For other reviewers, such as Stella Papamichael the history was irrelevant, and she advised her own readers to: 'Throw away the history
books and behold the majesty.'[7] In fact, Kapur has not done that himself. What he has done, in line with a great many adaptors of text for
film, is to take history as his starting point and reinvent it for a representative medium that works through images. A film is a story told in
pictures. What is odd about Kapur's approach is the way in which he
makes the audience's first and last experience of this film world that of
reading the screen like a 'virtual book'. Kapur's caption sequences capture audience interest in history, whilst presenting a fictional account
of it.

It is clear from the paratext which surrounded *Elizabeth: The Golden
Age* that those working on the film had researched the historical characters, settings and events, but due to reasons ranging from the desired
dramatic shape of the piece to the practicalities of securing still occupied buildings for the shooting, changes were knowingly made. The
impossibility of clearing the Thames for Elizabeth's barge shots meant
that they were actually shot on the River Cam and shots of the back
of St John's College were then used to superimpose shots of Elizabethan London. Kapur did not use CGI extensively, nor did he shoot
entirely on set at Shepperton. Instead he aspired to lend his film a
veneer of historical authenticity by shooting in locations that were
not merely sufficiently old-looking to suspend disbelief, but which
increased the dramatic impact of the scenes for which they were
used.

Kapur's audience will notice that he has a propensity to shoot in
cathedrals rather than the dark, panelled rooms in which much of the
business would have taken place. This enables him to get his crane
shots that at times reduce great monarchs to the size of insects – for
instance when Elizabeth is agonizing over the imminent execution of
Mary and we see her scurrying across the twelfth-century nave of Ely
Cathedral. In other scenes Ely Cathedral creates a context of grandeur
when Elizabeth needs it, as in the scene with Don Guerau, when she
promises 'I too can command the wind, sir. I have a hurricane in me
that will strip Spain bare, if you dare to try me!'[8] The more recent
Lady Chapel at Ely Cathedral, built 1321–1349, served as Elizabeth's
presence chamber in which she surveys the portraits of her would-be
suitors. Establishing Elizabeth as a viable marriage proposition and one
able to assure dynastic succession was an important part of the political game that she played with Europe. Justin Pollard, the historical

advisor for the film explained that the best way of communicating the marriage game was to squeeze the suitors into one scene:

> This involves compressing time, bringing together four suitors who were not, in fact, all suitable for marriage or considered at the same time. In truth they were not even all alive at the point in time this scene nominally takes place. But by this technique we can explain succinctly the range of Elizabeth's marriage options, the benefits and drawback they might bring, and demonstrate the increasing tension between the Queen and her ministers as the game dragged dangerously on.[9]

As Elizabeth prepares to meet the Armada, we see her first in a re-creation of the Map Room, Whitehall Palace, in a scene that is clearly an amalgamation of the Ditchley portrait (1592) by M. Gheeraerts the Younger and the Armada portrait (1588) by George Gower.[10] In the Ditchley portrait Elizabeth is depicted standing on a map of England and wears a string of pearls around her neck that reaches down to and below her waist to suggest her bodily purity. In the background the sun is coming through the clouds to dispel the storm, thereby endorsing Elizabeth's status as ruler by divine authority.[11] The Armada portrait (1588) by George Gower shows Elizabeth with her right hand on the globe pointing to America, whilst two paintings in the background depict moments in the war against the Spanish Armada, its threatening approach and its subsequent wrecking on coastal rocks. Elizabeth's virginal status is translated into political impregnability. Kapur amalgamates the political allegory of these portraits and adds a reference to the frontispiece of Dr John Dee's *General and Rare Memorials Pertayning to the Perfect Arte of Navigation* (1577), which Andrew and Catherine Belsey have described as 'a plea for the establishment of a British Empire'.[12] Clearly Kapur is keen to draw on the tradition of political representation, but the fact is that rather than dominating the picture, as she does in the portraits, here Elizabeth looks lost in the huge floor map with only a small replica of a ship – of state – to play with. We are suddenly reminded of the Elizabeth doll that has been dangling from the Infanta's hand since the opening scene.

Kapur manages to keep the threat of potential annihilation by Spain alive, even though the history books have spoiled any chances of a surprise ending being taken seriously. Elizabeth is indeed shown as weak and vulnerable in the planning stages of the defence against the Armada, but at Tilbury she is dressed in silver armour with a silver staff as she surveys her soldiers and fills their hearts with the fire to fight off the invaders. There is barely a line of resemblance to the speech that was later recorded as Elizabeth's Tilbury speech, and which was actually delivered after the defeat of the Armada at Gravelines. Hirst and Nicholson's substitute speech only demonstrates that English soldiers needed very little by way of verbal exhortation to fight for their queen. The fact that Elizabeth was 55 at Tilbury doesn't prevent Kapur from showing a fresh and feisty Elizabeth devoid of wrinkle or stain to further endorse the myth of her divinity. The ethical polarities that the film sets up are nowhere more apparent than during the apocalyptic battle between the forces of good and evil, in which Elizabeth is depicted in white light, and Philip crouches in the darkness of his private cell.

The exterior shots of the Escorial Palace were authentic, but the interior shots in which we observe Philip with Isabella were shot in Westminster Cathedral, the foundation stone of which was not laid until 29 June 1895. Philip's private moments with a candle were shot at Shepperton Studios. The attempt to invoke the monastic feel of Philip's private quarters of the Escorial Palace resulted rather in the evocation of a dark dungeon in which Philip had trapped himself.

Kapur cuts between Elizabeth at Tilbury and Philip in his palace so that when his candle is finally extinguished we are meant to feel that this is a divine judgement on the unjust claims of Spain to English soil. Indeed, in the aftermath of the defeat of the Armada, commemorative medals were issued which bore the inscription: 'Flavit et Dissipati Sunt' (He blew with His winds, and they were scattered).

Kapur does not emphasize Elizabeth's Protestant identity in the film, even whilst he portrays the Catholics as extremist conspirators. Catholicism becomes a convenient cover for terrorists who actually want power for themselves. Elizabeth's war with Spain and the execution of Mary Stuart are both understood in terms of defensive rather than aggressive actions. When Elizabeth challenges Don Guerau with the discovery of the Babington plot to overthrow her, he responds by accusing Elizabeth of bringing war upon herself by encouraging piracy against Philip's Spanish ships. He might have added to piracy, Elizabeth's refusal to marry Philip in 1559, the imprisonment of the Catholic Mary Queen of Scots, Elizabeth's support of the Dutch revolt, secretly in 1572 and openly in 1585, or, indeed, the repeated failures of his attempts to remove Elizabeth by more covert means. He doesn't mention her religion and she only banishes him when he suggests that the Virgin is a whore. In fact Kapur's Elizabeth shows little interest in the harvests either from Spanish ships or the New

World. Even when Ralegh informs her that he has stamped her Virgin name on his colony Elizabeth seems unimpressed. In this way Kapur exonerates her from the piracy and plundering of which her own subjects are accused, but from which she inevitably benefits. Elizabeth is much more interested, it seems, in the stories that Walter Ralegh has brought back from the New World, because they represent freedom.

In an interesting deflection, Kapur does show the devastation of the natural landscape, but this is presented as another sign of Philip II's evil. In a scene intended to identify Philip with the evil wizard Saruman in *The Lord of the Rings*, the king of Spain hacks down his forests to supply the wood for the building of the Armada that is destined for England. He complains to Robert Reston, a Jesuit, that 'Every tree that falls hurts me. I lose a part of myself.' Philip establishes himself as a sacrificial victim and the potential saviour of England. 'I sacrifice my country's forests to save the souls of a lost nation.' Whilst the trunks are hauled away for shipbuilding, the roots and branches are burned. Reston gazes excitedly on: 'The light of purifying fire.' We next see Reston in a London armourer's shop. Savage loads his newly purchased pistol for the assassination of Elizabeth, Reston begs the armourer's forgiveness and then snaps his neck. Jesuits are thereby depicted as a most violent and fanatical organization at the service of Philip.

Elizabeth's encounters with Ralegh, Walsingham and John Dee reveal three aspects of her character: as a desiring woman, a politician and as iron-willed in having forged such strength out of weakness. Kapur emphasizes the contrast between Mary's disappointment upon hearing that the plot to kill Elizabeth has failed with Elizabeth's anguish over signing Mary's death warrant and her subsequent agony at the moment of Mary's execution. To divert the attention from an historically intriguing Mary, Kapur ultimately makes that relationship about Elizabeth's own political stability. Elizabeth is reminded, as if she needed to be, 'you kill a queen, all queens are mortal'. Even her relationship with Mary, it turns out, is actually just another facet of the complex relationship she is having with herself.

Instead of shooting Mary's final days at a Fotheringhay Castle (the thirteenth-century Eilean Donan Castle for the purposes of the film since Fortheringhay Castle was razed in 1627), Kapur decided to move back to Chartley; the actual shooting location was Hatfield House, Hertfordshire. Kapur wanted to show the contrast between the conditions of her captivity in the earlier stages of the film with those in later scenes. The audience's sympathy is drawn toward Mary as she

is stripped of her earthly possessions. Kapur encourages us to agree
with Mary's protestations that she should command the same respect
as Elizabeth, but Mary had invited scandal, won the reproach of the
Scottish nobles and been forced to abdicate to secure her son's succession. Although historically shame attended Mary's life and did not stop
in the moment of her leaving it, Kapur preferred to leave out the double chop of the axe that was necessary to sever her head, the incident of
the little dog that ran from under her skirt, the wig that separated from
the head when the executioner held it up or, indeed, the twitching
corpse.[13] Kapur thereby lends a dignified fiction to Mary's departure
which curiously undermines Elizabeth whilst preserving the myth of
the divinity of queenship.

   The energetic, wily, darkly sexual, spymaster of *Elizabeth* is here old
Walsingham the bungler and the butt of Elizabeth's albeit understandable frustration. In almost every scene with her he is overpowered and
undermined. He sacrifices his health, his happiness, and even his fictitious, Catholic brother, in his tireless duty to an ungrateful queen.
The Long Gallery at Hatfield House became Walsingham's house in
the film. Maps, letters, reports and mirrors were placed in his study
to create the flavour of authenticity. Walsingham's account book was
recreated in as near as possible a hand to his own in an endeavour to
demonstrate the careful attention to the minutiae of history, a history
that is conveniently ignored in the creation of a brother for extra dramatic effect. Kapur seems to be in a constant struggle with himself
over the desire for history and the dramatic bonus of lying about it.

   Given the historical reality of Tudor torture chambers and the modern appetite for violence as entertainment, the torture sequences were
hardly shocking. Apparently, Catholics were prepared to give it all
up for a few pokes with a torch and the loss of body hair. This, of
course, contributed to the reinforcement of the idea of terrorism as
the last resort of cowards. Kapur juxtaposes the leniency of the queen
to terrorists compared to what they have in store for her. In this exploration of toleration versus fundamentalism, there can be no doubt
that Elizabeth is being set up as the icon of toleration, always at a
safe distance from Walsingham and his men who are doing the dirty
job of arresting, torturing and murdering the Catholic plotters in her
name. This becomes dramatically more interesting when even Bess
Throckmorton, the queen's Maid of Honour, is placed under suspicion because of her cousin's involvement in a plot against Elizabeth. By
foregrounding the role of Francis Throckmorton in the film in what is

an amalgamation of plots against Elizabeth, Kapur further emphasizes the dangers of assuming that the threat is external.

Walsingham, too, is presented with a dramatic conflict when he is faced with the choice of fidelity to the queen and fidelity to his own blood. Although showing Walsingham within his domestic arena adds a human dimension to his character, it also shows him compromising the integrity on which Elizabeth must rely for the safety of her realm, once again drawing attention to the fragility of security. Whilst Walsingham apparently has no qualms about executing all of the Catholic plotters he doesn't know, he decides to risk the safety of the queen and to spare his own brother.

Alison Weir objected most strongly to the way in which Ralegh was given prominence in this film whilst more significant characters in Elizabeth's court were pushed into the wings: 'Where is William Cecil, Lord Burghley, Elizabeth's chief minister? Where is Sir Francis Drake, vice-admiral with the English fleet?'[14] William Cecil was an invaluable advisor to Elizabeth throughout her reign, occupying the roles of Secretary of State and subsequently Lord High Treasurer, but Cecil was not best known for his tolerant attitude in matters of religion, believing as he did that people could not be divided in the service of God and united in the service of their country. This stance is, of course, unhelpful to the broader aim of the film which is to promote toleration over and above religious fundamentalism. Hirst and Nicholson have instead elided his role at Elizabeth's court with that of Walsingham's, as not only her chief advisor but an active agent against the terrorist threats that surround her. The screenwriters make the same elisions with Francis Drake and Walter Ralegh. We know that Ralegh had no role in the defence of England against the Spanish Armada, whilst Drake was second-in-command of the fleet. Although Drake earned a heroic reputation in England for his sea voyages, there were also a number of associations that would later be an encumbrance to his wider popularity, not least of all the fact that he was instrumental in the English slave trade. When looking for an Elizabethan hero for the twenty-first century Ralegh emerges as the likeliest choice not because of what he did, but because of what he did not do. Interestingly, Drake makes the briefest of appearances so that we don't confuse the two, in spite of the fact that Ralegh is doing his job. In the realm of fiction more noble and remarkable acts can always be attributed to him – such as the winning of Elizabeth's heart and the war against the Armada. Lord Charles Howard of Effingham actually led the attack, and had to beg Elizabeth for money to pay his starving and sick men afterwards.

Whilst there were, undeniably, more important figures at Elizabeth's court than Sir Walter Ralegh, he was not an insignificant individual. He was many things to many people: a courtier, knight, statesman, adventurer, sailor, poet and historian.[15] He had powerful friends and powerful enemies, too, which in what was undeniably a patronage culture was reflected in his shifting fortunes. Robert Naunton's *Fragmenta Regalia* (1644) described Ralegh as:

> a handsome and well-compacted person, a strong natural wit, and a better judgement, with a cold and plausible tongue whereby he could set out his parts to the best advantage, and to these he had the adjuncts of some general learning, which by diligence he enforced to a great augmentation, and perfection; for he was an indefatigable Reader, whether by Sea or Land, and none of the least observers both of men, and the times . . . [16]

Kapur gives prominence to Ralegh as a figure at Elizabeth's court, but it is in order to create a dramatic choice for Elizabeth. There is no attempt to create the charismatic character that was able to perform any role asked of him.

The story of Sir Walter laying down his 'cape' so that Elizabeth could avoid splashing her shoes does not occupy any firm ground in history; the anecdote being recorded for the first time by Thomas Fuller in 1663. However, its lack of historical status has not hindered the cape from becoming the synecdoche of Ralegh the courtier in subsequent representations of him throughout history and in every available representational medium. Even in his most recent memorial by Vivien Mallock, which now occupies a space in East Budleigh, Ralegh can be identified at a distance by his cape. That Kapur should choose to introduce Ralegh to his audience with the cape is hardly surprising, but he does it in such a way as to reinforce an underlying theme of the terrorist threat as ever present.

Because of the proximity of Ralegh's cape to the queen, it is interpreted as an assassination attempt, albeit with a weapon of last resort. Ralegh explains: 'a puddle in the way, majesty' which Elizabeth responds to with incredulity: 'a puddle'. She steps over it and continues into chapel, where she again muses: 'a puddle'! What seems insignificant turns out to be highly significant in the turning of Ralegh's fortunes, for with this unlikely introduction Ralegh is admitted to Elizabeth's court bearing tobacco, potatoes, and a couple of natives, Wanchese and Manteo, from the newly named Virginia.

With the help of a passing zebra, which obviously hasn't got off the same boat, the natives must do all of the work of evoking the exoticism of 'other worlds' in the film. The fact that Ralegh never actually went to Virginia, and introduced neither the potato nor tobacco to England, is irrelevant in the context of the film. Kapur's desire is only to appropriate the popular image of Ralegh for his filmic audience. In assigning the victory of the Armada to Sir Walter Ralegh, rather than the hurricane which wrecked many of the ships off the coast of Ireland, Kapur foregrounds Ralegh's role over what was at the time perceived to be God's role in the protection of England.

Whilst promoting an account of Ralegh that is not historically true, the film does however, contribute to the myth of Ralegh that has a history of its own within cultural representation. Ralegh's rebellious nature became translated over time into heroic resistance. By the early eighteenth century he was already assuming the role of national hero in plays such as George Sewell's *The Tragedy of Sir Walter Rawleigh* (1719) in which Sewell elides the religious with the nationalist spirit in his portrayal of Ralegh as 'an English Martyr'. It was as a 'valiant soldier and able statesman' that Ralegh was remembered in the Temple of British Worthies at Stowe School in 1735 between the statues of King William III and Sir Francis Drake. In the monumentalizing nineteenth century Ralegh continued to inspire the heroic models for every form of cultural representation from boys' adventure stories to historical paintings. One of the more famous of these paintings is Millais' 'The Boyhood of Ralegh' (1870), where, defined in terms of time and tide, the eternal storyteller, a cultural bridge between the Old World and the New in whom is seeded a vision of empire that would only be realized in Victoria's reign, Ralegh promises to be continually recycled in representations of England's greatness. In the great American industry of the twentieth century, the Film Business, Ralegh was not without a role in films that featured Elizabeth and her court, such as Michael Curtiz's *The Private Lives of Elizabeth and Essex* (1939), Walter Forde's *Time Flies* (1944) and Henry Koster's *The Virgin Queen* (1955). In the latter film especially, Michael Dobson and Nicola J. Watson note the way in which Ralegh represents the 'acceptable American face of Elizabeth, that which supersedes the obsolete Old World and exports all that is most important, enduring, and potent of Elizabethanism to become Americanness.'[17] In *Elizabeth: The Golden Age* Kapur continues to represent Ralegh in this way, whilst accommodating his broader theme of terrorist threat.

As Elizabeth sits in her private quarters in some despair surrounded by crumpled paper she takes out 'that same letter' that she resorts to in her 'weaker' moments. In spite of his numerous writings on a wide range of subjects Ralegh's letter to Elizabeth is the only reference to Ralegh as a writer in the film.[18] As Elizabeth and Ralegh sit in the fireplace, in the oddest of filmic references to *The Private Lives of Elizabeth and Essex*, she asks him to 'do something' for her that she hasn't known in a long time, 'something not to be spoken of afterwards'. Kapur teases his audience with the prospect of a love affair. Even in *Elizabeth* Kapur didn't show Robert Dudley and Elizabeth in bed after she had 'become a Virgin'; Dudley's betrayal of her works dramatically toward her decision to become one.[19] Kapur settles for a kiss, as Elizabeth must.

As the unholy triangle of Elizabeth, Ralegh and Bess crumbles, Elizabeth becomes hysterical, beating the newly married and pregnant Bess in plain sight of Walsingham and Ralegh. An increasingly annoying and feeble Walsingham shouts 'mercy' like a reluctant referee from the corner, and even Ralegh is unable to save his wife. With all of the dispassionate disappointment of a headmaster to a schoolboy he merely reproaches Elizabeth: 'This is not the queen I love and serve'. Although the romantic triangle was unhistorical, Elizabeth's violent reaction to the news of the unauthorized marriage of Bess and Ralegh was not. Ralegh's son was born on 29 March 1592 and kept secret, as Mark Nicholls documents:

> On 27 April Bess returned to court, taking up her duties as a maid of honour, still trying to hide the facts of marriage and motherhood, while Ralegh sailed on the first leg of an expedition in which a good part of his fortune was invested. He was back in Plymouth by mid-May, and then, belatedly, his secret came out. Elizabeth took his measure.[20]

It wasn't till 7 August that both Ralegh and Bess were sent to the Tower of London. In *Elizabeth: The Golden Age*, the marriage precedes the war against the Armada, Ralegh is released so he can deserve Elizabeth's forgiveness by fighting the Spaniards in her name, and the birth of his son Damerei is reserved for dramatic closure.

The film does not end with the defeat of the Armada in 1588, but tellingly with a scene at the home of Ralegh and Bess in 1592. Bess brings her screaming infant into the room for Elizabeth's blessing. In the moment that Elizabeth takes the baby in her arms it ceases its crying and even smiles. Elizabeth effects peace and harmony in the domestic realm, as in the public realm: 'They call me the Virgin Queen, I have no child, I am a mother to my people.' The main plot of the film, then, is not the Spanish invasion, or the domestic assassination attempts, or her relationship with the rival queen, Mary, or even her domestic court, but rather her hopeless romance with Ralegh that ends in marriage with Bess. Of all of the potential main plots, the Virgin Queen's romance was always going to be the hardest to write convincingly.

Suggestions for Further Reading

Stephen Greenblatt, *Sir Walter Ralegh: The Renaissance Man and His Roles* (New Haven, 1973).
Mark Nicholls and Penry Williams, 'Sir Walter Ralegh (1554-1618)' *Oxford Dictionary of National Biography*.
Anna Beer, *Bess: The Life of Lady Ralegh, Wife to Sir Walter* (London, 2004).
Garrett Mattingley, *The Defeat of the Spanish Armada* (London, 1959).
Colin Martin and Geoffrey Parker, *The Spanish Armada* (London, 1988).

12

Shakespeare in Love: Elizabeth I as *Dea ex Machina*[1]

Brett Usher

Legends beget legends. It is not for its many merits and ingenuities that John Madden's *Shakespeare in Love* (1998) will enter *The Filmgoers' Guide to Moderately Interesting Cinematic Facts* but for the remarkable circumstance that Dame Judi Dench, allotted less than eight minutes' screen-time out of the film's total of about 115, won an Oscar as Best Supporting Actress for her portrayal of Elizabeth I. As Thomas Betteridge has observed, ungallantly but pertinently, 'the power of the figure being portrayed' may perhaps have had as much to do with the matter as Dame Judi's performance. 'Was the Oscar really for Dench, or for that greatest of Elizabethan actors – Elizabeth herself?'[2]

Since mere historians are scarcely capable of sifting the truth behind the witterings of the Hollywood paparazzi we shall probably never know the truth. There may, for example, be some mileage in the rumour that, pipped at the post a year earlier for her *tour de force* as Queen Victoria in Madden's previous offering, *Mrs Brown*, Dame Judi was only receiving her belated due. Betteridge's point nonetheless remains irrefutable: the Hollywood moguls are unlikely to have dished out the Golden Apple if she had merely turned in an eight-minute guest-appearance as, say, the heroine's mother. They awarded it, as Paris awarded the original, partly in homage to one of the immortals.

The screenplay of *Shakespeare in Love*, which likewise won an Oscar, is credited jointly to Marc Norman and Sir Tom Stoppard. Where the division of labour lay remains officially off the record but the final product bears so many of the hallmarks of 'Stoppardian' comedy that

179

Plate 10 Dame Judi Dench as a regal Elizabeth in John Madden's historical romance *Shakespeare in Love*. Courtesy of Miramax Films, Universal Pictures, The Kobal Collection and Laurie Sparham for the image from the motion picture *Shakespeare in Love* (1998).

it has come to be regarded, unfairly it may be, as essentially his work.[3]
Now, 'Stoppardian' comedy presents many problems for the spectator as well as many delights. At its most dazzling it is frankly elitist,
dividing an audience into sheep and goats, the in-crowd and the rest.
A full appreciation of *Rosencranz and Guildenstern Are Dead*, the play
that catapulted Stoppard to fame back in the 1960s,[4] depends almost
entirely on a thorough working knowledge of Shakespeare's *Hamlet*.
For a full appreciation of his second major success, *Jumpers* (1972),
some familiarity with the basic tenets of philosophical enquiry during
the twentieth century is a desirable prerequisite. To get the most out
his third, *Travesties* (1974), you should ideally be reasonably conver-
sant with Oscar Wilde's *The Importance of Being Earnest*, the private life
of Vladimir Ilyich Ulyanov (Lenin), the European peregrinations of
James Joyce and the place of the Dadaist Movement in early twentieth-
century art. On occasions it is simply a question of familiarity with
a foreign language (well, French, anyway). In the first act of *Travesties*, the dotty, Swiss-domiciled English protagonist, presented with a
cheese sandwich, expostulates '*what a bloody country even the cheese has
got holes in it!!*' Shortly afterwards his butler remarks 'Yes sir – if I may
quote La Rochefoucauld, 'Quel pays sanguinaire, même le fromage
est plein de trous'. *Half* the audience guffaws with laughter.

Now the traditional function of the dramatist is to *unite* his audience, sending it away with a sense of having participated in a collective
experience and thus with a sense of corporate identity. Stoppard often
revels in doing the very opposite, confirming the *cognoscenti* in their
complacency and unsettling the *hoi polloi* by making them conscious
of their ignorance. And yet to deny his brilliance and say that you
didn't entirely enjoy your evening is to court disaster. While the real
cognoscenti will probably have the grace to keep silent those who hope
to be *counted* among the *cognoscenti* will almost certainly pounce: you
have ranked yourself with the *hoi polloi* and blustering condescension
will be your lot. 'But my dear fellow – well, I didn't understand *all* of
it, of course – but can't you *see* how brilliant it is?' For not a few Stop-
pardians who fall into this category it is a case, I venture to suggest, of
the Emperor's New Clothes.

The screenplay of *Shakespeare in Love* will make deft use of the
device of the Emperor's New Clothes in its denouement but it is
in the first place centred on a (totally daft and tongue-in-cheek)
theory as to how Shakespeare came to write one of his best-loved
plays, *Romeo and Juliet*. In some respects the script mirrors the play's
plot-mechanics. Like Juliet, for example, the heroine has a brisk and

efficient nurse (Imelda Staunton), who aids and abets her mistress. More subtly, Shakespeare's 'two households both alike in dignity' are here presented as the two rival theatres of London, Philip Henslowe's 'The Rose' in Southwark and Richard Burbage's 'The Curtain' in Shoreditch, homes, respectively, of the Admiral's Men and of the Lord Chamberlain's Men.[5]

Over and above all the ingenuity, *Shakespeare in Love* is a superbly crafted piece of *grand guignol*, happily romping its way through the London of '1593'. Street-scenes, river-scenes, costumes and playhouse sequences – the latter based on the modern reconstruction of Shakespeare's Globe Theatre on Bankside – all strike the right note for the sophisticated modern filmgoer. Elizabethan London might *just* have been like this – the constant juxtaposition of filth and sumptuousness, of bustle and languor: 'Merrie London' as the microcosm of 'Merrie England'. No place here for the sudden collapse of confidence which, modern historians are at pains to emphasize, overtook the nation during the 1590s, with its disastrous harvests and rising prices, increasing poverty and vagrancy, the demise in fairly rapid succession of many of its leading political figures, and an ever-intensifying debate about the succession to the Crown after the death of the childless Elizabeth.[6]

In this 'Stoppardian' world all remains comedic: we see no paupers lying half-dead in the street nor even (in marked contrast to twenty-first-century London) any beggars. The opening torture-scene should alert us for it is deliberately played for laughs. The fictitious Hugh Fennyman (Tom Wilkinson), who later becomes endearingly stage-struck, even gets away with his Laurence-Olivier-Richard-III voice for a line or three. Norman and Stoppard also skate with gusto into an area traditionally regarded as thin ice: the depiction of life backstage. Until the very recent past, it was a superstition that to write a successful play about 'the business' was impossible. Not even Noel Coward, ideally fitted for the task, risked it and only when Michael Frayn scored a brilliant success with *Noises Off* (1982) was that particular ghost finally laid. *Shakespeare in Love* accordingly enters the fray without reserve, modernizing outrageously as it goes ('Break a leg') and utilizing many a theatrical in-joke.

But why 1593, in particular? In the first place it was a responsible choice for writers who clearly elected – as Shekhar Kapur's script for *Elizabeth* (1998) did not – to stick to some basic chronological truths. According to received bibliographical wisdom, Shakespeare could have written *Romeo and Juliet* at any point between 1591 and 1597 and the screenplay requires moreover that he be presented as a more-or-less-established London playwright. But 1593 *in particular* because it allows the authors to introduce Christopher Marlowe 'of the mighty line', Shakespeare's hero and model, and the plot hinges in part on the fact that he died in a tavern brawl at Deptford in May 1593. Meanwhile, in one of its most extended theatrical in-jokes, the script slyly conjures up the theatre director's ultimate nightmare: during a sequence in which new recruits to the Admiral's Men are being auditioned, every single actor offers the most famous passage from Marlowe's *Dr Faustus*: 'Was this the face that launched a thousand ships? . . .'

Well then, in May 1593 Shakespeare (baptized in April 1564) has to be just a little over 29 years of age. Through the action, therefore, strides the young(ish) but still impressionable Will (Joseph Fiennes). When we meet him he is struggling to summon up his muse in order to complete a piece for the Admirals' Men called *Romeo and Ethel the Pirate's Daughter* and (yes, he has serious reservations about the title) is a bit stuck for ideas. Already married back in Stratford-upon-Avon, he now meets and falls hook, line and sinker for Viola (Gwyneth Paltrow), daughter of a rich London merchant by the outlandish name of Sir Robert de Lesseps.[7] Sir Robert's ability to provide Viola with a dowry has not escaped the attention of the penurious Earl of Wessex (Colin Firth). The script here crisply depicts the nature of Elizabethan realities: when Viola objects that she is not well enough born to marry him, her nurse replies 'Money is the same as well born'. And so it remains. That is why the British peerage survives as a political and social force (not *caste*) to this day.

Will only meets Viola because she longs to be an actor, dresses up as 'Thomas Kent', auditions for *Romeo and Ethel the Pirate's Daughter* and is cast as Romeo. Pursuing 'Thomas' back to the de Lesseps's mansion after their first encounter – 'he' claims to be a servant there – Will is accordingly confronted with Viola, who is very good at quick-changes. It takes him a long time to realize that they are one and the same – he does so in what must be counted one of the film's cleverest scenes[8] – but meanwhile their frantic, tragical–comical courtship and its sexual consummation inspires him to discard Ethel and shape the piece into the one we all know, *Romeo and Juliet*.

As the authors are perfectly well aware – although it is rather less clear whether they expect their audience to take them semi-seriously or not – this is complete and riotous nonsense. Shakespeare did not invent the plot at all. It was one of the best-known love-stories of its time well before Shakespeare got hold of it, rendered both into English verse and English prose. Arthur Brooke's verse *novella, The*

Tragicall Historye of Romeus and Juliet, had been published back in 1562 and Shakespeare, a rotten plotter himself, purloined it lock, stock and barrel. Indeed he seems to have known Brooke's effort off by heart.[9]

Unlike the love story of Romeo and Juliet, that of Will and Viola is 'star-cross'd' not because of any feud between their two families but because of several unnegotiable brickbats. In the first place Will is married already. Even if he wasn't, how could such a financially eligible young woman marry a mere player? Alchemically, Sir Robert's gold and Wessex's escutcheon will combine to produce that magical creation – an honour that she dreamed not of – Viola Countess of Wessex. And last, since earls – even penurious earls – are regarded by the monarch as royal 'cousins' and their alliances subject to royal approval, we learn that this one has been graciously sanctioned by the queen.

Ah yes, the queen, I had almost forgotten the queen. Re-create Elizabethan London and a boisterous tale of love and passion and how can you leave out Elizabeth herself – Astraea, Cynthia, Oriana, Gloriana, England's Eliza?

Well, you can. Almost. And you can certainly omit the clichés, the conventions and the claptrap with which most film and stage Elizabeths have been traditionally lumbered. There is only one myth about Elizabeth which Norman and Stoppard do not assiduously avoid – a salient fact about the script which appears to have occurred to none of the film's admirers, including the usually observant Michael Dobson and Nicola Watson.[10]

First, and most obviously, the story is not *about* the queen. We meet her, for a few fleeting seconds, only when the film has been running a full 10 minutes. No one has mentioned her up to this point but it now transpires that the Lord Chamberlain's Men have been summoned to Whitehall to present *Two Gentlemen of Verona*, here postulated as Will's most recent success (which it probably wasn't). And so *enter the Quene and her trayne*.

We are, it is true, presented *visually* with the traditional ageing monarch of the sumptuous wardrobe, the white pancake make-up and the flaming red wig. But Dame Judi's Elizabeth is not sketched as vain, merely as routinely dressed. Nor perforce is she tall, gaunt and stately. If the film's creators had wanted to present that particular image of Eliza then they might well have considered a couple of other Dames instead – Diana Rigg, say, or Maggie Smith. It would appear therefore that there is to be no attempt at an iconic Virgin Queen – a role in which Eliza's subjects would in any case have been surprised to learn that she was eventually to be cast by twentieth-century art historians.[11]

Within the *public* space, she sits *alone* on her dais. Although she has been followed into shot by a couple of routine ladies in waiting they take no part in the ensuing action. Nor is she hedged about by attendant, grim-faced ministers or by Hollywood-style 'lovers'. Bored at the outset, she is eventually diverted by the antics of Shakespeare's one and only stage-dog, Crab, who gets over-excited ('He's nervous: he's never played the Palace'). Elizabeth, steadily consuming sweetmeats, goes so far as to throw the animal one of them – thus demonstrating how 'English' she is[12] – but when the farce turns to poetic utterance, she slumbers. Is this the shape of things to come – a philistine 'English' monarch (the English being notoriously distrustful of the Arts) who only enjoys slapstick comedy and regards a trip to the theatre as an excuse for chomping her way through a box of chocolates? Does it also mean that we are going to be denied Gloriana?

Indeed it does. A full hour will elapse before we see Dame Judi again and meanwhile Gloriana has been knocked from her pedestal with witty finality by none other than Wessex. Truculently reminding Viola's nurse that, having consented to his marriage to the lady, the queen wishes to 'inspect' her, he is clearly vexed rather than impressed by Her Majesty's condescension:

> The queen, Gloriana Regina, God's chosen vessel, the radiant one who shines her light on us, is at Greenwich today and prepared during the evening's festivities to bestow her gracious favour on my choice of wife and if we're late for lunch the OLD BOOT will not forgive . . .

Traditional images of Elizabeth, it seems, are being discarded like items of luggage from a rickety wagon as we roll merrily along. No Virgin Queen, no Gloriana – and above all, it will transpire, no agonized, would-be lover of a younger man. As Betteridge points out, every screen Elizabeth from Sarah Bernhardt (*The Loves of the Queen*, 1912) via Flora Robson (*Fire Over England*, 1937) and Bette Davis (*The Private Lives of Elizabeth and Essex*, 1939) to Cate Blanchett (*Elizabeth*, 1998) is portrayed as fighting a personal battle between duty and love (usually for Robert Devereux, 2nd Earl of Essex) and accordingly much of the action takes place behind closed doors.[13] In *Shakespeare in Love* the queen will never be seen in private and patently – even though at first the film-buff is naturally tempted to make the elision — *Wessex is Not Essex*. The latter, Elizabeth's second 'sweet Robin' in succession to his stepfather, Robert Dudley, Earl of Leicester, was chivalrous, rash, impulsive, generous, the quintessential overgrown schoolboy. Wessex (never humanized with a Christian name in this screenplay) is unchivalrous, cold, remote and grasping.

Ah, but he has estates in Virginia, for which he is about to set sail. So the swelling act of the imperial theme, perhaps, as a subtext? An England conscious of its destiny as a great colonial and maritime power? Not a bit of it. These estates, for all we are told to the contrary, have been bestowed on Wessex or his father and are now mortgaged to the hilt. Viola's dowry will remedy the situation. Thus Wessex is no colonial adventurer, merely an opportunistic entrepreneur ('I fancy tobacco has a future') but in any case this Virginian *motif* has no more basis in fact than the inference that Shakespeare fashioned the plot of *Romeo* out of his personal experiences. England established no colonies on America's eastern seaboard until the following century and here the authors are merely making convenient use of a number of confused myths about Sir Walter Ralegh's disastrous attempts to do so in 1585 and 1587.[14] At Elizabeth's death England remained a remote outpost of Europe with no pretensions to imperial status beyond Henry VIII's declaration (strictly in order to repudiate papal claims to the contrary) that 'this realm of England is an Empire'.

And so, when the film has been running a full hour and 10 minutes, with most of our preconceptions about Elizabeth and her England comprehensively wrecked — either by sober attention to historical truth or else by a number of legitimate theatrical devices, Dame Judi is now allotted a further three minutes of screen-time in an oddly unsettling sequence compounded of pantomime and *realpolitik*. Alone on her dais once again, she is not in a good mood, clearly dislikes Wessex and seems to have decided to dislike Viola as well, scornfully dismissing her passionate assertion that a play can hold the mirror up to nature (and thus revealing in part why she dozed during *Two Gents*). 'Playwrights teach us nothing about love. They make it pretty, they make it comical, or they make it lust. They cannot make it true'. When Wessex wades in with both feet — 'nature and truth are the very enemies of play-acting. I'll wager my fortune . . . ' Elizabeth flattens him with the script's deadliest line: 'I thought you are here because you had none'.

When a squeaky voice from the crowd sings out '£50' — it is Will, dressed up, in a caricature of the nurse, as 'Miss Wilhelmina'[15] — Elizabeth elects (following a beady look in his direction which will

be explained later) to stand witness to the wager, stalking off with
a further contemptuous comment to Wessex. 'Have her then . . . but
you're a lordly fool. She's been plucked since I saw her last and not by
you. It takes a woman to know it . . . ' Does this make her jealous? An
ageing *voyeuse*? Or is it that she simply couldn't care less?

The plot now rattles along, propelled by the news of Marlowe's
death at Deptford and the melodramatic confusions which result.
Edmund Tilney, Master of the Revels (Simon Callow), has The Rose
closed when the atrocious urchin John Webster (Joe Roberts) tips him
off that 'Thomas Kent' is in fact a woman and proves it by stuffing a
mouse down her neck, thus revealing the flowing locks beneath the
wig which, in sober truth, could never have adequately concealed
them. As the Admiral's Men drown their sorrows in the local tavern Burbage appears and puts The Curtain at their disposal for the
premiere of *Romeo and Juliet*. Rehearsals are resumed, Will perforce
playing Romeo himself.

Meanwhile, back at the ranch, nothing can prevent the fateful marriage. But as all emerge from church, playbills advertising *Romeo and
Juliet* for that afternoon flutter in the wind, one hitting Wessex full in
the face. With the nurse's connivance, Viola escapes. Wessex puts two
and two together and arrives at the correct statistic. All make a bee-
line for The Curtain, where unfortunately the production now lacks
a Juliet, the voice of the boy-actor playing her having most inconve-
niently broken overnight. Of course, Viola has no hesitation in going
on in his stead but no sooner has the play swept to its triumphant
conclusion than Tilney and his men appear in order to make a few
judicious arrests 'in the queen's name'. He is stopped in his tracks by a
familiar voice: 'Have a care with my name, Mr Tilney, you will wear
it out.'

And so at last Dame Judi inherits her celluloid kingdom as *dea ex
machina* and as Shakespeare's patroness. This latter role was first thrust
upon Elizabeth in 1702 when John Dennis claimed it to be a 'tradition' that she had personally requested Shakespeare to depict Falstaff in
love, thus effectively 'commissioning' *The Merry Wives of Windsor*.[16] It
is necessarily the one enduring myth about the queen which Norman
and Stoppard have retained for without it there could be no obvious
excuse for introducing Elizabeth into the script at all. But their use of
it will be deftly handled, never passing the bounds of what *might* have
been.

In the interim, no matter that Elizabeth would never have attended
a public playhouse. No point in asking how she and her ladies made

their way to Shoreditch by coach without being spotted and loyally cheered. No earthly use in wondering where she could have been sitting to watch the performance without attracting attention. What follows is pure Disney and pure enjoyment. When Tilney blusters that there is a woman on stage he is brushed aside: 'The queen of England does not attend exhibitions of public lewdness so something is out of joint . . . Come here, Master Kent, let me look at you.'

Although it must be blindingly obvious to many present apart from Elizabeth that they have just been watching the new Countess of Wessex cavorting about in her wedding-dress, the queen serenely dons the Empress's New Clothes. 'Yes, the illusion is remarkable and your error, Mr Tilney, is easily forgiven but I know something of a woman in a man's profession, yes by God I do know about that.' It is the script's sole concession to the hoary old 'love *versus* duty' *motif* of all its predecessors. *Mais la farce est jouée* and Elizabeth now metes out her own particular form of poetic justice to the protagonists. Addressing Viola (not 'Thomas') she contents herself with 'That is enough from *you*, Master Kent.' In other words, kindly resume forthwith your *real* role as a peeress of my realm. To Wessex, skulking in the gallery: 'There was a wager, I remember, as to whether a play could show the very truth and nature of love. I think you lost it today.' You have, you lordly fool, married a 'Juliet' who clearly loves her 'Romeo', and not only on stage. To Shakespeare: 'Next time you come to Greenwich come as yourself . . . ' – rather than in ridiculous drag, you impudent wretch – 'and we will speak some more'. This last is said gently, with an affectionate smile. Will smiles too, but to himself. Elizabeth leaves.

A Shakespearean ending, then, for a Shakespearean playhouse. Outside, there are more pressing realities. Obviously Wessex cannot be satisfied with this comedy of masks and rushes out to confront Elizabeth before she reaches her coach. Keeping up the pretence, the queen feigns surprise that he is alone. 'Why, Lord Wessex, lost your wife so soon?' It is wounding and malicious and the thrust is not lost on him. The pretence, however, must be ripped away and he challenges her directly:

> Indeed, I am a bride short and my ship
> Sails for the New World on the evening tide.
> How's this to end?
> As stories must when love's denied.
> With tears and a journey . . . . Those whom God hath joined
> Together not even I can put asunder.[17]

Rescuing her preferred 'Shakespearean' ending from Wessex's attempt to wreck it, she throws in an afterthought to 'Thomas': 'Tell Master Shakespeare something more cheerful next time, for Twelfth Night.'

This hardly makes her 'the sponsor of cross-dressing', as Dobson and Watson oddly assert[18] – she commissions *a* play, not *the* play – but it does gather together many of the threads which have been woven into the plot.[19] As Stephen Warbeck's graceful music swells its way towards the credits, the film's final images are of three people *alone*, all sadder but wiser. 'A glooming peace this morning with it brings . . .' Elizabeth, *semper eadem*, powerless to alter social realities, resumes her place on an unshared throne, her excursion to Shoreditch a mere half-holiday from an otherwise inexorable routine. Will is cooped up in his lodgings penning the opening scene of *Twelfth Night*. Viola is seen walking into infinity on her preordained distant shore – the nearest the camera-work ever gets to Hollywood *kitsch*.

Behind the greatest comedy there always lies reality and that is what ultimately makes *Shakespeare in Love* a fine piece of filmmaking. It neatly prescribes its own definitions of reality by sidestepping 'gender' issues even before the proponents of that form of social history can begin sharpening their quills: it is simply *given* that Viola would love to go on the stage – what girl would not, at some stage of her development? – and there is nothing else to be read into it. Likewise the whole business of cross-dressing, about which much pseudo-psychological rubbish has been written, is deployed only in a kind of comedic inversion. Only two characters apart from Will and young Master Webster are allowed to notice that 'Thomas' is quite obviously Viola – Elizabeth herself and the boatman who rows Will and 'Thomas' to the de Lesseps's mansion in a sequence during which Will, gazing into 'Thomas's eyes, expatiates upon the beauty of Viola's. Polaxed when 'he' bestows a passionate kiss before leaping out of the boat, Will has scarcely recovered before the boatman, completely unphased by what he has just witnessed, casually says 'good night, m'lady'. Will stares at him in disbelief. 'Lady Viola de Lesseps', explains the boatman imperturbably, 'known her since she was this high . . . wouldn't deceive a child'. Will follows Viola into the house and with the simple 'Can you love a fool?' the whole concept of cross-dressing as a psychological *motif* is gaily consigned to oblivion.

As for more queenly realities, was it their self-imposed date of 1593 which prompted the authors into their almost relentless flight from fantasy in their presentation of Elizabeth? As with Viola's fixation for the theatre, it is simply *given* that she is a woman alone. In May 1593 she was almost exactly 60 years old. Her last official courtship had finally faded into nothing in 1581 and with it any last, lingering hope of a Tudor heir in the direct line from her father, Henry VIII. The euphoria of Armada Year (1588) was now clouded by the wintry economic climate of the decade which followed and the unsettling knowledge that the extinction of the Tudor dynasty was only a matter of time. Here, then, is no drama queen agonizing about the claims of love and duty. Duty is all that is left. Dench's Elizabeth is essentially a woman who may in truth have become profoundly bored with the burden of an office which only the accident of birth and then 'providential' survival has thrust upon her. This remarkably clear-eyed view of the queen is counterpointed in part by the fact that (with the curious exception of Marlowe) all the other 'historical' characters are gleefully fictionalized.[20] And perhaps the 'Stoppardian' *coup de theatre* with which Elizabeth takes her leave of the film – faced with a muddy puddle she finds no shimmering Ralegh doffing his cloak but only a bunch of fumbling non-entities hoping that someone else will make the gesture first – is meant to be as serious as it is obviously hilarious. A clutch of court poets excepted, no-one seems to regard her any longer as the desirable woman of their wildest dreams. She plunges, muttering, through the puddle: 'Too late, too late . . . ' Trip no further, once-pretty sweeting. Youth, like the rule of the Tudors, is the stuff that will not endure.

Suggestions for Further Reading

Stephen Greenblatt, *Will in the World: How Shakespeare Became Shakespeare* (New York, 2004).
Andrew Gurr, *Playgoing in Shakespeare's London* (Cambridge, 1987).
Andrew Gurr, *The Shakespearean Playing Companies* (Oxford, 1996).

13

The Private Lives of Elizabeth and Essex and the Romanticization of Elizabethan Politics

Paul E. J. Hammer

What can *The Private Lives of Elizabeth and Essex* tell us about Queen Elizabeth I or Robert Devereux, 2nd Earl of Essex? It will surely come as no surprise that this movie tells us very little about the historical Elizabeth or Essex. As the expensive cinematography which betokened its status as a prestige production suggests, *Private Lives* is a film which draws colour from the historical events of the final years of Elizabeth's reign, but it offers little meaningful illumination of those events. Given that it is a piece of popular entertainment which is very much a product of the 1930s – and of Hollywood culture in the 1930s, at that – it may seem otiose to begin by emphasizing the movie's historical inaccuracy. Yet the power and pervasiveness of movie images have undeniably had a profound impact upon both popular and academic understanding of Tudor and Stuart England. In the case of the Earl of Essex, whose place in modern historical consciousness is less prominent than that of Queen Elizabeth, the dramatic liberties which *Private Lives* takes with historical events has been a positive hindrance to a realistic understanding of the past. The role of Essex (and especially Errol Flynn's rather uncomfortable performance of it) unfortunately gave fresh and powerful impetus to a view of the historical Essex as a romantic and incompetent political dabbler – a caricature from which even serious scholars have broken free only in the last few decades.[1] In reality, Essex was a highly self-conscious

Plate 11 Revealed here are the unspoken gender hierarchies embedded in the film treatment of the relationship of Queen Elizabeth and Robert, Earl of Essex. Courtesy of Warner Bros., First National, The Kobal Collection and Bert Six for the image of Errol Flynn and Bette Davis from the motion picture *The Private Lives of Elizabeth and Essex* (1939).

and distinctly intellectual politician who pursued a coherent set of anti-Spanish policies with an almost missionary zeal and carefully cultivated public support. Nevertheless, the relationship between *Private Lives* and Elizabethan history is more complex than one of simple inaccuracy.

Like other movies, of course, *Private Lives* offers a window into the time and culture in which it was produced. As Renée Pigeon and Thomas Betteridge have argued, the depiction of Elizabeth in *Private Lives* is, for example, very different from that in *Fire Over England*, which was made in Britain only two years earlier. Compared to the latter's warning against the dangers of contemporary Fascism, *Private Lives* reflects a more distinctively American interest in individual psychology.[2] Michael Dobson and Nicola J. Watson have also noted how the figure of Essex reflects a profoundly anachronistic yearning for American-style democracy.[3]

As the earl suggests after his capture of the queen and her court, 'if this had been a freer time, if the people could elect, I'd have swept the country before me.' Such sentiments are wildly incongruous in the context of real Elizabethan political culture, which ascribed authority to the influence of God and preached that the overriding duty of the commons was obedience to their social superiors.[4] However, for all its historical inaccuracy, the story of Elizabeth and Essex presented in *Private Lives* is itself also part of a long historical tradition that extends back to the early seventeenth century. Within a generation of the deaths of Essex and Elizabeth, European dramatists began to trade upon the international fame of the queen and the earl to fashion plays which increasingly distorted, or ignored, the now stale complexities of Elizabethan politics and reshaped the story of Elizabeth and Essex into one of romance and tragedy.[5] The very public fame of both Elizabeth and Essex made it all the more appealing to create dramas around the imagined 'secret' lives which such famous figures supposedly led away from the public gaze. Crucial elements of *Private Lives* spring directly from these seventeenth-century romances and the film is very much their twentieth-century equivalent.

The immediate inspiration for *Private Lives* was *Elizabeth the Queen*, a play by the noted American dramatist Maxwell Anderson which had proved a critical success in 1930.[6] *Elizabeth the Queen* was written in a deliberately 'old-fashioned' format, the romantic tragedy in verse, and constituted the first of what subsequently became a loose trilogy of Tudor plays by Anderson (the others being *Mary of Scotland* in 1933 and *Anne of the Thousand Days* in 1948). All three plays focus on Tudor queens and explore the thirst for power and its human cost. In the case of *Elizabeth the Queen*, Anderson's prime source of information was clearly Lytton Strachey's *Elizabeth and Essex*, which was published in 1928 and tellingly sub-titled *A Tragic History*.[7] Strachey's *avant-garde* interpretation of Elizabethan history reflected a strongly Freudian interest in the psychology of the queen and the ways in which her relationship with Essex reflected, and finally re-opened, psychic wounds which she had received during her 'singular and horrible' childhood and adolescence. Paired with this emotionally damaged queen was an Essex who represented 'a psychology that was dominated by emotion instead of reason'.[8] Strachey's book therefore offered Anderson the raw materials of drama, as well as a rough framework of historical events in the 1590s and a variety of more specific information, such as the nature of Francis Bacon's advice to his patron Essex and Elizabeth's fury that her investment of £50,000 in the Cadiz expedition of 1596 brought Essex fame but failed to bring her a return on her money.[9] These points feature in both the play and the movie.

Anderson's dramatic requirements also encouraged him to distort, or wholly disregard, the historical record in other ways. Inevitably, many real events are de-contextualized and compressed together in order to create greater drama. Elizabeth's cool welcome for Essex upon his return from Cadiz, for example, actually occurred in August 1596, while the earl withdrew himself from court in early 1597 (being appointed Master of the Ordnance upon his return) and during the summer of 1598, when he and the queen sustained a 'great quarrel'. He departed for Ireland in March 1599. The scene in which Essex mocks Sir Walter Ralegh by dressing guardsmen in silver armour to mimic Ralegh's attire seems to be based upon an event which allegedly occurred in the tiltyard, but the earl's means of mocking Ralegh was the wearing of orange-tawny feathers rather than silver armour.[10] By transmuting this device into silver, Anderson makes Essex and Ralegh seem both petty and extravagant in a more powerful way than feathers could suggest. More significant changes are reflected in the play's *dramatis personae*. Presumably for reasons of simplifying the cast-list and plot, William Cecil, 1st Lord Burghley, the queen's famous Lord Treasurer and father of Sir Robert Cecil, is treated as living well beyond August 1598, when the real Burghley died. A whole host of other important figures in Elizabeth's last years are pruned out altogether. Anderson also plays fast and loose with the main female characters attending upon the queen, especially by inventing the character of Penelope Gray. Given her distinctive name, this character seems to be

based upon Lady Penelope Rich, who served as the romantic focus
of Philip Sidney's sonnet sequence *Astrophil and Stella* in the early
1580s.[11] However, Lady Rich was Essex's sister, not his would-be
lover. Lady Rich was also *persona non grata* at court throughout the
1590s because of her openly adulterous relationship with Charles
Blount, 8th Lord Mountjoy, and her attempt to intervene with the
queen on behalf of her brother in early 1600 backfired badly.[12] In
Anderson's fiction, the fraternal affection of the real Penelope is deliberately re-invented as romantic love in order to create a network of
thwarted love around the central relationship between Elizabeth and
Essex, with Penelope Gray becoming the pivot between two separate
romantic triangles: she vainly loves Essex and is, in turn, the unwilling
recipient of Sir Walter Ralegh's advances and the object of hopeless
adoration on the part of the queen's Fool.

The emphasis upon doomed love and the price to be paid for the
exercise of power helps to explain the greatest change which Anderson
makes to the historical record, by completely recasting the nature and
timing of Essex's rebellion against the queen. In both Anderson's play
and the film *Private Lives*, Essex's revolt is portrayed as arising from his
failure in Ireland and his acute sense of personal and strategic abandonment, having been cut off from contact with the queen and deprived
of all the necessities of war. In response, he turns his army upon
England and marches through London to take control of the court.
Elizabeth refuses all demands that she mount a military defence against
this advance and briefly becomes Essex's prisoner, before inducing him
to dismiss his troops. The earl's willingness to trust in the queen's
personal feelings for him proves spectacularly ill-judged when she
promptly orders his arrest for treason – resulting in his subsequent
trial and condemnation – in order to reassert her authority as queen.
Interestingly, given the extent to which these events diverge from reality, Anderson's use of dramatic licence here might almost be termed
an exercise in 'virtual' or counterfactual history rather than simple
invention.[13] Like the character in the play and the movie, the real
Essex felt abandoned and betrayed during his command in Ireland
in 1599 and actively considered taking precisely the course followed
by the dramatic character. Although he felt no romantic love for the
queen, his professions of obedience and zeal for her service might have
placed him in a similar quandary about how to reconcile his sincere
rhetoric with the reality of confronting his sovereign when backed by
armed force. In the event, however, the real Essex shrank from the
prospect of civil war. Instead, he returned from Ireland unannounced

on the morning of 28 September 1599 and famously burst into the queen's bedchamber at about 10 o'clock, where he found her 'newly up, the hair about her face'.[14] Although Elizabeth at first greeted him warmly, the earl's welcome soon turned cold. By the end of the day, he was confined to his chamber. Essex never saw the queen again and his life and career thereafter disintegrated with the riveting inevitability of a slow-motion train-wreck. Formally stripped of all his major offices in June 1600 and refused royal aid to stave off bankruptcy in October, he and his remaining band of supporters were stampeded into a premature and ill-conceived insurrection in the streets of London on 8 February 1601. This action finally brought his arrest and execution for treason. Like the character in the play and film, the real Essex enjoyed immense popularity with the commons, especially in London, and his death was widely attributed to the sinister manipulation of the queen by the earl's enemies.[15]

The screenplay for *Private Lives* was written by Norman Reilly Raine and Aeneas MacKenzie and their adaptation of Anderson's play further reshaped the Elizabeth and Essex story. Much of the self-conscious theatricality of Anderson's work is removed, including numerous Shakespearean touches which deliberately evoke the dramatic tradition in which Anderson saw himself as participating. The Elizabeth of the play receives Burbage and Hemmings into her presence and later tries to divert her attention from Essex's impending execution by calling upon actors to perform a scene between Falstaff and Prince Hal.[16] By contrast, although she still scorns the dangers presented by a performance of *Richard II*, the queen's comments in the film represent a considerably reduced allusion to Shakespeare. Further simplification for the movie can be seen in the removal of a series of lesser characters, including young female companions for the queen and her Fool. The excision of the latter character results in some of the Fool's observations about Essex's folly being transferred to Elizabeth, a point which is signalled in the movie by the queen's explicit mention of her Fool in connection with Ireland. The loss of the Fool also streamlines the role of Penelope Gray in the movie, removing her as the focus of the second love triangle with Ralegh and the Fool and thereby centring the film more fully on the Elizabeth and Essex relationship. The movie also adds an entirely new character, Mistress Margaret Radcliffe, to serve as a foil to the queen's romantic turmoil. As a naive young Maid of Honour, Mistress Radcliffe pines for an absent soldier, Captain Peter Finchley, and excites both jealousy and kindness from the queen for her uncomplicated love. News of Finchley's death in Ireland shows the queen that war fought in her name can turn even innocent passion into heartbreak. Finchley's death also underlines the cost and futility of war more generally. In contrast to *Fire Over England* (1937) and *The Sea Hawk* (1940), in which Queen Elizabeth and her subjects are shown as defiant in the face of Spanish aggression, *Private Lives* reflects a marked aversion to war. Set a full decade after the defeat of Spain's *Gran Armada* of 1588, *Private Lives* contrasts Essex's glory-seeking promotion of war with an ageing queen who is burdened down by years of enduring the conflict's human and financial toll. Where Essex seeks to escalate the war in pursuit of victory, she seeks to escape it. For an American audience who watched events in Europe in 1939–1940 with growing foreboding, Finchley's death and Essex's ultimate failure serve to underline the validity of Elizabeth's desire for peace.

The addition of the Mistress Radcliffe character is also significant because a real Mistress Margaret Radcliffe served as Maid of Honour to the real Queen Elizabeth in the late 1590s. However, the captain in Ireland for which the historical Mistress Radcliffe pined was not a suitor, but her brother, Sir Alexander Radcliffe. When he was killed while serving under Essex in Ireland in August 1599, Elizabeth commanded that the news be kept from her because she was 'determined to break it unto her herself'. The news proved shattering and Mistress Radcliffe starved herself to death three months later, shocking the court and prompting the queen to grant her a funeral at Westminster Abbey befitting a nobleman's daughter.[17] As Anderson had done in his creation of Penelope Gray, the scriptwriters for *Private Lives* therefore recast a real example of fraternal love at Elizabeth's court into a fictional romantic passion in order to emphasize the equally fictional romance between Elizabeth and Essex.

The scriptwriters also made changes which affected the character of Essex in *Private Lives*. The role of Francis Bacon was simplified to make him quicker to abandon the earl. Two new characters, Mountjoy and Knollys, are added to act as Essex's side-kicks in the movie. As with the addition of Mistress Radcliffe, these characters bear the names of real historical figures, but their rendering here as virtual servants of Essex represents a substantial distortion of reality.[18] Essex's fate in Ireland is also changed in a major way for the movie. In *Elizabeth the Queen*, Anderson shows Essex's desperation for news of the queen as being so great that he is apparently willing to torture a royal messenger to seek out her letters. His decision to turn his army against the court is made when he finally believes she has abandoned and betrayed him. By contrast, *Private Lives* explicitly shows Essex's sense of betrayal growing out of his military defeat by Tyrone's Irish forces. As with the screenplay writers' strategy in choosing historical names for their new characters, this change gives the film an added veneer of historical 'accuracy' because the real Essex was forced to conclude an embarrassing truce with Tyrone and personally met with him at a riverbank parley, loosely in the manner portrayed in the film.[19] However, the combination of costumes and cast involved in this part of the film also gives it a curious alternative frame of reference. The Irish who shoot at Essex's men (mainly with bows) look and behave very much like the Merry Men whom Errol Flynn had led in the film *The Adventures of Robin Hood* during the previous year, while Essex's English soldiers fight (and die) as unimaginatively as those of the Sheriff of Nottingham had done. The connection between the scenes in Ireland and *Robin Hood* is further reinforced by the individuals involved in their production. Michael Curtiz directed both movies and Flynn played the male lead in both films. Alan Hale, who plays a bluff Tyrone in *Private Lives*, had played a similarly bluff Little John. Olivia de Havilland, who plays Penelope Gray in *Private Lives*, had also been Maid Marian in *Robin Hood*. It is hard to know whether the alignment between the Tyrone's forces and Robin Hood and his Merry Men shows an instinctive American expression of sentimental sympathy for the Irish or simply represents a desire by those who had been involved in *Robin Hood* to transplant some of the elements of that movie's commercial success into their latest undertaking. Either way, this allusion to *Robin Hood* suggests that no amount of heroism on Essex's part could ever hope to prevail against the freedom-loving Irish.

The importance of action and visual splendour in cinema also encouraged a very different opening to *Private Lives* from the play upon which it was based. Anderson's play opens in distinctly Shakespearean manner, with four guards at Whitehall discussing the likely implications of Essex's return to court and the amorous possibilities which it might arouse for men such as themselves. The guards even speculate whether the queen really is a virgin. By contrast, *Private Lives* opens on a grand scale by cutting between the splendour of Essex and his army triumphantly marching through the streets of London after his victory at Cadiz and the varied reactions of those who observe the spectacle.[20] When the camera finally stops, it focuses on the queen's women looking down from the windows of the court in adoration of the earl. The character of Penelope Gray dominates these women and is clearly set up as a rival to the queen for the earl's attentions. However, the very opening shot of the film is not of the ladies of the court or the cheering crowds, but over the shoulders of a group of male courtiers who are soon afterwards revealed to be enemies of Essex. Although Elizabeth herself does not appear on screen for some minutes (and does so initially in the form of a silhouette), the opening shot seems to represent her point of view. Looking out from the gloom of an interior room at court, the camera can only catch a view of the approaching Essex and the excitement which he generates by sharing the perspective of those who hate him and by trying to bend its gaze around the obstacle which these courtiers represent.

The implication that Elizabeth has absorbed some of the criticism of Essex is further developed in another departure from Anderson's play. In *Elizabeth the Queen*, the characters of Elizabeth and Essex initially squabble in private and she warns him that financial necessity will impel her to oppose his request for the profits of ransoms from Cadiz. Elizabeth nevertheless acknowledges that ransoms constitute a traditional reward for victorious commanders and that she must eventually give way, as she does in the following scene. The queen's effort to assert her royal authority over Essex in the play is therefore shown as moderate and an essentially symbolic action which she warns him about in advance. In *Private Lives*, the kingly arrival of the victorious Essex and the step-by-step revelation of Bette Davis in the role of Elizabeth culminate in a very public meeting between the two characters, where the queen delivers a premeditated rebuke to Essex over his failure to repay her £50,000 investment in his Cadiz expedition which is deliberately intended to humiliate him. Essex's furious response results in her hitting him in full view of the assembled Court and precipitates his prolonged withdrawal to his house at Wanstead. The movie version of the clash between Elizabeth and Essex is consequently far more brutal and public than the equivalent scene in Anderson's play, which has no reference to Elizabeth striking Essex. This change by the film's scriptwriters reflects, once again, their twin goals of heightening the romantic tension between the characters of Elizabeth and Essex and giving the movie a superficial sheen of historical 'accuracy'. The historical Elizabeth did indeed strike Essex when he turned his back on her during an argument. Essex instinctively reached for his sword in response, only to be held back by the Lord Admiral. Before leaving the room, Essex told the queen and others present that 'he neither could nor would put up so great an affront and indignity, neither would he have taken it at King Henry the Eighth his hands'.[21] This shocking breach of protocol marked the start of the notorious 'great quarrel' which kept Essex away from court for several months over the summer of 1598. The real event therefore arose from debate about Ireland rather than Cadiz and occurred in the confines of the council chamber rather than the full glare of a formal court occasion, as the film would have it.

The effort to give *Private Lives* a gloss of loose historical accuracy and the substantial budget which was lavished upon costumes and grand sets marked out the film as a prestige production in its day. The use of technicolour also signalled its status as an important film for Warner Brothers. These efforts were rewarded with Academy Award nominations in five technical categories.[22] However, although it achieved a certain fame as Bette Davis's first performance in the iconic role of Queen Elizabeth, there is much about the movie that is rather unsuccessful. Errol Flynn's performance as Essex drew scathing reviews from some critics. In the opinion of *The New York Times*, Flynn was 'a good-looking young man who should be asked to do more in pictures than flash an even-toothed smile and present a firm jaw-line. His Essex lacked a head long before the headsman got around to him'.[23] Bette Davis's performance as Elizabeth now appears terribly mannered, with the tics and twitches which she uses to convey the queen's inner turmoil seeming excessive and distracting. Davis herself was nervous about playing a character so much older than herself – especially one as historically famous as Queen Elizabeth – and the tics seem like an over-earnest attempt to empathize with the old queen's psychology.[24] When Davis played Elizabeth again in *The Virgin Queen* 16 years later, the tics were banished. Perhaps a more fundamental problem with *Private Lives* was that the screenplay sought to retain as much as possible of Maxwell Anderson's much-lauded verse text, which gave the film a certain element of cultural prestige but resulted in an uneasy combination of grand cinematic gestures like the opening victory parade and a series of passionate scenes between the characters of Elizabeth and Essex which work rather less well in a movie than on a stage. As Thomas Betteridge has noted, 'Elizabeth and Essex battle away throughout the film but nothing changes, nothing really happens'.[25]

For Bette Davis, playing the role of Elizabeth was a 'dream of mine come true' and she sought to embrace the opportunity by recreating herself on the model of the historical Elizabeth.[26] When Charles Laughton, who had famously played the title role in *The Private Life of Henry VIII* (1933), visited the set, she greeted him 'Hi, Pop', to which Laughton replied, 'Ah! It's my favourite daughter!'[27] Davis's eyebrows were removed and her hairline was shaved back by two inches. She also flouted Michael Curtiz's instructions about her costume in order to wear 'authentic' dresses that were so heavy they left her exhausted and weighing only 80 pounds by the end of her six weeks of shooting.[28] However, Davis's commitment to the project was not shared by Errol Flynn. Indeed, the two leads famously battled away during the filming of *Private Lives* – the second and last movie which they made together – in a fashion which was oddly reminiscent of the struggle between their characters, Elizabeth and Essex.

Private Lives was always intended as a star vehicle for Davis and she was profoundly disappointed to be saddled with Flynn as her co-star, deeming him an inadequate actor for the role of Essex. Her anger grew further when she learned he would be paid more than her and that the movie's title would be changed – from *Elizabeth the Queen* to *The Knight and the Lady* – to give his character first billing.[29] Only her threat to walk out prompted a compromise choice, *Elizabeth and Essex*, which was finally discarded in favour of *The Private Lives of Elizabeth and Essex* for reasons of title rights.[30] Davis's emphatic choice for the part of Essex had been Laurence Olivier and, even 'when we were shooting the picture, all I could think of was all of Maxwell Anderson's blank verse going down the drain. I wanted Laurence Olivier'.[31] For his part, although he had enjoyed extraordinary box-office success, Flynn saw Davis as 'the great big star of the lot . . . the queen of Hollywood' and was determined not to be dominated by her. Flynn was infuriated that Davis forced him to rehearse Essex's grand arrival at court solely with her stand-in. When the time came for the first take of the scene in which Elizabeth strikes Essex, Davis failed to fake her punch and hit him in the jaw with her full force and wearing 'about a pound of costume jewellery' on her hand. As stunned by the unexpected blow as his character, Flynn withdrew to his dressing room and vomited repeatedly before deciding that, if Davis hit him again, 'that little jaw will have my fist in it'.[32] The result was a battle of wills between Davis and Flynn which frequently strained relations on the set and ensured that the supposedly passionate scenes between Essex and Elizabeth actually concealed mutual hostility.[33]

However, the interaction between the leading actors was more complex than merely a struggle between the 'queenly' Bette Davis and the wounded male pride of Errol Flynn. Flynn had won top billing over Davis in their first film together (*The Sisters* in the previous year) and she was determined to assert her pre-eminence on what she regarded as 'her' movie. Davis was also determined not to let herself be seduced and manipulated by Flynn, as many other actresses had been. Even though she was allegedly attracted to him, she refused to let herself become one of his conquests. As one of her biographers puts it – in terms strongly reminiscent of her character in *Private Lives* – 'pride in her was stronger than passion'.[34] To make matters worse, Flynn was allegedly the main reason why Davis had failed to secure the greatest prize of the day – the role of Scarlett O'Hara in *Gone with the Wind*.[35] *Private Lives* was Davis's consolation prize – her chance to reign, as it were – and she was determined to defend her bid to secure 'my career and my stardom forever'.[36] This not only entailed battling against Flynn, but also putting up with his flagrant, if unavailing, efforts to seduce Olivia de Havilland, who played Penelope Gray. For her part, de Havilland had to swallow the disappointment of coming from her major role as Melanie in *Gone with the Wind* to a supporting role beside Davis's Elizabeth, as well as fend off Flynn. Although the two women remained friendly, Flynn's efforts reproduced a virtual triangle of thwarted passion on the set which effectively reversed the feelings exhibited by their fictional characters.[37]

If the on-set antics of *Private Lives* associate it with the modern tradition of 'Hollywood Babylon', one creative choice which Maxwell Anderson made in his use of Strachey's *Elizabeth and Essex* directly connected both his play *Elizabeth the Queen,* and consequently *Private Lives,* to a much older and more significant historical tradition. Although Strachey mentions it only to dismiss its veracity, the romantic tale that Essex received a ring from the queen which would guarantee his pardon proved appealing enough to Anderson for him to appropriate it as a key feature of his play.[38] By offering both Elizabeth and Essex a means of saving his life and yet showing their inability to take that option, the device of the ring sharpens the drama of Essex's tragic death in both the play and the film. The ring story also undoubtedly appealed to Anderson because, like his Shakespearean allusions and his choice to write in blank verse, it connected his work to older dramatic traditions. The romantic myth of 'Essex and the ring' became a famous motif in European literature and a staple of seventeenth- and eighteenth-century works about Elizabeth and Essex. Although rings appeared in plays about Essex as early as the 1620s, the first appearance of a ring that would guarantee Essex's safety seems to have been in France in the late 1630s.[39] Thereafter, it quickly gained wide currency. The ring story was most fully elaborated in *The Secret History of the Most Renowned Q. Elizabeth*

and E. of Essex by a Person of Quality (1680), which was a translation of a French prose work of 1678. *The Secret History*, in turn,
inspired John Banks' hugely successful tragedy, *The Unhappy Favourite:
Or the Earl of Essex* (1681), which spawned a series of imitators of
its own in the mid-eighteenth century.[40] The ring story therefore
connects *Elizabeth the Queen,* and consequently *Private Lives,* to the
commercialized romantic imaginings about Elizabeth and Essex which
began to flourish a generation or two after their deaths. This is surely
the historical context in which *Private Lives* must be placed – not
in connection with the real events which the movie purports to
describe, but with the seventeenth- and eighteenth-century works
which offered eager audiences romantic fantasies about famous historical figures, who were otherwise unknowable as individual men
and women.

However, Anderson's use of the ring story breaks with the romantic
tradition of works like *The Secret History* and *The Unhappy Favourite*
in one significant way which gives his drama a distinctly twentieth-
century and American flavour. Although the ring offers Elizabeth and
Essex an immediate means of saving his life, neither character is able
to take that option – by conscious choice, rather than the intervention
of a malicious third party. The tragedy of Essex in both *Elizabeth the
Queen* and *Private Lives* is not that he and the queen are torn apart
by personal folly or ill fortune, but that the exercise of power itself is
ultimately incompatible with love. In Anderson's vision, power – or at
least the autocratic, hereditary authority represented by monarchical
power – is destructive of all those who wield it. Even for Elizabeth,
who uses her power in a conscientious way and ultimately places the
safety of her realm and royal authority above all else, the price of power
is shown to be barely less mortal than the penalty which Essex pays for
his failed bid to seize the throne. For all its technicolour glamour and
period costumes, *The Private Lives of Elizabeth and Essex* suggests that
this dilemma of power and the heart is insoluble in the Old World,
even in the England of Queen Elizabeth. If there is a solution to the
dilemma, the movie seems to hint, it can only be found in the New
World and in the American-style elections for which the character of
Essex seems so incongruously eager.

Suggestions for Further Reading

John Guy (ed.), *The Reign of Elizabeth I: Court and Culture in the Last Decade*
    (Cambridge, 1995).

P. E. J. Hammer, 'Sex and the Virgin Queen: Aristocratic Concupiscence and the Court of Elizabeth I', *Sixteenth Century Journal* 31, (2000), pp. 77–97.

P. E. J. Hammer, *The Polarisation of Elizabethan Politics: The Political Career of Robert Devereux, 2nd Earl of Essex, 1585–1597* (Cambridge, 1999).

P. E. J. Hammer, 'The Last Decade', *History Today* 53, no. 5, May 2003, pp. 53–9.

Wallace T. MacCaffrey, *Elizabeth I: War and Politics, 1588–1603* (Princeton, 1992).

14

Oliver Cromwell and the Civil Wars

John Morrill

Oliver Cromwell has been portrayed in the cinema on at least six occasions. This essay will dwell on the most recent three of them; but we ought to at least record what the earlier ones were. The first I know about is *The Vicar of Bray* (1937), a rather weak melodrama starring Stanley Holloway as the said vicar and with George Merritt having a cameo role as Cromwell. The next was *The Cardboard Cavalier* (1948), a farce in which Sid Field plays a barrow boy and Margaret Lockwood plays Nell Gwyn and in which Edmund Willard plays a killjoy Lord Protector (as a repressed rather than a heroic figure in the strait-laced words of Leslie Halliwell's *Film-goer's Companion*). And then in 1958 John le Mesurier was horribly miscast as Cromwell in *The Moonraker*, an under-funded adventure about a seventeenth-century Pimpernel helping Charles II to escape from Worcester. All three remind us that filmmakers see historical events as a starting point for fantasies that take us out of ourselves. And so long as they work on the assumption that they know that we know that that is all they are doing, no harm is done at all.

Since then, three films have appeared all of which, in their own way, relate more actively with the life of Cromwell and the years of civil war in ways that need to detain us a bit longer. They are *Witchfinder General* (1968), *Cromwell* (1970) and *To Kill a King* (2003). How relaxed can historians be about the way they present the past and relate to the way they present it?

Plate 12   Alec Guinness (Charles I) and Richard Harris (Oliver Cromwell) pose side
by side in Ken Hughes's *Cromwell*. Courtesy of Columbia, Irving Allen and
The Kobal Collection for the image of Alec Guinness and Richard Harris
from the motion picture *Cromwell* (1970).

The easiest of the films to discuss is *Witchfinder General* (1968) directed by Michael Reeves. Granted an 'X' certificate on release and an '18' on re-release, it is a bleak, disturbing account of Matthew Hopkins, a sexual sadist who enjoys torturing and killing women in the name of religion (although he only admits to doing it for money, his eyes and mouth tell us that his pleasure comes from more than the purse). There are a number of named places in East Anglia where Hopkins did indeed ply his trade – Brandeston, Hoxne, Lavenham – and some real historical characters. These include the man known at the time and since as the Witchfinder General (Matthew Hopkins); Oliver Cromwell who has a slightly unnecessary cameo part; Hopkins's assistant and 'enforcer' John Stearne; and the 'Laudian' vicar of Brandeston (played by Rupert Davies dressed to look exactly as William Laud is dressed in that most famous of portraits of him by Van Dyck). The forces of innocence and revenge are led by two fictional characters, John Lowes's niece Sarah and her lover/husband who is a New Model Cornet called Richard Marshall, and a whole series of bit parts of those who are one of the following: parliamentarian troopers; puritans assisting Hopkins in his witch-finding with varying degrees of wilful ignorance or shamefaced compliance; or women willing to scream very loudly when knives are shoved into any marks on their bodies by Hopkins's really nasty assistant John Stearne.

Little is known about the real Matthew Hopkins except for his witch-finding in the years 1645–1647 (he died of tuberculosis and was buried in Manningtree [Essex] on 12 August 1647). He was the son of an Essex minister but (unlike Vincent Price who plays him as a man in late middle age) he was in his twenties at the time when he generated the greatest of all English witch-crazes in East Anglia. In just two years (which overlapped with the end of the Great Civil War), about 250 people were tried as witches or tortured as part of a pre-trial procedure, and around 100 were executed. Hopkins brought the notion of pacts with the Devil (normally absent from English witchcraft accusations) into play, and his methods and obsessions are accurately caught by the film. What is most conspicuously absent is the trial at assizes that invariably preceded execution even in the chaotic days at the end of the Civil War. In the course of the film, Hopkins hangs four and burns three witches (one male and six female, about the right gender ratio, but wrong about the method of execution – they were all hanged). In the film, he is a stickler for only using approved tortures, but does not mind getting weak folk to claim to have heard confessions that they have not heard. In between the scenes of torture, death and

implied rape and fornication (screams again being an effective substitute for gratuitous action), there is rather a lot of time spent in soldiers
and others riding pell-mell in the great tradition of the Western.

The part of Cromwell is played by Patrick Wymark. He actually
looks like Oliver and the make-up artists did wonders to make the
warts realistic. Wymark had played Cromwell in an excellent BBC
Play for Today about the trial and execution of King Charles (*Cruel
Necessity* [1966]), and was fresh from playing an overbearing company boss in a successful TV series called *The Power Game*. But for
some reason the director wanted him to play Cromwell not as a new
Gideon, called from the plough to lead the armies of the Lord, but as
a Sandhurst-trained toff, every inch the career officer and gentleman.
A pity, it was an opportunity missed. In the end, Cromwell's presence
confuses rather than helps the film, which does not in general pretend
to be more than a horror film. The director (Michael Reeves) had
previously directed *Revenge of the Blood Beast* and *The Sorceress*; his star
was Vincent Price, master of *grand guignol* and fresh from playing in
a series of Edgar Allan Poe films from the Hammer Studios (I have
vivid memories of his manic operation of the eponymous machine
in *The Pit and the Pendulum* [1961] – indeed in the US the film was
released with the title *The Conqueror Worm*, the title of a Poe poem). As
Matthew Hopkins, he is sinister-camp rather than flamboyant-camp,
but none the worse for that. The hints of sexual arousal during the
torture scenes are genuinely disturbing. So the film comes across as a
horror movie, not a historical epic. The music (by Paul Ferris) mixes
chill with romance in a rather 1930s way, and makes no concession
to period music. And whenever necessary the clichés of the Gothic
are invoked: the dungeons owe more to Transylvania than to Stuart
Suffolk; and the inn scenes in which no woman is allowed to appear
with her breasts covered again leaves us in no doubt that we, as well as
Hopkins, are there as voyeurs not history students.

So the film makes few claims on us. It is true that the kind of voice
that (at least in 1968) evoked the Oxford Senior Common Room
(remember *Accident* [1967, dir. Joseph Losey]?) offers us a guide to the
historical background of the film. After a pre-credits hanging, then
the credits, and before an overlong scene in which Cornet Marshall
and his men see off some royalist horse-thieves, this mature Oxford
don tells us that in 1645 a civil war was raging, law and order was
breaking down, and sedulous and superstitious people were caught up
in reporting one another to Matthew Hopkins, lawyer and sadist. And
so of course, he actually was.

The film does base itself on an actual man who created the worst witch-craze in English History in exactly the areas mentioned in the film. Hopkins did prick witches and he did swim them (the scene in which this happens is one of the most effective and powerful). After that, the Gothic imagination takes over. Hopkins did not (as he boasts in the film) 'invent' burning as an alternative to hanging (more the reverse). The real Hopkins unlike the film Hopkins did not spare those who gave their bodies to his prick in the colloquial sense rather than the technical sense. Puritans and New Model soldiers did not cross themselves as a witch died; nor did good puritans kneel before an altar beyond a rood screen to make wedding vows in the face of heaven in the absence of a minister. But it hardly matters. What makes the film effective is that it combines three separate traditions. Firstly it draws on the tradition of implied and glimpsed violence of 1960s Hammer Horrors. Secondly it evokes the best aspects of the Western tradition (not just all that speeded-up riding across open country, but the lawless communities of intimidated civilians torn between the good individual (Richard Marshall) and the forces of evil (Hopkins and Stearne)). The third is that is uses period settings and locations to bring those together. And it has a truly shocking ending. Marshall, having seen Sarah tortured breaks free and starts hacking Hopkins to pieces with an axe; his men burst in and finish Hopkins off with a bullet. Marshall, snarling like a wolf that has its prey snatched from its maw, accuses them of robbing him of his revenge, and the camera cuts to Sarah, deranged and clearly ruined as a human being. The camera freezes and the credits role. *Cinema verité* it is not; historical realism is not suspected; *film noir* is suddenly anticipated.

The other two films focus much more on Cromwell, or in one case on the relationship between Cromwell and Charles I (*Cromwell* [1970]) and the other the relationship of Cromwell and Fairfax (*To Kill a King* [2003]). I am deeply indulgent of the first and deeply scornful of the second for reasons I have found hard to pin down. In part, no doubt, this is because against all expectation Richard Harris's Cromwell is far closer to my sense of the historical figure than Tim Roth's, but in larger part, I believe, it is because the former film is more relaxed about what it is claiming and not claiming about historicity and because it makes a more honest attempt to engage with the recoverable past. This is not straightforward. But I will try to explain what I mean.

Cromwell appeared in cinemas in 1970, and it was directed and written by Ken Hughes immediately after he had directed *Chitty Chitty*

Bang Bang and co-directed *Casino Royale*. But he had already shown his credentials in serious historical drama with his film on *The Trials of Oscar Wilde* (1960). So he was a versatile director who knew both how to entertain and how to challenge. This *Cromwell* was a large budget, ambitious production with not only two very large battle sequences, but with large crowds for the scene in which Charles I is executed and a realistically packed Parliament House throughout. It is assured in its story-telling and offers a coherent account of Cromwell's reluctant move from peace to war, from serving parliament to defying it, from seeking a settlement with the king to presiding over his trial and execution, from semi-retirement to reluctant taking on the Lord Protectorship. And it is based around two compelling central performances by Richard Harris as Cromwell and by Alec Guinness as Charles I. Harris was an Irish Catholic by birth, and a hell-raiser by profession (and he had just played King Arthur in *Camelot* and *A Man Called Horse* about a white American who goes native in the days of the Wild West), and so was a startling choice as Cromwell: but he rose brilliantly to the challenge. What he brought to the part was intensity, integrity, persuasiveness as a natural leader, and an extraordinary self-belief in himself as a man of destiny. There may be too much reliance on a brooding presence, looking out fiercely from under lowered eyebrows, but he combines a credible warmth with an equally credible tendency to burst forth into torrents of political rhetoric. He succeeds above all in showing a Cromwell who was regularly dragged along by events until he felt impelled to command them. For example, thinking he could make a deal with Charles I, he hangs a Leveller protestor for doubting his integrity. Finding that he had been fooled by the king, his rage and determination to avenge that wronged Leveller is convincingly relentless.

Even more compelling is Alec Guinness as Charles I. His face – apart from his eyes – is impassive. But those eyes, which stare with an extraordinary deadness when he is in stubborn vein, suddenly dart this way and that to reveal the underlying insecurity. This Charles is all too ready to sacrifice a wonderfully bluff and arrogant Strafford (here played with gusto by our friend Patrick Wymark as a coarse Yorkshireman), all too aware of the bad advice given by Henrietta Maria (an excellent cameo by Dorothy Tutin) but too much in love with her to brush her aside (one passionate kiss is enough to suggest the volcano behind the icy self-control). This is a man well able to command, and both the trial and execution scenes (which use actual words recorded of those events) are a high point of the film and a triumph both of acting and of direction. When Charles I and Cromwell are both on set, right and might are in perfect balance. It is this which sets this film apart as history and drama from _To Kill a King._

Cromwell is both deeply committed to visual accuracy and very relaxed about combining certain characters and events, or even fictionalizing them for dramatic purpose. Let us take each in turn. All the exteriors and interiors (such as the Palace of Westminster) are plausible – I especially like the attention to detail at mealtimes. Battle drill is good and weapons appropriately deployed (although the actual course of the battles is profoundly and deliberately incoherent). Clothes are generally appropriate to the period, although baddies tend to be overdressed and too gaudy – the first appearance of Robert Morley's outrageously vain Earl of Manchester being a leading example. Still, this has a good period feel without being slavish. When necessary (as when the New Model goes to war), seventeenth-century metric psalms are sung. At other times, Frank Cordell provides a kind of discreet 'epic background' music. But there is an interesting hybrid at the outset. Cromwell, standing besides an (undrained) fen pondering whether his future is to be in Old or New England, is tracked down by the unlikely pair of John Pym and Henry Ireton and asked to help them halt Charles I's misgovernment, by force if necessary, a suggestion he angrily rebuts. As this scene unfolds, the words 'Rejoice in the Lord' are sung, combined with verses from the Magnificat ('_He hath shewed the strength of his arm: he hath scattered the proud in the imagination of their hearts. He hath put down the mighty from their seats, and hath exalted the humble and weak_'). It is an inspired idea, getting close to the essence of the smouldering fire in Cromwell's belly, and set in a slightly astringent modern polyphony. History is made accessible in modern idiom but with a real regard to the actual history.

The film is, however, outrageously free in its combination of characters and events. Parliament is unicameral; the Earl of Manchester sits in this parliament and represents old corruption in 1640, 1647 and 1653; Pym dies in the film in 1647 (instead of 1643) and the Earl of Essex is still alive and well in 1653 (he died in 1646). Sir Edward Hyde (Nigel Stock) is rather well portrayed as an honourable trimmer in the early 1640s, but he becomes Cromwell's spy close to the king in 1647 and he actually testifies against him at his trial. Someone needs to explain the depths of Cromwell's duplicity. Rather than find a new character, one who had already changed sides once might as well serve. Cromwell leaps straight into the war as a colonel, is in charge at Naseby (actual date 14 June 1645) where his forces are supposedly outnumbered by the king's because Manchester fails to turn up to a rendezvous there. The Self-Denying Ordinance (actual date 3 April 1645) is thus re-dated to the period *after* Naseby. Cromwell does not have to conquer Ireland or Scotland in this film. Rather he retires from politics after the regicide and has to be recalled because the freedoms he thought he had secured by his victories are being withheld by a Rump persuaded by (oh dear!) a Sir Thomas Fairfax who never seems to have served in the army to perpetuate itself and by the Earl of Manchester to suppress a proposed commission into the corrupt practices of members. This leads to a rather splendid re-enactment of the actual events of 20 April 1653, again drawing on many of the words remembered by those actually present at the time. Quite a lot of this quite unnecessarily falsifies the facts of history. But the aim is manifestly to keep the narrative lines clear and the viewer able to follow a core narrative *that does testify to historical events.*

Events and people are changed to make the narrative flow; but the film is more concerned than almost any other to avoid anachronism, explaining the past in terms of the preoccupations of the present. As a study of the mind of Cromwell and as a *translation* of his values into accessible modern language the film has much to commend it. Cromwell's religious sincerity (as the king's) is constantly made clear and both sides are shown at their own forms of prayer on the eve of battle. Cromwell's commitment to government accountable to the people, his gradual radicalization as first he realizes that neither the threat of rebellion, nor defeat in war, not even *realpolitik* will make Charles rule as Cromwell yearns for him to do, are well translated. Leveller voices, Irish Catholic voices (in the form of a papal nuncio clad in Lenten violet, alas, and not cardinal red), and Charles's fear that his enemies would replace him with Prince Henry rather than Prince Charles, are important parts of the historical record well integrated into the narrative. And at the heart of the story is the study of irony and paradox of a Cromwell who makes a defiant speech when Charles enters with his soldiers to break parliament, but enters himself in much the same way to break that same parliament 12 years later; who sees himself as entrusted by a sacred mission by God no more and no less than Charles I sees himself entrusted with a sacred mission; and of a Charles I who is an authoritarian conservative and Cromwell who is an authoritarian liberal who knows better than the people do what is good for them. Their visions differ, but their sense of being the instruments of a divine plan is shared. (Cromwell, after all, did say in 1647 that government 'is for the people's good, not what pleases them').

As a Voice-of-the-BBC announcer tells us at the end, the future lay with Cromwell's vision; but the uneasiness of a man driven by an Ayatollah-like self-confidence devoid of personal ambition remains. This is a film which uses the filmmaker's poetic license to grapple with the realities of political power. What anyone seeing the film would take away from it is a fuzzy set of inaccurate details, and a clearer sense of what trained historians know to be the fundamental issues.

This leaves us with the most problematic film of the three: *To Kill a King* (2003), a £13.5-million flop that combines a wonderful feel for the material culture of civil-war England with a culpable disregard for the integrity of actual people and events from the past. Some exceptionally talented actors and support staff combine to make a film that is an utter failure at every level.

The film is 96-minutes long, but both the pre-credits and the end-credits take several minutes, padding out a film that had run out of money and worthwhile footage long before it reached the cutting room. The pre-credits open with a text (not a voice as with *Witchfinder General* but with an almost identical message) and then show the aftermath of battle – dead bodies in the mud or (stripped to their smalls) in heaps, some poor chap having his leg amputated, prisoners in chains (really?). This takes several minutes. At the end we have the longest, slowest credits I can remember. They are preceded with a rolling script making fatuous claims about the consequences of the Revolution and then by an endless list of acknowledgements (of amongst others a make-up trainee, a breaking down and ageing department, a generator driver, the firm that provided cherry pickers, and even the firm that did the photocopying). But no historical adviser is mentioned, because none was clearly used. After that and after the logo of Kodak who provided the film and Dolby who provided the sound, we get in tiny print the following statement: 'this film is based on history. However, certain characters and events have been combined and/or fictionalised for dramatic purpose'. The claim is made and therefore it is entirely reasonable to see in what sense (if any) that claim has substance.

The hero of the film is Thomas Fairfax, victor in the Great Civil War, and it explores his relationship with his best friend and second-in-command Oliver Cromwell (who wants to impose justice and liberty on the people in the face of a king who has learnt nothing from his defeat, in the face of politicians willing to take bribes to restore said sullen monarch) and his relations with his wife, who is portrayed as the daughter of a Royalist called de Vere (but see below). A host of other characters come and go inconsequentially, except for Denzil Holles, leader of a party of venal and corrupt professional politicians, who is oddly portrayed as Speaker of what appears to be a unicameral parliament. In order to spread justice and liberty, Cromwell is constantly getting out his carbine and shooting anyone who annoys him, so it is no surprise that he is determined to chop off the king's head and wash his hands in his blood. No sooner is the king dead, than he calls himself Lord General instead of Fairfax, and is saddened when the latter no longer seems his friend. Shortly thereafter he dons a cope and is invested with a sceptre, and looking more and more like Olivier's Richard III, descends into snivelling paranoia. Fairfax arranges for Sergeant Joyce to assassinate Cromwell, and when Joyce bungles it, he admits to Cromwell that he was behind the attempt. Cromwell orders him to be seized, taken to Tyburn and burnt alive. Happily, so great is everyone's respect for the upright Fairfax that they ignore Cromwell's orders and the former walks freely through their midst and out into the courtyard at Hampton Court to the roar of an adoring crowd. He returns to Yorkshire where for several years he lives in peace, making one last visit to see the dying Cromwell (hated by all but curiously still in power) to express regret that their friendship had not prospered.

Now I do not think that this can be safely described as a film based on history, but in which certain characters and events have been combined and/or fictionalized for dramatic purpose. Does it matter? I think it does for reasons we will come to; and I certainly think that one should be clear that this is not just the result of the money running out before the big outdoor scenes could be made.

The screenwriter was a novice and I will not name and shame her. In an interview with *The Times* on 20 May 2000 she boasted that she had learnt to write screenplays from a £10 book, and that a film producer was so impressed by her at a workshop run by his company that he put her in charge of writing the screenplay for a film with a $20-million budget. Her background was not in History – she had an English degree from Oxford – and in 2000, halfway through the filming, she could tell *The Times* that she was curious that no one had done a film about Cromwell since 1970: 'as I read more, I became more interested' she said, 'we were the first country to execute our king. It inspired the French Revolution.' How can £13.5 million be entrusted to someone so ignorant and so insouciant?

The production company's website even later in the production schedule was saying that Mike Barker (the director) 'intends to combine the scale of a film such as *Elizabeth* with the emotional and moral core of a work like *A Man for All Seasons*'. This gives us a self-definition against which to measure the scale of the film's failure. More specifically, Barker said he intended to examine the dichotomy between public and private, and 'to create a sense of the paranoia and edginess of politics at this most turbulent of times'. He added that 'the film will evoke the seventeenth century, but the style in which we edit and shoot will be more contemporary, more post-modern'. He called it an emotional thriller. Since these claims are far stronger, far more public, far more dangerous, than those of Michael Reeves or Ken Hughes, we need to take them much more seriously. For the film flatters to deceive.

First of all, it does succeed rather brilliantly in *evoking the seventeenth century*. From those pre-credit shots of the aftermath of battle, through the street scenes, the authentic interiors of country houses and great halls (with their central fireplaces), through the attention to detail in the dress of soldiers, civilians and noblemen and women (the hat-maker certainly deserves a place in the credits), this *looks* right. So we could easily be taken in and persuaded that the events described and the motivation of the leading actors are – as it is claimed, remember, by the makers on film and in publicity – based on History. No such claim is made by the makers of the other films and no such claim is implied.

But as my all-too-accurate account of the plot makes clear, History is not just adapted, events are not just elided; they are fundamentally altered to suit the needs of an earthbound plot. I am not going to labour the point, but I do need to get a sense of perspective. It is true that between 1645 and 1649 Charles I refused to negotiate seriously with those who had defeated him in war. It is true that he sought to divide and rule his opponents. It is true that Cromwell and Fairfax began with much the same view of the political settlement that would be just and right and drifted apart. It is true that at the time of the king's trial, Lady Fairfax made clear her opposition to what Cromwell was now doing, and that her public protest was assumed to mirror his private reservations. After that the plot collapses completely into unreality.

Nonetheless there are the germs here of a story worth exploring. It is a perfectly reasonable supposition that Fairfax was torn between the convictions of a comrade in arms and the convictions of the wife he took in his arms during their rare meetings. It is a proper sub-ject for imaginative recreation of how that tension might have played itself out. It is irritating that to make this point, Anne Fairfax has to be given a de Vere (earls of Oxford) father, rather than a battle-hardened puritan father called Horace Vere who spent his life in the service of the Protestant cause abroad. But it does help make this central point clear. Dougray Scott makes something of the part of Fairfax, not the ditherer of too much historical writing, but a man who oscillates between two courses of action, and who believes like a just man in the German Army in the 1930s that it is better to grit one's teeth and seek to mitigate abuses of power, than wash one's hands and walk away. Rupert Everett is not convincing as Charles I, not a patch on Alec Guinness. It doesn't help that he is far taller than any-one else in the movie (when so much of Charles's personality can be traced back to his being so short, with bandy legs caused by childhood rickets). There are glimpses of the surly self-pitying defiance, but in general this is a wooden performance that can never make up its mind whether Charles is to be a tyrant who wills his own fate or a martyr to Cromwell's self-righteousness.

The real catastrophe in the first half of the film (before it goes off the rails) is Tim Roth's portrayal of Cromwell. For this the blame must lie firmly with the screenwriter, closely followed by the actor and director. As Cromwell first comes into close-up at the beginning, what flashed straight into my mind was 'yon Cassius has a mean and hungry look'. This is a Cromwell driven 80 per cent by paranoia and 20 per cent by ambition. He rattles out lines about justice and liberty but without ever appearing to mean them. And before he even speaks, he is shown kicking a royalist prisoner around the head, and needing to be restrained by Fairfax from shooting him. It is not long before we see him personally supervising the torture of an MP to make him spill the beans about Charles I's bribery of Holles and others, and not long after that before he is shooting randomly those who stand in his way. Cassius gives way to a deranged Richard III who has the benefit of firearms. He even begins to stoop as though he is developing curvature of the spine. There is no space here for anyone to the Left of Cromwell, there is not one religious thought or fibre in his body, let alone word on his lips. 'You are no longer subjects' he tells the crowd as he shows them his hands dripping with Charles I's blood, 'you are citizens'. No wonder they looked stunned at this bizarre anachronism. Soon, as he rides through a market, he is shooting a hawker for selling badges with the king's head on them, shooting to maim, not to kill, so that Fairfax, in a supremely incomprehensible moment, shoots the man in the heart to put him out of his misery. This is used to be the emblem of the new tyranny (actually, we never see Charles's tyranny, only Cromwell's) and Fairfax's growing confusion about what to do for the best. But by now, the story has lost all contact with reality, so perhaps I should not leave it there.

I wish I did not have to add, but I think I must, that while, early on, some attempt is made to have a story that carries some basis in verifiable information, as we go along, the factual carelessness becomes breathtaking. If you are going to use a real historical figure as Fairfax's loyal trooper, that is to say George Joyce, why call him a sergeant both in 1646 and in 1653 (when he is made to attempt to assassinate Cromwell) when the real George Joyce was a cornet in 1646 and a colonel in 1653? If you are going to invent a member of the exiled court to visit Lady Fairfax so that she can tell them how to set up an escape for the king, why call him the Earl of York (when there was a perfectly good duke of York, the king's 12-year-old son) and lots of other less confusing titles? Why on earth does the king say that he conferred Fairfax's title on him (he didn't) and that if he doesn't toe the line, he will not confer the succession on any son the Fairfaxes have (an unthinkable thought for a man like Charles)? Why change the sequence so that the king's death warrant is signed before his trial starts, when the truth is startling enough? Why have Cromwell installed as Lord Protector by a clergyman dressed even more like Van Dyck's Archbishop Laud than the priest hanged as a witch in *Witchfinder General*. These are such unnecessary, pointless mistakes.

The film is a complete failure, not simply in terms of all the aims publicly stated by its writer and director, but as a study in human relationships. As the producers ran out of money, the film became more and more a study of a three-way relationship: husband torn between wife and buddy. And its greatest weakness is its utter failure to make any of those relationships credible or even interesting.

So the film has been a box-office flop. That will not stop it appearing endlessly as wallpaper on movie channels on the television for decades to come. But since it is such a failure, why waste time on writing about it, let alone worrying about it?

I suppose that I warn against the film because I have to consider what would have happened if the film had been bad history, but better box office. After all, the historical content in *To Kill a King* is no worse than the historical content in *Braveheart*, but the storytelling and technical excellence of the latter has had a wholly malign effect in giving a specious validation to nationalist feelings in Scotland and amongst the Scottish diaspora. Perhaps we do not think that matters. Would we feel the same if a film skilfully made by Holocaust deniers fed into neo-Nazism consciousness? Fine, but that is close to home. So can the falsification of events 350 years ago matter? Would a film as well made as *Braveheart* and as careless with History as *To Kill a King* but concerned with Cromwell's conquest of Ireland (with a polemic intended to see those events through the fevered imaginations of the present) be as harmlessly malign (thus far) as *Braveheart*?

The profession of History exists to allow people to understand themselves in space in time. It does this in three ways. The first purpose of History is to help us to understand how the past is *different* from the present ('the past is a foreign country; they do things differently there'). If we can learn to understand the very different ways in which men and women in the past understood themselves and made sense of the world they lived in, we can come to see how highly contingent is own understanding of our world. It makes us more tolerant of the differences between ourselves and others, and less sure that we have solved the problems of existence in ways superior to (rather than different to) the ways others have solved them. The second purpose of History is to teach us how the present is informed by the past; how there is a historical logic behind the way we are, the way we live, the way we relate to one another politically, economically, culturally. The third way is to investigate the second of these through the first – to assess the links between past and present without seeking to explain the past in the categories of the present. This is the highest form of History.

To understand why there was such widespread belief in witches and witchcraft in the seventeenth century is an example of the first; to understand the major Christian traditions in modern Britain and to understand how Britain became an unusually open and free culture is an example of the second; to understand why Britain had a revolution in the mid-seventeenth century (which involves interrogating the culturally relative term 'revolution') but not later is an example of the third.

We are moving into an age when the authority of the text is diminishing and the authority of the moving image is increasing. At schools, even colleges, as the habit of sustained reading diminishes, the use of film, including not only documentaries but feature films, is becoming more prominent. It is an influential medium of instruction, including instruction about History. When – and specifically when – feature films claim to be based on History, they are likely to be taken at face value. A film like *To Kill a King* which makes specious claims to being based on History is in danger of entering popular consciousness as a coarsening and destructive agent in developing an informed corporate memory of a formative period of History.

I do not want to be too strait-laced or alarmist about this. I am aware that one can create a political correctness about the past which is as unhealthy as is much political correctness about the present. But I have also seen the effect of Dan Brown's *The Da Vinci Code* in fanning anti-Catholic and anti-Christian feeling in Britain and elsewhere. People I know well, and who are confused about their residual post-Christian anxiety and guilt, have taken at face value a statement at the beginning of the book which reads: 'FACT: The Priory of Sion – a European secret society founded in 1099 – is a secret organisation. In 1975 Paris's *Bibliotheque National* discovered parchments known as *Les Dossiers Secrets,* identifying numerous members of the Priory of Sion, including Sir Isaac Newton, Sandro Botticelli, Victor Hugo and Leonardo da Vinci.' The Priory is in possession of the proof that Christ married Mary Magdalena, and had a child or children by her who have living descendants. When Dan Brown wrote this, the forgers of *Les Dossiers Secrets* and of the Priory of Sion had long since been exposed and some at least had confessed and recanted. Yet, many thousands now believe that *The Da Vinci Code* is a fictionalized account of a real history of a real alternative narrative of the life of Christ. Some of us care a lot about that. It is actually a classic adventure story with very clever puzzles and clues, not very well written but compellingly constructed. Its clever reliance in explaining puzzles relating to real places and real artefacts creates a veneer of verisimilitude which is reinforced by that bogus preface. The confusion of a real past with a fictionalized one through a false claim of factual accuracy has led to actual harm, against which one warns but does not censor.

There is no case for banning films that are bad History. But there is a case for trained historians to warn against them when, and only when, there is a danger that their claims to being historically based are being taken seriously. Stylistic conventions make this not a problem in the case of *Witchfinder General*; well-understood conventions of poetic licence makes this not a problem in the case of *Cromwell*. But the combination of public claim, careful attention to historical accuracy in relation to what we see as against what we hear makes *To Kill a King* an unimportant example of the kind of film that historians should warn against. No more, no less.

Suggestions for Further Reading

There are innumerable good biographies of Oliver Cromwell. The best recent ones are:

Peter Gaunt, *Oliver Cromwell* (Oxford, 1996).
J.C. Davis, *Oliver Cromwell* (Oxford, 2001).
John Morrill, *Oliver Cromwell* (Oxford, 2007)

Biographies of Fairfax and Charles I lack the same flair. But recommendable are:

M. A. Gibb, *The Lord General: A life of Thomas Fairfax* (London, 1938),
Charles Carlton, *Charles I: The Personal Monarch* (2nd edition, London, 1996).

There is a good popular biography of Matthew Hopkins, which should be backed up by some recent scholarship on him:

Richard Deacon, *Matthew Hopkins: Witchfinder General* (London, 1976).
J. A. Sharpe, *Instruments of Darkness: Witchcraft in England 1450–1750* (London, 1996), in which pp.128–47 concern Hopkins.

15

The Unfilmed Oliver Cromwell*

David L. Smith

This essay is intended to complement John Morrill's contribution to this volume by concentrating on those aspects of Oliver Cromwell that filmmakers have tended to neglect. This is therefore about dogs that did not bark in the night – or at any rate not during the films. I want to focus mainly on the two films that contain the two most extended cinematic portrayals of Cromwell, namely those by Richard Harris in *Cromwell* (1970) and by Tim Roth in *To Kill a King* (2003). Although made over 30 years apart, and despite their very evident differences of quality and approach, these two films raise fairly similar issues in terms of what they leave out.

Perhaps the most striking feature is that the Cromwell who appears in these films is Cromwell the military leader and/or Cromwell the regicide rather than Cromwell the Lord Protector. This thematic focus is closely linked to a corresponding chronological concentration, almost entirely on the 1640s and early 1650s. The Richard Harris Cromwell film concludes with the dissolution of the Rump Parliament, and there is then a closing shot of Cromwell's funeral effigy, complete with crown, orb and sceptre. The last 25 minutes or so of *To Kill a King* cover the period after 1649, but in a massively distorted manner that collapses the last nine-and-a-half years of Cromwell's life into series of garish, invented scenes. *Witchfinder-General* presents the Cromwell of the mid-1640s in a cameo role, and again this is very much Cromwell the soldier rather than Cromwell the Lord Protector. So why is this, and what do we lose as a result?

Much of the explanation surely lies in the fact that filmmakers have found Cromwell when he was fighting against Charles I a far more exciting subject than Cromwell when he was in power himself. Much of the force of Cromwell as played by Tim Roth or Richard Harris derives from the fact that this is an angry man, driven to righteous indignation – and ultimately armed resistance – against a tyrannical king. The Cromwell of the 1650s, and particularly the Lord Protector who from 1653 to 1658 was alternately exhilarated and tormented by power, is somehow a much less appealing subject. I suspect that many filmmakers would agree with a particularly candid passage in Christopher Hill's *God's Englishman*, interestingly published in the same year, 1970, that the Richard Harris Cromwell film was released. Hill admits:

> I sympathise with the ageing, disillusioned man who struggled on under the burden of the protectorate, knowing that without him worse would befall: who wanted to be painted 'warts and all'. But it is the boisterous and confident leader of the 1640s who holds my imagination, and whose pungent, earthy truths echo down the centuries. So long as men and women 'with the root of the matter in them' call in question those values of their society which deny our common humanity, so long indeed as the great issues of liberty and equality which Oliver raised remain unresolved, so long will he continue to fascinate, and the debate over him will continue.[1]

That passage is almost a commentary on, and an unintentional justification for, the Harris film. It not only reflects the politically radical atmosphere of the years around 1970, but also helps us to explain why filmmakers have concentrated on the portions of Cromwell's career that they have. In practice, it means that in the cinema Cromwell the ruler has consistently taken second place – and often no place at all – to Cromwell the crusader.

It is interesting to note that for the most part the same is also true of those television programmes that have been devoted to Cromwell. I am thinking, for example, of a Channel Four film about Cromwell that was broadcast in 2001, or of Richard Holmes's assessment of Cromwell in the BBC *Great Britons* series in 2002, which devoted only a few sentences to Cromwell's career after 1649.[2] In that sense, factual documentaries struggle as much as fictional films to do justice to the later Cromwell. The most notable exception that I have seen was a highly evocative episode of *Timewatch* in the mid-1980s in which an actor played out extracts from Cromwell's letters and speeches. These included some excerpts from the time of the Protectorate, and the programme caught something of Cromwell's complexity, inner turmoil and growing weariness.

More usually, however, the last phase of Cromwell's life, when he was Head of State, has been almost entirely neglected. With it, we lose not just a particular segment of Cromwell's career but also a whole dimension of his complex character. For it was in the years after 1653 that Cromwell wrestled with the dilemmas of power most painfully. It was in this period that his struggle to translate his ideals into some kind of reality became most acute. In his unbroken run of victories on the battlefields between 1642 and 1651, things had seemed so much more clear-cut: it was far easier to see the forces of good and evil, of right and wrong, personified in the two sides fighting each other. By contrast, in the complex politics of the Protectorate – the equivalent of the smoke-filled rooms of latter-day political wheeling and dealing – it was much more difficult for Cromwell to see his way clearly and to build a political and religious consensus. Those years were not as action-packed as his military career had been, nor did they witness anything as revolutionary as the trial and execution of the king; but they did have their dramatic episodes and they do offer important insights into his personality that cannot be gleaned from his earlier life.

In particular, the Protectorate was perhaps the phase of Cromwell's career that most graphically revealed his political and religious complexity, what Blair Worden has called his 'ideological schizophrenia'.[3] We see it in Cromwell's largely unsuccessful attempts to forge an effective working relationship with successive Protectorate Parliaments, where his belief in government by 'a single person and a Parliament' as a 'fundamental' co-existed uneasily with his frustration that most members did not share his commitment to a radical extension of liberty of conscience. We see a similar ambivalence in his temporary recourse to the more authoritarian expedient of the Major-Generals, established in 1655 to implement a 'reformation of manners', if necessary by coercive means. Perhaps the most profound inner tensions were those that became evident when Cromwell agonized for nearly three months in 1657 before declining Parliament's offer of the kingship. The Cromwell presented on film is almost always a figure battling on behalf of his ideals against opponents: his anger and frustration are reactions against their attempts to thwart those ideals, be this in the image of Richard Harris denouncing and dissolving the Rump, or the totally fabricated scene in which Tim Roth shoots a man for selling images of Charles I. What is missing from these depictions is the Cromwell divided against himself, the Cromwell torn apart by conflicting priorities and principles, the Cromwell weighed down by the burdens of power, the Cromwell who would have preferred 'to have lived under my woodside, to have kept a flock of sheep, rather than undertook such a place of government as this is'.[4] Those facets of his character and experience are absent mainly because Cromwell the Lord Protector has remained very largely unfilmed. The Cromwell of film faced many trials and tribulations, but he has not been portrayed as an ideological schizophrenic.

Perhaps a deeper reason why filmmakers have shied away from the later Cromwell is because the final phase of his career forces us, as it forced him, to confront the nature of failure. From the beginning of the English Civil War in 1642 until the king's execution in 1649, Cromwell's career was generally successful, despite some temporary setbacks and ultimately having to settle for an act of regicide that he had sought to avoid. From 1649 until the establishment of the Protectorate in 1653, his career was a somewhat more qualified success. But between the end of 1653 and his death in 1658, Cromwell's career was in many ways a failure. His last months, in particular, were lived in the shadow of disillusionment and despair. Cromwell's final speeches, to the short second sitting of the second Protectorate Parliament in January and February 1658, indicated that he was by then weary, overwrought, at times almost hysterical. Take this passage, for example, from his speech on 25 January 1658:

> I beseech you, what is the general spirit of this nation? Is it not that each sect of people . . . may be uppermost? That every sort of men may get the power into their hands, and that they would use it well. It were a happy thing if the nation would be content with rule. Content with rule, if it were but in civil things, and with those that would rule worst; because misrule is better than no rule, and an ill government, a bad one, is better than none. It is not that only, but we have an appetite to variety, to be not only making wounds, but widening those already made, as if we should see one making wounds in a man's side, and would desire nothing more than to be groping and grovelling with his fingers in those wounds . . . They would be making wounds, and rending and tearing, and making them wider than they are. Is not this the case?[5]

That is a very fine example of the kind of rhetoric that Cromwell was capable of delivering in his later years, but that has never been depicted – even in an adapted form – on film. Surely such a speech has enormous potential for powerful dramatic portrayal. Yet it also creates real difficulties. The language here is not only powerful but frankly disturbing, and would certainly not make for a comfortable cinematic experience. Furthermore, because it came so late in Cromwell's career it does not readily allow for closure on a more upbeat note. This is, of course, part of the key to Cromwell's perennial historical fascination; but for a film one can see why the earlier part of Cromwell's career, centred on his struggle against Charles I which ultimately led to the latter's execution, has seemed so much more appealing than attempting to portray an anguished soul struggling to come to terms with the disappointments of power.

Part of that anguish undoubtedly grew out of tensions within Cromwell's own make-up and collisions between different aspects of his beliefs. These tensions and collisions became ever more apparent during the course of the Protectorate. One of the worst aspects of Tim Roth's performance in *To Kill a King* is that he portrays Cromwell as a two-dimensional, violent, irrational monster, mowing down anyone who resists him, or even dares to think differently from him. He is not so much 'holier than thou' as 'angrier than thou', and strides belligerently through the film as though he is perpetually muttering 'out of my way – don't you know I've got a revolution to run?' There is no attempt to explore the far more interesting dilemmas of a man who wished to rule 'for [the people's] good not what pleases them'.[6] Nor is there even a hint of the ambivalences and internal contradictions of Cromwell that became such a besetting feature of his career, especially during the Protectorate.

One example will serve to illustrate what I mean. On 12 September 1654, Cromwell identified four 'fundamentals' of government: firstly, that no parliament should sit perpetually, and that new parliaments should be elected at regular intervals; secondly, that government should be 'by one single person and a Parliament'; thirdly, that there should be 'liberty of conscience' in religion; and finally, that control of the militia should be shared between parliament and the Lord Protector.[7] But what happened if some of these 'fundamentals' proved to be incompatible with others? What happened if, as in fact turned out to be the case, the majority of members of parliament with whom the Lord Protector had to govern were sceptical, if not downright hostile, towards an extension of 'liberty of conscience'? Cromwell was relatively unusual among godly Protestants in mid-seventeenth-century England in believing that God's elect were scattered among many different groups and denominations. This has never been depicted on film, yet it was a crucial aspect of his character. As he put it in September 1656,

That men that believe in Jesus Christ, ... men that believe the remission of sins through the blood of Christ and free justification by the blood of Christ, and live upon the grace of God: that those men that are certain they are so, they are members of Jesus Christ, and are to Him as the apple of His eye. Whoever hath this faith, let his form be what it will, [if] he [is] walking peaceably, without the prejudicing of others under another form, it is a debt due to God and Christ, and He will require it, if he, that Christian, may not enjoy this liberty.[8]

Cromwell's disregard for outward religious forms was reflected in his personal friendships with people as diverse as the Quaker leader George Fox and the former Anglican Archbishop of Armagh, James Ussher. Blair Worden and Colin Davis have shown that Cromwell did not seek religious toleration in a modern sense but rather wished to nurture peaceful co-existence between different religious groups as a way of ultimately reuniting God's people.[9] The problem was that his commitment to liberty of conscience differentiated him markedly from the majority of members of the Protectorate Parliaments who feared that such a policy would unleash what they regarded as 'errors, heresies and blasphemies'. There was thus a deep-rooted incompatibility between the two 'fundamentals' of liberty of conscience and government by 'a single person and a Parliament'.[10]

The inevitable consequence was that Cromwell faced an insoluble contradiction between different principles and priorities, a contradiction that helps to explain his inability to achieve a stable and effective working relationship with any parliament during the 1650s. He and the Protectorate Parliaments needed each other, yet found it impossible to work together, and this aroused a mutual sense of mistrust, frustration and bafflement. Cromwell's reactions and dilemmas were similar to those of someone in a relationship that they can neither break off nor make to work. Each time he met a new parliament he welcomed it in the hope that it might succeed where its predecessors had failed; but each time the mismatch between his priorities and those of the majority of members ensured that he was disappointed. None of these issues has ever been portrayed on film, and to present Cromwell as a fanatic driven by a monolithic ideology does less than justice to the inner conflicts that he himself never resolved, and perhaps only partially even recognized.

Such a portrayal is also impossible to square with contemporary accounts of him, be they positive or negative. Many of these accounts were far more successful at coping with the ambivalences of Cromwell's career and legacy than modern filmmakers have been.

None of the Cromwells portrayed on film – and especially not Tim Roth's – could plausibly have evoked the deeply enigmatic and ambiguous response expressed in Andrew Marvell's Horatian Ode.[11] These film portrayals are too morally and politically clear-cut to cope adequately with the idea of a noble failure, or a flawed achievement. Yet, when Cromwell died, those were precisely the intractable issues that haunted the more perceptive of his eulogists and early biographers. This is the kind of complex response that lies behind, for example, Thomas Sprat's wonderfully fresh and vivid line in 1659 that Cromwell had left 'behind a richer slime'.[12] Or take this passage, from one of the early lives of Cromwell, *The Perfect Politician*, by L.S., published in February 1660:

> After he had made use of all that could augment his interest, then humility condescended to look through his fingers at a crown; but still waiving the airy title of King, he rather chose to accept the substantial power of Protector. The *primum mobile* of his desires herein being somewhat satisfied, then Parliaments were rallied, and by him as familiarly routed . . . The pride and ambition which some say he was guilty of, may be easily excused as an original sin inherent in nature . . . His religion must not pass my pen. In this he was zealous, not altogether like the Pharisee that prayed in the Temple; but really often would he mourn in secret, and many times did his eyes in public distil tears at the nation's stubbornness.[13]

This is a far more complicated, ambivalent and subtle characterization of Cromwell than that portrayed in any film.

If ambiguity is one feature that is missing from cinematic depictions of Cromwell, gentleness is another. Perhaps the most moving account of the tender side of Cromwell's nature was provided by John Maidstone, the steward and cofferer of the protectoral household, in a letter that he wrote to John Winthrop a few weeks before the Restoration. According to Maidstone, Cromwell was

> naturally compassionate towards objects in distress, even to an effeminate measure; though God had made him a heart, wherein was left little room for any fear, but what was due to himself, of which there was a large proportion, yet did he exceed in tenderness towards sufferers.[14]

That passage captures an aspect of Cromwell's personality that on film is only really glimpsed – and then all too briefly – in the Harris portrayal. Even that is slightly too spiky and not sensitive enough, but it is still better than anything else that the cinema has achieved.

Furthermore, it remains difficult to see how the filmed Cromwell could have evoked the most persistent criticism of the historical Cromwell that sprang from all points along the political and religious spectrum, namely that he was a canting hypocrite. To portray him merely as an exemplar of the principle that all power corrupts is a gross over-simplification. Such a two-dimensional view does not begin to do justice to the mixture of grudging admiration, disapproval and regret that Cromwell increasingly evoked towards the end of his life, as caught, for instance, in this letter that the Cheshire Parliamentarian Robert Duckenfield wrote to him in March 1655:

> I desire to imitate Caleb and Joshua in the wilderness, as near as may be, and not to seek a confederacy with those who limit God to their passions, and against whom God hath an evident controversy, & c. I believe firmly, that the root and tree of piety is alive in your lordship, though the leaves thereof, through abundance of temptations and flatteries, seem to me to be withered much of late; yet I hope time and experience will have a good influence upon your lordship (*Deo juvente*) & c.[15]

It is difficult to imagine Tim Roth's Cromwell prompting such a delicately balanced reaction from anyone.

Film has thus left out much that might explain Cromwell's capacity to inspire ambivalent feelings among his contemporaries. Ironically, however, it also omits the episode in his career that, more than any other, has made him an object of passionate hatred, especially within Ireland and the Irish diaspora, namely Cromwell's conquest of Ireland in 1649–1650. There has never been any attempt to depict on film that campaign in general, or the notorious events at Drogheda and Wexford in particular. They are not even mentioned in either of the two films that I am concentrating on here. Perhaps this part of Cromwell's career is simply too controversial to handle, and to attempt to film episodes where feelings have run so deep for so long is just too difficult. It may well be that the resurgence of troubles in Ireland in the years after 1969 made it even less likely that filmmakers would wish to dwell on Cromwell's career in Ireland. Furthermore, any filmmaker has to bear in mind likely audiences, and the sensitivities of the large Irish community in the United States have no doubt been an important consideration. Cromwell's association with atrocities in Ireland, and the complex nature of his responsibility for them, must surely be crucial in explaining why Hollywood studios have generally avoided dealing with Cromwell. It is probable that British filmmakers have been influenced by the lead of their American colleagues in likewise preferring to steer clear of this subject. Cromwell's actions in Ireland were too disturbing and too morally problematic to lend themselves readily to cinematic portrayal. Current research is generating important revisionist accounts that suggest that Cromwell's record in Ireland may command some degree of understanding and respect;[16] but it is virtually impossible to do justice to such scholarly insights in the context of a film.

However, the fact that Cromwell's treatment of Scotland has also been almost completely neglected on film suggests that the omission of Ireland is part of a broader problem of Anglocentricity in the way that Cromwell has been portrayed. Scotland receives one glancing mention in *To Kill a King*, and none at all in the Richard Harris film. The Cromwell of film is very much an English Cromwell. He is never portrayed doing anything outside England, or even showing very much interest in developments abroad. This is perhaps partly because Cromwell's more attractive side has seemed to be most evident in England, but it probably also owes something to a pervasive Anglocentricity that scholars have only really begun to challenge during the past 20 years or so. Such historiographical developments are too recent to have had any impact on film as yet.

This Anglocentricity, together with the lack of interest on the part of filmmakers in Cromwell's years as Lord Protector, may help to explain another curious phenomenon, which is the almost complete neglect on film of his foreign policy. With the exception of the disastrous Western Design, this has often been seen as one of the more successful aspects of Cromwellian rule, yet it barely features on film. This is in marked contrast with for example Elizabeth I, whose stand against the Spanish Armada has been the subject of numerous film depictions. Admittedly, to say 'I may have the body of a weak and feeble women, but I have the heart and stomach of a King, and a King of England too' may lend itself to cinematic portrayal rather more easily than Cromwell uttering phrases like: 'Your great enemy is the Spaniard. He is. He is a natural enemy . . . The Spaniard is your enemy . . . Truly he hath an interest in your bowels'.[17] But the fact that filmmakers can readily adapt such quotations if they so wish suggests that there may be deeper reasons for the lack of film treatments of his foreign policy. Cromwell was, for instance, among those English rulers and warriors who did not receive a heroic film portrayal during the Second World War, a fact that may indicate that it was – at least in those days – acceptable to portray royal patriots, or those who fought on their behalf (such as Lord Nelson), but not to portray republican patriots. A film about Cromwell may have been no more comfortable a prospect in the 1940s than a battleship named Cromwell (Winston Churchill's idea, vetoed by King George V) had been during the First World War. It is also possible that the lack of glorification of Cromwell as a patriotic leader during the Second World War may be partly explained by the reluctance of Churchill and his government to risk offending the powerful Irish–American lobby at a time when they were heavily reliant on the goodwill of a Democratic President of the United States. At any rate, Cromwell peering beyond England's shores, waging war against Spain or the Dutch Republic, or even organizing assistance for the persecuted Protestants of the Vaudois, all remain among the unfilmed aspects of his career.[18]

Cromwell thus emerges on film as a little Englander. Ironically, this can be related to a final insoluble tension within his own beliefs, which again has entirely escaped the camera's eye, and which stems from Cromwell's view of England as an elect nation. Convinced that the English were a chosen people, Cromwell repeatedly encountered the problem of how to affirm the godly so that they eventually became coterminous with the nation as a whole. In furthering this process, how were the interests of the godly minority to be reconciled with those of the people more generally? It was an issue that preoccupied Cromwell and one that he addressed frequently in his speeches. He hoped desperately that the two interests could be reconciled, and he clutched at any potential settlement that he thought might achieve this, as for example when he told the parliamentary framers of the Humble Petition and Advice in April 1657:

> I think you have provided for the liberty of the people of God, and for the liberty of the nation. And I say he sings sweetly that sings a song of reconciliation betwixt these two interests! And it is a pitiful fancy, and wild and ignorant to think they are inconsistent. Certainly they may consist![19]

Always, however, he was disappointed, and such words have something of the character of whistling in the dark. Yet they show Cromwell to have been a reflective if unsystematic religious thinker, and they reveal a more pensive side of his nature that belies the man of action so often portrayed on screen. The difficulty is that his reflections sometimes led him into areas of thought that were too sophisticated and ultimately too intractable to lend themselves to film treatment. The Cromwell who, like his own admired 'russet-coated captain', 'knows what he fights for, and loves what he knows'[20] is much easier to film; but there was so much more to Cromwell than that, especially during the latter part of his career.

A further irony is that despite this Anglocentric presentation of Cromwell, he has not proved to be an attractive subject for the recent vogue of English heritage films.[21] Cromwell has, so to speak, lost out twice over: he is generally presented on film as a little Englander, and yet he has not lent himself readily to the makers of English heritage films which have proved so popular during the 1980s and 1990s. There are a number of possible reasons for this. First, these films engage with issues of Englishness and English national identity, and from this perspective Cromwell is a distinctly problematic and controversial figure. His religious radicalism and republicanism sit uncomfortably with national traditions that are often associated with monarchy and an established Church. The contrast with a figure like Elizabeth I, who was the subject of one of the most successful heritage films in 1998, is very striking. Compared to Elizabeth, Cromwell is a far less consensual and more angular individual, and as a result he is less well suited to appeal to a broad audience. The relationship between Englishness and republicanism remains highly contested, as does the issue of an established Church of England: on such questions Cromwell is identified with attitudes that seem too divisive and contentious to recommend themselves naturally to the makers of heritage films and quality costume drama.

It is likely that there are also several other reasons why the makers of such films have fought shy of Cromwell. In a number of ways, he fails to meet some of the most important criteria which Andrew Higson has identified as characteristic of this genre of films. Cromwell's life does not really provide much in the way of romantic love interest or sexual politics, nor does it contain elements that might appeal to a specifically female audience (here again Elizabeth I provides an instructive contrast).[22] Moreover, Cromwell offers filmmakers very little opportunity for the 'aesthetics of display'. The architectural locations with which he is readily associated are either not unique to him (Whitehall, Hampton Court), or relatively obscure and undistinguished (Huntingdon, Ely). Likewise, an era of puritan austerity affords little scope for lavish costumes or visually appealing spectacles. Heritage films have often been closely linked with English literature, either as direct literary adaptations or via more indirect forms of inspiration, but here again Cromwell has missed out. The canonical writers who engaged most vividly with his career, John Milton and Andrew

Marvell, did not produce the kind of accessible literary oeuvre that lends itself easily to film treatment.[23] All these considerations, together with the concerns about the American market examined above, probably explain why Cromwell has not figured in the wave of English heritage films for which he might, at first sight, appear to offer an appropriate subject.

An examination of the unfilmed Cromwell thus tells us much both about what filmmakers have thought heroic in him, and about what they have found too problematic, too unattractive, or simply too difficult to film. In general, the nature of failure, disillusionment, and the moral and political dilemmas of power have seemed less appealing than the vision of Cromwell leading a crusade against a tyrannical king. As a result, film portrayals of Cromwell to date have done less than justice to him, and especially to the later years of his life. It will be fascinating to see whether this situation is ever even partially redressed in the future.

Suggestions for Further Reading

Barry Coward, *The Cromwellian Protectorate* (Manchester, 2002).

J. C. Davis, *Oliver Cromwell* (London, 2001).

John Morrill, 'Oliver Cromwell', in *The Oxford Dictionary of National Biography* (Oxford, 2004).

David L. Smith (ed.), *Cromwell and the Interregnum* (Oxford, 2003).

16

*Winstanley**

Christopher Durston

Kevin Brownlow and Andrew Mollo's 90-minute, black-and-white film *Winstanley*, which appeared in 1975, is an interesting and important piece of work both in terms of its historiographical significance and cinematic merit. Directed by two young, but highly respected filmmakers and students of film history, it tells the story of the ill-fated attempt by the Digger visionary, Gerrard Winstanley, to set up a communal farm on St George's Hill near Weybridge in Surrey in 1649. After briefly sketching-in the historical background, Winstanley's early career and the sequence of events during 1649, this essay will consider the treatment the story receives in the film, how the film was devised and created, and in particular how it differed from the novel, *Comrade Jacob*, upon which it was based. It will conclude with some comments on the filmmakers' 'take' on the story and a brief assessment of the impact of the film over the last 30 years.

II

The 20 years between 1640 and 1660 were some of the most dramatic and momentous in English history. The 1640s witnessed a full-scale Civil War, the public trial and execution of the English monarch, and the establishment of a short-lived republic. The exceptional nature of these years also gave rise to a great deal of political and religious debate, and led to the emergence of radical political groups like the Levellers, who believed that power lay with the people, that government was a trust, that the vote was the birthright of all adult males, and that all were equal before the law. The 1650s meanwhile saw England under

Plate 13 Kevin Brownlow's *Winstanley* used mainly amateur actors and most unusually focused on scenes of everyday life in early-modern England. Courtesy
of BFI and The Kobal Collection for the image of Jonathan Walton, Muriel
Higgins and Don Higgins from the motion picture *Winstanley* (1975).

the control of a military regime with a strong puritan flavour which wished to impose its own strict moral and religious values on the English people, but which was also committed to a wide measure of religious toleration for law-abiding Trinitarian Protestants.

In these circumstances the religious conformity of the pre-war period broke down and significant numbers of people began to opt out of the national Church and join the ranks of the radical sects. In the early 1650s groups of Ranters, who believed their elect status had freed them from any obligation to observe the contemporary moral code, denied the existence of sin and even of a transcendent deity. They also allegedly met in public houses to smoke tobacco, drink alcohol, engage in casual sex and perform parodies of conventional religious services. As we shall see below, some of them were to turn up on the Digger collective farm and to prove a very disruptive influence there. The 1650s also witnessed the emergence and spectacular growth of the Quaker movement, which challenged the established religious system by rejecting predestination and all set liturgical forms, and by refusing to show the customary deference to their social betters. Gerrard Winstanley's Diggers, who will be discussed in detail below, were another of these radical religious groups that grew out of the dislocation and confusion of the post-Civil War years in England.

A number of twentieth-century historians were fascinated by these radical groups and the way their ideas seemed so far in advance of their time. This was particularly true of the Marxist Oxford historian, Christopher Hill, who in works like his seminal *The World Turned Upside Down* of 1972 praised them for their anti-authoritarianism and rejection of the Protestant work ethic.[1] All this attention and admiration led to some exaggeration of their contemporary importance. In the mid-1980s Hill's championing of the Ranters in particular was severely criticized by J. C. Davis, who argued that he had been unduly attracted to the group's rejection of the social and moral norms of their day and as a result had greatly exaggerated its contemporary significance.[2] While many of today's historians would argue that Davis's criticisms of Hill were somewhat overstated, they would be careful to stress that only a very small percentage of the population of mid-seventeenth-century England was ever attracted to the positions outlined by the radicals and that they had only a limited impact upon contemporary events. Some, however, would nonetheless still argue that the radical sects were of great importance in that they destroyed forever the older belief that Church and State should be coterminous and thus helped to shape the subsequent multi-denominational character of English Christianity.

III

Gerrard Winstanley was born in Wigan in 1609 into a mercer's family.[3] In 1630 he was apprenticed to the widow of a London merchant tailor, Sarah Gater. In 1638 he was admitted a freeman of the Merchant Taylors' Company, and the following year he moved into his own residence in the parish of St Olave, Jewry, in the city. In September 1640 he married Susan King, the daughter of a London barber-surgeon, who owned some land in Cobham in Surrey. The outbreak of the Civil War in 1642 had a serious adverse effect on trading conditions in London and elsewhere, and within 18 months Winstanley's recently established business had failed and he was declared bankrupt. At the end of 1643 he travelled down to Cobham where with the help of his father-in-law he obtained a small house and made a living as a grazier. The post-war economic disruption of the late 1640s once again, however, badly disrupted his personal finances.

During the middle years of the 1640s he steadily became more radical in his religious beliefs. After abandoning the established Church of England, he may have briefly joined a gathered Baptist Church in the Cobham area, before eventually concluding that all outward forms of religious worship were superfluous. Thereafter he began to develop a set of highly personal, mystical religious beliefs, based on a socially radical reading of scripture and the promptings of God's spirit which he believed spoke directly to him in trances and dreams. These ideas were outlined in a number of early pamphlets including *The New Law of Righteousness*, published in January 1649 a few days before Charles I's execution, where he argued that the private ownership of property was the root not only of social inequality but also of all human sinfulness.

On Sunday 1 April 1649 Winstanley and his friend the former New Model Army soldier, William Everard, led a small group of followers on to common heathland at St George's Hill in Walton parish, Surrey, and started to sow a number of vegetables. This represented a defiant act of trespass, as the land was the property of the local landowners who used it to graze their livestock. Winstanley justified the act in a tract published in late April, *The True Levellers Standard Advanced*, in which he argued that the earth had been created as 'a common treasury' for the whole of mankind. Over the next few months around 90 poor people, mostly from the local area, came to join them and to form the nucleus of the Digger collective farm. The local landowners were greatly disturbed by the Diggers' actions and referred the matter to the head of the army, Thomas Fairfax. Fairfax, however, exhibited some sympathy for the community, a number of whose members had recently fought under him and his local commander, Captain John Gladman, and initially did not consider the matter important enough to intervene. The landowners thus took their own direct action, attacking the community on several occasions and destroying its crops.

As a result of this harassment, in August 1649 the community moved to Little Heath in Cobham parish several miles away. This brought them on to the land of the rector of West Horsley, John Platt, who now led a concerted campaign against them, both by orchestrating fresh attacks on their settlement and by complaining to the Council of State that they were violent and dissolute in their lifestyle. At the start of 1650 Winstanley again defended the Diggers' cause in his tract *A New Yeers Gift to Parliament and the Armie*. But John Platt and his landowning neighbours remained thoroughly unconvinced by his arguments, and on Good Friday 1650 Platt led 50 men in an attack that finally destroyed the Digger settlement, burning it to the ground and forcing its inhabitants to disperse. A number of other Digger communities which had sprung up in the south-east during the same year met a similar fate.

A disillusioned Winstanley spent the remainder of the 1650s in the Cobham area. At some point during that decade or the early 1660s he joined the rapidly growing Quaker movement, which shared many of his radical religious beliefs. His own economic fortunes improved after he was given a grant of land by his father-in-law, and following the Restoration of Charles II in 1660 he even held local office for a while. Following his wife's death in the early 1660s, he remarried in 1664 and became the father of a son the following year. He died in London in 1676.

IV

The film *Winstanley* attempts to give a faithful and historically accurate account of the events at St George's Hill and Little Heath in 1649 and 1650. It begins, however, with an atmospheric prologue set to music from Prokofiev's opera, *Alexander Nevsky*, which sketches in the tumultuous events of the period leading up to April 1649. In dramatic scenes that some critics have seen as homage to early silent filmmakers like Eisenstein, the prologue portrays the final battles of the Civil War, the famous debates in Putney Church in late 1647 over what form of post-war political settlement the New Model Army should support, the subsequent mutiny by Leveller soldiers at Corkbush Field near Ware in Hertfordshire, and the summary execution of the ringleaders by the army commanders, Fairfax and Cromwell.

The mood then abruptly changes, becoming much quieter and more tranquil as the film moves to depict the early days of the Digger settlement and uses Winstanley's own words to explain his motives for founding the communal farm. From the outset Winstanley is portrayed as a gentle and kindly idealist, who is easily discouraged when presented with the evidence of the uncharitable behaviour of his contemporaries. His friend, William Everard, by contrast is shown as a wild and impetuous, perhaps even slightly deranged, activist. Early scenes show the arrival of the first recruits to the farm, many of whom are depicted as desperately poor, sick and hungry, and initially highly suspicious of the warm welcome they receive from the Diggers. The film then switches to Parson John Platt's substantial rectory to record the tensions between the authoritarian and rigid Presbyterian minister and his unhappy and pregnant wife, Margaret, who incurs her husband's wrath by reading one of Winstanley's pamphlets over dinner. These details of the Platts' troubled marital relationship and Margaret's attraction for Winstanley and his ideas have no basis in historical fact but, as we shall see below, were taken from the novel that originally inspired the film. Subsequent scenes include an angry exchange between Winstanley and Platt over the role of organized religion and the responsibility of the rich towards the poor; Winstanley's audiences with the local lord of the Manor, Sir Francis Drake, and later with Thomas Fairfax; and Fairfax's subsequent visit to the Digger community. Margaret Platt, meanwhile, becomes increasingly drawn to Winstanley. Following the birth of her child, she consults him on several occasions and offers him financial support to sustain the settlement which he reluctantly accepts.

The middle section of the film is taken up with the escalating assaults on the settlement by Platt's henchmen, and the resultant divisions within the Diggers between those, like Winstanley, who counsel against retaliation and others who wanted to strike back against their attackers. It also covers the arrest and subsequent release of a number of Diggers for trespass, and the appearance of Winstanley and some of his followers before Kingston magistrates, where they are refused permission to conduct their own defence. The film also deals in some detail with the arrival at the settlement of a group of blaspheming and hedonistic Ranters. They refuse to work in the fields, smoke tobacco and make sexual advances to some of the Digger women. Their leader also attempts to undermine Winstanley's leadership of the community; he is highly critical of his motives for founding the community and accuses him of being motivated by pride and ambition. The later scenes of the film portray Margaret Platt's decision to join the Diggers, her rapid disillusionment with the miserable realities of life for the Diggers, and her outraged departure after one of the Ranters 'goes naked for a sign' in front of her. She then returns to the rectory to submit to her husband and to confirm his prejudices by regaling him with stories of scandalous Digger practices. The last scenes of the film portray the final destruction of the settlement and the triumphant return of Platt to his village amid the cheers of his parishioners. It closes with a shot of the deserted settlement with a voice-over reading a passage from Winstanley's *A New Yeers Gift to Parliament and the Armie*

> And here I end, having put my arm as far as my strength will go to advance righteousness: I have writ, I have acted, I have peace: and now must I wait to see the spirit do his own work in the hearts of others: and whether England shall be the first land, or some other, wherein truth shall sit down in triumph.

V

By the time they embarked on the filming of *Winstanley* in the late 1960s, Kevin Brownlow and Andrew Mollo already had a growing reputation as talented filmmakers. Brownlow was the author of several respected studies of early silent movies, and the pair had also produced and directed the 1965 film, *It Happened Here*, a counterfactual account of life in Nazi-occupied Britain during the 1940s that had received much praise for its authenticity and attention to period detail. As Brownlow later explained in an interview in the journal *Cineaste*, the idea for the second film came about when, shortly after the appearance of *It Happened Here*, Miles Halliwell, a boyhood friend of Andrew Mollo and schoolteacher from Farnham in Surrey who had had a small part in the previous film, gave the two filmmakers a copy of a novel about the Diggers, *Comrade Jacob* by David Caute.[4]

Caute, a left-wing academic and fellow of All Souls, Oxford, who would go on to write a number of academic studies of the French Marxist intellectuals, published the novel in 1961. Its title probably contained a reference to the story of Jacob and Esau from the Bible, which Winstanley referred to on occasions in his own writings, and perhaps also to the sixteenth-century German mystic, Jacob Boehme, whose ideas might have influenced the Digger leader. Perhaps through an earlier mutual membership of the British Communist Party, Caute knew Christopher Hill, the Marxist tutor in early-modern history at Balliol College and an expert on the English Civil War, whom he consulted while writing the book. As a result, the novel is very well informed and gives a historically accurate account of the Digger story. Caute, however, makes no attempt to hide his strong admiration for Winstanley and his ideas, portraying the Digger leader as the sane voice of communism and a man 'with his feet on the ground and his head in the clouds'.[5] All the rich landowners in the book are shown in an extremely negative light, and Winstanley's tormentor, Captain John Gladman, is portrayed as acquisitive and vindictive, and as one of the proto-capitalist economic improvers about whom Hill wrote so extensively in his own books.

One of the oddest and least attractive features of Caute's novel is its gender sub-plot. The author depicts the Platts as very unhappily married, and Margaret Platt moreover is described as extremely unattractive physically. Winstanley indeed refers to her as 'almost grotesquely unlovely' and 'the negation of all womanly fragility, with a faintly distasteful odour'.[6] Margaret also puts forward proto-feminist, anti-men opinions, and is sexually aggressive towards the innocent Winstanley, who Caute makes a widower although in reality his wife Susan was still alive and was probably with him on St George's Hill. Although Caute's Winstanley is sexually frustrated, he rejects Margaret's advance as he finds her physically repellent. He subsequently, however, forms a strong physical and emotional attachment to a young woman Judith who arrives at the Digger settlement with his old friend from London, Robert Coster. A love triangle develops, and eventually on finding Gerrard and Judith enjoying an intimate tête-à-tête, the insanely jealous Margaret Platt flies into a rage and stops the financial subsidies which have been keeping the Digger community going through the winter months.

Whatever this story might suggest about Caute's own attitudes to women and sex, most of it was wisely left out of the film. After Brownlow and Mollo had spent some time doing their own research by reading Winstanley's tracts and contemporary accounts of the St George's Hill experiment amongst the Thomason Tracts in the British Library, they quickly realized that it was a complete fabrication. Under the influenced of their female script adviser, Marina Lewycka, and perhaps also of the nascent women's movement of the late 1960s and early 1970s, they decided not to include Caute's sexual sub-plot, even though they recognized it would have lent a more racy edge to the film and perhaps added to its box-office appeal. In his 1980 *Cineaste* interview Brownlow intimated that they had found the story rather distasteful and felt that Caute had let his imagination run away with him. They had also baulked at trying to persuade an actor to play a hideously ugly woman. Thus, while they retained for the film script the story of the unhappy Platt marriage and the fact that Margaret Platt was strongly attracted to Winstanley, they presented her not like Caute as an alarming and voracious sexual predator, but rather as 'a romantic middle class person, in love with the idea that the Diggers represent, but blind to the reality'.[7]

VI

Initially Brownlow and Mollo who knew little about seventeenth-century history were slow to see the cinematic potential of *Comrade Jacob*. They warmed to the project, however, after immersing themselves in Winstanley's own writings, and then spent some considerable time trying to find backers for the project, before eventually receiving a small grant of around £17,000 from the British Film Institute. Brownlow's original plan was to employ professional actors, but Mollo felt that for both aesthetic and financial reasons they should use amateurs and suggested that Miles Halliwell should play Winstanley. Halliwell agreed and began to research the Civil War period and the early development of the Quaker movement. His middle class, home-counties accent was quite wrong for the Lancastrian Winstanley, but as his attempts at a northern accent were in Brownlow's phrase, 'pure Worker's Playtime' they decided he should use his normal voice.[8] It was Halliwell who enlisted a number of other members of the cast: his wife Alison played Margaret Platt, and a school colleague William Everard. Sid Rawle, who played the Ranter leader, was heavily involved in the squatting movement in Camden at the time. In the end all the cast, except Jerome Willis who played Thomas Fairfax, were amateurs. Brownlow later told *Cineaste* that the use of amateur actors reinforced the sense of realism he was trying to achieve and that 'the occasional rough delivery serves to remind you that these are ordinary people'. He also commented: 'When you consider that virtually no one in the cast had appeared before a camera in their lives, the conviction they bring to their roles is a tribute to each of them.'[9]

The film took fully eight years to shoot. As most of the actors had other jobs, much of the filming took place at weekends, and financial difficulties also slowed progress on occasions. The scenes in and around the Digger settlement were filmed on Surrey heathland near Churt, a number of the interior scenes were shot at Chastleton House in Oxfordshire (recently opened to the public by the National Trust), and the court scene was filmed at Malmesbury in Wiltshire. As he had with *It Happened Here*, Andrew Mollo spared no pains to make the film as accurate as possible. After researching the period extensively, he borrowed seventeenth-century armour from the Tower of London, enlisted the help of the battle reconstruction group, the Roundhead Association, and went to great lengths to ensure that the clothes, shoes, weapons, agricultural implements and breeds of animal were all authentic. The filming also often took place in bad weather, with the resultant footage further emphasizing the privations suffered by the Diggers. At the end of shooting, a rough cut of the film was shown to Christopher Hill, who suggested a number of changes to enhance the period accuracy.

Kevin Brownlow told *Cineaste* in 1980 that the mood of the film had been influenced by the engravings made by Jacques Callot during the Thirty Years' War, as well as by early German silent movies, like von Gerlach's *Chronicles of the Grey House* and Dreyer's *The Parson's Widow*. He also stated that he had tried to recapture the feel of the seventeenth-century Dutch and Flemish paintings he had studied in the Rijksmuseum in Amsterdam.[10] Much of the resultant film was reflective and sombre in feel, and some of the interior shots of Margaret Platt working or reading do call to mind the Dutch interiors of Vermeer and others. The film was also very successful in depicting the harsh realities of life for the lower orders of early-modern England; the fact that it was shot in black and white was important here, as this seemed only to emphasize the bleakness of the situation faced by most of those who joined Winstanley's community.

VII

Kevin Brownlow argued in 1980 that the aim of the film was to paint as true a picture as possible of the Digger story. He told the *Cineaste* interviewer that *Winstanley* was not a political film, but rather 'a trip in a time-machine back to the seventeenth century', adding: 'There is no point whatever in making a historical film, unless you are going to show what happened. Fiction interests me less and less.'[11] He went on to admit, however, that in their depiction of Gerrard Winstanley they had to play down the Digger leader's mystical qualities, as these would simply have been too difficult to capture on film, as they possessed neither the creative imagination nor the budget of a Fellini. Furthermore neither he nor Mollo made any secret of their great admiration for Winstanley or what he called his 'heroic attempt to change the way people lived'. Those viewing the film are left in no doubt that the Diggers had right on their side and that their opponents were the representatives of an oppressive and indefensible social system. Occasionally some of Winstanley's adversaries, such as Sir Francis Drake's wife, do provide some insight into the religious and ideological underpinning to the hierarchical seventeenth-century social order, but most often characters like Parson Platt are simply shown as heartless, uncharitable and only out to protect their economic interests. In this sense, and contrary to the aspirations of most modern historiography, the film does take a moral stance and is quicker to condemn rather than explain.

Brownlow also firmly rejected the suggestion that the film was meant to have any contemporary relevance or draw any lessons for the time in which it was created. But here too, he was perhaps a little disingenuous. He admitted that he believed Winstanley to have been 'a couple of hundred years ahead of his time', and the casting of Sid Rawle (cf p. 240) – the 1970s hippie who was involved with groups of squatters who illegally occupied empty properties – as the Ranter leader inevitably lent a contemporary edge to the story and invited comparisons between the Diggers and the twentieth-century homeless. The confrontations between the hardworking and God-fearing Diggers and the indolent and morally suspect Ranters may also have parallels in the 1970s disagreements between the 'drop-out' hippie movement and groups of more politically engaged revolutionary socialists.

Writing in *Historical Journal of Film, Radio and Television* in 2000, John Tibbetts, a lecturer in cinema studies at the University of Kansas, argues that the film gives 'a presentist view of history' and that Brownlow and Mollo 'project contemporary concerns and considerations onto the screen of a meticulously constructed past'. He saw the film as reflecting 1970s concerns over hippies and squatting, and even suggested that the film's band of amateur 'outsider' actors may have drawn unconscious parallels between their own filmmaking project and the Diggers' efforts and aspirations.[12] This view must be taken seriously. There can be little doubt that, despite the directors' firm intention to portray the realities of seventeenth-century life and the great pains they took to keep the details authentic, by adopting an unashamedly pro-Digger line the film does reflect the contemporary concerns of the time of its creation. Gerrard Winstanley is shown as the upholder of the mid-twentieth-century values of egalitarianism, personal liberty and religious autonomy, and as an individual engaged in a heroic but uneven struggle with the forces of political, economic and religious dogmatism and oppression. The film's directors, and many of the political and social radicals of the 1960s and 1970s, would undoubtedly have empathized with him in this fight. Consciously or unconsciously, they probably also drew parallels between his failure to put right the social evils of his day and the inability of the political, social, cultural revolutionaries of the 1960s to transform their own world permanently.

VIII

Reaction to the film was generally, though not universally, positive. Predictably, Christopher Hill raved about it; his 1975 *Past and Present* review – the only film review ever to appear in that august academic journal – described it as 'meticulously accurate' and enthused about its 'imaginative reconstruction', claiming that it revealed more about the ordinary people of seventeenth-century England than a score of textbooks.[13] Subsequently it has received many plaudits from film buffs and cinema scholars alike, although John Tibbetts has been less complimentary, criticizing it for its weak acting and desultory plot.[14] The film has broken no box-office records and rarely now receives screenings, but it has played a significant part in the resurgence of interest in Gerrard Winstanley and the Diggers over the last 30 years, which has seen them emerge as early pioneers of the 'green' movement and as the heroes of environmental lobbyists, like George Monbiot, and groups like 'The Land is Ours'. In 1999, the 350th anniversary of the Digger episode, this latter group staged a second symbolic mass trespass on St Georges's Hill – now ironically the site of the luxury residences of some of the south-east's wealthiest individuals. Like the scholarly writing of historians, no film can ever fully capture the realities of life for our ancestors. *Winstanley* is, nonetheless, a brave and, on the whole, highly successful attempt to retell an important and until recently sadly neglected aspect of our national story.

Suggestions for Further Reading

J. C. Davis and J. D. Alsop, 'Gerrard Winstanley', *Oxford Dictionary of National Biography* (Oxford, 2004).

Christopher Hill, *The World Turned Upside Down: Radical Ideas in the English Revolution* (London, 1972).

J. C. Davis, *Fear, Myth and History: The Ranters and the Historians* (Cambridge, 1986).

17

Why Don't the Stuarts Get Filmed?

Ronald Hutton

Let me begin this chapter by making it plain that I know perfectly well that I have given it a nonsensical title. The Stuarts do get filmed: in fact they have been filmed more often than most other royal families in world history. Thanks to the historical development of the industry (with the centre of power in it rapidly shifting to the English-speaking world), and the sheer survival powers of the British monarchy, British dynasties have always been particular favourites of the broad screen. Among those, the Stuarts emerge very respectably as the third in popularity, featuring in at least 24 films, and also making a considerable impact on television drama. The House of Saxe-Coburg-Gotha, alias Windsor, is a little too recent to be handled easily except through the medium of documentary. Furthermore, its members have generally been too routinely respectable to make exciting subjects. With the single colossal exception of Victoria, the Hanoverians are generally of little interest unless they go mad: there is a trickle of films that include the Georges, but no sustained cinematic tradition. The Anglo-Saxons and Normans have no presence as individuals, except for the single one who happens to be called 'Great'. That leaves the Tudors and Plantagenets in the lead, and the latter do it, in historical terms, largely by cheating. For one thing there are simply so many of them, and for another, they get a lot of help from Shakespeare. Even so, they would still not beat the Stuarts were it not for the large number of walk-on parts accorded to Richard the Lionheart in features about Robin Hood or Ivanhoe. To put it another way, if you stretch

Plate 14 Nell Gwyn (Anna Neagle) and Charles II (Cedric Hardwicke) sublimate their carnal desires with a hearty meal in Herbert Wilcox's *Nell Gwyn*. Courtesy of British and Dominions and The Kobal Collection for the image of Anna Neagle and Cedric Hardwicke from the motion picture *Nell Gwyn* (1934).

the royal Stuarts to their full dynastic extent, to take in Mary Queen of Scots and Bonnie Prince Charlie, they easily exceed the number of appearances put in by the Plantagenets. Mary is, indeed, a royal figure with a genuinely pan-Continental appeal on both stage and screen that most other British monarchs have lacked. To carry out that stretching exercise, however, would itself be a cheat, because, in cinematic as in historical tradition, Mary Queen of Scots belongs firmly to the Tudor family soap opera. Part of the reason for her popularity is, indeed, her association with that genre. What distorts the entire record of British royal appearances on film is, simply, the remarkable impact of the Tudors. For a dynasty that reigned for a relatively short time, and whose members made few of the glorious achievements – such as conquests – traditionally associated with great monarchs, its screen presence is amazing. Even a bit-player in the family like Lady Jane Grey gets a starring role of her own in three movies,[1] and the balance of interest in this collection of essays speaks for itself.

Put like that, I could have quite comfortably and understandably have given this chapter an anodyne, objective and euphonious title such as 'The Stuarts on Celluloid'; but I didn't, because I wanted to enter the subject from an angle that asked some pointed questions about it. There are really two in which I am interested here, and both can be posed by additions to my chosen title. They are: 'Why don't the Stuarts get filmed as often as the Tudors?'; and 'Why don't the Stuarts get filmed memorably?' The second question rescues the first from being ill-considered. Without it, that first question might seem to be better worth asking as 'Why doesn't any other British Royal Family get filmed as often as the Tudors?' With it, we have a problem worth confronting. When you open a classic work on cinematic costume drama, such as Joseph Roquemore's *History Goes to the Movies*,[2] you find no entry on the Stuart period whatsoever. There have been far more films set in seventeenth-century France than in Britain of the same period, and they have been made by French, British and American companies. Those that have been made featuring the seventeenth-century Stuarts have tended either to be B-movies or critical and commercial failures. Perhaps the greatest award that any of them has ever won was the Oscar for Best Costumes picked up by the Columbia Pictures blockbuster *Cromwell*, in 1970, which was both an anti-Stuart story and at best a very mixed critical success in every other respect.

This is in strikingly sharp contrast to the profile that the period has in national culture as a whole. Both in traditional British and

American historiography, it is the one in which the titanic struggles were fought out that established the Anglo-American tradition
of representative government and religious toleration. It was also the
one in which most of the early American colonies were established.
Marked by such events as the Gunpowder Plot, the Civil War, the
regicide, and the Glorious Revolution, it hardly lacks for drama, and
none of the Stuarts of the time are themselves colourless characters.
Even the clothes are gorgeous. The epoch has been well served by
popular fiction, and there has been a constant stream of television
documentaries devoted to its events, which have increasingly blurred
the boundary with film drama by using reconstructions employing
professional actors and actresses. When re-enactment societies began
to appear, from the late 1960s, those devoted to the English Civil War
were not only the earliest, but have remained the largest, in Europe.
There would therefore appear to be the perfect substructure for cinematic interest, and yet that interest has remained fitful, and often
marginal.

Part of the problem may be that the Stuarts do not belong solidly to
one kingdom – either Scotland or England – as the Tudors are identified with the English kingdom and later royal families with a more
well-integrated Britishness. Another may be that they do not appear
to be a family, in the way that the Tudors are: there are too many of
them, and they generally get on too well. Once Henry VII, the only
real ratings-destroyer in the bunch, is shunted off into Shakespeare or
a BBC television series, the Tudors essentially take up just two generations of interlocking personalities, who often do terrible things to each
other. Having said that, much the same is true of the later Stuarts, and
it is notable that at the end of the 1960s a successful British television
series actually did turn them into a family soap. It was, admittedly, not
actually about them, but *The First Churchills*, the intertwined careers
of the Duke and Duchess of Marlborough that spanned the reigns of
five of them. Nonetheless, the personal dynamics between those five,
and the political fallout from them, did make for gripping and popular
TV. The lesson is, unfortunately, that it takes a series to cope wholesale with events as drawn-out and complex as those between 1670 and
1714.

When the events concerned are separated, however, there should
still be rich pickings for screenplays. The career of the Duke of Mon-
mouth, after all, mixes sex, politics and tragedy in a film-sized package,
and the Scottish nationalism that has picked up on William Wallace,

Rob Roy and Culloden might have found an obvious centre-point for a story in the Glencoe massacre.

None of this, however, has actually occurred. The government of James II forms a malevolent background presence to the plot-lines of *Lorna Doone* and *Captain Blood*, but no more than that. William of Orange may have been a hero to Macaulay, but is apparently not to anybody in the film industry, and none of the glitter that surrounds Elizabeth, Victoria and Mary Queen of Scots seems to have rubbed off on Queen Anne. This plausibly enough reflects the general dimness of the period in national memory since the late nineteenth century; you have to get as far as the Spanish Main before it starts becoming exciting.

Not much of an improvement is found if we bounce to the other extreme of the period and the reign of James VI and James I. As a film character he reaps the reward that he so self-consciously sowed, in his shyness of the public and dislike of display, his rejection of heroic posturing and his commitment to balance and reconciliation. As a result he is the only British monarch to reign between 1558 and 1685 whom most of the modern public simply cannot picture, and that is not cinema. Charles I does better, partly because of his dramatic end, and partly because of Van Dyke, both reflecting his much greater instinctual sense of style. As everybody perceived from Charles himself onward, whatever else the regicide was, it was great theatre. It also gave that king the opportunity for his most distinguished portrayal on screen, by Sir Alec Guinness in *Cromwell,* which has been the most self-conscious attempt so far to turn Stuart history into an epic. Apart from the clothes, Sir Alec's performance was the one thing that most critics seemed to find successful about it. The polarization between his personality as Charles, and that of Richard Harris as Cromwell, was the main dramatic axis on which the film turned. Charles invited some sympathy, as elegant, genteel, human and touchingly vulnerable, but was also presented as shifty, weak and obtuse, and the leading figure in an exploitative and unjust social and economic system. As such, he acted as the embodiment of all to which Cromwell was ultimately opposed, and Cromwell was designed completely to attract the sympathies of the film's audience.

Charles's followers, the Civil War Royalists, have long been at the centre of a curious contrast between popular and cinematic tradition. In the former, they have long attracted considerable sympathy and interest, and still do. Any member of a modern Civil War re-enactment society knows that the single biggest problem of the job lies in finding recruits who want to be in the Parliamentarian army. This popularity actually was, at first, reflected in the cinematic record, with the additional twist that most celluloid representations of the king's adherents have concentrated on their activities during the post-war period, of parliamentarian and then republican supremacy. This not only reduced costs, by doing away with battle scenes, but enabled them to be represented as the underdogs, upholders of the values of a more decent, old-fashioned and genteel world in the face of a repressive and joyless modernity.

What is truly significant about these treatments, however, is that they almost all date from before World War II. That war destroyed the atmosphere of reactionary sentimentality in which the older screen-plays had thrived, and royalist sympathies then took a different, and more sophisticated, form, to which I shall come in a moment. The only reappearance of the Civil War Royalist swashbuckler during the late twentieth century was thanks to Hammer Films, which during the 1960s made a series of B movies or double-feature items that – consciously or not – represented re-creations of Edwardian melo-dramas with colour and sound. The relevant one here is *The Scarlet Blade*, in 1963, which dealt with an unsuccessful attempt by a royalist underground to rescue and save Charles I. What made this production especially significant was the length to which it went to turn the king's partisans into counter-cultural icons. Predictably, they were all good-looking and fun-loving, while the Parliamentarians were all grim and glowering killjoys. More imaginatively, settings and characters were taken from Captain Marryat's Victorian best-seller, *The Children of the New Forest*, which succeeded both in placing the film in a venerable political and cultural tradition and relating the Royalists directly, and as if organically, to the natural world and thus an essential Englishness. At one point they were even made to take refuge with a camp of gyp-sies, represented as natural allies: equally marginalized, persecuted and romantic figures.

It is significant that even such desperate measures did not work. Within 10 years, Britain was full of young men who looked and dressed more like Cavaliers than anybody had done for three centuries, and in the name of a boisterous counter-culture pitted against Puri-tanism. The old party of High Church and King, however, just did not make a credible enough match for a revolutionary modern movement to feature seriously as imagined progenitors, and it was radical Puri-tanism, as represented by the Diggers and Ranters, that won the hippy heart instead. It was left to a television series, made in the early years of

Thatcherism, to disinter Victorian and Edwardian royalist nostalgia in its full-blown form. *By the Sword Divided*, screened in 1983, traced the fortunes of a doomed family of royalist aristocrats through the Civil War, portraying them as having a simple, old-fashioned decency associated with a timeless rural world: a kind of Midland English *Gone with the Wind*. It even had a heroic Prince Rupert. By contrast, the Parliamentarians were not merely the usual parade of hard-faced grey men associated with the genre, but included an even older figure of royalist satire: the lecherous and scheming hypocrite, dedicated to his own upward social mobility. The inevitable triumph of this figure, and his cause, functioned implicitly as an unhappy tribute to the unstoppable power of modernity. Appropriately enough, the series itself seemed to become a victim of the same forces, winning little acclaim, producing no television imitators, and having no impact on the wide screen.

Where royalism has proved most effective has been in combination with the one seventeenth-century Stuart to have real star quality: and that is Charles II. With at least 15 films to his credit, he is the third most popular British king in cinema history, and the remainder of this chapter must be devoted to him. Were it not for the bit-parts in Robin Hood and Ivanhoe adventures that inflate Richard the Lionheart's record, Charles would in fact trail behind Henry VIII alone. He has been portrayed by actors as diverse as Sir Cedric Hardwicke, George Sanders, Douglas Fairbanks Jnr, Sam Neill and John Malkovich. If Henry's wide appeal is proved, among much else, by the fact that he could be played by Sid James, then Charles does almost as well by counting Vincent Price among his *alter egos*.

Charles's cinematic career spans the entire twentieth century, but with some significant change in tone. His Victorian history-book reputation was as a lazy, lecherous and unpatriotic monarch, and this is exactly how he is portrayed in films made before the First World War. What changed everything was a process that I have described in my most recent book: the makeover that Charles's reputation underwent after the war, as part of the general rejection of things Victorian by smart society.[3] He became represented as the most charming and cultured of all British monarchs: affable, witty, sophisticated, tolerant and worldly wise. This image certainly reflected actual traits in his personality, but had been greatly enhanced by Tory authors in the early eighteenth century, creating a king with which to embarrass the last Stuarts and the Hanoverians much as the cult of Elizabeth had developed to show up the early Stuarts. After the war it was worked up in turn by a series of non-academic writers to create a new, less stuffy, kind of monarch, fit to preside over the Roaring Twenties. The momentum and success of this revamping of Charles's reputation was sufficient to carry it right through the next four decades and unite authors as different as the Tory Sir Arthur Bryant and the socialist George Bernard Shaw.

Its impact on cinema was profound, and took two different forms. One was to integrate Charles, in his younger self, into the swash-buckling tradition of heroic royalist resistance and conspiracy. Charles had of course himself dictated the script for this, in his own account of his escape from England after the battle of Worcester, in which he featured as the most daring, intelligent and resourceful figure in the entire episode.[4] The most striking expression of Charles as Cavalier hero occurred just after World War II, in what in my opinion is the most finely crafted film yet made about the seventeenth-century Stuarts: *The Exile*, made at Hollywood, released in 1946 and produced and written by, and starring, Douglas Fairbanks Jnr.[5] It is technically beautifully filmed, with heavy use of the conventions of Gothic cinema, and has both a fast-moving plot and a coherent ideology. It portrays Charles himself as a classic swashbuckling champion in his own right. It also articulates a view of monarchy as the natural, and popular, government of the English people, reflecting the general admiration among the Western allies for the conduct of George VI and Elizabeth Bowes-Lyon during the war. Cromwell's government, by contrast, is associated with those of the Axis powers and of Stalin's Russia: at once brutal, militarized and cheerless. Its headquarters is a vast hall, with no furniture but an armed guard lurking behind every pillar. The villain of the tale, sent out from this bunker to murder Charles, is Colonel Ingram, the very stereotype of a pitiless, ascetic, black-clad puritan fanatic. The measure of the two men is doubly taken in the final tremendous sword duel between them. Charles wins it physically, out-fighting his opponent, but also morally, by revealing a better sense of the greatness of the country that they both claim to represent: when Ingram tells him 'You must die that England may live', his royal opponent snaps back 'Twaddle! England will live whether you or I die.'

One of the cleverest alignments of the film is the way in which it equates the Restoration with the end of a period of deprivation and austerity equivalent to that prevailing in the post-war conditions of its own time. Charles is a kind of May King, waiting to bring back summer to his realm. If England languishes (visually) in shadow without him, even a foreign land which contains him – in this case the Netherlands – is a sea of flowers, and his loyal followers in exile, however impoverished, are graceful and joyous. More soberly, he is represented as the ideal people's monarch, refusing opportunities to reclaim his throne by conspiracy and waiting for a general call for his return. When tempted by the distractions of love (embodied in a sweet farm-girl called Katie) he sets them aside after his companion Sir Edward Hyde reminds him of his responsibilities to the English: 'You are their past, future, memory, emblem, flag.' If all this may strike some of us as a polar opposite to the historical Charles, the film was all the more successful for its brazen indifference to that. It inspired two imitations: *The Cardboard Cavalier*, in 1949, which was also partly a send-up; and *The Moonraker* in 1958, which reused the story of Charles's escape after Worcester as an opportunity to field a new set of romantic adventurers from the royalist underground.

Alongside the screenplays which combined the young Charles with the tradition of heroic Cavalier resistance there also flourished, from the 1920s, those which represented him as the worldly and mature monarch. Here he had a lot of help from one of his historical pals, Nell Gwyn. To deploy Nell by his side achieved a number of aims at once. It neutralized his older reputation as a lecher and adulterer by associating him with the right sort of girlfriend, a woman of the people who acted as personification of his natural populism and pop-ularity. It helped, of course, that she was an actress, somebody who would have been a film star herself in another 300 years. In the context of the period after World War I, moreover, one legendary aspect of her career was especially effective: the story that she had inspired Charles to found the Royal Hospital at Chelsea for crippled and indigent vet-erans. It also aided Nell and Charles, however, that one filmmaker was especially fond of them: Herbert Wilcox, who filmed their story three times over, in 1926, 1934 and 1954.

The 1934 version, starring his wife Anna Neagle, was probably the most popular film to date that has involved a Stuart king, being reis-sued in 1941 and 1948, to comfort another generation of servicemen: it accordingly deserves extended treatment, and makes a particularly good contrast with *The Exile*. Charles is a hero in both, but *Nell Gwyn* makes him an older, calmer and more worldly one: the successful monarch rather than the apprentice one. It opens with a dramatic claim to historical accuracy, announcing that the script was taken ver-batim from the actual words of the leading characters and making its first shots views of Samuel Pepys's diary and the Peter Lely portrait of Nell to establish its apparent roots in the reality of the past. In truth, at times it did lift well-known quotations from contemporary sources, but most of the plot and dialogue was wildly unhistorical. Its protestations of careful research seem, rather, to have been a device to make an audience at that period more inclined to accept the essential amorality of Nell's character and situation, and the joyful salacity of the film's tone, which constantly celebrates (by implication) her sexual union with Charles. It is never admitted that Charles had a wife, and Nell's rival is always portrayed as another girlfriend, the aristocratic (and foreign) Duchess of Portsmouth, whose favour with the king makes it virtually a patriotic duty for an Englishwoman to seduce him. Nonetheless, the atmosphere is one of eulogy for good and loose living, which must have been calculated as having an especial appeal in the era of the Great Depression.

The film has, moreover, cultural resonances which would have had further implications for the period. Charles is portrayed, as he would be in *The Exile*, as the ideal people's monarch: tolerant, generous and gracious, equally at home when receiving bejewelled ambassadors or boozing in London taverns with old soldiers (which he seems to do as a matter of course, and without guards). Nell represents the perfect social and personal foil for him, the chirpy Cockney: sharp-witted, irreverent, brave and impulsively kind-hearted. What is represented here is a natural alliance between an old-fashioned monarchy and aristocracy and an old-fashioned working-class populace, the former naturally responsible and responsive, and the latter naturally loyal and supportive. The middle classes are conspicuously absent and the system of parliamentary government more or less irrelevant. It is a nostalgic and reactionary view of politics, reflecting that embedded in the Churchillian Conservatism of the time, and embodied wholesale in Sir Arthur Bryant's best-selling contemporary biography of Charles. Significantly, none of this sufficed to make the film a huge success. It was only undertaken at all because of the massive popular appeal of one about a Tudor king, Alexander Korda's study of Henry VIII, which had been screened the previous year. It never itself got above fourth place in the annual *Film Weekly* poll of best British movies, and its celebration of extra-marital sexuality gave it serious problems in obtaining release in America. For a film about a Stuart, that is about as good as things get.

These, then, were just some of the movies that celebrated the second Charles as the ideal king for the sophisticated British. It is probably significant that the 1940s were a particularly fertile decade for them, the association of his court with flamboyant costume and pleasure acting to offset the dreariness of much actual life in those years. In addition to the two reissues already cited, and the two swash-bucklers, we have also *Hudson's Bay* in 1940 and *Forever Amber* in 1947, both reminders that the American film industry could find him equally attractive. The latter film, directed by Otto Preminger, made an interesting contrast with both *The Exile* and *Nell Gwyn*. Its political sympathies were directly opposed, making the Civil War Royalists dashing but dissolute, and Charles a capricious tyrant: self-centred, lecherous and very clearly an adulterer as well as a rake, who single-handedly reduces the moral tone of his realm. Decency, in his realm, lingers among country folk – automatically presumed to be Puritans and Republicans – and flowers anew in the American colonies that give hope for the future. Nonetheless, Charles still emerges as the most interesting character in the story: urbane, intelligent, witty, cyn-ically sophisticated and wearily aware of his own shortcomings. He gets all the best lines in a film not generally noted for its script.

Like the celebrations of the young Charles, those of the mature king petered out in the 1950s, with *The King's Thief*.[6] The drift of cinema towards social realism and more radical politics during the next two decades had no place for him, even though the eulogization of him as the wittiest, sexist and most affable of British kings continued into the 1970s in the pop histories of Lady Antonia Fraser and Richard Ollard.[7] I really believed that the work of John Miller and myself, in the 1980s and 1990s, might finally have killed off the 1920s legend of Charles II, by revealing a monarch so unpleasant that he could never be made a credible hero again.[8] In doing so, of course, I underesti-mated the functional constraints that operate on scriptwriters. In 2003 the BBC made a series about Charles starring Rufus Sewell, which resurrected the legend of the compassionate, humane and worldly-wise monarch wholesale. It was revealing in this context to read the interview with the writer of it published in the *Radio Times* when it was screened. She admitted candidly that the only biography of him that she found to be of any help was that by Antonia Fraser, from the 1970s, which supplied her with a king who could be most readily and sympathetically dramatized.

Gazing back over the whole screen career of Charles II, it is appar-ent that even this star of the family has only limited appeal. In the last analysis, a drawing-room hero, for such the mature king essentially was, even in legend, has a limited impact on the modern imagination. Even in his Cavalier incarnation, he remains too much a denizen of a cultivated, aristocratic, world, which lingered in some respects until the 1950s, but has since completely gone.

It is time to return to my original pair of questions. It must be apparent that there is a complex of different reasons why the Stuarts have not been filmed as often, nor especially memorably, as the Tudors. Those factors still operate, and one might consider them to be reinforced by the general Americanization of world cinema, the particular collapse of the British industry, and the concurrent growth of the sense that a republic, with a capitalist economy and a strong sense of individual rights, should be the normal system of government for any nation in the present world. It is also possible, however, that these developments may actually produce an increased frequency of appearances by the Stuarts on screen, and there are three straws in the wind that make me suppose that.

First comes that great rarity, an appearance by James I, and moreover in a film produced by a major Hollywood studio. The reason why it generally escapes notice is that it is a Walt Disney children's cartoon, the sequel to *Pocahontas*. In keeping with its predecessor, and with the company's desperate attempts to live down its conservative image, *Pocahontas II* was unambiguously in favour of Native Americans, environmentalism, pacifism, feminism, and the presumed inherent decency of ordinary working Europeans. Its targets consisted of machismo and greed in general, and the greatest villainy is represented by the English court aristocracy. In this context, James comes off predictably badly, appearing at once capricious, stupid, brutal and weak. In the end, he gets put in his place by his intelligent, humane and perceptive wife. The second feature is the last cinematic appearance to date of Charles I, in Kenneth Leader's disastrous *To Kill a King*, released in 2003. He features as a surly, doomed tyrant whom not even as able an actor as Rupert Everett can bring to life.

The third is the 1996 American film *Restoration*. This is not the most recent representation of Charles II; Rupert Everett made a cameo performance in *Stage Beauty* (2004) and John Malkovich in *The Libertine* (2005) – but it is arguably the most significant. Played by Sam Neill, it makes a wholesale re-creation of the hostile Victorian view of Charles, as a capricious and selfish despot, ruthlessly exploiting men and women alike. His court is an exemplar of false values, in which a royal lapdog is treated like a princess and aristocrats dress in satin and silk but regard breaking wind as the summit of wit. All genuine humanity and virtue in his realm is found among social outcasts and persecuted religious radicals, and, in a precise inversion of the magical politics of *The Exile*, the rottenness of the regime is mirrored in the calamities suffered by the land, in the form of the Great Plague and Great Fire of London. Only at the very end is Charles redeemed by a gesture of generosity, and – again in an inversion of traditional representations – this is because he is infected by the humanity of an ordinary person, acting as solvent on the inherent nastiness of his class and office. Nonetheless, the fact that he can be redeemed, however tardily and momentarily, shows that a potential for sympathetic treatment lingers in the image of this king that is available to none of the rest of his family.

None of these straws actually weigh very much, of course. Despite the supporting talents of Meg Ryan, Sir Ian McKellen and Hugh Grant, *Restoration* made almost no impact. The financial troubles and commercial failure of *To Kill a King* are notorious, and *Pocahontas II* did not even get an entry in Halliwell's film guide. What I am suggesting here is that it is possible that if feeling against monarchy and aristocracy grows stronger in Western culture, and especially in those aspects of it most under the influence of America, such as film, the Stuarts may actually find a new role. This will resurrect that which most of them have long occupied in the English liberal and radical tradition, and which has surfaced in some of the earlier films discussed above: as the principal enemies of evolving Anglo-American representative democracy, religious toleration and human rights. As heroes it is possible – though not certain – that their day is done. As villains, foils and fall-guys they may have a new and glorious career before them on the wide screen. Should this occur, however, it is likely that Charles II will be the last to succumb to wholesale demonization: as the 1920s reinvented him as an ideal modern monarch for those who like their rulers sophisticated and entertaining, so he remains the Stuart best suited to the most charismatic of modern forms of entertainment.[9]

Suggestions for Further Reading

Arthur Bryant, *King Charles II* (London, 1931).
Antonia Fraser, *King Charles II* (London, 1979).
Ronald Hutton, *Charles II, King of England, Scotland and Ireland* (Oxford, 1989).
John Miller, *Charles II* (London, 1991).

Notes

1. Introduction: It's Only a Movie

1. Woodrow Wilson's foremost biographer, Arthur Link, is sceptical that Wilson made the comment about Griffith's film; see Arthur S. Link, *Wilson: The New Freedom* (Princeton, NJ, 1956), p. 253. Also see Richard Schickel, *D. W. Griffith* (London, 1984), pp. 269–70 and 619 n5. I would like to thank Susan Doran, Lori Anne Ferrell, Judith Richards and David L. Smith for reading earlier versions of this introduction and for their helpful comments. The views expressed, however, are my own and they bear no responsibility for them.
2. Robert Brent Toplin, *Reel History: In Defense of Hollywood* (Lawrence, KS, 2002), pp. 92–7.
3. Robert Rosenstone, *History on Film/Film on History* (Harlow, 2006), p. 45.
4. On the influence of *Gone with the Wind* on American culture see Bruce Chadwick, *The Reel Civil War: Mythmaking in American Film* (New York, 2001), pp. 187–9 and 212–31 as well as Jim Cullen, *The Civil War in Popular Culture: A Reusable Past* (Washington, DC, 1995), pp. 67–9. As both of these authors have observed, the film modified and ameliorated the racial politics of Margaret Mitchell's novel and presented a somewhat more positive portrait of Reconstruction (Chadwick, *Reel Civil War*, pp. 195–8 and Cullen, *Civil War in Popular Culture*, pp. 82–64). There is a trenchant discussion of the political and historiographical messages of the film *Gone with the Wind* in Alan T. Nolan, 'The Anatomy of the Myth', in Gary W. Gallagher and Alan T. Nolan (eds), *The Myth of the Lost Cause and Civil War History* (Bloomington, IN, 2000), pp. 30–1.
5. Robert Rosenstone, 'Oliver Stone as Historian', in Robert Brent Toplin (ed.), *Oliver Stone's USA: Film, History and Controversy* (Lawrence, KS, 2000), p. 14.
6. For detailed consideration of the heritage film, see Andrew Higson, *English Heritage, English Cinema: Costume Drama Since 1980* (Oxford, 2003). In this work, Higson avoids consideration of the historical film as such and assumes that 'the costume drama label covers all period films, whether they depict actual historical figures or clearly fictional figures' (p. 12).
7. See the chapter in this volume by David Smith for discussion of this point.

8. See the chapters in this volume by Thomas Freeman, Susan Doran and Ronald Hutton.

9. Pierre Sorlin, *The Film in History: Restaging the Past* (Totowa, NJ, 1980), p. 21.

10. For criticisms of the historical accuracy of *The Mission*, see James Schofield Saeger, 'The Mission and Historical Missions: Film and the Writing of History', in Donald F. Stevens (ed.), *Based on a True Story: Latin American History at the Movies* (Wilmington, DE, 1997), pp. 63–84.

11. Flora Lewis, 'New Film by Costa-Gavras Examines the Chilean Coup', *New York Times*, 7 February 1982.

12. Quoted in George F. Custen, *Bio/Pics: How Hollywood Constructed Public History* (New Brunswick, NJ, 1992), pp. 38–9.

13. Gary Wills, *John Wayne's America: The Politics of Celebrity* (New York, 1997), p. 217.

14. Chadwick, *Reel Civil War*, p. 233.

15. Eric Foner, 'Hollywood Invades the Classroom', *New York Times*, 20 December 1997.

16. Robert Brent Toplin, *History by Hollywood: The Use and Abuse of the American Past* (Urbana and Chicago, 1996), pp. 139–40.

17. Quoted in E. W. Marsh, *James Cameron's Titanic* (London and Basingstoke, 1998), p. 126.

18. *The Mirror*, 16 April 1998.

19. *Daily Mail*, 11 September 1998.

20. Danae Brook, 'Elizabeth I is Known as the Virgin Queen. So Why Does a New Film Show Her Having Sex with a Courtier?', *The Mail on Sunday*, 13 September 1998.

21. Eric Foner and John Sayles, 'Eric Foner and John Sayles', in Ted Mico, John Miller-Monzon and David Rubel (eds), *Past Imperfect: History According to the Movies* (New York, 1995), p. 17.

22. For examples of this see Higson, *English Heritage*, pp. 242–3.

23. Hodding Carter, ' "JFK" Stonewalls History', Newspaper Enterprise Association column, 13 January 1992.

24. George Will, 'Oliver Stone Gives Paranoia a Bad Name', *New Orleans Times-Picayune*, 23 December 1991.

25. David Beilin, 'The Big Lies of *JFK*', *New York Times Magazine*, 17 February 1992; Toplin, *History by Hollywood*, pp. 72–6.

26. Severin Carrell, 'Don't Airbrush UK Out of History, Smith Urges Hollywood', *The Independent*, 5 June 2000; Lucy Ward, 'Economics of Truth: MPs Attack Rewriting of Wartime History for Box Office Gain', *The Guardian*, 7 June 2000; and Sarah Schaefer, 'Blair: US Films Are an Affront to Britain', *The Independent*, 8 June 2000.

27. Audrey Gillan, 'Small Town Gangs Up on Tinseltown', *Scotland on Sunday*, 8 March 1998; Jim McBeth, 'Hollywood Offers Titanic

Apology to Small Town', *The Scotsman*, 8 April 1998; and Kevin Jackson, 'The Titanic Hero They Couldn't Sink', *The Mail on Sunday*, 17 May 1998.

28. Dorothy Grace-Elder, column, *Scotland on Sunday*, 12 April 1998.
29. 'It's a Titanic Liberty with the Truth', *The Mirror*, 16 April 1998 (original emphasis).
30. Pierre Berton, *Hollywood's Canada* (Toronto, 1975).
31. See Jack Shaheen, *Reel Bad Arabs: How Hollywood Villifies a People* (New York, 2001), a book, which while overstated in its conclusions, provides ample evidence of the bias and ill-will in historical films about the Middle East. For a more nuanced view of some of these film treatments see Richard Francaviglia, 'Crusaders and Saracens: The Persistence of Orientalism in Historically Themed Films about the Middle East', in Richard Francaviglia and Jerry Rodnitzky (eds), *Lights, Camera, History: Portraying the Past in Film* (College Station, TX, 2007), pp. 53–90; and John Aberth, *A Knight at the Movies: Medieval History on Film* (New York and London, 2003), pp. 63–107.
32. Malcolm X with Alex Haley, *The Autobiography of Malcolm X* (London, 1966), p. 106.
33. Wills, *John Wayne's America*, pp. 202–6.
34. Abreth, *Knight at the Movies*, pp. 91–106; and Toplin, *Reel History*, p. 24.
35. See Abreth, *Knight at the Movies*, pp. 135–47 for a discussion of *El Cid* as Nationalist propaganda. The film's financing was a result of the DuPont family's sales of oil to Franco's Spain. The DuPonts were paid in unexportable Spanish pesetas and used this money to pay the production costs of films like *El Cid*, which were made in Spain for international markets. The films would be sold around the world and the profits would be received in convertible currencies. (See Norma Borzman, *The Red and the Blacklist* [Kilmarnock and London, 2005], p. 296.) There was thus every incentive for the filmmakers not to offend Franco's government.
36. John Guy, *Thomas More* (London, 2000), p. 1.
37. Harold M. Foster, *The New Literacy: The Language of Film and Television* (Urbana, IL, 1979), p. 3.
38. Sam Wineburg, *Historical Thinking and Other Unnatural Acts* (Philadelphia, 2001), pp. 232–55.
39. David M. Chambers, *Hooded Americanism: The First Century of the Ku Klux Klan, 1865–1965* (Garden City, NY, 1965), pp. 25–32; and Kenneth T. Jackson. *The Ku Klux Klan in the City, 1915–30* (New York, 1967), pp. 3–4.
40. Chadwick, *Reel Civil War*, pp. 130 and 134.
41. Catherine Clinton, *Tara Revisited: Women, the War and the Plantation Legend* (New York, 1995), p. 205.

42. Chadwick, *Reel Civil War*, p. 80.
43. Toplin, *History by Hollywood*, pp. 172–4.
44. Tom Wicker, *One of Us: Richard Nixon and the American Dream* (New York, 1991), p. 585.
45. William K. Everson, *American Silent Film* (New York, 1978), p. 87.
46. For examples and discussion of this see Robert Brent Toplin, 'In Defense of the Filmmakers' in *Lights, Camera, History*, pp. 113–14; and Toplin, *Reel History*, pp. 1–2.
47. For examples of this see Higson, *English Heritage*, pp. 235–41.
48. Bryan Mealer, 'Gangs of New York', *Esquire*, October 2001, p. 148.
49. For these see J. Matthew Gallman's review of the film in *Journal of American History* 90 (2003), p. 1125; and David Henkin's review of the film in *American Historical Review* 108 (2003), p. 620.
50. Marsh, *James Cameron's Titanic*, pp. 29–41.
51. Ibid., p. xiii.
52. Ibid., pp. 88–90.
53. Lynch makes this remark in his commentary on the DVD of the film.
54. Shortly after the *Titanic* went down, Freud's *Selected Papers on Hysteria and other Pyschoneuroses* was published and the following year, a major work, his *Interpretation of Dreams* appeared in an English translation.
55. Simon Schama, 'Clio at the Multiplex: What Hollywood and Herodotus Have in Common', *New Yorker*, 19 January 1998, pp. 39–40.
56. Daniel Walkowitz, 'Visual History: The Craft of the Historian-Filmmaker', *Public Historian* 7 (1985), p. 60.
57. Quoted in Daniel Nathan, Peter Berg and Erin Klemyk, ' "The Truth Wrapped in a Package of Lies": Hollywood, History and Martin Scorsese's *Gangs of New York*' in *Lights, Camera, History*, p. 108.
58. Natalie Z. Davis, *Slaves on Screen: Film and Historical Vision* (Cambridge, MA, 2000), p. 128.
59. See the discussion of this in Toplin, 'In Defense of the Filmmakers', p. 130. Toplin suggests that the box-office failure of Ang Lee's *Ride with the Devil* was to due its lack of moral certainties and dramatic resolution of the problems raised in the film.
60. Walkowitz, 'Visual History', p. 58.
61. Mark C. Carnes, 'Hollywood History', *American Heritage* (September 1995), p. 83.
62. Robert A. Rosenstone, 'History in Images/History in Words: Reflections on the Possibility of Really Putting History on Film', *American Historical Review* 93 (1988), p. 1178.
63. Geoffrey C. Ward, 'Refighting the Civil War', in Robert Brent Toplin (ed.), *Ken Burns's The Civil War: Historians Respond* (New York, 1996), p. 147 (original emphasis). Robert Toplin has also described how a projected film, for American public television, on the Port Royal Experiment – an attempt during the Civil War to bring landownership,

freedom and education to former slaves on the sea islands off the shores of Georgia and South Carolina – foundered over the difficulty in writing a script that did justice to the broad social and economic issues involved. Ultimately a film was made about Charlotte Forten, who had gone to the sea islands to teach the former slaves and who left a diary describing her experiences (Toplin, *Reel History*, pp. 140–4).

64. David Thomson, *Warren Beatty and Desert Eyes: A Life and a Story* (New York, 1987), p. 409.
65. Julianne Pidduck, *La Reine Margot* (New York and London, 2005), pp. 72 and 97–8.
66. Toplin, *Reel History*, pp. 155–6.
67. David Herlihy, 'Am I a Camera? Other Reflections on Film and History', *American Historical Review* 93 (1988), p. 1189.
68. Ian Kershaw, 'The Past and the Box: Strengths and Weaknesses' in David Cannadine (ed.), *History and the Media* (Basingstoke, 2004), p. 121.
69. Ian Jarvie, 'Seeing Through Movies', *Philosophy of the Social Sciences* 8 (1978), p. 378.
70. Rosenstone, 'History in Images/History in Words', p. 1178.
71. Natalie Davis has suggested that filmmakers list the sources they consulted in the film credits (*Slaves on Screen*, pp. 131–2). This would be useful as starting place for examination of the film as a historical text, although its benefit for the audience would be limited. Davis has also suggested that filmmakers might incorporate references to their sources within the narrative of the film (*Slaves on Screen*, pp. 132–6). It is doubtful, however, that filmmakers would be willing to do this. Another possibility is that the sources used and, indeed, the historical basis of a film could be discussed on a DVD. This, however, while perfectly possible, depends on the willingness of filmmakers to cooperate.
72. David Cesarani and Peter Longerich, 'The Massaging of History', *Guardian*, 7 April 2005.
73. Charlotte Higgins, 'Bunker Film "Is too Kind to Nazis"', *The Guardian* 5, April 2005.
74. Toplin, 'In Defense of the Filmmakers', p. 129 (original emphasis in quote).
75. Rosenstone, *History on Film/Film on History*, p. 37.
76. Ibid., p. 30.
77. Robert A. Rosenstone, '*JFK*', in Alan Rosenthal (ed.), *Why Docudrama? Fact-Fiction on Film and TV* (Carbondale, IL, 1999), p. 339.
78. Rosenstone, *History on Film/Film on History*, p. 118.
79. Herlihy, 'Am I a Camera?', pp. 1186–92.
80. Greg Walker, *The Private Life of Henry VIII* (London, 2003); and for Pidduck's book see n. 65 above.
81. Davis, *Slaves on Screen*, p. 36.
82. Eric Josef Carlson, 'Teaching Elizabeth Tudor with Movies', Sixteenth Century Journal, 38 (2007), pp. 419–28.

2. A Tyrant for All Seasons: Henry VIII on Film

1. Quoted in Greg Walker, *The Private Life of Henry VIII* (London and New York, 2003), p. 22. I would like to thank Susan Doran, Dale Hoak, Peter Marshall, Alec Ryrie and Ethan Shagan for reading earlier versions of this chapter and for their helpful comments.

2. Eric Bana, who plays Henry VIII in the recent film *The Other Boleyn Girl*, does not strike the pose, but throughout the film he wears variations on the Holbein costume in different colours.

3. Walter Ralegh, *The History of the World* (London, 1614), sig. A4v. (The spelling and punctuation of this quotation have been modernized.)

4. John Foxe, *The Ecclesiastical History Contayning the Actes and Monuments of these Latter and Perilous Dayes . . .* (London, 1570), p. 1478. (The spelling and punctuation of this quotation have been modernized).

5. A. F. Pollard, *Henry VIII* (London, 1902), pp. 1–3, 180–9, 222–3, 245–50 and 288–97.

6. Paul Tabori, *Alexander Korda* (New York, 1959), p. 131.

7. See Francis Hackett, *Henry the Eighth* (New York, 1929), pp. 346–7.

8. Hackett, *Henry the Eighth*, pp. 358–9. This incident appears to be based on the Spanish ambassador's report that Catherine Howard intervened with Henry to secure Sir Thomas Wyatt's release (*CSP Spanish, 1538–42*, p. 314).

9. Hackett, *Henry the Eighth*, p. 352. Greg Walker observes that there are 'strong similarities' between Hackett's biography and the screenplay to *The Private Life of Henry VIII*, although he also points out that the characterizations of Anne of Cleves and Catherine Parr in the film differ from Hackett's portrayal of them (Walker, *Private Life*, p. 35). But this last fact hardly precludes Korda and his scriptwriters from having drawn heavily on Hackett's biography.

10. Alfred S. Shivers, *The Life of Maxwell Anderson* (New York, 1983), pp. 227–8 and 'Maxwell Anderson files Libel Action', *Publishers Weekly*, 4 June 1949, p. 2301.

11. Maxwell Anderson, 'How a Play Gets Written: Diary Retraces the Steps', *New York Herald Tribune*, 21 August 1949.

12. Cf. Martin Hume, *The Wives of Henry VIII* (London, 1905), pp. 127–8 with Maxwell Anderson, *Anne of the Thousand Days* (New York, 1977), Act I, scene 2. Hereafter this work will be cited as *AOTTD*.

13. Hume, *Wives of Henry VIII*, p. 187.

14. *AOTTD*, Act I, scene 5.

15. Cf. Hackett, *Henry the Eighth*, pp. 226, 245 and 255 with *AOTTD*, pp. 25 and 28–30. Admittedly, Anderson could have taken this material from other sources; rumours that Henry bedded Anne's mother circulated during his reign and were repeated by Catholic historians (Eric Ives, *The Life and Death of Anne Boleyn* (Malden, MA and Oxford, 2004),

pp. 15–16). But there is no evidence of Anderson using sources besides Hume and Hackett.

16. Cf. Hackett, *Henry the Eighth*, p. 231 with *AOTTD*, Act I, scene 3.
17. *AOTTD*, Act II, scene 1.
18. Hackett, *Henry the Eighth*, p. 244.
19. Ibid., pp. 121–3, 332 and 419.
20. Hume, *Wives of Henry VIII*, pp. 445–9; quotation on p. 447.
21. R. W. Chambers, *Thomas More* (London, 1935), p. 366.
22. Chambers, *Thomas More*, p. 382. For Chambers's very negative assessment of Henry VIII also see pp. 375–85.
23. Walker, *Private Life*, p. 26.
24. Klaus Kremeier, *Die Ufa-Story: Geschichte eines Filmkonzerns* (Munich, 1992), p. 72.
25. Karol Kulik, *Alexander Korda: The Man Who Could Work Miracles* (London, 1975), pp. 30–1.
26. Kulik, *Alexander Korda*, pp. 90–1.
27. Kulik discusses the significance of the marginalization of Catherine and Jane in the film (Kulik, *Alexander Korda*, p. 90).
28. Walker, *Private Life*, p. 85.
29. Charles Higham, *Charles Laughton: An Intimate Biography* (London, 1976), p. 44.
30. This is shrewdly analyzed in Walker, *Private Life*, pp. 75–7.
31. Bolt, *A Man for All Seasons*, p. vii.
32. The lines about diplomacy were cut from the film, but they appear in the published version of the script (Arthur Wimperis, *The Private Life of Henry VIII*, ed. E. Betts [London, 1934], pp. 14–15).
33. Walker, *Private Life*, p. 57.
34. Ibid., pp. 55, 58 and 60–4.
35. Ibid., pp. 57–60.
36. Ibid., p. 60.
37. Kulik, *Alexander Korda*, p. 252.
38. Sue Harper, *Picturing the Past: The Rise and Fall of the British Costume Film* (London, 1994), pp. 16 and 21–2; also see Walker, *Private Life*, pp. 34–5 and 58–9.
39. Walker, *Private Life*, pp. 4–6.
40. Harper, *Picturing the Past*, p. 36.
41. Jeffrey Richards, *The Age of the Dream Palace: Cinema and Society in Britain, 1930–9* (London, 1984), p. 263.
42. Richards, *Dream Palace*, pp. 264–9; and Harper, *Picturing the Past*, pp. 53–5.
43. Both of these films were released in 1953. One was a lightweight live-action Disney film, *The Sword and the Rose*, which took the already colourful story of Charles Brandon's marriage to Henry VIII's sister and gilded it with swordfights and cross-dressing. The other film was *Young Bess*, the story of the childhood and adolescence of Elizabeth, in which

Charles Laughton reprised the role of Henry VIII. This latter film is discussed in more detail in Judith Richard's chapter.

44. Anderson, 'How a Play Gets Written', p. 2.
45. *AOTTD*, Act II, scene 7. Henry's early desire to reign well is also discussed on *AOTTD*, Act I, scene 4.
46. *AOTTD*, Act I, scene 5 and ACT II, scene 4.
47. Bolt, *A Man for All Seasons*, p. xx.
48. In the film, Henry is shown praying in his chapel for the strength to do whatever is necessary to secure the succession. But the film then subverts Henry's apparent sincerity by having Catherine of Aragon walk out of the shadows and gaze at Henry reproachfully.
49. These quotations are taken from interviews on the DVD of *Henry VIII*.
50. Edward Herbert, *The Life and Reign of King Henry the Eighth* (London, 1672), p. 639.

3. Saints and Cinemas: *A Man for All Seasons*

1. Hugh Trevor-Roper, *Renaissance Essays* (London, 1986), p. 27.
2. Majie Padberg Sullivan, 'The Now and Future Gold Mine', *Moreana* 4, no. 15 (1967), 204. See also Bernard Basset, *Born for Friendship: The Spirit of Sir Thomas More* (London, 1965), p. 188: 'Millions of Englishmen had hardly heard his name when Robert Bolt . . . drew and held such impressive audiences.'
3. Adrian Turner, *Robert Bolt: Scenes from Two Lives* (London, 1998), pp. 162–9, 226, 251; Fred Zinnemann, *An Autobiography* (London, 1992), p. 199.
4. James R. Nicholl, 'More Captivates America: The Popular Success of *A Man for All Seasons*', *Moreana* 13, no. 51 (1976); Joel N. Super, 'Fred Zinnemann, *A Man for All Seasons* (1966), and Documentary Fiction', in Arthur Nolletti (ed.), *The Films of Fred Zinnemann* (Albany, NY, 1999), pp.157–9; Bosley Crowther, ' "A Man for All Seasons": A Sturdy Conscience, a Steadfast Heart', *New York Times*, 13 December 1966.
5. Nolletti, 'Conversations with Fred Zinnemann', *Films of Fred Zinnemann*, p. 31.
6. Bolt, 'Preface', in *A Man for All Seasons* (Canadian Education Edition, Toronto, 1963), pp. xv–xvi.
7. Bolt, *Man for All Seasons*, pp. 25–6. Cf. R. S. Sylvester and D. P. Harding (eds), *Two Early Tudor Lives* (New Haven and London, 1962), p. 225.
8. Redgrave was originally scheduled to play Margaret, but had to withdraw due to stage commitments: Zinnemann, *Autobiography*, pp. 205–6.
9. Bolt, *Man for All Seasons*, pp. 23, 48, 62–3.
10. This oath, recognizing Anne as queen and her children as lawful heirs, was imposed on all adult males in 1534: More was the only English layman to refuse it.

11. '*A Man for All Seasons*, London July 1960', http://www.guardian.co.uk/arts/curtainup/story. See also the remark of the influential film critic Pauline Kael that 'Bolt's presentation of More's martyrdom is so totally one-sided that we don't even get to understand *that* side: *Kiss Kiss Bang Bang* (Boston, 1968), p. 154.

12. See, for example, Michael Anderegg, 'A Myth for All Seasons: Thomas More', *Colorado Quarterly* 23 (1975), p. 296.

13. Bolt cited the authority of Chambers on a historical point in an interview with the critic Ronald Hayman: Hayman, *Robert Bolt* (London, 1969), p. 81. See the comment of Gilbert Storari, 'From Elizabeth I to Elizabeth II: Two Popular Views of Thomas More', *Moreana* 8, no. 30 (1971), p. 28, that Bolt 'seems to have done hardly any reading outside one book'.

14. J. Duncan M. Derrett, 'The Trial of Sir Thomas More', *English Historical Review* 79 (1964) pp. 449–77; G. R. Elton, *Policy and Police: The Enforcement of the Reformation in the Age of Thomas Cromwell* (Cambridge, 1972), pp. 409–17.

15. These points are made by E. E. Reynolds, 'The Significance of *A Man for All Seasons*', *Moreana* 6 (1969), pp. 36–7.

16. William J. Sheils, 'Catholic Saints and English Identity: The Canonization of Thomas More and John Fisher, 1935.' I am very grateful to Dr Sheils for allowing me to read this important paper in advance of its publication.

17. *Moreana* 4, no. 13 (1967), pp. 112–14; 4, no. 14 (1967), pp. 120–1; 5, no. 17 (1968), pp. 73–90.

18. Germain Marc'hadour, 'Fred Zinnemann and *A Man for All Seasons*', *Moreana* 20, no. 79 (1983), p. 54.

19. G. R. Elton, 'Sir Thomas More and the Opposition to Henry VIII', *Bulletin of the Institute of Historical Research* 41 (1968) pp. 19–34; 'Thomas More, Councillor', *Studies in Tudor and Stuart Politics and Government* (4 vols, Cambridge, 1974–1992, I), pp. 129–54; 'The Real Thomas More?', in P. N. Brooks (ed.), *Reformation Principle and Practice* (London, 1980), pp. 21–31.

20. G. R. Elton, 'Sir Thomas More and the Opposition to Henry VIII', *Moreana* 4, no. 15 (1967), pp. 285–303.

21. R. W. Chambers, *Thomas More* (London, 1935), p. 291.

22. Elton, 'The Real Thomas More?', p. 24; 'Thomas More and Thomas Cromwell', *Studies in Tudor and Stuart Politics and Government*, IV, p. 145.

23. Richard Marius, *Thomas More* (London, 1985), quote at p. xxiv.

24. Elizabeth Furlong Alkaaoud, 'A Man for Our Season: Marius on More', *Moreana* 27, nos 101–2 (1990), p. 47.

25. Noting that it followed Roper's version of More's fateful conversation with Richard Riche (p. 501).

26. Richard Marius, 'Looking Back', *Moreana* 26, no. 100 (1989), p. 557.
27. Richard Marius, 'A Man for All Seasons', in Mark C. Carnes *et al.* (eds), *Past Imperfect: History According to the Movies* (London, 1996), pp. 70–3. The itemizing of inaccuracies itself contains a howler, when it is said that 'English did replace Latin as the language of worship' (p. 72) in Henry's reign, though as this appears in a marginal mini-essay, perhaps a researcher rather than Marius himself is to blame.
28. Bolt, 'Preface', p. xviii.
29. Jasper Ridley, *The Statesman and the Fanatic: Thomas Wolsey and Thomas More* (London, 1982), preface, pp. 290–3.
30. Bolt, *A Man for All Seasons*, pp. 52–3. The passage represents a deliberate misquoting of a speech of Galileo's in Berthold Brecht's *Leben des Galilei*, to which *A Man for All Seasons* is in some measure a riposte. See Turner, *Bolt*, p. 162.
31. Anthony Kenny, *Thomas More* (Oxford, 1983), pp. 93–7. See also Anderegg, 'Myth for All Seasons', pp. 303–4.
32. J. Roquemore, *History Goes to the Movies* (New York, 1999), pp. 353–4.
33. John Guy, *Thomas More* (London, 2000), p. 1.
34. Letter from Anne Marie Drew, reproduced in *Moreana* 29, nos 111–12 (1992), p. 166.
35. Cited in Louis L. Martz, *Thomas More: The Search for the Inner Man* (New Haven and London, 1990), p. 3.
36. Christopher Smith, 'A Drama for All Times? *A Man for All Seasons* Revived and Reviewed', *Moreana* 25, no. 98 (1988), pp. 53–6.
37. Martz, *Thomas More*, p. 3.
38. E. E. Reynolds, 'Significance of *A Man for All Seasons*', 34; review in *The Tablet*, quoted in *Moreana* 4, no. 14 (1967), pp. 120–1.
39. Sullivan, 'The Now and Future Gold Mine', p. 204.
40. 'Screening Reality: Some Difficulties Discussed', *The Clergy Review*, 72, no. 11, 414–15, cited in *Moreana* 24, no. 95 (1987), p. 63.
41. Clarence H. Miller, 'Thomas More, a Man for All Seasons: Robert Bolt's Play and the Elizabethan Play of Sir Thomas More', *Moreana* 27, no. 104 (1990), pp. 106–7. It is interesting to note that a remarkably similar objection (that of ignoring the devotional dimension) has been levelled by another of the Yale team, John Headley, at one of the sternest critics of Bolt's veracity: 'John Guy's *Thomas More*: On the Dimensions of Political Biography', *Moreana* 37, nos 143–4 (2000).
42. Bolt, 'Preface', pp. xii–xiv; Turner, *Bolt*, pp. 162.

4. *Anne of the Thousand Days*

1. Geneviève Bujold won the Golden Globe Award for Best Actress, Charles Jarrott won Best Director and the movie also won Best Screenplay.

2. A. Shivers, *The Life of Maxwell Anderson* (New York, 1983), p. 228.
3. *New York Times*, 21 January 1970.
4. Robert Rosenstone, *Visions of the Past: The Challenge of Film to Our Idea of History* (Cambridge, MA, 1995), p. 129.
5. G. R. Elton, *Henry VIII: An Essay in Revision* (London, 1962). This pamphlet first emphasized the role of Henry's personality in explaining his record as king. J. J. Scarisbrick, *Henry VIII* (London, 1968). See also D. R. Starkey, *The Reign of Henry VIII: Personality and Politics* (London, 1991).
6. A. F. Pollard, *Henry VIII* (London, 1902).
7. J. Woolfson, 'Morison, Sir Richard (c.1510–1556)', *Oxford Dictionary of National Biography* (Oxford, 2004). Morison's 1539 tract *Exhortation to Styrre up All Englishemen to the Defence of their Country* praised Henry for bringing true religion to England and defending it from foreign powers.
8. Diarmaid MacCulloch, 'Henry VIII and the Reform of the Church' in his *The Reign of Henry VIII* (London, 1995), pp. 159–80.
9. D. R. Starkey (ed.), *Henry VIII: A European Court in England* (London, 1991), pp. 8–13. See also *The Reign of Henry VIII*.
10. R. S. Sylvester (ed.), *The Life and Death of Cardinal Wolsey* by George Cavendish (London, 1959). Cavendish, Wolsey's gentleman usher, provides a first-hand observation of Wolsey by a close and loyal servant.
11. An important alternative view is offered by Peter Gwyn, *The King's Cardinal: The Rise and Fall of Thomas Wolsey* (London, 1990). Gwyn argues that Wolsey worked mainly to increase royal authority rather than his own power.
12. On Wolsey and the annulment see Scarisbrick, *Henry VIII*, pp. 198–304 and Gwyn, *King's Cardinal*, pp. 501–48. On his mission to France and the role of France in the break with Rome see Glenn Richardson, 'Eternal Peace, Occasional War: Anglo-French Relations under Henry VIII', in Susan Doran and Glenn Richardson (eds), *Tudor England and its Neighbours* (London, 2005), pp. 44–69, esp. pp. 48–60.
13. G. R. Elton, *The Tudor Revolution in Government* (Cambridge, 1953); 'Tudor Government: The Points of Contact; III the Court', in *Transactions of the Royal Historical Society*, 5th ser., 26 (1976), pp. 211–28; Christopher Coleman and D. R. Starkey (eds), *Revolution Reassessed* (Oxford, 1986); See also John Guy, 'Thomas Wolsey, Thomas Cromwell and the Reform of Henrician Government', in MacCulloch (ed.), *The Reign of Henry VIII*, pp. 35–57.
14. P. Friedmann, *Anne Boleyn, A Chapter of English History, 1527–1536* (2 vols, London, 1884); the first genuinely scholarly account of Anne's life and significance.
15. E. W. Ives, *The Life and Death of Anne Boleyn* (Oxford, 2004), esp. pp. 101–26; D. R. Starkey, *Six Wives: The Queens of Henry VIII* (London, 2004), pp. 346–68. See also *The Reign of Henry VIII*.

16. R. W. Hoyle, 'Percy, Henry Algernon, Sixth Earl of Northumberland (c.1502–1537)', *Oxford Dictionary of National Biography*. The Fifth Earl was hardly a 'clodhopper' but he was far from a stable character, quarrelling with his brothers and his wife, whom he disinherited, while making excessive grants of land to his gentry clients.

17. Ives, *Anne Boleyn*, pp. 14–17, 37–9.

18. Ibid., pp. 34–6; 63–80, cf. Starkey, *Six Wives*, pp. 275–8, who argues that Henry was interested in Anne by late 1524 and that Wolsey's intervention was probably made in June 1525.

19. Cavendish, *Cardinal Wolsey*, pp. 31–6. The film echoes Cavendish's view of these events and their consequences. Starkey endorses this view while Ives is more sceptical about its reliability.

20. Ives, *Anne Boleyn*, pp. 81–92; Starkey, *Six Wives*, pp. 277–85.

21. Ives, *Anne Boleyn*, pp. 205–87; Maria Dowling, *Humanism in the Reign of Henry VIII* (Beckenham, 1986); Starkey, *Six Wives*, pp. 368–407 *et seq.*; E. W. Ives, 'Anne Boleyn and the Early Reformation in England: The Contemporary Evidence', *Historical Journal*, 37 (1994), pp. 389–400; G. W. Bernard, 'Anne Boleyn's Religion', *Historical Journal*, 36 (1993), pp. 1–20 offers a dissenting view. See also T. S. Freeman, 'Research, Rumour and Propaganda: Anne Boleyn in Foxe's 'Book of Martyrs', *Historical Journal*, 38 (1995), pp. 797–819.

22. Ives, *Anne Boleyn*, pp. 306–64; Starkey, *Six Wives*, pp. 554–83.

23. G. W. Bernard, 'The Fall of Anne Boleyn', *English Historical Review*, 106 (1991), pp. 584–610; 'The Fall of Anne Boleyn: A Rejoinder', *English Historical Review*, 107 (1992), pp. 665–74.

24. R. M. Warnicke, *The Rise and Fall of Anne Boleyn: Family Politics at the Court of Henry VIII* (Cambridge, 1989); 'The Fall of Anne Boleyn Revisited', *English Historical Review*, 108 (1993), 653–65. This Tudor conspiracy theory to outdo all others has no hard evidence to commend it.

25. G. Walker, 'Rethinking the Fall of Anne Boleyn', *The Historical Journal*, 45 (2002), pp. 1–29.

26. The film elides 'the oath' as set down by the 1534 Act of Supremacy with the provisions of the Act of Succession of the same year which declared Mary illegitimate and recognized Elizabeth as Henry's heir. They were then both bastardized after Anne's death in 1536 before being restored to the succession in 1544.

27. *New York Times*, 21 January 1970.

5. Lady Jane Grey on Film

* Versions of this paper were presented at City University of New York Graduate Center and at the University of Kansas. I am very grateful for the valuable suggestions that I received. I am deeply grateful to Frank Prochaska, historical consultant for the 1986 *Lady Jane* film, for his help

on this project. Particular thanks to Carolyn Biltoft, Jo Carney, Amy Gant and Lena Orlin for their thoughtful ideas and support.

1. David Mathew, *Lady Jane Grey: The Setting of the Reign* (London, 1972), p. 160.
2. Barrett L. Beer, *The Political Career of John Dudley, Earl of Warwick and Duke of Northumberland* (Kent, OH, 1973), p. 165.
3. The earliest film about Jane, *Lady Jane Grey; Or, The Court of Intrigue*, was made in 1923 and was 22 minutes in length. Unfortunately the film does not seem to have survived. It was directed by Edwin Greenwood and the script was by Eliot Stannard. Nina Vanna played Jane; Charles Barratt the Duke of Northumberland; Forbes Dawson was King Edward; Charles Dane the Duke of Suffolk; and John Reid, Guildford Dudley. The same year as *The Court of Intrigue* a film called *The Virgin Queen* was released as was *The Loves of Mary, Queen of Scots*. I am grateful to the checklist of Renaissance films in Rowland Wymer's ' "The Audience Is only Interested in Sex and Violence." Teaching the Renaissance on Film.' [http://www.shu.ac.uk/wpw/renaissance/wymer.htm] Jane is also a character in the Prince and the Pauper films but because of issues of length and theme I am not addressing the characterization of Jane in these films.
4. It is worth noting that Warwick was never appointed Lord Protector.
5. Frank Prochaska, 'The Many Faces of Lady Jane Grey.' *History Today* 35, no. 10 (October 1985), p. 40.
6. E-mail from Frank Prochaska to Carole Levin, 4 May 2005.
7. J. G. Nichols (ed.) 'The Chronicle of Queen Jane and Two Years of Queen Mary', *Camden Society*, original series 48 (London, 1850), pp. 54–9.

6. From Hatfield to Hollywood: Elizabeth I on Film

* I would like to thank Eric Josef Carlson and Alan and Bathsheba Doran for their helpful comments on an earlier draft of this essay.

1. See Marcia Landy (ed.), *The Historical Film* (London, 2001), pp. 7–8.
2. Cynthia Behrman, *Victorian Myths of the Sea* (Ohio, 1977), pp. 30–7, 113–16; Leonée Ormond, ' "The Spacious Times of Great Elizabeth": The Victorian Vision of the Elizabethans', *Victorian Poetry* 25.3 (1987), pp. 29–46.
3. *The Times*, 19 July and 25 October 1888. See also Roland Quinault, 'The Cult of the Centenary, *c.*1784–1914', *Historical Research* 71 (1998), pp. 314–16, 322. The medal is in the National Maritime Museum.
4. Published in 1905, it remained popular well into the 1950s, see *History Today* (June, 2002). It is now on the Internet.

5. See also Ormond, 'The Spacious Times', pp. 29–32.
6. James Anthony Froude, *History of England from the Fall of Wolsey to the Defeat of the Spanish Armada* (New York, 1878) vol. 13, pp. 580–7.
7. Mandell Creighton, *Queen Elizabeth* (London, 1899), pp. 197–200.
8. Arthur D. Innes, *Leading Figures in English History, Tudor and Stewart Period* (London, 1931), p. 91
9. Innes, *Leading Figures*, p. 112.
10. J. E. Neale, *Queen Elizabeth I* (London, 1934), pp. 64–5, 70, 249, 293–4.
11. Neale, *Queen Elizabeth*, p. 212; Innes, *Leading Figures*, pp. 112–13.
12. It was released in the United States on a very limited basis as *Drake the Pirate*.
13. *The Times*, 15 May 1935.
14. *The Times*, 29 April 1935; Sue Harper, *Picturing the Past: The Rise and Fall of the British Costume Film* (London, 1994), p. 40.
15. Michael Todd Bennett, 'Anglophilia on Film: Creating an Atmosphere for Alliance, 1935–1941,' *Film and History* 27 (1997), p. 7 suggested that the film was the 'first film shown in America that commented upon the Spanish Civil War'. However, I'm unconvinced that the filmmakers had Franco rather than Hitler primarily in mind.
16. Neale, *Queen Elizabeth*, pp. 202–3, 257–82. See also, for example, Katherine Anthony, *Queen Elizabeth* (London, 1929), pp. 169–70, 176.
17. Neale, *Queen Elizabeth*, pp. 177–8, 252, 316. For a different judgement see Christopher Haigh, *Elizabeth I* (London, 1988), p. 38.
18. *Sight and Sound* 6, no. 22 (1937), pp. 98–9.
19. Letter to *The Times*, 17 March 1937.
20. *Sight and Sound* 6, no. 22 (1937), pp. 98–9.
21. Doubting its authenticity are Susan Frye, 'The Myth of Elizabeth at Tilbury', *Sixteenth Century Journal* 23 (1992), pp. 95–114; and Frances Teague, 'Queen Elizabeth in her Speeches', in S. P. Cerasano and M. Wynne-Davies (eds), *Gloriana's Face: Women, Public and Private in the English Renaissance* (Detroit, 1992), pp. 67–9. But, Janet M. Green disagrees in ' "I My Self": Queen Elizabeth's Oration at Tilbury Camp', *Sixteenth Century Journal* 28 (1997), pp. 421–42.
22. Cited in Sue Harper, *Women in British Cinema, Mad, Bad and Dangerous to Know* (London, 2000), p. 25.
23. An extract from Kenneth Barrow, *Flora* (1981) in the files of the British Film Institute.
24. See Will Coster's chapter. This point is made clear in the screenplay of the film Rudy Behlmer (ed.), *The Sea Hawk* (Madison, Wisconsin, 1982), pp. 20–5.
25. Bennett, 'Anglophilia on Film', p. 10.
26. Even though the film's press books did not draw attention to contemporary parallels, Kenneth McCaleb could write 'History

Repeats – in England and in Hollywood' in *New York Mirror*. See Bennett, 'Anglophilia on Film', p. 13.

27. This foreword was omitted on the screen because of legal difficulties arising out of Louis Parker's play *Drake*; Behlmer *Sea Hawk*, pp. 59, 209.
28. This view is shared by H. Mark Glancy, *When Hollywood Loved Britain: The Hollywood British Film 1939–45* (Manchester, 1990), p. 101.
29. Anthony, *Queen Elizabeth,* especially pp. 253–4.
30. Alfred S. Shivers, *Anderson* (Boston, 1976), pp. 80–5 and *The Life of Maxwell Anderson* (New York, 1983), pp. 39–40. For Schiller and Scott and the 'well-established tradition', see Ormond, 'The Spacious Times', p. 31.
31. Eric H. Rideout, *The American Film* (1937) thought it could 'arouse aught but fury in those who respect the memory of Queen Elizabeth of England'.
32. This follows closely Elizabeth's words in Maxwell's play: 'It was you or I . . . The one of us must win. And I must always win.'
33. A. F. Pollard, *The History of England from the Accession of Edward VI to the Death of Elizabeth 1547–1603* (1910), pp. 179–80. Historians today are more inclined to see Elizabeth as a sincere Protestant. See, for example, Susan Doran, 'Elizabeth I's Religion: The Evidence of her Letters', *Journal of Ecclesiastical History* 51 (2000), pp. 699–720.
34. Lawrence G. Avery, *Dramatist in America: Letters of Maxwell Anderson 1912–1958* (Chapel Hill, NC, 1977), p. 311.
35. Barbara Leaming, *Bette Davis* (London, 1999), pp. 157, 166.
36. Trailers can be seen along with the film on DVD.
37. See letters in Rudy Behlmer (ed.), *Inside Warner Bros. (1935–1951)* (London, 1985), pp. 96, 100.
38. *The Black Rose* (1950), *Quo Vadis?* (1951), *Ivanhoe* (1952), *The Robe* (1953), *Julius Caesar* (1953), *Knights of the Round Table* (1953) together with several films about Robin Hood.
39. Laurence Olivier's *Hamlet* (1948) and *Richard III* (1955) and Orson Welles's *Macbeth* (1948) and *Othello* (1952).
40. This is the view of Michael Dobson and Nicola J. Watson, *England's Elizabeth: An Afterlife in Fame and Fantasy* (Oxford, 2002) but Judith Richards in this volume disagrees. According to the BFI files, 6 years before the film was produced the Hollywood producer, Sidney Franklin, had suggested an adaptation of Margaret Irwin's novel which was not taken up in England but left to Hollywood.
41. James Morgan, 'Coronationiana USA'. *Sight and Sound* (1953), p. 43.
42. Sir Arthur Salisbury MacNalty described the princess as a 'warm-hearted, impulsive and affectionate' girl who 'fell in love with' the dashing Thomas Seymour. *Elizabeth Tudor: The Lonely Queen* (London, 1954), p. 100.

43. See, for example, Yvonne French, *Six Great Englishwomen* (London, 1953), pp. 13–14: 'This episode was a turning point in the girl's life. It crushed her softer feelings . . . It made her less human, but it reinforced her character, taught her to trust no-one, to learn self-reliance, and gain an inward strength.'

44. For further criticisms, see Carole Levin and Jo Eldridge Carney, 'Young Elizabeth in Peril: From Seventeenth-Century Drama to Modern Movies', in Carole Levin, Jo Eldridge Carney and Debra Barrett-Graves (eds), *Elizabeth I: Always Her Own Free Woman* (Aldershot, 2003), pp. 228–9.

45. Since her own day there had been speculations that Elizabeth was infertile. The possibility was discussed in Lytton Strachey, *Elizabeth and Essex: A Tragic History* (Penguin reprint London, 2000), pp. 23–4 and dismissed by MacNalty, *Elizabeth*, pp. 225–7.

46. Henry Harington (ed.), *Nugæ Antiquæ*, 2 vols (1769–75); Lucy Aitkin, *Memoirs of the Court of Queen Elizabeth* (London, 1818), vol.2, especially pp. 499–500.

47. Haigh, *Elizabeth I*, pp. 87, 93, 96, 98.

48. For alternative views, see Anna Beer, *Bess: The Life of Lady Ralegh, Wife to Sir Walter* (London, 2004); Susan Doran, *Elizabeth* (London, 2003).

49. Before this Irene Worth starred as Elizabeth in the Italian-made *Seven Seas to Calais* (1962).

50. Interestingly college students today do not react to her in the same way; see Eric Carlson, 'Teaching Elizabeth Tudor with Movies', *Sixteenth Century Journal* 38 (2007), pp. 419–28.

51. www. jclarkmedia.com/jarman/jarman02jubilee.html

52. Renée Pigeon, '"No Man's Elizabeth": The Virgin Queen in Recent Films', in Deborah Cartnell, I. Q. Hunter and Imelda Whelehan (eds), *Retrovision: Reinventing the Past in Film and Fiction* (London, 2001), pp. 20–1.

53. A point perceptively made by Thomas Betteridge in 'A Queen for All Seasons: Elizabeth I on Film', in Susan Doran and Thomas S. Freeman (eds), *The Myth of Elizabeth* (Basingstoke, 2003), pp. 255–56.

54. Interview with Kapur, 19–26 November 1998, www.bostonphoenix.com. See also A. Higson, *English Heritage, English Cinema: Costume Drama Since 1980* (Oxford, 2003), pp. 194–255.

55. See chapter by Christopher Haigh.

56. See, for example, Margaret L. King, *Women of the Renaissance* (Chicago, 1991); Theodora A. Jankowski, *Women in Power in the Early-Modern Drama* (Urbana and Chicago, 1992); Carole Levin, *The Heart and Stomach of a King: Elizabeth I and the Politics of Sex and Power* (Philadelphia, 1994).

57. Frances Yates, *Astraea: The Imperial Theme in the Sixteenth Century* (1975); Roy Strong, *The Cult of the Virgin Queen* (1977); Stephen Greenblatt,

Renaissance Self-Fashioning: From More to Shakespeare (Chicago, 1980); Louis Adrian Montrose, 'Shaping Fantasies: Figurations of Gender and Power in Elizabethan Culture', *Representations* 2 (1983), pp. 61–94; and Susan Frye, *Elizabeth I: The Competition for Representation* (Oxford, 1993). For a critique of these approaches, see Helen Hackett, *Virgin Mother, Maiden Queen: Elizabeth I and the Cult of the Virgin Mary* (1995) and Susan Doran, 'Virginity, Divinity and Power', in Susan Doran and Thomas S. Freeman (eds), *The Myth of Elizabeth* (Basingstoke, 2003), pp. 171–99.

7. Lady in Waiting: Young Elizabeth Tudor on Film

1. Margaret Irwin, *Young Bess* (New York, 1945).
2. *Variety Film Reviews*, 29 April 1953.
3. For this role and two others in the same year (in *The Actress* and *The Robe*), Jean Simmons won the Best Actress Award from the US National Board of Review.
4. The magazine *Seventeen*, published in Philadelphia from 1944 exemplified how that new group was identified, and by the later 1950s, as an arbiter of exciting teenage fashion and demure female sexuality it reached from the States to Britain, and beyond to such English-speaking outposts as Australia and New Zealand.
5. See Lesley Johnson, *The Modern Girl Girlhood and Growing up* (Buckingham, 1993).
6. John Walker (ed.), *Halliwell's Film and Video Guide*, 16th edition (London, 2001).
7. The edition of Neale used throughout this essay is J. E. Neale, *Queen Elizabeth I* (Harmondsworth, 1960).
8. Neale, *Queen Elizabeth*, pp. 20, 21.
9. Although not discussed here, David Starkey's television series on Elizabeth continued to work essentially within Neale's paradigm of the conventionally heroic Elizabeth.
10. Irwin, *Young Bess*, pp. 309–10.
11. This conclusion is based on intermittent anecdotal discussion among mature female students of history.
12. Natalie Z. Davis, *The Return of Martin Guerre* (Harmondsworth, 1985), p. viii.
13. For a more recent (but comparably concerned) discussion of similar issues, see the review essay by Scott Hendrix, 'Reflections of a Frustrated Film Consultant', *Sixteenth Century Journal* 35, no. 3 (Fall, 2004), pp. 811–14.
14. Neale, *Queen Elizabeth*, p. 34.
15. *A Speciall Grace . . . at Yorke . . . . in November 1558*. STC 7599.
16. *The Letters and Papers, Foreign and Domestic, of Henry VIII*, ed. J. S. Brewer, J. Gairdner and R. H. Brodie (London, 1862–1932), xi, 132.

17. Maria Dowling, *Humanism in the Age of Henry VIII* (London, 1986), p. 234.
18. A very public display of Mary's defiance of the Edwardian religious forms at a time when she was under considerable pressure to conform, is reported in J. G. Nichols (ed.), The diary of Henry Machyn *Camden Society* original series 42 (London, 1848) for March 1551, pp. 4–5.
19. For a more detailed discussion of this episode, see Sheila Cavanagh, 'The Bad Seed: Princess Elizabeth and the Seymour Incident', in Julia M. Walker (ed.), *Dissing Elizabeth: Negative Representations of Gloriana* (Durham, NC, 1998), pp. 13–29.
20. See, for example, the letter Elizabeth wrote to Mary in October probably in 1552, in which she appears to apologize for being a less frequent correspondent than her sister. The letter is reproduced in several collections including Leah S. Marcus, Janel Mueller, and Mary Beth Rose (eds), *Elizabeth 1 Collected Works* (Chicago, 2000), pp. 37–8.
21. Linda Pollock, *With Faith and Physic The Life of a Tudor Gentlewoman Lady Grace Mildmay 1552–1620* (London, 1993), p. 27.
22. *Calendar of State Papers Venetian*, vol II, 1509–1519, 1085.
23. As summarised Ian Kershaw, 'The Past on the Box: Strengths and Weaknesses', in David Cannadine (ed.), *History and the Media* (Basingstoke, 2004), pp. 119–20.

8. Kapur's *Elizabeth*

1. Arundhati Roy, 'The Great Indian Rape-Trick', 22 August 1994, at www.sawnet.org/books/writing/roy_bq1.html
2. Kapur interview in *Pitch Weekly*, 25 November 1998, at www.tipjar.com/dan/kapur.htm
3. Tim Bevan in 'The Making of *Elizabeth*', on the DVD version of *Elizabeth*, 1998.
4. Bevan quoted in 'The Genesis of *Elizabeth*', at virgil.org/sdswo/courses/renaissance-poetry/Elizabeth-genesis.pdf
5. Alison Owen quoted in 'The Genesis of *Elizabeth*'.
6. Michael Hirst in 'The Making of *Elizabeth*'.
7. Bevan in 'Interviews with Cast and Crew', on the DVD version of *Elizabeth*.
8. Susan Doran, *Monarchy and Matrimony: The Courtships of Elizabeth I* (London, 1996).
9. Shekhar Kapur quoted in *Oxford Student*, at www.oxfordstudent.com/1999-06-03/news/10
10. Owen quoted in 'The Genesis of *Elizabeth*'.
11. Kapur and Cate Blanchett in 'Interviews with Cast and Crew'.
12. Kapur quoted in a review by David Walsh, 3 December 1999, at www.wsws.org/arts/1998/dec1998/eliz-d03.shtml

13. Owen in 'The Making of *Elizabeth*'.
14. Kapur quoted in *Guardian Review*, 2 October 1998.
15. Kapur interview in *Pitch Weekly*.
16. Kapur quoted in *Oxford Student*.
17. Kapur quoted in 'Talking with...Shekhar Kapur', at www.geocities. com/Hollywood/Theater/5640/interviews/Elizabeth/Shekhar.html
18. Janet Maslin in *New York Times*, 6 November 1998.
19. Kapur in 'Talking with...Shekhar Kapur'.

9. *Mary Queen of Scots* (1971)

1. *The Times*, 30 March 1972.
2. *The Times*, 18 February 1971.
3. *The Times*, 24 February 1973.
4. *The Times*, 24 July 1971.
5. Notes to Donizetti's *Maria Stuarda*, English National Opera (London, 1998–1999), pp. 22–8.

10. The Armada, War and Propaganda in the Cinema

1. F. Nietzsche, 'The Uses and Disadvantages of History for Life', in O. Stern (ed.) and trans. R. J. Hollingdale, *Untimely Meditations* (Cambridge, MA, 1991), p. 69.
2. S. Harper, *Women in British Cinema, Mad, Bad and Dangerous to Know* (London, 2000), pp. 24–5.
3. C. Drazin, *Korda, Britain's Only Movie Mogul* (Basingstoke, 2002).
4. Sabatini also wrote other books that would become classic swashbuckler films including *Scaramouche* in 1921 and *Captain Blood* in 1922.
5. A. Thomas, *The Cinema of the Sea, A Critical Survey and Filmography, 1925–1986* (London, 1988), pp. 12–15.
6. H. M. Glancy, *When Hollywood Loved Britain, The Hollywood British Film* (Manchester, 1999), pp. 100–1.
7. G. Vidal. *Screening History* (London, 1992), p. 42. Vidal makes the same claim for another Korda wartime epic, *That Hamilton Women* (1941), see, pp. 46–56, which is known to have been Churchill's favourite film.
8. Notably the Tilbury Speech, see W. Churchill, *A History of the English-Speaking Peoples, II: The New World* (London, 1956), p. 100.
9. W. S. Maltby, *The Black Legend in England* (Durham, 1971).
10. H. Kamen, *The Spanish Inquisition* (London, 1965) and his *The Spanish Inquisition: A Historical Revision* (London, 1998). For the definitive statement of how the inquisition was seen in the 1930s, see C. Roth, *The Spanish Inquisition* (London, 1937).
11. G. W. Sanderlin (ed.), *Bartolomé de las Casas; A Selection of his Writings* (New York, 1971).

12. G. Gascoigne, *The Spoyle of Antwerpe* (London, 1576).

13. I am grateful to Tom Freeman for his observation of this point.

14. C. Martin and G. Parker, *The Spanish Armada* (1988, 2nd edition, Manchester, 1990), pp. 249–59.

15. G. Mattingly, *The Defeat of the Spanish Armada* (London, 1959), p. 201.

16. N. Z. Davis, ' "Any resemblance to Persons Living or Dead": Film and the Challenge of Authenticity', *Yale Review* 76 (1987), pp. 457–82.

17. W. Wood, *Elizabethan Sea Dogs, A Chronicle of Drake and His Companions* (New Haven, 1918).

18. W. S. W. Vaux (ed.), *The World Encompassed by Sir Francis Drake* Hakluyt Society, first series, 16 (London, 1854); C. W. Ellot (ed.), *Voyages and Travels: Ancient and Modern, with Introductions, Notes and Illustrations* (New York, 1910).

19. C. Kingsley, *Westward Ho!* (London, 1855) and H. Newbolt, *Admirals All* (London, 1897). See ' "That Golden Knight": Drake and His Reputation', *History Today* 46, no. 1(1996), pp. 14–21.

20. J. S. Corbett, *Drake and the Tudor Navy*, 2 vols (London, 1899).

21. Most obviously, H. Kelsey, *Sir Francis Drake: The Queen's Pirate* (New Haven, 1998).

22. M. Dobson and N. J. Watson, *England's Elizabeth: An Afterlife in Fame and Fantasy* (Oxford, 2004), p. 287.

23. D. Loades, *England's Maritime Empire: Seapower, Commerce and Policy 1490–1690* (Harlow and New York, 2000); N. A. M. Rodger, *The Safeguard of the Sea: A Naval History of Britain. Vol. 1, 660–1649.* (London, 1997).

24. K. R. Andrews (ed.), *English Privateering Voyages to the West Indies 1588–1595*, Hakluyt Society, 2nd Series, 111 (Cambridge, 1959) and his *Elizabethan Privateering: 1585–1603* (Cambridge, 1964) and *Trade, Plunder and Settlement. Maritime Enterprise and the Genesis of the British Empire, 1480–1630* (Cambridge, 1984).

25. J. Sedgewick, 'Cinema-going Preferences in Britain in the 1930s', in J. Richards (ed.), *The Unknown 1930s: An Alternative History of the British Cinema 1929–39* (London 1998), p. 33.

26. J. Richards and D. Sheridan (eds), *Mass Observation at the Movies* (London, 1987), pp. 66, 77, 112, 124, and 167.

27. S. Richards, *The Rise of the English Actress* (Basingstoke, 1993), p. 150.

28. Glancy, *When Hollywood Loved Britain,* p. 100. The other films were *Captain Blood* (1935), *The Charge of the Light Brigade* (1936), *The Prince and the Pauper* (1937), *The Adventures of Robin Hood* (1938) and *The Private Lives of Elizabeth and Essex* (1939).

29. C. R. Koppes and G. D. Black, *Hollywood Goes to War, How Politics, Profits, and Propaganda Shaped World War II Movies* (New York, 1987), pp. 17–47 and C. Shindlet, *Hollywood Goes to War, Films and American Society, 1939–1952* (London, 1979).

30. Allen Rostron, ' "No War, No Hate, No Propaganda" – Promoting Films About European War and Fascism During the Period of American Isolationism', *Journal of Popular Film and Television* 30 (2002), p. 86. A. Rostron, ' "No War, No Hate, No Propaganda" ', p. 86.
31. Glancy, *When Hollywood Loved Britain*, p. 102.
32. Ibid., p. 1.
33. Vidal. *Screening History*, p. 33.

11. *Elizabeth: The Golden Age*: A Sign of the Times?

1. See Thomas Betteridge, 'A Queen for All Seasons: Elizabeth I on Film', in Susan Doran and Thomas S. Freeman (eds), *The Myth of Elizabeth* (Basingstoke, 2003), pp. 242–59.
2. See *Variety* website: http://www.variety.com.
3. See Kapur's website: http://www.shekharkapur.com/goldenage/.
4. Stephen Moss 'Film-making Is an Adventure', *The Guardian*, 1 November 2007.
5. Philip French: 'Elizabeth: The Golden Age', *The Observer*, 4 November 2007.
6. Roger Ebert 'Elizabeth: The Golden Age', *The Sunday Times*, 12 October 2007.
7. Stella Papamichael 'Elizabeth: The Golden Age (2007)', 2 November 2007, http://www.bbc.co.uk/.
8. Winchester Cathedral served as Old St Pauls for the space in which we see Elizabeth praying.
9. See Justin Pollard, the historical advisor for *Elizabeth: The Golden Age* at http://www.shekharkapur.com/goldenage/archives/. Throughout the making of the film Justin Pollard contributed to Kapur's diary to explain some of the reasons for their choices and the obstacles that faced them in trying to create an authentic Elizabethan England.
10. See Andrew Belsey and Catherine Belsey, 'Icons of Divinity: Portraits of Elizabeth I', in Lucy Gent and Nigel Llewellyn (eds), *Renaissance Bodies: The Human Figure in English Culture c. 1540–1660* (London, 1995), pp. 11–35.
11. In the preface to the King James Bible (1611) Elizabeth was depicted as the bright occidental star, but James is no less than 'the sun in his strength', a direct reference to the Messiah in Apocalypse 1.16.
12. See Belsey and Belsey, 'Icons of Divinity', p. 15.
13. See Jenny Wormald, *Mary, Queen of Scots* (London and New York, 2001).
14. Alison Weir, 'Another View: Historian Alison Weir on Elizabeth: The Golden Age', Interview by Paul Arendt, *The Guardian*, 6 November 2007.
15. Stephen Greenblatt, *Sir Walter Ralegh: The Renaissance Man and His Roles* (New Haven, 1973).

16. Robert Naunton, *Fragmenta Regalia* (London, 1641).
17. Michael Dobson and Nicola J. Watson, *England's Elizabeth: An Afterlife In Fame and Fantasy* (Oxford, 2002).
18. See 'What Remains of Rawleigh/Raleigh/Ralegh (1554–1618)', *Entertext* 6 (2007), 867–90.
19. Mark Nicholls and Penry Williams, 'Ralegh, Sir Walter (1554–1618)', *Oxford Dictionary of National Biography.*
20. Ibid.

12. *Shakespeare in Love*: Elizabeth I as *Dea ex Machina*

1. The phrase was first used to describe Elizabeth's role in the film by Michael Dobson and Nicola J. Watson, *England's Elizabeth: An Afterlife in Fame and Fantasy* (Oxford, 2002), p. 262. I am grateful to Tom Freeman not only for first drawing my attention to this study but also for generously presenting me with a copy.
2. Thomas Betteridge, 'A Queen for All Seasons: Elizabeth I on Film', in Susan Doran and Thomas S. Freeman (eds), *The Myth of Elizabeth* (London, 2003), pp. 242–59 (at p. 259, note 9).
3. One version of the film's genesis is that Stoppard was called in to 'polish' an original screenplay by Norman. The first attempt to make it (1992) fell through and it was finally put into production with a script further 'revised' by Stoppard. I gain this information from websites pertaining to both Norman and Stoppard.
4. First staged on the Edinburgh Festival fringe in 1966, the play was taken up by the National Theatre and produced at the Old Vic in 1967.
5. When The Rose is closed by order of the Master of the Revels, Burbage (Martin Clunes) magnanimously offers The Curtain for the premiere of *Romeo and Juliet*, thus in effect 'turning their "households" rancour to pure love' (*Romeo and Juliet*, II. 3, 91–2). In reality, the Admiral's Men and the Lord Chamberlain's Men frequently joined forces during this early period. Furthermore, the former are not recorded at The Rose until 1594: E. K. Chambers, *The Elizabethan Stage* (4 vols; Oxford, 1923), vol. 2, pp. 135–9, 193–4, 409.
6. For an attempted overview of the 1590s, see John Guy (ed.), *The Reign of Elizabeth I: Court and Culture in the Last Decade* (Cambridge, 1995).
7. The name is absent from any roll call of the rich merchants of Elizabethan London and there seems no obvious reason why the authors should have wished to remind their audience that Ferdinand de Lesseps was the creator of the Suez Canal.
8. See below, p. 182.
9. John Dover Wilson (ed.), *Romeo and Juliet* (New Cambridge Shakespeare, 1954), p. xi. A prose version of the tale, *The Story of Romeo*

and Julietta, appeared in William Painter's *The Palace of Pleasure* (1567). For a modern reprint of the latter and further comments on Brooke's poem, see T. J. B. Spencer, ed., *Elizabethan Love Stories* (London, Penguin Shakespeare Library, 1968), pp. 16–18, 51–95; and Frederick S. Boas, *Queen Elizabeth in Drama and Related Studies* (London, 1950), pp. 59–60.

10. 'Judi Dench's ... commanding ... impersonation ... has been perhaps the most conspicuously successful of all screen Elizabeths, and it manages to combine and reinflect [*sic*] so many of the possible roles and positions by which the last four centuries of English culture have made meaning for Elizabeth that even the most cursory attention to her part in the film might sum up a good deal of our study': Dobson and Watson, *England's Elizabeth*, p. 262.

11. It has been demonstrated that there was no attempt in her portraits to emphasize her status as Virgin until the 1580s; that thereafter the device was used for strictly *political* ends, in part to offset feelings of unease about the succession; that there is no evidence that the queen herself encouraged such iconography; and that her subjects' own perception of her would have been derived not from the emblematic portraits adorning the picture-galleries of the rich but merely from the routine imagery perpetuated on the coins in their pockets and purses: Susan Doran, 'Virginity, Divinity and Power: The Portraits of Elizabeth I', in Susan Doran and Thomas Freeman (eds), *The Myth of Elizabeth*, pp. 171–93. It may be added that the profile on her coinage is hardly flattering and was not dramatically altered until the very end of the reign. Until 1600 she is depicted as long-nosed, her hair flowing down over a small ruff and surmounted by a large imperial (that is, closed) crown. Only with what is technically known as the 'Sixth Issue' of 1601–1602 is that image changed. The flowing locks are replaced by the familiar, tightly curled hair-style of the later portraits, which is fully contained within a larger ruff and surmounted by a much *smaller* imperial crown. Perhaps in compensation, she now holds a sceptre (symbol of royal authority and dignity) but her profile is altered *to incorporate a double chin*. What price, then, the ageless virgin?

12. Dobson and Watson, *England's Elizabeth*, p. 264.

13. Betteridge, 'A Queen for All Seasons', pp. 242–3. Note that Hugh Ross Williamson's *Queen Elizabeth* (1947), a stage-vehicle for Edith Evans, likewise takes place entirely within private apartments.

14. For which see Dobson and Watson, *England's Elizabeth*, pp. 283–7. Ralegh's doomed enterprise has been most recently explored in Lee Miller, *Roanoake: Solving the Mystery of England's Lost Colony* (London, 2000).

15. He had affected this disguise in order to escape from Viola's bedroom when Wessex arrived to collect her. Why Wessex should have allowed 'her' to accompany them to Greenwich is not apparent.

16. For the increasingly bizarre myths which came to surround the supposed relationship between the queen and her 'national poet', see Dobson and Watson, *England's Elizabeth*, pp. 121–38.
17. This is of course my own re-arrangement of the text into rough-and-ready blank verse. The Shakespearean rhyming couplet does, however, seem implied and the whole is reminiscent of the closing sequence of *Love's Labours Lost*, where Princess Katherine and her ladies banish their lovers for a year and a day ('That's too long for a play').
18. Dobson and Watson, *England's Elizabeth*, p. 263.
19. Earlier Will has said: 'I dreamt last night of a shipwreck. And you were cast ashore in a far country.' Shakespeare's Viola is a spirited girl who dresses up as a youth for protection in an alien environment and then meets a man she falls in love with. The puritanical (but secretly lecherous) Tilney, closing theatres right, left and centre, may perhaps serve as Malvolio and Burbage as an embryonic Toby Belch.
20. For example, Anthony Sher presents Dr John Dee as Shylock, metamorphosed after his enforced retirement into a fervent student of Freud, Adler and Jung.

13. *The Private Lives of Elizabeth and Essex* and the Romanticization of Elizabethan Politics

1. P. E. J. Hammer, *The Polarisation of Elizabethan Politics: The Political Career of Robert Devereux, 2nd Earl of Essex, 1585–1597* (Cambridge, 1999), pp. 1–7.
2. Renée Pigeon, 'Gloriana Goes to Hollywood: Elizabeth I on Film, 1937–1940', in William F. Gentrup (ed.), *Reinventing The Middle Ages and the Renaissance: Constructions of the Medieval and Early Modern Periods*, Arizona Studies in the Middle Ages and the Renaissance, 1 (1998), 109–21; Thomas Betteridge, 'A Queen for All Seasons: Elizabeth I on Film', in Susan Doran and Thomas S. Freeman (eds), *The Myth of Elizabeth* (Basingstoke, 2003), pp. 248–54.
3. Michael Dobson and Nicola J. Watson, *England's Elizabeth: An Afterlife in Fame and Fantasy* (Oxford, 2002), pp. 277–80.
4. See, for example, the famous 'homily on obedience', most conveniently printed as 'An Exhortation, Concerning Good Order and Obedience, to Rulers and Magistrates', in Arthur F. Kinney (ed.), *Elizabethan Backgrounds: Historical Documents of the Age of Elizabeth I* (Hamden, CT, 1990), pp. 60–70.
5. See, for example, the play text about the death of Essex from the local Rhetoricians' Chamber in the small Zeeland village of 's-Gravenpolder, which survives in two manuscript copies, dated 1629 and 1694: Wim

Husken, 'Queen Elizabeth and Essex: A Dutch Rhetoricians' Play', *Leeds Studies in English*, new series, 32 (2001), pp. 151–70.

6. For the text of *Elizabeth the Queen*, see Maxwell Anderson, *Eleven Verse Plays, 1929–1939* (New York, 1965), pp. 1–131.

7. Lytton Strachey, *Elizabeth and Essex: A Tragic History* (London, 1928). References here are to the Penguin edition of 1950, reprinted in 1985.

8. Strachey, *Elizabeth and Essex*, pp.19, 160. For discussion of Strachey's interpretation of Elizabeth I and its influence on works of the 1920s–1950s, see Dobson and Watson, *England's Elizabeth*, pp. 221–9.

9. Strachey, *Elizabeth and Essex*, pp. 73–4, 78–80.

10. [Edward Hyde, later earl of Clarendon], 'The Difference and Disparity Between the Estates and Conditions of George Duke of Buckingham and Robert Earl of Essex', in *Reliquiae Wottonianae: Or a Collection of Lives, Letters [and] Poems . . . by . . . Sir Henry Wotton Kt.* (4th edition, London, 1685) [Wing W3651], p. 190. The date of Essex's 'glorious feather-triumph' is uncertain. According to Hyde, Essex 'caused two thousand Orange-tawny feathers, in despight of Sir Walter Ralegh, to be worn in the Tilt-yard, even before Her Majestie's own face'. It is unclear if Ralegh had tried to clothe his followers in orange-tawny feathers, but some contemporary libels against Ralegh seem to slander him as a jackdaw, the bird of borrowed feathers (see, for example, http://extra.shu.ac.uk/emls/texts/libels/essex_ralegh_section/A11. html).

11. For Lady Penelope Rich, see *Oxford Dictionary of National Biography*. Anderson emphasizes the importance of her name in the opening of Act Two, when the Fool rhapsodizes over her qualities as the embodiment of her namesake in classical mythology: 'all that this early Penelope began has a later Penelope completed' (Anderson, *Eleven Verse Plays*, p. 55). Anderson's choice of Gray as his character's surname seems to reflect her inability to inspire love from Essex rather than allude to any historical figure, such as Essex's bitter enemy (and *quondam* protégé) Thomas 15th Lord Grey of Wilton.

12. Arthur Collins, *Letters and Memorials of State . . . from the Originals at Penshurst Place* (2 vols, London, 1746), 2, p. 172.

13. Such 'reimagined' history has recently become an accepted sub-genre of history: for example, Niall Ferguson (ed.), *Virtual History: Alternatives and Counterfactuals* (London, 1997) and Robert Cowley (ed.), *What If? The World's Foremost Military Historians Imagine What Might Have Been* (New York, 1999).

14. Collins, *Letters and Memorials*, 2, p. 127.

15. See, for example, the materials and commentaries printed on the 'Early Stuart libels' website (http://purl.oclc.org/emls/texts/libels).

16. The Elizabeth of Anderson's play tries to find a comforting mirror for herself in the character of the royal Hall, but the scene actually reveals her

as being more like the blundering and prideful Falstaff. Elizabeth herself seems to recognize the parallel when Falstaff calls for 'a play extempore', as she has just done, and halts the performance (Anderson, *Eleven Verse Plays*, 120).

17. Collins, *Letters and Memorials*, 2, pp. 118, 141–2. It seems likely that the scriptwriters (or their researchers) drew their inspiration for the Mistress Radcliffe character and other changes suggesting greater historical verisimilitude from the materials published in G. B. Harrison, *A Second Elizabethan Journal: Being a Record of Those Things Most Talked of During the Years 1595–1598* (London, 1931) and idem, *A Last Elizabethan Journal: Being a Record of Those Things Most Talked of During the Years 1599–1603* (London, 1933). References here are to the 1974 reprint of Harrison's *Journals*.

18. As noted above, Lord Mountjoy, was the lover of Essex's sister Penelope, a nobleman who ultimately became Essex's successor as commander in Ireland. Sir William Knollys was Essex's uncle, Comptroller of the Queen's Household and a member of the privy council in his own right. There are entries for both men in the *Oxford DNB*.

19. Harrison, *Last Journal*, pp. 39–40.

20. The effort and expense that went into this opening parade encouraged the Warner Brothers studio to re-use some of the footage in two later films, *The Adventures of Don Juan* (1949) and *The Story of Mankind* (1957).

21. W. Camden, *The History of the Most Renowned and Victorious Princess Elizabeth* (4th edition, London, 1688) [Wing C363A], p. 556. Camden's account of the incident is printed in Harrison, *Second Journal*, p. 287.

22. The nominations were for cinematography (colour), art direction, sound recording, score and special effects.

23. Quoted in Tino Balio, *History of the American Cinema. Vol. 5. Grand Design: Hollywood as a Modern Business Enterprise, 1930–1939* (Berkeley, CA, 1995), p. 205.

24. Whitney Stine, *No Guts, No Glory: Conversations with Bette Davis* (London, 1990), p. 32. Davis was aged 30 in 1939, while the character of Elizabeth is in her late sixties.

25. Betteridge, 'A Queen for All Seasons', p. 252.

26. Bette Davis, *The Lonely Life: An Autobiography* (London, 1962), p. 188.

27. Davis, *Lonely Life*, p. 189. Significantly, she felt she could admit her nervousness at playing Elizabeth to 'Henry VIII in person' (ibid.).

28. Stine, *No Guts*, p. 39; Lawrence J. Quirk, *The Passionate Life of Bette Davis* (London, 1990), pp. 201, 209; Barbara Leaming, *Bette Davis: A Biography* (London, 1992), pp. 139, 141.

29. Davis (probably correctly) also interpreted the suggestion of *The Knight and the Lady* as an in-joke by the male studio executives which implied Queen Elizabeth was 'a lady of the night': Whitney Stine, *Mother*

Goddam: The Story of the Career of Bette Davis, With a Running Commentary by Bette Davis (London, 1975), p. 120.

30. Stine, *Mother Goddam*, p. 220; Quirk, *Bette Davis*, p. 156, 202; Leaming, *Bette Davis*, p. 139. The final title deliberately paralleled that of Laughton's British movie of 1933.
31. Stine, *No Guts*, p. 32. Davis claimed that 'in all our scenes together I used to dream that Laurence Olivier was Essex': Stine, *Mother Goddam*, p. 121.
32. Errol Flynn, *My Wicked, Wicked Ways* (London, 1960), pp. 221–7.
33. See, for example, Davis' approach to kissing Flynn: Stine, *No Guts*, p. 32.
34. Quirk, *Bette Davis*, pp. 140–1, 156.
35. Davis was supposedly offered the role of Scarlett on the condition that she accept Flynn as Rhett Butler – a condition which she refused to accept (Stine, *No Guts*, pp. 19–81; Quirk, *Bette Davis*, pp. 138ff.).
36. Davis, *Lonely Life*, p. 185.
37. Quirk, *Bette Davis*, p. 204. De Havilland performed opposite Flynn in numerous movies and his long and maladroit pursuit of her sometimes verged on the obsessive: Flynn, *Wicked*, pp. 179–80.
38. Strachey, *Elizabeth and Essex*, pp. 166–7.
39. For an example of a ring being used to validate Elizabeth's unsuccessful bid to save Essex in a Dutch drama which seems to date from the 1620s, see Husken, 'Queen Elizabeth and Essex', pp. 157, 165. For French interest in the Essex story, see C. J. Gossip, 'Politics and Tragedy: The Case of the Earl of Essex', in K. Cameron and E. Woodrough (eds.), *Ethics and Politics in Seventeenth-Century France: Essays in Honour of Derek A. Watts* (Exeter, 1996), pp. 223–31.
40. Dobson and Watson, *England's Elizabeth*, pp. 89–90.

15. The Unfilmed Oliver Cromwell

* I am most grateful to John Morrill and to the editors of this volume for their very helpful comments on an earlier draft of this paper.

1. Christopher Hill, *God's Englishman* (London, 1970), pp. 266–7.
2. Richard Holmes, 'Oliver Cromwell', in John Cooper (ed.), *Great Britons: The Great Debate* (London, 2002), pp. 56–66.
3. Blair Worden, *The Rump Parliament, 1648–1653* (Cambridge, 1974), p. 69.
4. S. C. Lomas (ed.), *The Letters and Speeches of Oliver Cromwell with Elucidations by Thomas Carlyle* (3 vols, London, 1904) [hereafter cited as Lomas-Carlyle], III, pp. 188–9 (Cromwell to the second Protectorate Parliament, 4 February 1658).
5. Lomas-Carlyle, III, pp. 174–5 (Cromwell to the second Protectorate Parliament, 25 January 1658). Charles L. Stainer (ed.), *Speeches of Oliver*

Cromwell, 1644–1658 (1901), p. 378, omits the words 'widening those already made', but this does not affect the overall sense of this passage.

6. Lomas-Carlyle, III, p. 345 (Cromwell to the 'Council of War' at Reading, 16 July 1647).

7. Lomas-Carlyle, II, pp. 381–5 (Cromwell to the first Protectorate Parliament, 12 September 1654).

8. Lomas-Carlyle, II, p. 536 (Cromwell to the second Protectorate Parliament, 17 September 1656).

9. Colin Davis, 'Cromwell's Religion', in John Morrill (ed.), *Oliver Cromwell and the English Revolution* (Harlow, 1990), pp. 181–208; reprinted in David L. Smith (ed.), *Cromwell and the Interregnum* (Oxford, 2003), pp. 139–66; Blair Worden, 'Toleration and the Cromwellian Protectorate', in W.J. Sheils (ed.), *Persecution and Toleration: Studies in Church History* 21 (1984), pp. 199–233.

10. David L. Smith, 'Oliver Cromwell, the First Protectorate Parliament, and Religious Reform', *Parliamentary History* 19 (2000), pp. 38–48; reprinted in *Cromwell and the Interregnum*, pp. 167–81.

11. On this, see especially the masterly discussion in Blair Worden, 'Andrew Marvell, Oliver Cromwell, and the Horatian Ode', in Kevin Sharpe and Steven N. Zwicker (eds), *Politics of Discourse: The Literature and History of Seventeenth-Century England* (Berkeley and Los Angeles, 1987), pp. 147–80.

12. *Three Poems upon the Death of His Late Highness Oliver, Lord Protector of England, Scotland and Ireland* (London, 1659), p. 20; quoted in Morrill, *Oliver Cromwell and the English Revolution*, p. 275.

13. 'L.S.', *The Perfect Politician: Or, A Full View of the Life and Actions (Military and Civil) of O. Cromwel* (London, 1659[/60]), pp. 347, 349–50.

14. Thomas Birch (ed.), *A Collection of the State Papers of John Thurloe, Esq.* (7 vols, London, 1742), I, p. 766 (John Maidstone to John Winthrop, 24 March 1659[/60]).

15. Birch, *State Papers of John Thurloe*, III, p. 294 (Robert Duckenfield to Cromwell, 23 March 1654[/5]). After the Israelites escaped from Egypt and were crossing the desert, Caleb and Joshua were 2 of the 12 whom Moses sent into Canaan to spy out the Promised Land. Whereas the other 10 spies thought the land unconquerable, Caleb and Joshua were the only two who trusted God's promise and advocated going on. As a result, God rewarded their faithfulness by allowing them alone to enter the Promised Land, while the others of the Exodus generation died wandering in the wilderness.

16. In particular John Morrill, 'The Drogheda Massacre in Cromwellian Context', in David Edwards, Padraig Lenihan and Clodagh Tait (eds), *Age of Atrocity: Violence and Political Conflict in Early Modern Ireland* (Dublin, 2007), pp. 242–65. I am most grateful to Professor Morrill for showing me this article prior to publication.

17. Lomas-Carlyle, II, pp. 511, 512, 518 (Cromwell to the second Protec-
    torate Parliament, 17 September 1656).
18. The fullest study of Cromwell's foreign policy is Timothy Venning,
    Cromwellian Foreign Policy (London, 1995).
19. Lomas-Carlyle, III, p. 101 (Cromwell to the representatives of the second
    Protectorate Parliament, 21 April 1657).
20. Lomas-Carlyle, I, p. 154 (Cromwell to Sir William Spring and Maurice
    Barrowe, September 1643).
21. On these films, see Andrew Higson, *English Heritage, English Cinema:
    Costume Drama Since 1980* (Oxford, 2003), to which this and the
    following paragraph are indebted.
22. Higson, *English Heritage, English Cinema*, pp. 194–256.
23. See especially Blair Worden, *Literature and Politics in Cromwellian England:
    John Milton, Andrew Marvell, Marchamont Nedham* (Oxford, 2007).

16. *Winstanley*

* A VHS video copy of the film is available from the British Film Institute
  website www.bfi.org.uk.

1. Christopher Hill, *The World Turned Upside Down: Radical Ideas in the
   English Revolution* (London, 1972); see also *A Turbulent Seditious and
   Factious People* (Oxford, 1988).
2. J. C. Davis, *Fear, Myth and History: The Ranters and the Historians*
   (Cambridge, 1986).
3. The ensuing biographical information is taken from Gerrard
   Winstanley's *Oxford Dictionary of National Biography* entry by J. C. Davis
   and J. D. Alsop.
4. Lenny Rubenstein, 'Winstanley and the Historical Film: An Interview
   with Kevin Brownlow', *Cineaste* 10/4 (1980), pp. 22–5.
5. David Caute, *Comrade Jacob* (London, 1961), p. 21.
6. Ibid., p. 58.
7. Rubenstein, 'Winstanley and the Historical Film', pp. 22–3.
8. The comment is from Kevin Brownlow's obituary for Miles Halliwell,
   The Independent, 26 November 2004.
9. Rubenstein, 'Winstanley and the Historical Film', p. 24.
10. Ibid., p. 25.
11. Ibid., pp. 23, 25.
12. John C. Tibbetts, 'Kevin Brownlow's Historical Films. *It Happened
    Here* (1965) and *Winstanley* (1975)', *Historical Journal of Film, Radio and
    Television*, June 2000.
13. Christopher Hill, 'Notes and Comments', *Past and Present* 69 (1975),
    p. 132.
14. Tibbetts, 'Kevin Brownlow's Historical Films'.

17. Why Don't the Stuarts Get Filmed?

1. *Lady Jane Grey* (1923); *Tudor Rose* (Robert Stevenson, 1936); *Lady Jane* (Trevor Nunn, 1986). All credits are to directors.
2. (New York, 1999).
3. Ronald Hutton, *Debates in Stuart History* (Basingstoke, 2004), pp. 135–42.
4. See Ronald Hutton, *Charles II* (Oxford, 1989), pp. 67–70.
5. And I am grateful to Jeffrey Richards for first drawing my attention to it.
6. Robert Z. Leonard, USA, 1955.
7. Antonia Fraser, *King Charles II* (London, 1979); Richard Ollard, *The Image of the King* (London, 1979).
8. Hutton, *Charles II*; John Miller, *Charles II* (London, 1991).
9. This prediction seems to be borne out in his latest portrayal in *The Libertine*, where John Malkovich plays him as charming intelligent and politically astute even though he is portrayed as devious, manipulative and disloyal.

Index

Fictional characters do not appear in this index. Films set in the Tudor and Stuart periods are indexed separately; otherwise they are listed under Films.